Currencies, Commodities and Consumption

Currency values, prices, consumption and incomes are at the heart of the economic performance of all countries. In order to make a meaningful comparison between one economy and another, economists routinely make use of purchasing power parity (PPP) exchange rates, but while PPP rates are widely used and well understood, they take a lot of effort to produce and suffer from publication delays. *Currencies, Commodities and Consumption* analyses the strengths and weaknesses of two alternatives to PPP. First, the so-called Big Mac Index, which uses hamburger prices as a standard of measurement, and second, a less well-known technique which infers incomes across countries based on the proportion of consumption devoted to food. Kenneth W. Clements uses international macroeconomics, microeconomic theory and econometrics to provide researchers and policy makers with insights into alternatives to PPP rates and make sense of the ongoing instability of exchange rates and commodity prices.

KENNETH W. CLEMENTS has been at The University of Western Australia since 1981 as Winthrop Professor of Economics and since 2008 BHP Billiton Research Fellow at the UWA Business School. In 2009, his book (coauthored with X. Zhao) *Economics and Marijuana* was published by Cambridge University Press. He is a Fellow of the Academy of Social Sciences in Australia and in 2009 received from the Australian Learning and Teaching Council a Citation for Outstanding Contributions to Student Learning.

Currencies, Commodities and Consumption

KENNETH W. CLEMENTS
Business School, The University of Western Australia

CAMBRIDGE
UNIVERSITY PRESS

University Printing House, Cambridge CB2 8BS, United Kingdom

One Liberty Plaza, 20th Floor, New York, NY 10006, USA

477 Williamstown Road, Port Melbourne, VIC 3207, Australia

314-321, 3rd Floor, Plot 3, Splendor Forum, Jasola District Centre, New Delhi - 110025, India

79 Anson Road, #06-04/06, Singapore 079906

Cambridge University Press is part of the University of Cambridge.

It furthers the University's mission by disseminating knowledge in the pursuit of education, learning and research at the highest international levels of excellence.

www.cambridge.org
Information on this title: www.cambridge.org/9781107014763

© Kenneth W. Clements 2013

First published 2013
First paperback edition 2015

A catalogue record for this publication is available from the British Library

Library of Congress Cataloging in Publication data
Clements, Kenneth W., 1950–
 Currencies, commodities and consumption / Kenneth W. Clements,
 Business School, The University of Western Australia.
  pages cm
 Includes bibliographical references and indexes.
 ISBN 978-1-107-01476-3
 1. Consumer price indexes. 2. Cost and standard of living. 3. Purchasing
 power parity. 4. Foreign exchange. I. Title.
 HB225.C54 2012
 339.3–dc23   2012033995

ISBN 978-1-107-01476-3 Hardback
ISBN 978-1-316-60111-2 Paperback

Contents

Figures

Tables

About the author and contributors

The Author

Kenneth W. Clements has been at The University of Western Australia since 1981 as Winthrop Professor of Economics and since 2008 as BHP Billiton Research Fellow at the UWA Business School. His research has been supported by a series of grants from the Australian Research Council, and he has published recently in journals such as the *American Journal of Agricultural Economics*, *Journal of Business*, *Journal of International Money and Finance* and *International Statistical Review*. In 2009, his book (coauthored with X. Zhao), *Economics and Marijuana*, was published by Cambridge University Press. He is a Fellow of the Academy of Social Sciences in Australia and in 2009 received from the Australian Learning and Teaching Council a Citation for Outstanding Contributions to Student Learning.

Contributors

DONGLING CHEN has a PhD from The University of Western Australia and is an economist with the Shanghai Municipal Authority.

MEI-HSIU CHEN has a PhD from The University of Western Australia and is a Lecturer in Accounting and Finance at University of Western Australia.

RENÉE FRY has a PhD from the Australian National University and is Associate Professor in Economics at Australian National University.

GRACE GAO has a PhD from The University of Western Australia and is a Research Associate in Economics at University of Western Australia.

YIHUI LAN has a PhD from The University of Western Australia and is Associate Professor in Finance at University of Western Australia.

SHI PEI SEAH has a master's degree in Financial Mathematics from The University of Western Australia and is a consultant with Pricewater-houseCoopers.

THOMAS SIMPSON has a Bachelor of Commerce with honours degree from The University of Western Australia and was a Research Assistant in Economics at University of Western Australia.

Acknowledgements

In carrying out the research reported in this book, I would like to acknowledge the substantial assistance received from a number of sources over an extended period of time. First, there are those individuals with whom I have collaborated directly: Dongling Chen, Mei-Hsiu Chen, Renée Fry, Grace Gao, Yihui Lan, Shi Pei Seah and Thomas Simpson, whose names are listed at the commencement of the relevant chapters as contributors.

The contributors and I have received helpful comments, criticism and encouragements from Kym Anderson, Garry Barrett, Mardi Dungey, Mark Hazell, Judy Hensen, Zhang Hongtao, Carol Howard, Aimee Kaye, Geoffrey Kingston, Emily Laing, Liang Li, Bill Malcolm, Bob Marks, Bob McColl, Ganesh Viswanath Natraj, Chris O'Donnell, Matt Polasek, Ye Qiang, Ranjan Ray, David Sapsford, Jeffrey Sheen, Jiawei Si, Larry Sjaastad, MoonJoong Tcha, George Verikios, Don Weatherburn, David Wesney and Xueyan Zhao. I benefitted from the excellent research assistance of Andrew Ainsworth, Renae Bothe, Mei-Hsiu Chen, Joan Coffey, Grace Gao, Mei Han, Ze Min Hu, Callum Jones, Aya Kelly, Yihui Lan, Vitaly Pershin, Shi Pei Seah, Jiawei Si, Tom Simpson, Eleni Stephanou, Stepháne Verani, Patricia Wang, Robin Wong and Clare Yu. I am very grateful to Jiawei Si (again) for his excellent work with the production of this book. I also acknowledge the helpful comments received from anonymous readers, as well as encouragement and guidance from Chris Harrison, Publishing Director (Social Sciences), Cambridge University Press. In additional, Josephine Lane, Assistant Editor, Economics and Management Cambridge University Press, and International Science Editing provided valuable assistance in the production of the book.

I have presented earlier versions of some of this research at the Economic Measurement Group Workshops, Centre for Applied Economic Research, The University of New South Wales in 2008 and 2011, the 2006 conference on 'The Economics of Commodity Prices and Exchange Rates' held at The University of Western Australia, the 2006 Conference of Economists, Curtin University, the UWA Business School Forum on 'The GFC Mark II', September 2011, and seminars at Monash University and UWA. I have benefitted from these opportunities to trial ideas and the feedback received from participants, but needless to say, I have not been able to incorporate all of the many comments and suggestions received.

A shorter version of Chapter 2 of this book appeared as K. W. Clements, Y. Lan and S. P. Seah, 'The Big Mac Index Two Decades On: An Evaluation of Burgernomics', *International Journal of Finance and Economics* 17: 31–60, 2012. A shorter version of Chapter 3 appeared as K. W. Clements and R. Fry, 'Commodity Currencies and Currency Commodities', *Resources Policy* 33: 55–73, 2008. Chapter 4 appeared as K. W. Clements, 'Three Facts about Marijuana Prices', *Australian Journal of Agricultural and Resource Economics* 48: 271–300, 2004 (and that paper formed the basis for part of K. W. Clements, 'The Pricing of Marijuana', chapter 3 in K. W. Clements and X. Zhao, *Economics and Marijuana: Consumption, Pricing and Legalisation*, Cambridge University Press, 2009). A shorter version of Chapter 7 appeared as K. W. Clements and D. Chen, 'Affluence and Food: A Simple Way to Infer Incomes', *American Journal of Agricultural Economics* 92: 909–26, 2010. I acknowledge the willingness of these journals to permit the use of that material in this book and thank the referees and editors for constructive comments and suggestions on earlier versions. The front cover pictures are copyrighted by iStockphoto and are used with permission.

This research was supported in part by grants and other forms of assistance I received from the Australian Research Council, ACIL Tasman, AngloGold Ashanti, BHP Billiton, WA Department of Industry and Resources and the Business School, The University of Western Australia. The views expressed herein are not necessarily those of the supporting bodies.

Finally, I want to express my appreciation for the productive research environment provided by the Business School of The University of Western Australia. Staff, students and the Deanery of the School have all helped to make this research possible.

Kenneth W. Clements

1 Introduction

KENNETH W. CLEMENTS

1.1 Overview

Currency values, prices, consumption and incomes are intimately linked and are at the heart of the economic performance of all countries. For example, a fundamental issue in geopolitics is the size of the Chinese economy and how fast it is growing: Is it really now larger than that of Japan? Is it likely to grow to become bigger than the US economy within the planning horizon?[1] Are the Chinese official statistics credible? If China is doing so well, why does the average Chinese consume so little, and why does there appear to be so much poverty? What is the appropriate exchange rate to use to convert RMB into dollars? If the RMB is undervalued, as claimed by the US administration, using the current rate would skew the result towards a larger gap between the two economies. These and related questions are at the forefront of contemporary discussions around the world that involve basic concepts of economics and measurement. As the issues are controversial, complex and far from settled, their understanding requires a serious research effort. This book takes a fresh approach to the area using a mixture of international macroeconomics, microeconomic theory and econometrics.

To make them comparable across countries, gross national product (GNP) and income data obviously need to be expressed in a common unit. In view of the notorious volatility of market exchange rates and their pronounced cyclical swings, these rates are particularly unsuitable for such comparisons. A popular approach is to use the purchasing power parity (PPP) exchange rates published by the International

---

[1] *The Economist* magazine has an interactive web page devoted to the relative size of the Chinese economy. At default growth rates, China is estimated to overtake the United States in 2019. See www.economist.com/blogs/dailychart/2010/12/save_date.

Comparison Program (ICP) of the World Bank; these are rates that equalise the cost of market baskets across countries. Although PPP rates are fast dominating this area, they are not without problems, including the vast resources needed to collect the underlying detailed information on prices and the long publication delays (of the order of five years). This book contains an in-depth investigation of two alternative approaches. The first is the Big Mac Index (BMI), popularised by *The Economist* magazine, which uses hamburger prices as the standard of measurement. At first glance, the hamburger standard might seem too narrow and an unpromising basis for serious income comparisons. However, this book establishes that the BMI contains substantial information regarding economic fundamentals, making it a viable alternative for cross-country income comparisons. In addition, as this index is shown to possess substantial predictive power, it can also be used to gauge the likely future course of currency values, a feature of considerable value to financial markets. And, of course, while not all McDonald's outlets are open for business 24/7, Big Mac prices are readily available on a high-frequency basis.

A second approach to the measurement of incomes internationally is a revealed-preference one. According to Engel's law, the proportion of consumption devoted to food (the food share) declines with income. Much research has established the validity of this law, and there is now a deep understanding of the nature of the dependence of the food share on income. Food shares of a reasonable quality are published regularly by most countries (even the poorest), and as these are pure numbers that are independent of currency values and price levels, they are readily comparable across countries. Accordingly, after adjusting for price differences, these shares can be combined with the income sensitivity of consumption to infer incomes across countries, an approach that can be described as reverse engineering of Engel's law. This book demonstrates that this is a viable approach for making reliable international income comparisons.

Commodity exporting countries, such as Australia, Canada, South Africa, Norway, New Zealand, and a number of developing economies, represent an important group for which world markets for commodities – minerals, energy and agricultural products – play a significant role in determining economic conditions. Here commodity markets can be responsible for prosperity, slumps and, always, volatility. The wide swings experienced by these countries can provide laboratory evidence for the rest of the world on the behaviour of economies under extreme conditions. This book analyses the two-way links between commodity prices and currency values in the form of the theory of so-called commodity currencies and currency commodities. Also included is an analysis of the determinants and patterns of certain specific commodity prices over time, countries and markets.

In many countries, consumption accounts for approximately three-quarters of GDP. An understanding of consumption patterns is of fundamental importance to appreciating the nature of the economy and the underlying affluence of consumers. In comparing consumption across countries, a major issue is the comparison of like with like. In what sense can consumers in, say, New York be compared in a meaningful way with those in New Delhi? Certainly, incomes and the prices in these cities differ, but allowances can be made for these observable differences. Do systematic differences remain after controlling for these factors? In other words, are tastes different in different countries? A related topic is the international variability of the quality of goods consumed. This book addresses these issues and provides measures of dispersion of prices, incomes and quality internationally.

In summary, this book covers considerable but interrelated territory in providing insights into the measurement and understanding of currency values, prices, consumption and incomes across countries. The book has three parts, and in what follows, each is briefly described.

1.2 Exchange rates and prices

There is an almost insatiable appetite for research to enhance understanding of exchanges rates, their links to economic fundamentals, their impact on competitiveness, their substantial volatility and how business and government can best manage foreign exchange risk. Part I contains two chapters. The first (Chapter 2) contains a comprehensive account of the theory of PPP, the formal link between currency values and prices, and how it can be applied to the BMI, which is published annually by *The Economist* magazine. The index has now been in existence for almost a quarter of a century, and *The Economist* describes it as the most popular single item in the whole magazine. This chapter contains a unified account of PPP theory, introduces a new generalisation of the theory that is dubbed 'stochastic PPP' and then uses the BMI in extensive empirical testing of the theory.

This chapter demonstrates the considerable information on the likely future course of currency values contained in the BMI. In particular, it is established that once the BMI is modified appropriately, those currencies identified as being undervalued subsequently appreciate, and vice versa, a finding of significant value to importers, exporters and investors. The BMI thus reflects economic fundamentals and can be used as a reliable conversion factor in cross-country comparisons of incomes, earnings, prices and so on. In short, while not perfect, at a cost of less than $ 10 per year, the BMI seems to provide good value for money. This chapter also contains in one place all available historical values of the BMI and its components (i.e., exchange rates and prices), which will be valuable to researchers.

The second chapter in Part I (Chapter 3) addresses the interactions between commodity prices and currency values. This is particularly relevant for commodity exporting countries, for which world commodity prices are an important driving force for exchange rates and the overall state of the economy. For these countries, commodity prices lead to an important modification to PPP theory. An additional factor that needs to be accounted for is the fact that because some of these countries are such substantial producers, they possess pricing power in world markets.

This chapter starts with the well-known theory of commodity currencies, according to which the value of the currency of a commodity exporting country moves in sympathy with world commodity prices. Thus a commodity boom appreciates the currency, which squeezes the country's noncommodity exporters and firms in the import competing sector. The appreciation also lowers the prices of imports at home, which enhances the real income of consumers and is an indirect way of distributing the benefits of the boom. The flip side of the theory of commodity currencies is called 'currency commodities' and refers to commodities whose world prices are substantially affected by variations in currency values. This involves the controversial case in which some commodity exporting countries possess hidden market power so that they are to some degree price-makers in commodity markets. This pricing power means that producers can pass on to customers cost increases or what amounts to the same thing, lost revenue due to an appreciating currency. This is a departure from the usual 'small country' assumption, whereby world prices are taken as given. The simultaneous existence of commodity currencies and currency commodities can account for at least part of the turbulence in commodity markets that seems to go hand in hand with volatility in the foreign exchange market. The theory of currency commodities and how they interact with commodity currencies is new and rich and offers considerable insight into the workings of the markets for foreign exchange and commodities. These matters are discussed at length in this chapter, which also contains an empirical application of the theory.

1.3 Commodity prices

Part II of this book deals with the pricing of commodities. It starts with the controversial case of marijuana (Chapter 4). The Australian Crime Commission made available unique information on marijuana prices, obtained from undercover drug busts. These prices have declined substantially, a decline that is much greater than that for most agricultural products. Why has this occurred, and what are the implications? One possible reason is that productivity in this industry has surged because of the hydroponic revolution, whereby the majority of Australian marijuana is now grown indoors under ideal conditions. Hydroponic growing techniques have enhanced productivity and reduced costs, with some of the benefits passed on to consumers in the form of lower prices. Another possible reason for the price decline is that laws have become softer and penalties have been reduced. In this chapter, marijuana prices are systematically compared with other commodity prices to emphasise just how rapidly they have fallen. This chapter also shows that patterns in prices can be used to divide Australia into three broad regions: (1) Sydney, where prices are highest; (2) Melbourne and Canberra, which have somewhat lower prices; and (3) everywhere else, where marijuana is cheapest. An exploratory analysis indicates the extent to which the price decreases have stimulated marijuana consumption and reduced growth in the consumption of a substitute product, alcohol.

Next, in Chapter 5, world prices for and quantities of major metals over the last half-century are analysed. These are summarised in the form of index numbers of changes in prices and quantities, their volatility and their covariation. This chapter also uses matrix comparisons as a way to conveniently compare the price of each metal with all others. In addition, some new results on the sensitivity of metal prices to changes in supply are presented.

1.4 International patterns for incomes, prices and consumption

Measurement of the comparative affluence of countries – and under-standing the reasons lying behind the differences – is one of the most basic issues in economics. Part III of this book is devoted to analytic explorations of differences in incomes, prices and consumption across countries, with an emphasis on measurement.

The most recently published ICP data for more than one-hundred countries are used to investigate the dispersion of incomes, prices and consumption. There are substantial differences across countries in these data. For example, in the richest countries, on average, food accounts for less than 5 per cent of consumers' budgets, whereas this rises to more than 50 per cent for the poorest; and per capita incomes in the richest countries are of the order of 200 times larger than those in the poorest. While such large differences can be useful in identifying empirical regularities that otherwise would be hidden, coming to grips with diversity of this magnitude is itself a challenge requiring special approaches.

Chapter 6 shows that the dispersion of the distribution of prices in poor countries is substantially higher than that in rich countries and that the relative price of food has a systematic tendency to decline as countries become richer. As relative prices are closely related to incomes, a model is developed that shows that the price of luxuries increases with income growth, and vice versa for necessities. This model provides a link between price dispersion and incomes that leads to several interesting concepts, including minimum variance income and dispersion-equivalent income, the income needed to compensate for higher dispersion. This chapter also contains an analysis of the welfare cost of higher dispersion in poorer countries.

Chapter 7 proposes an alternative measure of incomes across coun-tries, the inverse of the food budget share (the proportion of total consumption devoted to food). Using this share for cross-country com-parisons has several attractions. As mentioned previously, the food share is a pure number that is independent of currency units, which makes it readily comparable across time and countries. In addition, fairly reliable information on the food share is available in most coun-tries within a reasonable time frame. By contrast, there tends to be long delays in the publication of the ICP data. Finally, the relation between this share and income is one of the most studied in economics and is enshrined in Engel's law (the food share falls as income rises or, equivalently, the income elasticity of food is less than unity). In this chapter, it is established that after making a simple adjustment for price differences, the food share can be used to compare incomes across widely different countries. All that is required in addition to the food share and prices is numerical values for two parameters: the food income elasticity and the income elasticity of the marginal utility of income. This new approach permits the economic performance of countries to be monitored in a more timely manner than was previously possible. However, this approach to income measurement, like all others, is necessarily imperfect. As a partial way to recognise this, the uncertainty of the results is highlighted by presenting the probability distribution of the income of one country relative to another.

1.5 Notes on the literature

There is no single source that deals with the broad sweep of topics included in this book, which is not surprising given the tendency to compartmentalise and specialise in economics and finance. However, previous research has dealt separately with parts of the subject matter of this book, and important prior work is mentioned below.

Exchange rates and prices

There is a large body of literature on this topic that ranges from the most abstract academic level to material for practitioners. A selection of well-regarded scholarly books on exchange rate economics includes those by De Grauwe (2005), Dornbusch (1991), Isard (1995), MacDonald (2007), Manzur (2008), Ong (2003) and Sarno and Taylor (2002). Another related book is by Prasada Rao (2009), which mostly deals with the PPPs produced by the ICP. The book assesses the methodologies used, usually on the basis of index number theory, suggests alternative approaches and analyses estimates from the IPC and elsewhere.

Commodity prices

The pricing of commodities is a rapidly changing area of research with contributions from financial institutions, governments and international agencies concerned with economic development and academics.

A selection of reasonably recent books at the academic end of the spectrum includes those by Grynberg and Newton (2007), Manzur (2003), Sarris and Hallam (2006), Tyers and Anderson (1992) and Winters and Sapsford (1990). There is a tendency for these works to give more weight to agricultural prices instead of metals. Older books by Malenbaum (1978) and Tilton (1990) deal with world metal markets but focus mostly on quantities rather than prices. Tcha (2003) addresses the gold market. Greenaway and Morgan (1999) provide a collection of important articles on commodity prices and related areas.

International patterns for prices, consumption and incomes

This is an emerging area, and interest in the topic now seems to be accelerating with the publication of the latest instalment of data on 146 countries by the ICP (2008). Books dealing with cross-country consumption economics are those by Chen (1999), Lluch et al. (1977), Selvanathan (1993), Selvanathan and Selvanathan (2003), Theil (1996), Theil et al. (1989), Theil and Clements (1987) and Theil and Suhm (1981). Additional influential articles on this topic include those by Cranfield et al. (2002), Goldberger and Gamalestos (1970), Houthakker (1957), Lluch and Powell (1975), Neary (2004), Pollak and Wales (1987), Rimmer and Powell (1996) and Seale and Regmi (2006).

References

Chen, D. L. (1999). *World Consumption Economics*. Singapore: World Scientific Publishing.

Cranfield, J. A. L., P. V. Preckel, J. S. Eales and T. W. Hertel (2002). 'Estimating Consumer Demands Across the Development Spectrum: Maximum Likelihood Estimates of an Implicit Direct Additivity Model'. *Journal of Development Economics* 68: 289–307.

De Grauwe, P., ed. (2005). *Exchange Rate Economics: Where Do We Stand?* Cambridge, MA: MIT Press.

Dornbusch, R. (1991). *Exchange Rates and Inflation*. Cambridge, MA: MIT Press.

Goldberger, A. S., and T. Gamalestos (1970). 'A Cross-Country Comparison of Consumer Expenditure Patterns'. *European Economic Review* 1: 357–400.

Greenaway, D., and C. W. Morgan (1999). *The Economics of Commodity Markets*. Cheltenham: Edward Elgar.

Grynberg, R., and S. Newton, eds. (2007). *Commodity Prices and Development*. Oxford University Press.

Houthakker, H. S. (1957). 'An International Comparison of Household Expenditure Patterns, Commemorating the Centenary of Engel's Law', *Econometrica* 25: 532–51.

International Comparison Program (ICP) (2008). *Global Purchasing Power Parities and Real Expenditures*. Washington, DC: The World Bank. Available at: www.worldbank.org.

Isard, P. (1995). *Exchange Rate Economics*. Cambridge University Press.

Lluch, C., and A. A. Powell (1975). 'International Comparison of Expenditure Patterns'. *European Economic Review* 5: 275–303.

Lluch, C., A. A. Powell and R. Williams (1977). *Patterns in Household Demand and Saving*. Oxford University Press.

MacDonald, R. (2007). *Exchange Rate Economics: Theories and Evidence*. Milton Park, UK: Routledge.

Malenbaum, W. (1978). *World Demand for Raw Materials in 1985 and 2000*. New York: McGraw-Hill.

Manzur, M., ed. (2003). *Exchange Rates, Interest Rates and Commodity Prices*. Cheltenham: Edward Elgar.

Manzur, M., ed. (2008). *Purchasing Power Parity*. Cheltenham: Edward Elgar.

Neary, J. P. (2004). 'Rationalising the Penn World Table: True Multilateral Indices for International Comparisons of Real Income'. *American Economic Review* 94: 1411–28.

Ong, L. L. (2003). *The Big Mac Index: Applications of Purchasing Power Parity*. London: Macmillan.

Pollak, R. A., and T. J. Wales (1987). 'Pooling International Consumption Data'. *Review of Economics and Statistics* 69: 90–9.

Prasada Rao, D. S., ed. (2009). *Purchasing Power Parities of Currencies: Recent Advances in Methods and Applications*. Cheltenham: Edward Elgar.

Rimmer, M. T., and A. A. Powell (1996). 'An Implicitly Additive Demand System'. *Applied Economics* 28: 1613–22.

Sarno, L., and M. P. Taylor (2002). *The Economics of Exchange Rates*. Cambridge University Press.

Sarris, A., and D. Hallam, eds. (2006). *Agricultural Commodity Markets and Trade: New Approaches to Analysing Market Structure and Trade*. Cheltenham: Edward Elgar.

Seale, J. L., and A. Regmi (2006). 'Modelling International Consumption Patterns'. *Review of Income and Wealth* 52:603–24.

Selvanathan, E. A., and S. Selvanathan (2003). *International Consumption Comparisons: OECD versus LDC*. Singapore: World Scientific.

Selvanathan, S. (1993). *A System-Wide Analysis of International Consumption Patterns*. Dordrecht: Kluwer.

Tcha, M. J., ed. (2003). *Gold and the Modern World Economy*. London: Routledge.

Theil, H. (1996). *Studies in Global Econometrics*. Dordrecht: Kluwer.

Theil, H., C.-F. Chung and J. L. Seale, Jr. (1989). *International Evidence on Consumption Patterns*. Greenwich, CT: JAI Press.

Theil, H., and K. W. Clements (1987). *Applied Demand Analysis: Results from System-Wide Approaches*. Cambridge, MA: Ballinger.

Theil, H., and F. E. Suhm (1981). *International Consumption Comparisons: A System-Wide Approach*. Amsterdam: North-Holland.

Tilton, J. E., ed. (1990). *World Metal Demand: Trends and Prospects*. Washington, DC: Resources for the Future.

Tyers, R., and K. Anderson (1992). *Disarray in World Food Markets: A Quantitative Assessment*. Cambridge University Press.

Winters, L. A., and D. Sapsford, eds. (1990). *Primary Commodity Prices: Economic Models and Policy*. Cambridge University Press.

PART I

Exchange rates and prices

2 | *Purchasing power parity and the Big Mac Index*

KENNETH W. CLEMENTS, YIHUI LAN,
AND SHI PEI SEAH

2.1 Introduction

In 1972, just prior to the collapse of the Bretton Woods system of fixed
exchange rates, the US dollar cost about 40 British pence. By 1985,
the dollar had appreciated to 90 pence, but by the end of December
2008, it had fallen back to 67 pence. As such substantial changes in
currency values over the longer term are commonplace in a world of
floating exchange rates, understanding the valuation of currencies is a
significant intellectual challenge and of great importance for economic
policy, the smooth functioning of financial markets, and the financial
management of international companies.

While exchange-rate economics is a controversial area, a substantial body of research now finds that over the longer term, exchange
rates are 'anchored' by price levels. This idea is embodied in purchasing power parity (PPP) theory, which states that the exchange rate is
proportional to the ratio of price levels in the two countries. To illustrate, Figure 2.1 uses annual data to plot the exchange rate (relative to
the US dollar) of the United Kingdom and Japan and the ratio of their
price levels to that of the United States. British prices increased relative
to those in the United States over the past thirty years, whereas those
of Japan decreased. According to PPP theory, the British pound should
have depreciated (an increase in the pound cost of the dollar), and the
Japanese yen should have appreciated. This is what in fact happened.
Even though at times the exchange rate deviates substantially from the
price ratio, there is a distinct tendency for this ratio to play the role of
the underlying trend, or anchor, for the exchange rate. That is to say,
while the exchange rate meanders around the price ratio, over time it
has a tendency to revert to this trend value, so the ratio can be thought
of as the 'underlying value' of the currency. Figure 2.1 thus provides
some prima facie evidence in favour of PPP over the long term.

13

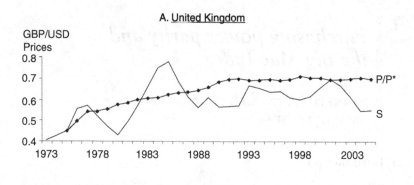

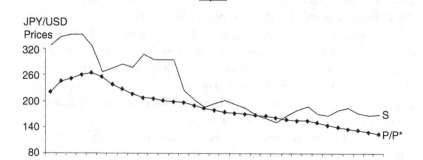

Figure 2.1 Exchange rates and prices, 1973–2007.

Note: The price levels are consumer price indices. The base year for each country (Britain 2002, Japan 2006) is chosen to minimise the deviations from parity, $S - P/P^*$. This amounts to assuming that PPP holds on average over the thirty-three years and determines nothing more than the 'average' height of the relative price curve.

Sources: International Monetary Fund, International Financial Statistics, and Pacific Exchange Rate Service (http://pacific.commerce.ubc.ca/xr/data.html).

A new and simple way of making PPP comparisons was introduced in 1986 by *The Economist* magazine. This involves using the price of a Big Mac hamburger at home and abroad as the price ratio that reflects the underlying value of the currency. This price ratio is known as the 'Big Mac Index' (BMI), and it forms the basis for 'burgernomics'. When compared with the actual exchange rate, the BMI purports to give an indication of the extent to which a currency is over- or undervalued according to the law of one price. '[Seeking] ...to make exchange-rate theory more digestible' (*The Economist*, 9 April 1998), the BMI has been published over a lengthy period for an increasing number of currencies (now more than forty) and is claimed to be a successful new product from a number of perspectives. In the words of *The Economist*:

The [Big Mac] Index was first served up in September 1986 as a relatively simple way to calculate the over- and under-valuation of currencies against the dollar. It soon caught on. Such was its popularity that it was updated the following January, and has now become the best-known regular feature in *The Economist*.[1]

In an instructive metaphor, *The Economist* (26 August 1995) describes the approach underlying the BMI in the following terms:

Suppose a man climbs five feet up a sea wall, and then climbs down twelve feet. Whether he drowns or not depends upon how high above sea-level he was when he started. The same problem arises in deciding whether currencies are under- or over-valued.

The current exchange rate is analogous to the position of the man on the sea wall, and the PPP rate is the sea-level. Thus, whether the currency is priced correctly by the market is determined by reference to its PPP value. Identification of the PPP value of a currency with the sea-level also accords with the idea that 'water finds its own level', so over time, the currency should tend to revert to its PPP value. While an informal currency-pricing model, the BMI is rooted in PPP theory and provides a fascinating example of the productive interplay among fundamental economic research, journalism, and financial markets.

[1] From 'Ten Years of the Big Mac Index', published on *The Economist* website (www.economist.com; accessed 14 July 1999). *The Economist* also publishes other similar PPP gauges. The 'Coca-Cola map' appeared in the magazine in 1997 and shows a strong positive correlation between per-capita consumption of Coca-Cola in a country and that country's quality of life. In 2004, the 'Tall Latte Index' was proposed, which is based on the price of a cup of tall latte coffee at Starbucks in more than thirty countries. This index provides roughly similar, albeit not identical, results to the BMI. Inspired by such single-good indices, other institutions have devised similar measures, such as the 'iTunes Index' featured in *Business Review Weekly*, an Australian business magazine, in August 2006, and the 'iPod Index' compiled by CommSec Australia in January 2007 (James, 2007a, 2007b).

The literature on PPP in general is large and growing, and several good surveys are available, including Froot and Rogoff (1995), Lan and Ong (2003), MacDonald (2007), Rogoff (1996), Sarno and Taylor (2002), Taylor and Taylor (2004), and Taylor (2006). Early contributors to academic research on the BMI include Annaert and Ceuster (1997), Click (1996), Cumby (1996), Ong (1997), and Pakko and Pollard (1996), whereas more recent papers include Chen et al. (2007), Clements and Lan (2010), Lan (2006), and Parsley and Wei (2007); a comprehensive review of the 'burgernomics' literature is provided later in this chapter. As a way of illustrating professional interest in PPP, we conducted a keyword search for the term 'purchasing power parity' or 'PPP' in Factiva.[2] As a basis for comparison, we also searched for four broad economic terms – 'inflation', 'unemployment', 'interest rate', and 'exchange rate' – and another relatively narrow term, 'foreign direct investment' (or 'FDI'), together with the 'BMI'. Figure 2.2 plots on the left-hand axis the number of articles published on each topic in each of the past three decades. As this axis uses a logarithmic scale, the change in height of the bars from one decade to the next indicates the exponential rate of growth for each topic. The right-hand vertical axis gives the average growth rate, on an annual basis, for each topic. It can be seen that PPP has grown at an average annual rate of about 25 per cent per annum, which ranks immediately below that of foreign direct investment, whereas the BMI has almost the same growth rate as FDI at 32 per cent. Thus, while the number of articles on PPP and the BMI are still smaller than the four broader areas, this topic is clearly of substantial professional importance and growing rapidly.

As the BMI is now a mature product, a broad evaluation of its workings and performance is appropriate. We show that although it is not perfect, the index offers considerable insight into the operation of currency markets. In Section 2.2 we set the scene by discussing PPP theory in some detail by providing a geometric exposition, among other things. Then follows in Section 2.3 an account of the workings of the BMI, where it is established that it is subject to serious bias. Once the index is adjusted for this bias, we show in Section 2.4 that exchange rates tend to revert to the mean, roughly speaking, after a period of about four years. Section 2.5 examines the predictive ability

---

[2] For an earlier analysis along these lines, see Lan (2002).

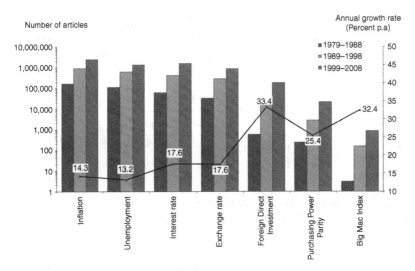

Figure 2.2 The growth of economic research.
Source: Factiva (http://global.factiva.com/sb/default.aspx?NAPC=S&
fcpil=en); keyword search conducted in July 2010.

of the BMI and establishes that overvalued (undervalued) currencies subsequently depreciate (appreciate). How equilibrating adjustments are split between changes in the nominal rate and inflation is discussed in Sections 2.6 and 2.7. The possible role of the US dollar in generating common shocks to all other currencies is explored in Section 2.8. Section 2.9 contains a survey of the literature on 'burgernomics', and concluding comments are given in Section 2.10.

2.2 Three versions of PPP

This section gives an account of PPP theory by presenting the three versions: absolute, relative, and stochastic. This material provides the theoretical underpinnings for the remainder of this chapter.

Let P_i denote the domestic price of good i in terms of domestic currency and P_i^* denote the price of the same good in the foreign country in terms of foreign currency. With zero transaction costs and no barriers to international trade, arbitrage equalises the cost of the good expressed in terms of a common currency:

$$P_i = SP_i^* \tag{2.1}$$

where S is the spot exchange rate (the domestic currency cost of a unit of foreign currency). Equation (2.1) is known as the 'law of one price'. The 2×2 structure of prices can be summarised as follows:

Currency	Location	
	Home	Foreign
Home	P_i	SP_i^*
Foreign	P_i/S	P_i^*

As prices in a given row are expressed in terms of the same currency, they are comparable 'rowwise', not 'columnwise'.

Further, let w_i and w_i^* denote the share of good i in the economy at home and abroad, with $\sum_{i=1}^{n} w_i = \sum_{i=1}^{n} w_i^* = 1$, where n is the number of goods. Then, multiplying both sides of equation (2.1) by w_i and summing over $i = 1, \ldots, n$, we obtain

$$\sum_{i=1}^{n} w_i P_i = S \sum_{i=1}^{n} w_i P_i^*$$

As the left-hand side of this equation is a share-weighted average of the n prices at home, it is interpreted as a price index, which we write as $P = \sum_{i=1}^{n} w_i P_i$. However, as the right-hand side of the equation applies domestic weights to foreign prices, it is not a conventional price index. To make some progress, we need the simplifying assumption that the foreign and domestic weights coincide so that $\sum_{i=1}^{n} w_i P_i^* = \sum_{i=1}^{n} w_i^* P_i^* = P^*$, an index of the price level abroad. Thus we have

$$P = SP^* \tag{2.2}$$

which is an economywide version of condition (2.1). We can interpret P as the domestic-currency cost of a basket of goods at home, whereas P^* is the cost of the same basket abroad. Thus SP^* converts this foreign currency cost into domestic-currency units, and the ratio $P/(SP^*)$ is a measure of the relative price of the two baskets. Expressing equation (2.2) as $S = P/P^*$, we obtain the *absolute version of PPP*, whereby the exchange rate is the ratio of domestic to foreign prices. Using lowercase letters to denote logarithmic values of variables, we obtain

$$s = p - p^* \tag{2.3}$$

Writing $r = p - p^*$ for relative prices, the preceding can be expressed as $s = r$. Next, we define the home country's *real exchange rate* as

$$q = \log \frac{P}{SP^*} \qquad (2.4)$$

which is the logarithmic relative price of the two baskets. According to absolute PPP, the real exchange rate $q = p - s - p^* = r - s = 0$ and is constant. When $q > 0$, prices at home are too high relative to those abroad, and the currency is said to be 'overvalued in real terms', and vice versa. If there is a tendency for the real rate to revert to the PPP value, a nonzero value of q signals some form of disequilibrium, calling for future readjustments of prices and/or the exchange rate.

Before proceeding, it is worthwhile to emphasise the restrictive conditions under which absolute parity holds. The assumption of zero transport costs and other barriers to trade rules out a 'wedge' between foreign and domestic prices. It also serves to exclude from PPP considerations all nontraded goods, those goods which do not enter into international trade due to prohibitive transport costs. As in a developed economy nontraded goods constitute something like 70 per cent of gross domestic product (GDP), their exclusion would seem to limit drastically the applicability of PPP theory, at least in its absolute form. Below we return to transport costs, and in the next section we return to the related issue of nontraded goods. A further restrictive condition underlying PPP is the assumption that the market basket associated with the price index is identical in the two countries.

We now present a geometric exposition of PPP theory. The left graph of panel A in Figure 2.3 presents the absolute PPP relationship, which is a 45-degree line passing through the origin. As this PPP line has a unit slope, any combination of s and r that lies on the line satisfies $s = r$, so the real exchange rate $q = r - s = 0$. On this PPP line, an increase in the relative price from r_1 to r_2, for example, leads to an equiproportional depreciation of the nominal exchange rate s, as illustrated by the movement from point A to B, whereby $s_2 - s_1 = r_2 - r_1$. The PPP ray acts as a boundary that divides up the exchange-rate/price space into two regions of mispricing. As shown on the right-hand graph in panel A, points above the ray indicate an undervaluation of the home-country currency ($q < 0$), where s is too high and/or r is too low. In this

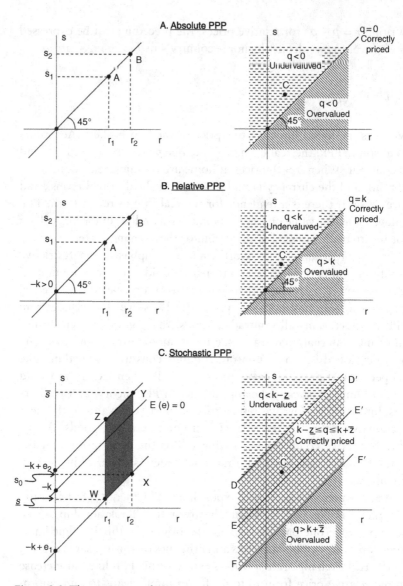

Figure 2.3 The geometry of PPP.

region, the price of the domestic basket P is below that of the foreign basket SP^*. Conversely, points below the PPP ray represent an overvalued domestic currency $(q > 0)$. Only at the boundary between these two regions is the currency correctly priced $(q = 0)$.

Let us now consider transport costs and any other barriers to the free flow of goods across borders that inhibit the equalisation of prices. With transport costs and other barriers, rather than having equation (2.1), we now have a generalisation $P_i = S(1 + T_i)P_i^*$, where T_i measures the proportionate wedge between domestic and foreign prices, which for short we term 'transport costs'. If these costs are approximately constant over time, then

$$\hat{P}_i = \hat{S} + \hat{P}_i^* \tag{2.5}$$

where a circumflex (^) represents relative change $(\hat{x} = dx/x)$. Equation (2.5) represents a weaker version of the law of one price because it is formulated in terms of changes not levels. We then can weight as before and aggregate over goods to obtain

$$\hat{P} = \hat{S} + \hat{P}^* \tag{2.6}$$

where $\hat{P} = \sum_{i=1}^{n} w_i \hat{P}_i$ is the change in the cost of the basket of goods at home, and $\hat{P}^*$ is the corresponding change for the foreign country. As these measures are share-weighted averages of the (infinitesimal) changes in the n individual prices, they are interpreted as Divisia price indexes. Integrating equation (2.6), we obtain $P = KSP^*$, where K is a constant of integration or, in logarithmic form,

$$s = p - p^* - k \tag{2.7}$$

This is the *relative version of PPP*. Since $\hat{x} = dx/x = d(\log x)$, equation (2.7) implies

$$\hat{S} = \hat{P} - \hat{P}^* \tag{2.8}$$

where $\hat{P}$ and $\hat{P}^*$ are interpreted as inflation at home and abroad, respectively. In words, the proportionate change in the exchange rate is equal to the inflation differential. Thus high-inflation countries experience depreciating currencies and vice versa, which is the open-economy version of the quantity theory of money. It is to be noted that equation (2.8) is just a rearrangement of equation (2.6). Note also that relative PPP expressed in equation (2.7) includes absolute PPP as a special case where $k = 0$ or $K = 1$ in $P = KSP^*$. To summarise, relative parity implies that the exchange rate is proportional to the price ratio, with the factor of proportionality not necessarily equal to unity. Under absolute parity, the proportionality factor is unity, so the exchange rate equals the price ratio.[3]

Geometrically, under relative PPP, the relationship between s and the relative price $r = p - p^*$ is a straight line of the form $s = r - k$, which is presented on the left graph of panel B in Figure 2.3. Along this line, the real exchange rate is $q = r - s = k$, which is constant. This relative PPP line also has a unit slope but an intercept $-k \neq 0$. Again, as we move up the line from A to B, an increase in the relative price still leads to an equiproportional depreciation in the nominal exchange rate such that $s_2 - s_1 = r_2 - r_1$. As before, points above the relative PPP line correspond to an undervaluation of the domestic currency $(q - k < 0)$, and those below the line correspond to an overvaluation $(q - k > 0)$, but in comparison with absolute PPP, the boundary between the two regions is now 'vertically displaced', as indicated by the graph given on the right-hand side of panel B in Figure 2.3.

Panel C in Figure 2.3 gives the case of *stochastic PPP*. [4] If we denote the stochastic deviation from relative parity by e with $E(e) = 0$ and variance σ^2, the real exchange rate then is the random variable $q = k - e$, with $\text{var}(q) = \sigma^2 > 0$, so q obviously is not constant. Initially, suppose for simplicity that e is a discrete random variable and that $e_1 < 0$ and $e_2 > 0$ are its only possible values. When the shock is $e_1 < 0$, we obtain a new, lower 45-degree line, $s = -k + e_1 + r$, which has an intercept of $-k + e_1$; similarly, $e_2 > 0$ results in the upper line in the left graph of panel C. Consider the situation in which $\underline{s}$ is the exchange rate and r_1 is the relative price so that we are located at the point W on the left graph of panel C. If there is now the same increase in the relative price as before, so that r rises from r_1 to r_2, then, in the presence of the shock e_1, we move from W to the point X with the rate depreciating

---

[3] A further issue about the distinction between absolute and relative PPP should be noted. Almost invariably statistical agencies publish information on the cost of a basket of goods in the form of a price index that has an arbitrary base, which determines the proportionality constant K. Such indexes can only be used for calculations of relative parity, not absolute.

[4] For an earlier rendition of stochastic PPP, see Lan (2002). For related work, see MacDonald and Stein (1999). Note also that MacDonald (2007, p. 42) considers PPP within an environment in which there are transaction costs in moving goods from one country to another. According to this broader version of PPP, there exists a 'neutral band' within which exchange rates and prices can fluctuate.

to s_0. However, if the shock is e_2, the same relative price r_2 leads to an exchange rate of $\bar{s}$, as indicated by the point Y. More generally, if relative prices change within the range $[r_1, r_2]$, and if the shocks can now vary continuously within the range $[e_1, e_2]$, then the exchange-rate/relative-price points lie somewhere in the shaded parallelogram WXYZ. Thus the relationship between the exchange rate and prices is $s = r - k + e$, which is the stochastic version of PPP. Due to the random shocks e, the exchange rate and prices are no longer proportionate. It is to be noted that the height of the shaded parallelogram exceeds its base, which accords with the idea that exchange rates are much more volatile than prices in the short run (Frenkel and Mussa, 1980). However in the long run, as $E(e) = 0$ and thus $E(s) = r - k$, relative PPP holds, and the expected value of the real exchange rate $E(q) = k$ is constant. Here k is the long-run, or equilibrium, value of the real exchange rate.

Therefore, in the case of stochastic PPP, the real exchange rate q is not constant and fluctuates around k, so exchange rates and prices are scattered around the 45-degree line. This is in contrast to relative PPP, in which q is a constant value for any combination of s and r and all (s, r) pairs located exactly on the 45-degree line. In other words, stochastic PPP means that there exists a 'neutral band' around the 45-degree line that contains values of the exchange rate and prices that identify the currency as being 'correctly priced'. Under relative PPP, these points are interpreted as deviations from parity. Obviously, the width of the band is the key to this approach: If it is sufficiently wide, then all possible configurations of exchange rates and prices would be contained in the band, and the approach would be vacuous. On the other hand, if the band is sufficiently narrow, all observations would locate outside it, and the approach always would be rejected. One way to strike a balance between the 'too wide' and 'too narrow' band problems is to proceed probabilistically.

Consider the probability distribution of the real exchange rate q with $E(q) = k$ and $var(q) = \sigma^2$. We commence with the symmetric case in which the probability of the exchange rate being undervalued $(q - k < 0)$ is $\alpha/2$, and the same $\alpha/2$ is the probability of the currency being overvalued $(q - k > 0)$, where $0 < \alpha < 1$. In other words, we can interpret $\alpha/2$ as the mass in each tail of the distribution, so our task is to characterise the location of the tails. According to Chebyshev's inequality,

$$\Pr\left(\left|q - k\right| > c\right) \leq \frac{\sigma^2}{c^2}$$

where c is a positive constant. We interpret c as defining the boundary so that $\alpha = \sigma^2/c^2$ or $c = \sqrt{\sigma^2/\alpha}$. Thus the lower bound is $k - \sqrt{\sigma^2/\alpha}$, and the upper bound is $k + \sqrt{\sigma^2/\alpha}$. The region of correct pricing is indicated in the area between the lines DD' and FF' on the right graph of panel C, which is defined by

$$k - \underline{z} \leq q \leq k + \bar{z} \qquad\qquad\qquad\qquad (2.9)$$

where $\underline{z} = \bar{z} = \sqrt{\sigma^2/\alpha}$. The points above the line DD' which correspond to the case $q < k - \underline{z}$ indicate that the currency is undervalued, whereas points below the line FF' $(q > k + \bar{z})$ identify overvaluation. Statistically, if we have a number of observations on q, $\alpha \times 100$ per cent of these would lie outside the band, and the remaining $(1 - \alpha) \times 100$ per cent would lie inside it. In this situation, the deviations are symmetric around the mean, so there are equal probabilities of currency under-valuation and overvaluation and $\underline{z} = \bar{z}$. In the more general case, the distribution of q is asymmetric, and the long-run relative PPP line EE' does not lie midway between the two boundaries DD' and FF'.

The preceding analysis does not hinge on q following any particular probability distribution – it is distribution-free. If we have information on the form of the distribution, then this additional information can be used to tighten the neutral band. Consider for the purpose of illustration the case of the normal distribution, whereby $q \sim N(k, \sigma^2)$ and $\alpha = 0.05$. Under normality,

$$\Pr\left[-1.96 < \frac{q - k}{\sigma} < 1.96\right] = 1 - \alpha = 0.95$$

so the neutral band for q is $[k - 1.96\sigma, k + 1.96\sigma]$. Contrast the width of this band with that implied by Chebyshev's inequality [equation (2.9)]. With $\alpha = 0.05$ as before, we have $\underline{z} = \bar{z} = \sqrt{\sigma^2/\alpha} = \sqrt{20}\sigma = 4.47\sigma$, so the neutral band is $[k - 4.47\sigma, k + 4.47\sigma]$. Thus the width of the band under normality is $2 \times 1.96\sigma$, whereas under Chebyshev's inequality it is $2 \times 4.47\sigma$, so the additional information that the distribution is normal results in a shrinkage of the band width by about 50 per cent.

It is worth noting that this approach to currency valuation resembles hypothesis testing. To see this, imagine the existence of an unknown 'true' state of the world in which the currency is priced either correctly or incorrectly, and we observe only whether or not the exchange-price configuration is located within the neutral band. There are four possible outcomes of the application of this approach:

1. When the currency is in fact priced correctly and stochastic PPP identifies this situation accurately; that is, the (s, r) point is located in the neutral band. Since the inference is correct, the procedure works satisfactorily.
2. When the currency is in fact priced correctly but stochastic PPP yields the conclusion that it is undervalued or overvalued. There is an $\alpha \times 100$ per cent probability of this incorrect inference being drawn, which is analogous to a Type I error.
3. When the currency is in fact priced incorrectly but stochastic PPP indicates that the currency is priced correctly. This is similar to the case of a Type II error.
4. When the currency is in fact priced incorrectly and stochastic PPP accurately indicates that the currency is priced incorrectly. In this situation, the correct inference is drawn.

This taxonomy is summarised in the following table:

True currency pricing	Does (s, r) lie in the neutral band?	
	Yes	No
Correct	Reliable inference	Type I error
Incorrect	Type II error	Reliable inference

To conclude this section, consider an arbitrary combination of s and r that is represented by the same point C in all three right-hand graphs of Figure 2.3. Since C lies above the PPP ray in panels A and B, both absolute PPP and relative PPP indicate that the currency is undervalued. However, according to stochastic PPP (panel C), the currency is priced correctly because point C lies within the neutral band. This situation is likely to be frequently encountered in practice, with many apparent departures from parity simply associated with the inherent volatility of currency markets. For example, some departures may be insufficient to justify the costs of moving goods internationally and/or taking a currency position, especially if they are expected to reverse themselves soon. Therefore, to value a currency, it is crucial that the proper distinction be made between the three versions of PPP.

2.3 The workings of the Big Mac Index

The preceding section highlighted the restrictive conditions under which absolute parity holds, *viz.*, (1) the absence of barriers to international trade, which also rules out nontraded goods, and (2) identical baskets underlying the price indexes in the home and foreign countries. The weaker condition of relative PPP largely avoids the first problem, which accounts for its more frequent use in practice, but the problem of identical baskets remains. Surprisingly, the BMI uses absolute parity in the context of a single-good basket, a Big Mac hamburger. In this section we illustrate the workings of the BMI, and as it purports to have much to say about the workings of the real-world currency markets, we assess how the BMI deals with the preceding two restrictive conditions and how it performs in practice.

Though just a single good, a McDonald's Big Mac hamburger has a variety of tradable ingredients, such as ground beef, cheese, lettuce, onions, bread, and so on, and a number of nontradable ingredients, such as labour, rent, and electricity, as well as other ingredients such as cooking oil, pickles, and sesame seeds. By estimating the Big Mac cost function using the prices of the various ingredients, Parsley and Wei (2007) recover the recipe in 'broad' basket form. They find that the shares of important ingredients are

Ingredient	Cost share (%)	
Tradable		
Beef	9.0	
Cheese	9.4	
Bread	<u>12.1</u>	30.5
Nontradable		
Labour	45.6	
Rent	4.6	
Electricity	<u>5.1</u>	55.3
Other		<u>14.2</u>
Total		100.0

We thus can regard the price of a Big Mac as being the cost of a basket of inputs, just as P in the preceding section is the cost of a market basket of goods. By comparing the price of a Big Mac in the United States and other countries, *The Economist* magazine judges whether currencies are priced correctly based on the idea that a Big Mac should cost the same everywhere around the world when using a common currency. Since the basket associated with the prices can be considered almost identical in the home and foreign countries, the BMI cleverly avoids problem 2 above associated with absolute PPP. But since transport costs and other trade barriers are not allowed when comparing prices, this is an application of absolute PPP.

As discussed in the preceding section, the arbitrage foundation of absolute parity applies to traded goods only. But the prices of non-traded goods also can be related across countries for at least two reasons. First, if there is substitution between traded and nontraded goods in production and consumption, then in a broad class of general equilibrium models, the change in the price of nontraded goods $\hat{P}_N$ is a weighted average of the changes in the prices of importables and exportables $\left(\hat{P}_M, \hat{P}_X\right) : \hat{P}_N = \omega \hat{P}_M + (1 - \omega)\hat{P}_X$, where $0 \leq \omega \leq 1$. Thus, if nontraded goods are good substitutes for importables, the weight ω is large, so the relative price P_N/P_M is approximately constant, whereas a large value of $1 - \omega$ implies that P_N/P_X is approximately constant (see Sjaastad, 1980, for details). Provided that the weight ω is approximately the same at home and abroad, if PPP equalises the prices of traded goods across countries, then there is at least a tendency for the same to be true for their weighted average, the price of nontraded goods. However, as this link is based on substitution in production and consumption, it could possibly take some time for these relative price changes to work themselves through the economy and for there to be full adjustment.

A second mechanism that links prices of nontraded goods across countries is expectations. If producers of nontraded goods know of the preceding link between their prices and those of traded goods (at least in an approximate sense), they reasonably may use it as a basis for their expectations. This could then mean that in setting prices, these producers employ as a short-cut the rule: Increase prices as soon as the exchange rate depreciates. An example is the Pedro the plumber in Buenos Aires, who puts up his prices as soon as the peso falls. This type of expectations mechanism may be quite rapid in its operation, especially if there has been a long history of inflation and depreciation. These two arguments can provide a rationale for the inclusion of elements of the cost of nontraded goods in PPP calculations, such as the BMI.

Figure 2.4 reproduces the table from the Big Mac article published in *The Economist* of 26 July 2008. As can be seen from column 4 of the table, the implied PPP of the dollar is just the ratio of the domestic Big Mac price in domestic currency (column 2) to that in the United States in terms of dollars (first entry in column 2). This ratio is the purchasing power of one US dollar in terms of Big Macs. However, the actual exchange rate, presented in column 5, may not be the same as this PPP exchange rate. Column 6 is the percentage difference between the PPP exchange rate and the actual exchange rate, a positive (negative) value of which indicates overvaluation (undervaluation) of a currency. An overvalued currency indicates that domestic prices are higher than foreign prices [$P/(SP^*) > 1$] and vice versa. Take as an example Brazil, the fourth country from the top of the list in the table. The first and forth entries in column 2 of the table show that it costs $ 3.57 to buy a Big Mac in the United States and 7.50 reals in Brazil. Thus the implied PPP exchange rate is $7.50/3.57 = 2.10$, as indicated by the third entry of column 4. As the actual exchange rate is 1.58 (the cost of $ 1 in terms of the real), the Brazilian real is overvalued by $(2.10 - 1.58)/1.58 = +33$ per cent (the third entry in column 6 of the table). Given the value of the real and US prices, Brazilian prices are too high, so a movement towards parity would require some combination of a fall in Brazilian prices and a depreciation of the real.

Tables 2A.1 and 2A.2 in Appendix 2A at the end of this chapter contain the implied PPP exchange rates and nominal exchange rates of all countries that have their Big Mac data published at least once in *The Economist* since the inception of the BMI in 1986. Tables 2.1 and 2.2 are the companion tables for the twenty-four countries that have all data available over the period of 1994–2008; these data will be used in all computations that follow. In the preceding paragraph we showed that for Brazil in 2008, the BMI is as much as 33 per cent above the market exchange rate. An element-by-element comparison of the third row of Table 2.1 with that of Table 2.2 reveals that there are similar large differences in most other years for this country. As will be discussed further below, the same problem of large deviations

The McCurrency menu

The hamburger standard

(1)	Big Mac prices In local (2)	(3)	Implied PPP[†] of the (4)	actual (5)	Under (−)/ over(+) valuation aganist (6)
United States[‡]	$3.57	3.57	–	–	
Argentina	Peso 11.0	3.64	3.08	3.02	+2
Australia	A$3.45	3.36	0.97	1.03	−6
Brazil	Real 7.50	4.73	2.10	1.58	+33
Britain	£2.29	4.57	1.56[§]	2.00	+28
Canada	C$4.09	4.08	1.15	1.00	+14
Chile	Peso 1,550	3.13	434	494	−12
China	Yuan 12.5	1.83	3.50	6.83	−49
Czech Republic	Koruna 66.1	4.56	18.5	14.5	+28
Denmark	DK28.0	5.95	7.84	4.70	+67
Egypt	Pound 13.0	2.45	3.64	5.31	−31
Euro Area**	€3.37	5.34	1.06[††]	1.59	+50
Hong Kong	HK$13.3	1.71	3.73	7.80	−52
Hungary	Forint 670	4.64	187.7	144.3	+30
Indonesia	Rupiah 18,700	2.04	5,238	9,152	−43
Japan	Yen 280	2.62	78.4	106.8	−27
Malaysia	Ringgit 5.50	1.70	1.54	3.2	−52
Mexico	Peso 32.0	3.15	8.96	10.2	−12
New Zealand	NZ$4.90	3.72	1.37	1.32	+4
Norway	Kroner 40.0	7.88	11.2	5.08	+121
Poland	Zloty 7.00	3.45	1.96	2.03	−3
Russia	Rouble 59.0	2.54	16.5	23.2	−29
Saudi Arabia	Riyal 10.0	2.67	2.80	3.75	−25
Singapore	S$3.95	2.92	1.11	1.35	−18
South Africa	Rand 16.9	2.24	4.75	7.56	−37
South Korea	Won 3,200	3.14	896	1,018	−12
Sweden	Skr38.0	6.37	10.6	5.96	+79
Switzerland	SFr6.50	6.36	1.82	1.02	+78
Taiwan	NT$75.0	2.47	21.0	30.4	−31
Thailand	Baht 62.0	1.86	17.4	33.4	−48
Turkey	litre 5.15	4.32	1.44	1.19	+21
UAE	Dirhams 10.0	2.72	2.80	3.67	−24
Colombia	Peso 7,000	3.89	1,960	1,798	+9
Costa Rica	Colones 1,800	3.27	504	551	−8
Estonia	Kroon 32.0	3.22	8.96	9.93	−10
Iceland	Kronur 469	5.97	131	78.6	+67
Latvia	Lats 1.55	3.50	0.43	0.44	−2
Lithuania	Litas 6.90	3.17	1.93	2.18	−11
Pakistan	Rupee 140	1.97	39.2	70.9	−45
Peru	New Sol 9.50	3.20	2.66	2.9	−10
Philippines	Peso 87.0	1.96	24.4	44.5	−45
Slovakia	Koruna 77.0	4.03	21.6	19.1	+13
Sri Lanka	Rupee 210	1.89	58.8	111	−47
Ukraine	Hryvnia 11.0	2.19	3.08	5.03	−39
Uruguay	Peso 61.0	2.55	17.1	23.9	−29

*At current exchange rates
†Purchasing-power parity; local price divided by price in the United States
‡Average of New York, Chicago, Atlanta and San Francisco §Dollars per pound
**Weighted average of prices in euro area ††Dollars per euro
Source: McDonald's; *The Economist*.

Figure 2.4 Example of Big Mac table.
Source: Derived from *The Economist*, 26 July 2008, p. 88.

Table 2.1 Implied PPP exchange rates for twenty-four countries, 1994–2008

Country	1994	1995	1996	1997	1998	1999	2000	2001	2002	2003	2004	2005	2006	2007	2008	Mean	SD	CV (× 100)
Argentina	1.57	1.29	1.27	1.03	0.98	1.03	1.00	0.98	1.00	1.51	1.50	1.55	2.26	2.42	3.08	1.50	0.63	41.8
Australia	1.07	1.06	1.06	1.03	1.04	1.09	1.03	1.18	1.21	1.11	1.12	1.06	1.05	1.01	0.97	1.07	0.06	5.79
Brazil	652	1.04	1.25	1.23	1.21	1.21	1.18	1.42	1.45	1.68	1.86	1.93	2.07	2.02	2.10	44.9	168	374
Britain	0.79	0.75	0.76	0.75	0.72	0.78	0.76	0.78	0.80	0.73	0.65	0.61	0.63	0.58	0.64	0.72	0.07	10.1
Canada	1.24	1.19	1.21	1.19	1.09	1.23	1.14	1.31	1.34	1.18	1.10	1.07	1.14	1.14	1.15	1.18	0.08	6.53
Chile	412	410	403	496	488	518	502	496	562	517	483	490	503	459	434	478	45.8	9.57
China	3.91	3.88	4.07	4.01	3.87	4.07	3.94	3.90	4.22	3.65	3.59	3.43	3.39	3.23	3.50	3.78	0.29	7.76
Czech Republic	21.7	21.6	21.6	21.9	21.1	21.9	21.7	22.0	22.6	20.9	19.5	18.4	19.0	15.5	18.5	20.5	1.94	9.46
Denmark	11.2	11.5	10.9	10.6	9.30	10.2	9.86	9.74	9.94	10.2	9.57	9.07	8.95	8.14	7.84	9.81	1.05	10.7
Euro area	1.09	1.08	1.07	1.03	0.96	1.04	1.02	1.01	1.07	1.00	0.94	0.95	0.95	0.90	0.94	1.00	0.06	6.00
Hong Kong	4.00	4.10	4.20	4.09	3.98	4.20	4.06	4.21	4.50	4.24	4.14	3.92	3.87	3.52	3.73	4.05	0.23	5.76
Hungary	73.5	82.3	90.7	112	101	123	135	157	184	181	183	173	181	176	188	143	42.1	29.5
Japan	170	169	122	122	109	121	117	116	105	96.7	90.3	81.7	80.6	82.1	78.4	111	28.7	25.9
Malaysia	1.64	1.62	1.59	1.60	1.68	1.86	1.80	1.78	2.02	1.86	1.74	1.72	1.77	1.61	1.54	1.72	0.13	7.56
Mexico	3.52	4.70	6.31	6.16	6.99	8.19	8.33	8.62	8.80	8.49	8.28	9.15	9.36	8.50	8.96	7.62	1.73	22.7
New Zealand	1.25	1.27	1.25	1.34	1.35	1.40	1.34	1.42	1.59	1.46	1.50	1.45	1.44	1.35	1.37	1.39	0.09	6.74
Poland	13478	1.47	1.61	1.78	2.07	2.26	2.19	2.32	2.37	2.33	2.17	2.12	2.10	2.02	1.96	900	3480	386
Russia	1261	3491	4025	4545	4688	13.8	15.7	13.8	15.7	15.1	14.5	13.7	15.5	15.2	16.5	1211	1902	157
Singapore	1.30	1.27	1.29	1.24	1.17	1.32	1.28	1.30	1.33	1.22	1.14	1.18	1.16	1.16	1.11	1.23	0.07	5.86
South Korea	1000	991	975	950	1016	1235	1195	1181	1245	1218	1103	817	807	850	896	1032	155	15.0
Sweden	11.1	11.2	11.0	10.7	9.38	9.88	9.56	9.45	10.4	11.1	10.3	10.1	10.6	9.68	10.6	10.3	0.64	6.17
Switzerland	2.48	2.54	2.50	2.44	2.31	2.43	2.35	2.48	2.53	2.33	2.17	2.06	2.03	1.85	1.82	2.29	0.24	10.7
Taiwan	27.0	28.0	27.5	28.1	26.6	28.8	27.9	27.6	28.1	25.8	25.9	24.5	24.2	22.0	21.0	26.2	2.34	8.91
Thailand	20.9	20.7	20.3	19.3	20.3	21.4	21.9	21.7	22.1	21.8	20.3	19.6	19.4	18.2	17.4	20.3	1.39	6.82

Notes:
1. The implied PPP exchange rate for country c in year t is defined as P_{ct}/P_t^*, where P_{ct} is the price of a Big Mac hamburger in country c during t, and P_t^* is the corresponding price in the United States.
2. SD = standard deviation; CV = coefficient of variation.

Source: The Economist

from parity occurs for most other countries. As under absolute parity these differences should be zero, this is not particularly encouraging for the proposition that BMI has economic content.

One other feature of Tables 2.1 and 2.2 is worthy of note. The last columns of these tables give the coefficients of variations of the implied PPPs and exchange rates in each country, and Figure 2.5 is the associated scatter. The points corresponding to Brazil, Poland and Russia are located far away from those for the other countries owing to the volatility of monetary conditions in these countries associated with currency redenominations. The left panel of Figure 2.5 shows that in seventeen of the remaining twenty-one countries, as the points lie above the 45-degree line, the implied PPPs are less volatile than the corresponding exchange rates. This difference between the behaviour of exchange rates and prices was noted long ago by Frenkel and Mussa (1980), who attributed it to the essential distinction between the natures of asset and goods markets. The exchange rate is the price of foreign money and, as such, behaves like the prices of other assets traded in deep, organised markets such as shares, bonds, and some commodities. The determination of asset prices tends to be dominated by expectations concerning the future course of events. As expectations change due to the receipt of new information, which is unpredictable, the net result is that changes in asset prices themselves are largely unpredictable, giving rise to the substantial volatility of these prices. By contrast, goods prices tend to be determined in flow markets, in which expectations play a much less prominent role. It is for this reason that goods prices tend to be more tranquil over time, reflecting changes in the familiar microeconomic factors of incomes, supply conditions, and so on. The Big Mac data reflect this difference between the volatility of asset and goods prices.

Under PPP, $P = SP^*$ or $P/(SP^*) = 1$. It is convenient to measure disparity logarithmically, so for country c in year t, we define $q_{ct} = \log\left[P_{ct}/\left(S_{ct}P_t^*\right)\right]$ as in equation (2.4), where we referred to this measure as the real exchange rate. This q_{ct}, when multiplied by 100, is approximately the percentage difference between P_{ct}/P_t^* and S_{ct}, the measure of disparity (or under- or overvaluation) used by *The Economist* (given in column 6 of the table in Figure 2.4). Under absolute PPP, $q_{ct} = 0$. Table 2.3 and Figure 2.6 give q_{ct} for each of the twenty-four countries over the fifteen-year period, and as can be seen, there are frequent departures from absolute PPP. Additionally, in the majority of countries, q_{ct} fluctuates substantially around its mean over

Table 2.2 Nominal exchange rates for twenty-four countries, 1994–2008

Country	1994	1995	1996	1997	1998	1999	2000	2001	2002	2003	2004	2005	2006	2007	2008	Mean	SD	CV (× 100)
Argentina	1.00	1.00	1.00	1.00	1.00	1.00	1.00	1.00	3.13	2.88	2.94	2.89	3.06	3.09	3.02	1.93	1.04	53.6
Australia	1.42	1.35	1.27	1.29	1.51	1.59	1.68	1.98	1.86	1.61	1.43	1.30	1.33	1.17	1.03	1.46	0.26	17.6
Brazil	949	0.90	0.99	1.06	1.14	1.73	1.79	2.19	2.34	3.07	3.17	2.47	2.30	1.91	1.58	65.0	245	376
Britain	0.69	0.62	0.66	0.61	0.60	0.62	0.63	0.70	0.69	0.63	0.56	0.55	0.53	0.50	0.50	0.61	0.07	10.9
Canada	1.39	1.39	1.36	1.39	1.42	1.51	1.47	1.56	1.57	1.45	1.37	1.25	1.12	1.05	1.00	1.35	0.18	12.9
Chile	414	395	408	417	455	484	514	601	655	716	643	593	530	527	494	523	99.9	19.1
China	8.70	8.54	8.35	8.33	8.28	8.28	8.28	8.28	8.28	8.28	8.26	8.26	8.03	7.60	6.83	8.17	0.44	5.40
Czech Republic	29.7	26.2	27.6	29.2	34.4	35.6	39.1	39.0	34.0	28.9	26.5	24.5	22.1	21.1	14.5	28.8	6.85	23.8
Denmark	6.69	5.43	5.85	6.52	7.02	6.91	8.04	8.46	8.38	6.78	6.22	6.06	5.82	5.46	4.70	6.56	1.10	16.8
Euro area	0.88	0.74	0.79	0.87	0.93	0.93	1.08	1.14	1.12	0.91	0.83	0.81	0.78	0.74	0.63	0.88	0.15	16.5
Hong Kong	7.73	7.73	7.74	7.75	7.75	7.75	7.79	7.80	7.80	7.80	7.80	7.79	7.75	7.82	7.80	7.77	0.03	0.39
Hungary	103	121.	150	178	213	237	279	303	272	224	211	204	206	180	144	202	57.6	28.6
Japan	104	84.2	107	126	135	120	106	124	130	120	112	107	112	122	107	114	12.8	11.2
Malaysia	2.69	2.49	2.49	2.50	3.72	3.80	3.80	3.80	3.80	3.80	3.79	3.81	3.63	3.43	3.20	3.38	0.55	16.4
Mexico	3.36	6.37	7.37	7.90	8.54	9.54	9.41	9.29	9.28	10.5	11.5	10.9	11.3	10.8	10.2	9.09	2.16	23.8
New Zealand	1.74	1.51	1.47	1.45	1.82	1.87	2.01	2.47	2.24	1.78	1.64	1.40	1.62	1.28	1.32	1.71	0.34	19.8
Poland	22433	2.34	2.64	3.10	3.46	3.98	4.30	4.03	4.04	3.89	3.86	3.31	3.10	2.75	2.03	1499	5791	386
Russia	1775	4985	4918	5739	5999	24.7	28.5	28.9	31.2	31.1	29.0	28.3	27.1	25.6	23.2	1580	2445	155
Singapore	1.57	1.40	1.41	1.44	1.62	1.73	1.70	1.81	1.82	1.78	1.72	1.66	1.59	1.52	1.35	1.61	0.16	9.71
South Korea	810	769	779	894	1474	1218	1108	1325	1304	1220	1176	1004	952	923	1018	1065	216	20.3
Sweden	7.97	7.34	6.71	7.72	8.00	8.32	8.84	10.2	10.3	8.34	7.58	7.41	7.28	6.79	5.96	7.92	1.20	15.2
Switzerland	1.44	1.13	1.23	1.47	1.52	1.48	1.70	1.73	1.66	1.37	1.28	1.25	1.21	1.21	1.02	1.38	0.21	15.5
Taiwan	26.4	25.7	27.2	27.6	33.0	33.2	30.6	32.9	34.8	34.8	33.5	31.1	32.1	32.8	30.4	31.1	3.02	9.73
Thailand	25.3	24.6	25.3	26.1	40.0	37.6	38.0	45.5	43.3	42.7	40.6	40.5	38.4	34.5	33.4	35.7	7.19	20.1

Notes:

1. The nominal exchange rate is the domestic currency cost of one US dollar. An increase thus implies a depreciation of the domestic currency and vice versa.

2. SD = standard deviation; CV = coefficient of variation.

Source: The Economist.

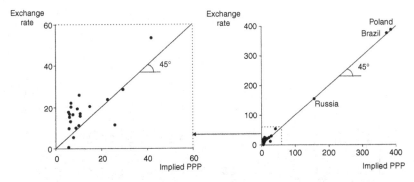

Figure 2.5 The volatility of exchange rates and prices, 1994–2008 (coefficients of variation; percentages).

the fifteen-year period; the exceptions to this general rule are Britain, China and Hong Kong. One striking pattern is the one-sided nature of the disparities. Among the twenty-four countries under investigation, eight countries – Australia, China, Hong Kong, Malaysia, Poland, Russia, Singapore and Thailand – always have undervalued currencies. The currencies of Britain, Demark and Switzerland are always overvalued, whereas the Czech koruna, the Hungarian forint and the Mexican peso are undervalued in all but one year. Moreover, the Swedish krona is overvalued in all years except one. Thus, for almost $8 + 3 + 3 + 1 = 15$ cases out of a total of twenty-four, the BMI declares the currencies to be continuously (or almost continuously) over- or undervalued for each of the fifteen years. These strings of persistent disparities over a fairly lengthy period in almost two-thirds of the cases raise serious questions about the credibility of the BMI as a pricing rule for currencies. To assess the current value of a currency, it would seem desirable for a robust pricing rule to appropriately incorporate past mispricing. The sustained nature of the departures from PPP, departures that are distinctly one-sided, means that past mispricing is largely ignored by the BMI. Below we explore further this problem.

To test the significance of the pattern of deviations from parity, we employ two tests, one based on a contingency table and the other a runs test. Consider again the signs of successive pricing errors. If these errors are independent, then the probability of the currency being over- or undervalued in year $t + 1$ is unaffected by mispricing in year t. To examine this hypothesis, in Table 2.4 we tabulate the mispricing for all

Table 2.3 Real exchange rates for twenty-four countries, 1994–2008

Country	1994	1995	1996	1997	1998	1999	2000	2001	2002	2003	2004	2005	2006	2007	2008	Mean	SE	t-value
Argentina	44.80	25.70	24.00	3.25	-2.37	2.84	-0.40	-1.59	-113.70	-64.38	-67.27	-62.37	-30.39	-24.47	2.01	-17.62	11.05	-1.60
Australia	-28.75	-24.56	-18.14	-22.21	-37.76	-37.71	-48.74	-51.66	-43.42	-37.46	-24.49	-20.21	-23.79	-14.53	-6.38	-29.32	3.35	-8.74
Brazil	-37.51	14.76	23.32	14.65	6.04	-35.42	-42.07	-43.51	-48.15	-60.35	-53.41	-24.71	-10.80	5.77	28.49	-17.53	7.90	-2.22
Britain	13.89	18.86	13.57	19.81	17.66	23.02	17.90	11.36	14.74	14.86	15.02	11.62	16.26	15.96	24.91	16.63	0.99	16.76
Canada	-11.14	-15.20	-11.53	-15.53	-26.46	-20.47	-25.82	-17.39	-16.04	-20.54	-21.88	-15.14	1.37	8.03	13.60	-12.94	3.04	-4.25
Chile	-0.44	3.60	-1.35	17.32	7.06	6.79	-2.36	-19.19	-15.27	-32.64	-28.54	-19.02	-5.18	-13.83	-12.91	-7.73	3.62	-2.14
China	-79.90	-78.91	-71.92	-73.15	-76.13	-70.92	-74.16	-75.35	-67.48	-81.83	-83.36	-87.94	-86.32	-85.70	-66.82	-77.32	1.75	-44.29
Czech Republic	-31.20	-19.53	-24.47	-28.76	-48.91	-48.56	-59.06	-57.04	-40.83	-32.53	-30.86	-28.55	-14.86	-30.76	24.45	-31.43	5.21	-6.03
Denmark	51.49	75.30	62.33	48.98	28.09	38.80	20.41	14.13	17.07	41.23	43.04	40.33	43.05	39.91	51.21	41.03	4.26	9.63
Euro area	21.39	37.17	30.17	16.77	3.50	11.33	-5.28	-11.61	-4.67	9.53	12.31	15.65	19.39	19.92	40.61	14.41	3.87	3.72
Hong Kong	-65.88	-63.54	-61.25	-63.89	-66.53	-61.32	-65.07	-61.60	-55.05	-60.87	-63.29	-68.66	-69.42	-79.85	-73.89	-65.34	1.54	-42.55
Hungary	-33.77	-38.51	-50.33	-46.34	-74.45	-65.55	-72.55	-65.69	-38.90	-21.42	-14.05	-16.29	-13.13	-2.27	26.28	-35.13	7.40	-4.74
Japan	49.14	69.39	13.15	-3.65	-21.05	0.82	9.99	-6.89	-21.15	-21.61	-21.88	-26.83	-32.84	-39.59	-30.87	-5.59	7.94	-0.70
Malaysia	-49.54	-42.94	-44.65	-44.68	-79.51	-71.44	-74.68	-75.87	-62.99	-71.45	-77.95	-79.63	-71.59	-75.45	-73.10	-66.36	3.54	-18.74
Mexico	4.70	-30.44	-15.47	-24.93	-20.00	-15.27	-12.23	-7.46	-5.37	-21.57	-33.23	-17.06	-18.89	-23.90	-12.92	-16.94	2.52	-6.73
New Zealand	-32.88	-17.19	-16.21	-7.67	-30.05	-29.01	-39.46	-55.54	-34.50	-19.98	-9.02	3.53	-12.09	5.25	3.90	-19.39	4.53	-4.28
Poland	-50.95	-46.79	-49.44	-55.66	-51.36	-56.44	-67.41	-55.10	-53.36	-51.48	-57.61	-44.55	-39.10	-30.68	-3.47	-47.56	3.83	-12.41
Russia	-34.20	-35.61	-20.03	-23.32	-24.67	-58.31	-59.39	-74.07	-68.91	-72.06	-69.31	-72.64	-55.97	-51.81	-33.92	-50.28	5.10	-9.85
Singapore	-19.21	-9.62	-8.71	-14.98	-32.38	-27.29	-28.78	-33.16	-31.72	-37.96	-41.24	-34.37	-31.42	-27.17	-19.90	-26.53	2.56	-10.36
South Korea	21.07	25.40	22.40	6.12	-37.25	1.35	7.58	-11.50	-4.63	-0.19	-6.41	-20.61	-16.59	-8.19	-12.73	-2.28	4.43	-0.51
Sweden	33.01	42.32	49.58	33.05	15.86	17.15	7.85	-8.43	1.37	28.32	30.65	30.95	38.00	35.43	58.00	27.54	4.63	5.95
Switzerland	54.29	81.12	70.93	50.59	41.62	49.50	32.40	36.03	42.14	52.88	52.45	50.10	51.85	42.32	57.94	51.08	3.23	15.84
Taiwan	2.09	8.63	1.25	1.79	-21.70	-14.19	-9.28	-17.71	-21.34	-29.81	-25.82	-23.88	-28.28	-39.97	-36.95	-17.01	3.88	-4.39
Thailand	-19.25	-17.31	-21.83	-30.20	-67.76	-56.37	-55.05	-74.25	-67.31	-67.36	-69.31	-72.64	-68.51	-64.05	-65.40	-54.44	5.41	-10.07
Mean	-8.28	-1.58	-4.36	-10.11	-24.94	-21.53	-26.90	-31.80	-30.81	-27.44	-26.89	-24.29	-19.14	-18.32	-4.91	-18.75	2.75	-5.95
SE	7.83	8.73	7.64	6.79	7.04	7.28	7.03	6.64	7.01	7.53	7.73	7.66	7.40	7.49	8.22	6.75	1.97	
t-value	-1.06	-0.18	-0.57	-1.49	-3.54	-2.96	-3.83	-4.79	-4.39	-3.65	-3.48	-3.17	-2.58	-2.44	-0.60	-2.78		-9.54

Notes:

1. The real exchange rate for country c in year t is defined as $q_{ct} = \log\left(P_{ct}/S_{ct}P_t^*\right)$, where P_{ct} is the price of a Big Mac hamburger in country c during t, P_t^* is the corresponding price in the United States, and S_{ct}, is the nominal exchange rate, defined as the domestic currency cost of US$1. A positive value of q_{ct} implies that the domestic currency is overvalued in real terms and vice versa.

2. All entries, except those in the last row and column, are to be divided by 100.

3. SE = standard error of the mean, which is a multiple $1/\sqrt{k}$ of the corresponding standard deviation, where $k = 15$ is the number of observations for the row means and $k = 24$ is the number of observations for the columns means. The t-values provide a test of the hypothesis that the means are zero.

4. The second-to-last entry in the second-to-last column, 2.75, is the standard error of the grand average, calculated as the standard deviation of all $24 \times 15 = 360$ observations divided by $\sqrt{360}$. The corresponding t-value is presented in the right-bottom entry of the table.

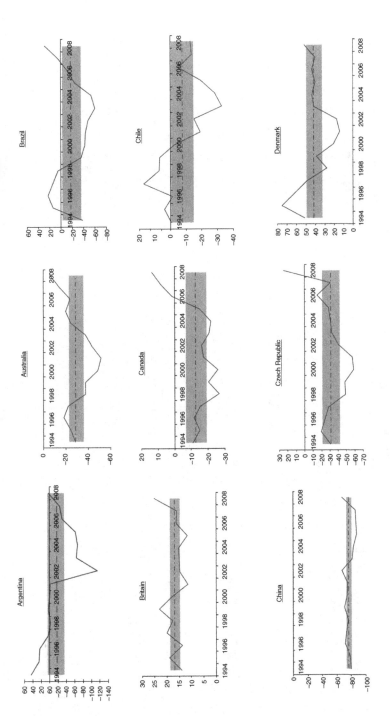

Figure 2.6 Big Mac real exchange rates for twenty-four countries, 1994–2008. (Means indicated by dashed-dotted lines; two standard error bands shaded; all × 100.)

35

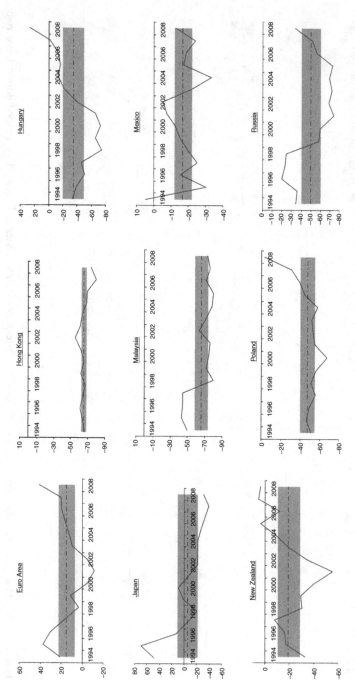

Figure 2.6 (*cont.*)

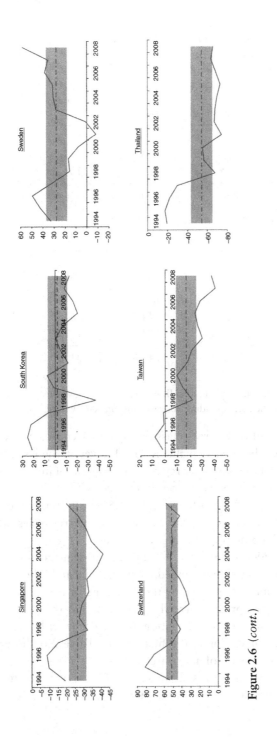

Figure 2.6 (*cont.*)

37

Table 2.4 *Contingency tables test of serial independence of mispricing, one-year horizon*

Mispricing in year t	Mispricing in year $t + 1$		Total
	Undervalued	Overvalued	
I. Observed			
Undervalued	221	14	235
Overvalued	15	86	101
Total	236	100	336
II. Expected under independence			
Undervalued	165	70	235
Overvalued	71	30	101
Total	236	100	336
III. Squared deviations			
Undervalued	19.0	44.7	63.7
Overvalued	44.1	104.1	148.2
Total	63.1	148.8	211.9

Note: The (i, j)th element of panel III is $(O_{ij} - E_{ij})^2/E_{ij}$, where O_{ij} and E_{ij} are the corresponding observed and expected values.

currencies in all years, cross-classified by sign in consecutive years t and $t + 1$. As the observed χ^2 value is 211.9 (given in the last entry of the last column of the table), we reject the hypothesis of independence on a year-on-year basis. Next, we repeat this test with the horizon extended from 1 year to 2, 3, ..., 14, and Table 2.5 reveals that independence is again rejected over most of these longer horizons regardless of whether or not overlapping observations are omitted.

Now consider a runs test. A 'run' is a subsequence of consecutive numbers of the same sign immediately preceded and followed by numbers of the opposite sign or by the beginning or end of the sequence. If a currency is priced correctly, it is expected that the number of runs in the signs of the deviation is consistent with that of a random series. For example, the first row of Table 2.6 shows that for Argentina, the signs of its q are $+ + + + - + - - - - - - - - +$, which comprise five runs. If there are T observations and positive and negative values occur randomly, then the number of runs R is

Table 2.5 *Test of serial independence over various horizons*

Horizon (years)	Observed χ^2 value, with overlapping observations	
	Included	Excluded
1	211.9	211.9
2	162.1	81.3
3	120.0	41.6
4	93.0	24.1
5	74.7	23.5
6	52.1	18.0
7	37.7	2.5
8	33.7	6.7
9	35.5	8.8
10	26.3	8.8
11	18.5	5.7
12	13.1	5.7
13	4.8	2.1
14	1.4	1.4

Note: Under the null of independence, the test statistic follows a χ^2 distribution with one degree of freedom. The critical value of $\chi^2_{.05}(1)$ is 3.8 and $\chi^2_{.01}(1)$ is 6.6.

a random variable with mean $E(R) = (T + 2T_+T_-)/T$ and variance $\text{var} R = 2T_+T_-(2T_+T_- - T)/T^2(T-1)$, where T_+ and T_- are the total number of observations with positive and negative signs, respectively, with $T_+ + T_- = T$. Asymptotically, the distribution of R is normal, and the test statistic $Z = [R - E(R)]/\sqrt{\text{var} R} \sim N(0,1)$. The results, given in Table 2.6, show that the null hypothesis of randomness is rejected in a substantial number of countries. Although this result is subject to the qualification that this test has only an asymptotic justification, there seems to be considerable evidence against the hypothesis of randomness.

Next, we test whether or not the disparities are significantly different from zero, which amounts to a test of bias in the BMI. The shaded regions of Figure 2.6 are the two-standard-error bands for the mean exchange rates. These bands include zero only for Argentina, Chile, Japan and South Korea, so we can reject the hypothesis that $q = 0$ for the remaining twenty countries. In Figure 2.7 we present the mean real

Table 2.6 *Runs tests for absolute parity*

Country	Sequence of signs of disparities	Number of runs Observed R	Number of runs Expected E(R)	Standard deviation $\sqrt{\mathrm{var}R}$	Test statistic Z
Argentina	+ + + + − + − − − − − − − − +	5	8.20	1.79	−1.79
Australia	− − − − − − − − − − − − − − −	1	1.00	0.00	+∞
Brazil	− + + + + − − − − − − − − + +	4	8.20	1.79	−2.35
Britain	+ + + + + + + + + + + + + + +	1	1.00	0.00	+∞
Canada	− − − + + + − − − − + + +	2	5.80	1.14	−3.33
Chile	− + − + + + − − − − − − −	5	6.87	1.43	−1.31
China	− − − − − − − − − − − − −	1	1.00	0.00	+∞
Czech Republic	− − − − − − − − − +	2	2.87	0.34	−2.55
Denmark	+ + + + + + + + + + + + +	1	1.00	0.00	+∞
Euro Area	+ + + + + + − + + + + + +	3	5.80	1.14	−2.45
Hong Kong	− − − − − − − − − − − − −	1	1.00	0.00	+∞
Hungary	− − − − − − − − − − − +	2	2.87	0.34	−2.55
Japan	+ + + − − + + − − − − −	4	7.67	1.64	−2.23
Malaysia	− − − − − − − − − − − −	1	1.00	0.00	+∞
Mexico	+ − − − − − − − − − − −	2	2.87	0.34	−2.55
New Zealand	− − − − − + − + +	4	5.80	1.14	−1.58
Poland	− − − − − − − − − −	1	1.00	0.00	+∞
Russia	− − − − − − − − − −	1	1.00	0.00	+∞
Singapore	− − − − − − − − − −	1	1.00	0.00	+∞
South Korea	+ + + + − − + − − + + + + + + +	4	8.20	1.79	−2.35
Sweden	+ + + + + − − + + + + + + + +	3	2.87	0.34	0.39
Switzerland	+ + + + − − − − − − − − −	1	1.00	0.00	+∞
Taiwan	+ + + + − − − − − −	2	6.87	1.43	−3.41
Thailand	− − − − − − − − − −	1	1.00	0.00	+∞

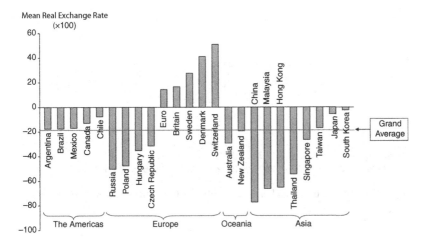

Figure 2.7 The geography of money: Over/undervaluation of currencies, 1994–2008 averages.

exchange rates with countries grouped into four regions. This figure reveals that all currencies except those for the five high-income European regions/countries – the Euro area, Britain, Sweden, Denmark and Switzerland – are undervalued on average. It is notable that among the Asians, the currencies of China, Malaysia, Hong Kong and Thailand are all substantially undervalued.[5] As exchange rates are expressed relative to the US dollar, some inferences about the value of the dollar can be drawn by averaging disparities over all nondollar currencies, as is done in the third-last row of Table 2.3. Thus we see that in 2008, on average, the twenty-four currencies were undervalued by about 5 per cent, which is equivalent to saying that the US dollar is overvalued by this amount. The value of the dollar over time thus is given by the entries of the third-last row of Table 2.3 with the signs changed. Figure 2.8 plots these values of the dollar, and as can be seen, it was most overvalued around 2001 and has been falling since then. The

---

[5] The productivity-bias hypothesis of Balassa (1964) and Samuelson (1964) says that the currencies of rich (poor) countries are overvalued (undervalued). While it is true that in Figure 2.7 the five countries (regions) with $q > 0$ all have high incomes, countries with $q < 0$ include Canada, Australia, New Zealand, Hong Kong, and Singapore, all of which probably also should be classified as rich. Thus the evidence in Figure 2.7 does not provide unambiguous support for the productivity-bias hypothesis.

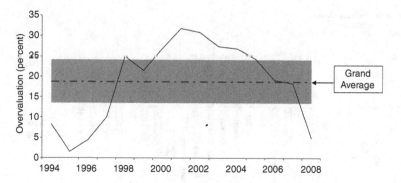

Figure 2.8 The value of the US dollar, 1994–2008. (Mean indicated by dashed-dotted line; two standard error band shaded.)

obvious qualification to this measure is that all twenty-four countries are equally weighted in valuing the dollar. More complex weighting schemes could be easily explored, but these would be unlikely to change the broad conclusion of an overvalued but falling dollar.

Given the 1997 Asian financial crisis, it is natural to divide the whole fifteen-year period into subperiods, before and after 1997, as in Table 2.7. There are two notable features here: (1) In the majority of countries, currencies become more undervalued (or less overvalued) following the Asian crisis. (2) The changes in the means over the two periods are mostly significant. The results of testing the hypothesis that the real exchange rate is zero can be summarised as follows:

	Period		
	1994–1997 (%)	1998–2008 (%)	1994–2008 (%)
Significantly positive	29	21	21
Significantly negative	54	79	67
Insignificant	17	0	13
Total	100	100	100

Thus we see that sustained mispricing is almost the rule for the BMI. If the BMI is meant to play the role of the long-term or equilibrium exchange rate, to which the actual rate is attracted, then an under- or overvaluation would signal subsequent equilibrating

Table 2.7 *Mean real exchange rates (logarithmic ratios × 100; standard errors × 100 in parentheses)*

Country	Period			t-value for equality of means
(1)	1994–1997 (2)	1998–2008 (3)	1994–2008 (4)	(5)
Argentina	24.44 (8.49)	−32.92(11.72)	−17.62(11.05)	3.96
Australia	−23.41 (2.22)	−31.47 (4.38)	−29.32 (3.35)	1.64
Brazil	3.80(13.92)	−25.28 (8.69)	−17.53 (7.90)	1.77
Britain	16.53 (1.63)	16.66 (1.26)	16.63 (0.99)	−0.07
Canada	−13.35 (1.17)	−12.79 (4.18)	−12.94 (3.04)	−0.13
Chile	4.78 (4.32)	−12.28 (3.90)	−7.73 (3.62)	2.93
China	−75.97 (2.01)	−77.82 (2.30)	−77.33 (1.75)	0.61
Czech Republic	−25.99 (2.56)	−33.41 (7.05)	−31.43 (5.21)	0.99
Denmark	59.53 (6.00)	34.30 (3.71)	41.03 (4.26)	3.58
Euro area	26.38 (4.55)	10.06 (4.39)	14.41 (3.87)	2.58
Hong Kong	−63.64 (0.95)	−65.96 (2.06)	−65.34 (1.54)	1.02
Hungary	−42.24 (3.74)	−32.55(10.03)	−35.13 (7.40)	−0.91
Japan	32.01(16.63)	−19.26 (4.49)	−5.59 (7.94)	2.98
Malaysia	−45.45 (1.42)	−73.97 (1.43)	−66.37 (3.54)	14.15
Mexico	−16.53 (7.72)	−17.08 (2.36)	−16.94 (2.52)	0.07
New Zealand	−18.49 (5.25)	−19.72 (6.01)	−19.39 (4.53)	0.16
Poland	−50.71 (1.86)	−46.41 (5.21)	−47.56 (3.83)	−0.78
Russia	−28.29 (3.89)	−58.28 (4.91)	−50.28 (5.10)	4.79
Singapore	−13.13 (2.45)	−31.40 (1.72)	−26.53 (2.56)	6.09
South Korea	18.75 (4.31)	−9.92 (3.68)	−2.28 (4.43)	5.06
Sweden	39.49 (4.01)	23.19 (5.66)	27.54 (4.63)	2.35
Switzerland	64.23 (7.16)	46.30 (2.39)	51.08 (3.23)	2.38
Taiwan	3.44 (1.74)	−24.45 (2.76)	−17.01 (3.88)	8.54
Thailand	−22.15 (2.84)	−66.18 (1.79)	−54.44 (5.41)	13.12
Mean	−6.08 (1.89)	−23.36 (2.99)	−18.75 (3.48)	4.48

adjustments of the exchange rate and/or prices. But lengthy periods of substantial, sustained, and significant mispricing demonstrate that such a mechanism is not at work. In a fundamental sense, the BMI fails, so the Big Mac metric of currency mispricing cannot be taken at face value. In large part, the reason for this failure is that the

BMI relies on absolute PPP, which ignores barriers to the international equalisation of prices. Fortunately, a simple modification of the BMI restores its predictive power, as is shown in the section after the next.

To summarise this section, we have established the following:

- The BMI uses the cost of a Big Mac hamburger as the metric for judging whether or not a currency is mispriced. As this product is made according to approximately the same recipe in all countries, the BMI avoids one of the major problems usually associated with absolute PPP – that the baskets underlying price indexes at home and abroad are likely to be substantially different, so the ratio of the indexes reflects a combination of compositional disparities, as well as currency fundamentals.
- A well-known empirical regularity is that exchange rates are more volatile than prices. The Big Mac prices reflect this regularity.
- There are substantial, sustained and significant deviations of exchange rates from the BMI. The under- and overvaluations of currencies based on the BMI published by *The Economist* cannot be accepted as a reliable measure of mispricing. The BMI needs to be enhanced before it has substantial practical power.

2.4 The bias-adjusted BMI and the speed of adjustment

The preceding discussion implies that the BMI is a biased indicator of absolute currency values. Thus, rather than absolute PPP holding in the form of $S = P/P^*$, we have $S = B(P/P^*)$, where B is the bias, or $s = b + p - p^*$ in logarithmic terms. This, of course, is just the relative PPP of Section 2.2 with $B = 1/K$ or $b = -k$. In this section we analyse the extent to which the bias-adjusted BMI tracks exchange rates by formulating it in terms of changes over time, $\Delta s = \Delta p - \Delta p^*$.

To proceed, we have to specify the length of the horizon for exchange-rate and price changes.[6] For any positive variable X_t ($t = 1, \ldots, T$), define $\Delta_{(h)} x_t = \log X_t - \log X_{t-h}$ as the h-year

---

[6] For related analyses, see Flood and Taylor (1996), Isard (1995, p. 49), Lothian (1985), and Obstfeld (1995).

logarithmic change and $\Delta^{(h)}x_t = (1/h)\Delta_{(h)}x_t$ as the corresponding annualised change, $h = 1,\ldots,T - 1$, $t = h + 1,\ldots,T$. As $\Delta^{(h)}x_t = (1/h)\sum_{s=0}^{h-1}(x_{t-s} - x_{t-s-1}) = (1/h)\sum_{s=0}^{h-1}\Delta_{(1)}x_{t-s}$, the annualised change over a horizon of h years is the average of the h one-year changes. Writing $r_{ct} = p_{ct} - p_t^*$ for the Big Mac price in country c in terms of that in the United States (as before), relative PPP implies that for horizon h, $\Delta_{(h)}s_{ct} = \Delta_{(h)}r_{ct}$, or dividing both sides by h,

$$\Delta^{(h)}s_{ct} = \Delta^{(h)}r_{ct} \tag{2.10}$$

Equation (2.10) states that exchange-rate changes are equal to the relative-price changes, with changes expressed as annual averages. To examine the content of this equation, we initially set $h = 1$ and plot one-year exchange-rate changes against the corresponding price changes for all countries. The graph on the top left-hand corner of Figure 2.9 contains the results. As can be seen, there is considerable dispersion around the solid 45-degree line, with a root-mean-squared error (RMSE) of 14 per cent.[7] In the other panels of the figure, as the horizon h increases, the points become noticeably closer to the 45-degree line, and the RMSE falls continuously to end up at a little over 2 per cent for $h = 14$ years. To clarify matters, Figure 2.10 provides a blow-up of the graphs for $h = 1, 6$, and 12.

To shed more light on the decrease in volatility as the horizon increases, consider the following parsimonious data-generating process for the real exchange rate:

$$q_t = \alpha + \beta q_{t-1} + \varepsilon_t \tag{2.11}$$

where α and β are constants, and the random disturbance term ε_t is iid, independent of q_{t-1}, with a zero mean and variance σ_ε^2. Figure 2.6 showed that there is considerable persistence in the behaviour of q over time, which could be consistent with model (2.11) with a high value of β. The stationarity of the real rate implies that $0 < \beta < 1$ and the variance of q is $\sigma^2 = \sigma_\varepsilon^2/(1 - \beta^2)$. On the other hand, if q follows a random walk, we have $\beta = 1$, so $q_t = \alpha + q_{t-1} + \varepsilon_t = (t - t_0)\alpha + q_{t_0} +$

---

[7] This RMSE is the square root of the ratio of $\sum_c\sum_t(\Delta_{(1)}r_{ct} - \Delta_{(1)}s_{ct})^2$ to the number of observations, which measures the dispersion of real exchange rate changes over a one-year horizon.

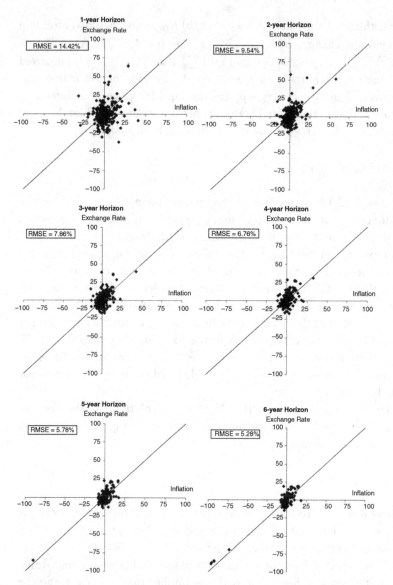

Figure 2.9 Scatter plots of exchange rates and prices, twenty-four countries, 1994–2008. (Annualised logarithmic changes × 100.)

Note: To facilitate presentation, the cases in which the annualised logarithmic changes (× 100) exceeded 100 per cent have been omitted. These cases are included in the computation of the RMSEs.

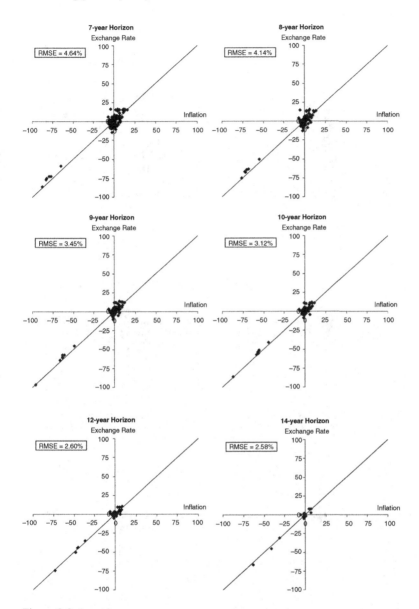

Figure 2.9 (*cont.*)

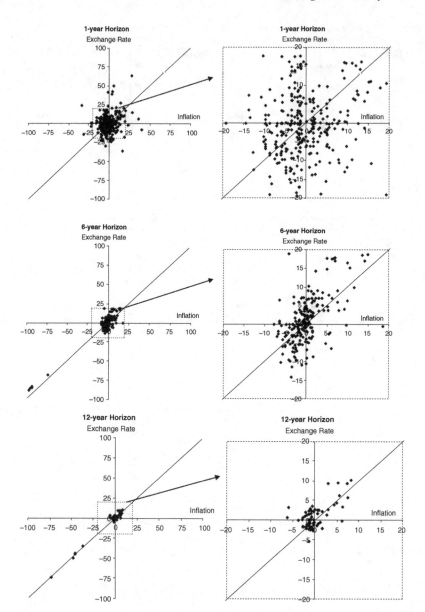

Figure 2.10 Blow-up of scatter plots of exchange rates and prices, twenty-four countries, 1994–2008. (Annualised logarithmic changes × 100.)

Note: To facilitate presentation, the cases in which the annualised logarithmic changes (× 100) exceeded 20 per cent have been omitted. These cases are included in the computation of the RMSEs.

$\sum_{s=t_0+1}^{t} \varepsilon_s$, where q_{t_0} is the initial value. Hence its variance at time t is $\sigma_t^2 = (t - t_0)\sigma_\varepsilon^2$ if the initial value is treated as fixed.

To examine the variance of the annualised change over horizon h, $\Delta^{(h)}q_t$, consider first the stationary case, in which $0 < \beta < 1$. Equation (2.11) implies that $q_t - q_{t-h} = \beta(q_{t-1} - q_{t-h-1}) + \varepsilon_t - \varepsilon_{t-h}$ ($h > 0$), which can be written as $\Delta^{(h)}q_t = \beta\Delta^{(h)}q_{t-1} + \Delta^{(h)}\varepsilon_t$, so

$$\text{var}\left[\Delta^{(h)}q_t\right] = \beta^2 \text{var}\left[\Delta^{(h)}q_t\right] + \frac{2}{h^2}\sigma_\varepsilon^2 - \frac{2\beta}{h}\text{cov}\left[\Delta^{(h)}q_{t-1},\varepsilon_{t-h}\right]$$

The covariance term in this equation is

$$\text{cov}\left[\Delta^{(h)}q_{t-1},\varepsilon_{t-h}\right] = \begin{cases} \begin{aligned} &\text{cov}[q_{t-1} - q_{t-2},\varepsilon_{t-1}] \\ &\quad = \text{cov}[q_{t-1},\varepsilon_{t-1}] = \sigma_\varepsilon^2 \quad \text{if } h = 1 \\ &\text{cov}[q_{t-1} - q_{t-h-1},\varepsilon_{t-h}] \\ &\quad = 0 \quad \text{if } h > 1 \end{aligned} \end{cases}$$

so

$$\text{var}\left[\Delta^{(h)}q_t\right] = \begin{cases} \dfrac{2(1-\beta)}{1-\beta^2}\sigma_\varepsilon^2 = \dfrac{2}{1+\beta}\sigma_\varepsilon^2 & \text{if } h = 1 \\[2ex] \dfrac{2}{h^2(1-\beta^2)}\sigma_\varepsilon^2 & \text{if } h > 1 \end{cases} \qquad (2.12)$$

Therefore, we can see that $\text{var}\left[\Delta^{(h)}q_t\right]$ decreases when the horizon h increases for the stationary case. This is represented in panel A of Figure 2.11 by the reciprocal quadratic curve of the form $\text{var}\left[\Delta^{(h)}q_t\right] \propto 1/h^2$, with $\beta = 0.06$.

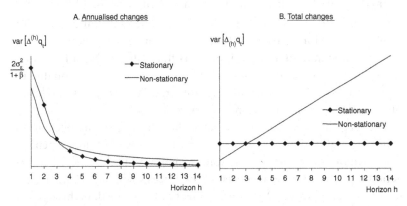

Figure 2.11 Variances of exchange-rate changes.

If $\beta = 1$, equation (2.11) implies that $q_t - q_{t-h} = h\alpha + \sum_{s=t-h+1}^{t} \varepsilon_s$. When divided by h, we have $\Delta^{(h)} q_t = \alpha + \frac{1}{h}\sum_{s=t-h+1}^{t} \varepsilon_s$, so

$$\text{var}\left[\Delta^{(h)} q_t\right] = \frac{1}{h^2} \text{var}\left[\sum_{s=t-h+1}^{t} \varepsilon_s\right] = \frac{\sigma_\varepsilon^2}{h} \tag{2.13}$$

which is represented in panel A of Figure 2.11 by the reciprocal curve of the form $\text{var}\left[\Delta^{(h)} q_t\right] \propto 1/h$. We can see that here $\text{var}\left[\Delta^{(h)} q_t\right]$ also declines, but at rate h, which is slower than in the stationary case. This contrast is more apparent by considering total volatility, defined as $\text{var}[\Delta_{(h)} q_t] = h^2 \text{var}\left[\Delta^{(h)} q_t\right]$. From equation (2.12) for $h > 1$ and equation (2.13), we have

$$\text{var}[\Delta_{(h)} q_t] = \begin{cases} \frac{2}{1-\beta^2} \sigma_\varepsilon^2 & \beta < 1 \\ h\sigma_\varepsilon^2 & \beta = 1 \end{cases} \tag{2.14}$$

which is constant when $\beta < 1$ and increases linearly when $\beta = 1$, as indicated in panel B of Figure 2.11.

Equation (2.14) is a key result that shows that when the real rate is stationary, the total volatility is constant as the length of the horizon expands, whereas it increases in the nonstationary case. Although this is based on the simple $AR(1)$ model, the implications carry over to more general cases. For a given horizon h, the RMSE of Figure 2.9 is the standard deviation of the annualised changes or an estimate of $\sqrt{\text{var}[\Delta^{(h)} q_t]}$. Thus $h \times$ RMSE is the standard deviation of the total changes $\sqrt{\text{var}[\Delta_{(h)} q_t]}$, which under stationarity also will be constant with respect to h. We use the RMSEs from Figure 2.9 in Figure 2.12 to plot $h \times$ RMSE against the horizon. As can be seen, total volatility increases first and after about four years fluctuates within a band that is less than 10 percentage points wide. It seems not unreasonable to interpret this evidence as saying real rates are stationary; that is, relative purchasing parity holds at longer horizons.

The preceding analysis shows that as the PPP adjustment mechanism is not evident until after a longish period, the speed of adjustment of exchange rates to prices is not rapid, which presumably reflects transaction costs, informational costs, sticky prices owing to contracts and menu costs, and so on. Over the medium term of more than three years, though, the tendency for exchange rates to reflect PPP is clear. In the

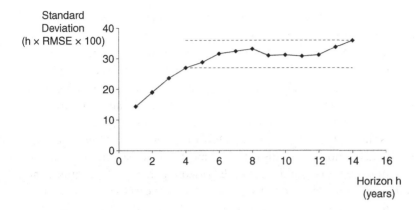

Figure 2.12 Total volatility and the horizon.

context of a discussion of Section 2.2, it seems that stochastic PPP with a relatively high value of the variance σ^2 is the way to think of the relationship between exchange rates and prices in the short term.[8]

2.5 Does the BMI predict future currency movements?

In this section we examine the predictive power of the BMI by asking the question, Can a currency be expected to appreciate (depreciate) in the future if it is currently undervalued (overvalued)? And if it does mean revert in this manner, how long does it take? For an early analysis along these lines, see Cumby (1996).

Since our objective is to examine the information contained in the current BMI regarding future currency values, we start by defining the horizon for future changes in the real rate as

$$\Delta_{(h)}q_{t+h} = q_{t+h} - q_t \tag{2.15}$$

which is the future change in q from the year t to $t + h$. This total change in q over h years is just the sum of the corresponding h annual changes, $\Delta_{(h)}q_{t+h} = \sum_{s=0}^{h-1} \Delta_{(1)}q_{t+h-s}$. Regarding current mispricing, the use of q_t would not be satisfactory due to the bias identified in Section 2.3. Instead, we use

$$d_t = q_t - \bar{q} \tag{2.16}$$

---

[8] See Appendix 2A.2 for more details.

with $\bar{q}$ the sample mean, which can be interpreted as the equilibrium exchange rate. Thus, now the currency is overvalued (undervalued) if $d_t > 0(< 0)$. Under PPP, deviations from parity die out, so if $d_t > 0(< 0)$, the future value q_{t+h} decreases (increases) relative to the current value q_t. To examine whether this is the case, we plot in Figure 2.13 the subsequent changes $\Delta_{(h)}q_{t+h}$ against d_t using the twenty-four-country Big Mac data for horizons of $h = 1, \ldots, 14$ years. PPP predicts that the points should lie in the second and fourth quadrants of the graphs, and Figure 2.13 shows that this is indeed mostly the case, with the pattern becoming more pronounced as the horizon increases. To examine the statistical significance of this pattern, we first carry out a χ^2 test of the independence of $\Delta_{(h)}q_{t+h}$ and d_t.[9] The test statistic is contained in the top box of each graph in Figure 2.13 and is significant for all horizons except fourteen years (for which there are few observations), so we can reject independence. Figure 2.14 plots the test statistic against the horizon h, and it can be seen that a maximum is reached for a horizon of $h = 5$ or 6, so in this sense the current deviation best predicts subsequent changes over a five- or six-year horizon.

In each panel of Figure 2.13 we also report the least-squares estimates of the predictive regression

$$\Delta_{(h)}q_{t+h} = \eta^h + \phi^h d_t + u_t^h \qquad (2.17)$$

where, for horizon h, η_h is the intercept, ϕ^h is the slope, and u_t^h is a zero-mean disturbance term. Panel A of Table 2.8 reproduces the estimates of this regression in the first line for each horizon, whereas column 6 reproduces the χ^2 values discussed in the preceding paragraph; the information in column 7 will be discussed subsequently. To examine the effect of inclusion of an intercept, we report for each horizon the slope coefficient when the intercept is suppressed, and the results are qualitatively similar. Panel B of Table 2.8 redoes the analysis with nonoverlapping observations only, and in all four sets of results – overlapping and nonoverlapping, with and without an intercept – the slope coefficient is significantly negative, indicating that the adjustment goes in the expected direction.

[9] This test is based on a 2×2 contingency table with rows for the sign of d_t and columns for the sign of $\Delta_{(h)}q_{t+h}$.

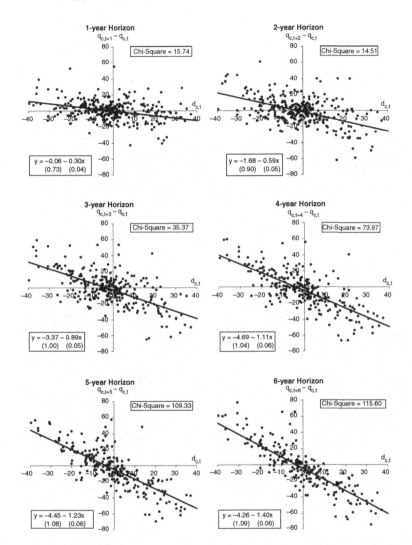

Figure 2.13 Scatter plots of future real exchange rates against current deviations from parity, twenty-four countries, 1994–2008. (Logarithmic changes × 100.)

Note: To facilitate presentation, the cases in which the annualised logarithmic changes (× 100) exceeded 80 per cent have been omitted. These cases are included in the regression and the chi-square value.

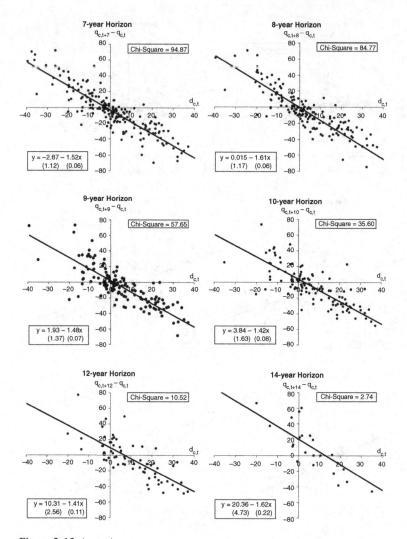

Figure 2.13 (*cont.*)

To further interpret equation (2.17), we combine equations (2.15), (2.16) and (2.17) to obtain

$$q_{t+h} = \left(\eta^h - \phi^h \bar{q}\right) + \left(\phi^h + 1\right) q_t + u_t^h \qquad (2.18)$$

Under PPP, q_{t+h} converges to the equilibrium value $\bar{q}$, so

$$\eta^h = 0 \quad \text{and} \quad \phi^h = -1 \qquad (2.19)$$

Chi square value

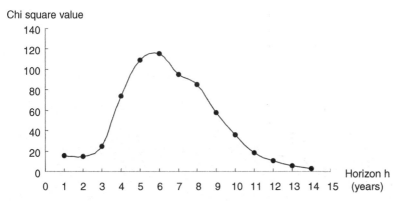

Figure 2.14 Predictive value of deviations from parity: Chi-square value against horizon.

A test of restriction (2.19) reveals whether or not there is full adjustment to mispricing over horizon h. The F-statistics for equation (2.19) are presented in columns 7 and 13 of Table 2.8 for the overlapping and nonoverlapping cases. For the purposes of testing, the results for the nonoverlapping case are more reliable, and as can be seen from panel B, the F-statistic is minimised for a three-year horizon and is not significant. The F-statistic is also not significant for a six-year horizon but is significant for all other horizons. These results point to the conclusion that, roughly speaking, over a period of three to six years there is more or less full adjustment of the rate to mispricing.

Panel A of Figure 2.15 plots the estimated intercepts and slopes, η^h and ϕ^h, against the horizon when overlapping observations are omitted. Three comments can be made. First, the intercepts are negative for all horizons up to ten, but many of the 95 per cent confidence intervals include zero. Second, the slope generally decreases with h, and the 95 per cent confidence interval includes -1 for horizons three to six years as well as seven years. As the absolute value of ϕ^h is the fraction of the total adjustment that occurs over horizon h, it is reasonable for a larger share of the adjustment to be completed over a longer horizon. Third, we should possibly pay more attention to the estimated slope rather than the intercept. If, for some reason, the equilibrium rate differs from the mean $\bar{q}$, then the difference would be absorbed into the intercept, which becomes nonzero even if PPP holds.

Table 2.8 *Predictive regressions, real exchange rates, twenty-four countries, 1994–2008* $[q_{c,t+b} - q_{c,t} = \eta^b + \phi^b d_{c,t} + u^b_{c,t}]$ *(standard errors in parentheses)*

Horizon b	A. With overlapping observations						B. Without overlapping observations					
	Intercept $\eta^b \times 100$	Slope ϕ^b	No. of observations	R^2	χ^2	F	Intercept $\eta^b \times 100$	Slope ϕ^b	No. of observations	R^2	χ^2	F
(1)	(2)	(3)	(4)	(5)	(6)	(7)	(8)	(9)	(10)	(11)	(12)	(13)
1	−0.06 (0.73)	−0.30 (0.04)	336	0.14	15.74	143.39*	−0.06 (0.73)	−0.30 (0.04)	336	0.14	15.74	143.39*
		−0.30 (0.04)	336					−0.30 (0.04)	336			
2	−1.68 (0.90)	−0.59 (0.05)	312	0.31	14.51	35.67*	−0.36 (1.38)	−0.59 (0.08)	168	0.27	6.65	15.54*
		−0.59 (0.05)	312					−0.58 (0.08)	168			
3	−3.37 (1.00)	−0.89 (0.05)	288	0.48	35.37	8.29*	−2.22 (1.49)	−0.87 (0.09)	96	0.52	19.84	2.17
		−0.88 (0.06)	288					−0.88 (0.09)	96			
4	−4.69 (1.04)	−1.11 (0.06)	264	0.60	73.97	11.86*	−6.46 (2.00)	−1.10 (0.10)	72	0.65	24.50	5.42*
		−1.10 (0.06)	264					−1.06 (0.10)	72			
5	−4.46 (1.08)	−1.23 (0.06)	240	0.66	109.33	16.63*	−5.94 (1.93)	−0.88 (0.11)	48	0.56	19.37	4.83*
		−1.23 (0.06)	240					−0.96 (0.12)	48			
6	−4.26 (1.09)	−1.40 (0.06)	216	0.74	115.60	33.48*	−4.23 (1.98)	−1.04 (0.10)	48	0.69	30.86	2.40
		−1.41 (0.06)	216					−1.05 (0.11)	48			
7	−2.87 (1.12)	−1.52 (0.06)	192	0.77	94.87	43.46*	−0.14 (3.17)	−1.42 (0.16)	48	0.64	19.86	3.65*
		−1.54 (0.06)	192					−1.42 (0.15)	48			
8	0.02 (1.17)	−1.62 (0.06)	168	0.80	84.77	50.14*	−6.71 (4.46)	−1.51 (0.21)	24	0.70	10.29	7.80*
		−1.61 (0.06)	168					−1.67 (0.19)	24			
9	1.94 (1.37)	−1.48 (0.07)	144	0.74	57.65	22.20*	−5.94 (3.12)	−1.26 (0.15)	24	0.77	6.40	6.75*
		−1.44 (0.07)	144					−1.34 (0.13)	24			

10	3.84 (1.63)	−1.43 (0.08)	120	0.72	35.60	13.54*	−4.16 (3.06)	−1.38 (0.14)	24	0.81	2.67	8.17*
		−1.34 (0.08)	120					−1.48 (0.13)	24			
11	8.02 (2.08)	−1.47 (0.10)	96	0.70	18.50	11.67*	0.22 (2.22)	−1.55 (0.10)	24	0.91	2.67	18.01*
		−1.23 (0.09)	96					−1.54 (0.09)	24			
12	10.31 (2.56)	−1.41 (0.11)	72	0.68	10.52	8.96*	4.05 (1.89)	−1.42 (0.09)	24	0.92	2.90	11.55*
		−1.12 (0.01)	72					−1.33 (0.08)	24			
13	13.07 (3.40)	−1.43 (0.14)	48	0.68	5.94	7.77*	5.94 (2.89)	−1.53 (0.14)	24	0.85	2.90	7.58*
		−1.10 (0.13)	48					−1.39 (0.13)	24			
14	20.37 (4.73)	−1.62 (0.22)	24	0.71	2.74	9.61*	20.37 (4.73)	−1.62 (0.22)	24	0.71	2.74	9.61*
		−1.16 (0.26)	24					−1.16 (0.26)	24			

Notes:

1. The χ^2 statistics of columns 6 and 12 test the hypothesis of the independence of $q_{c,t+b} - q_{c,t}$ and $d_{c,t}$. Under the null, χ^2 has one degree of freedom.

2. The F-statistics of columns 7 and 13 test the joint hypothesis of $\eta^b = 0$ and $\phi^b = -1$. Under the null, F has degrees of freedom equal to 2 and $N-2$, where N is the number of observations.

3. An asterisk (*) indicates significance at the 5 per cent level.

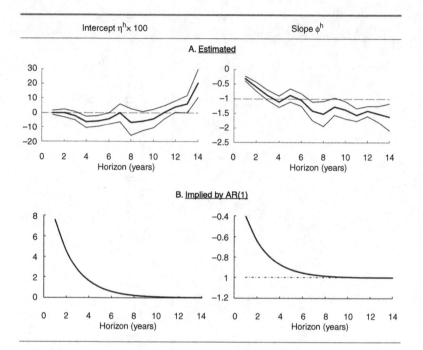

Figure 2.15 Time paths of estimated and implied parameters.
Note: In panel *A* the thick lines are estimated parameters, whereas the thinner lines are the 95 per cent confidence limits.

Next, consider as an illustrative example the $AR(1)$ case [equation (2.11)] $q_t = \alpha + \beta q_{t-1} + \varepsilon_t$ so that

$$q_{t+h} = \frac{\alpha(1 - \beta^{h-1})}{1 - \beta} + \beta^h q_t + \sum_{j=1}^{h} \beta^{h-j} \varepsilon_{t+j} \qquad (2.20)$$

Equating the intercepts and slopes of the right-hand sides of equations (2.18) and (2.20), we have $\left(\eta^h - \phi^h \bar{q}\right) = \alpha \left(1 - \beta^{h-1}\right)/(1 - \beta)$, $\left(\phi^h + 1\right) = \beta^h$, or

$$\eta^h = \bar{q}\beta^h \left(1 - \frac{1}{\beta}\right), \qquad \phi^h = \beta^h - 1 \qquad (2.21)$$

We use $\bar{q} = -0.2$, the grand average from the Big Mac data, and $\beta = 0.6$, as before, in equation (2.21) to plot the intercept η^h and slope ϕ^h against h, and panel B of Figure 2.15 gives the results. As these plots do not match those of panel A too well, it seems that the actual data-generating process is somewhat more complex than the simple $AR(1)$ model.

Since the work of Meese and Rogoff (1983a, 1983b), the random-walk model has become the 'gold standard' by which to judge the forecast performance of exchange-rate models. Accordingly, we compare the forecasts from the BMI and the bias-adjusted BMI with those from a random walk. Under the BMI, absolute parity holds, and the forecast real exchange rate at any horizon h is zero, $q_{t+h} = 0$; the bias-adjusted BMI, as represented by equations (2.17) and (2.19), implies that $q_{t+h} = \bar{q}$, and the random walk predicts no change, $q_{t+h} = q_t$. We compute the RMSE of the forecasts over all currencies and years for horizons $h = 1, ..., 14$, and Figure 2.16 shows that the random-walk model outperforms the BMI for all horizons, which is the familiar Meese-Rogoff result. However, the figure also reveals that beyond a one-year horizon, the bias-adjusted BMI beats the random walk. For example, for a four-year horizon, the RMSE is about 40 per cent for the BMI, 30 per cent for the random walk, and something less than 20 per cent for the bias-adjusted BMI. This is an encouraging result for the bias-adjusted BMI.

This section can be summarised as follows:

- The direction of future changes in currency values is clearly not independent of current deviations from parity. Overvalued currencies subsequently depreciate, whereas undervalued currencies appreciate.
- The adjustment to deviations from parity tends to be more or less fully complete over a period of three to six years.
- The bias-adjusted BMI beats the random-walk model for all but one-year horizons, demonstrating that it has considerable predictive power regarding future currency values.

2.6 The split between the nominal rate and prices

In this section we examine the relationship between mispricing and the two components of the real exchange rate – the nominal exchange rate and inflation – over different horizons in the future. From the definition

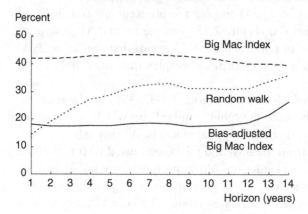

A. With overlapping observations

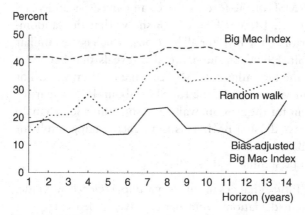

B. Without overlapping observations

Figure 2.16 The quality of three sets of exchange-rate forecasts (RMSE).

of the real exchange rate, $q_t = \log\left[P_t / \left(S_t P_t^*\right)\right]$, and using the previous change notation of $\Delta_{(h)} x_{t+h} = \log\left(X_{t+h} / X_t\right)$, we have the identity

$$\Delta_{(h)} q_{t+h} = -\Delta_{(h)} s_{t+h} + \Delta_{(h)} r_{t+h} \tag{2.22}$$

where, for example, $\Delta_{(h)} r_{t+h} = \Delta_{(h)} p_{t+h} - \Delta_{(h)} p_{t+h}^*$ is the cumulative inflation differential over h years in the future. Equation (2.22) decomposes the future change in the real rate into the corresponding changes in the nominal rate and the inflation differential. A positive value of $\Delta_{(h)} q_{t+h}$ means that the inflation differential exceeds the nominal depreciation of the exchange rate, which amounts to a real appreciation over an h-year horizon.

To examine the mean-reverting behaviour of the two components over different horizons, consider predictive regressions analogous to equation (2.17):

$$-\Delta_{(h)}s_{t+h} = \eta_s^h + \phi_s^h d_t + u_{st}^h, \quad \Delta_{(h)}r_{t+h} = \eta_r^h + \phi_r^h d_t + u_{rt}^h \quad (2.23)$$

where, for horizon h, $\eta_s^h, \phi_s^h, \eta_r^h$, and ϕ_r^h are parameters, d_t is current mispricing defined by equation (2.16), and u_{st}^h and u_{rt}^h are zero-mean error terms.[10] The parameters in equations (2.17) and (2.23) satisfy

$$\eta_s^h + \eta_r^h = \eta^h, \quad \phi_s^h + \phi_r^h = \phi^h \quad (2.24)$$

whereas the errors satisfy $u_{st}^h + u_{rt}^h = u_t^h$. To interpret model (2.23), for simplicity, we set the two intercepts $\eta_s^h = \eta_r^h = 0$ and the error terms to their expected value of zero so that $-\Delta_{(h)}s_{t+h} = \phi_s^h d_t$ and $\Delta_{(h)}r_{t+h} = \phi_r^h d_t$. Adding both sides of these two equations then gives $\Delta_{(h)}q_{t+h} = \left(\phi_s^h + \phi_r^h\right) d_t$ or $d_t = \Delta_{(h)}q_{t+h} \Big/ \left(\phi_s^h + \phi_r^h\right)$. Substituting this expression for d gives

$$-\Delta_{(h)}s_{t+h} = \lambda^h \Delta_{(h)}q_{t+h}, \quad \Delta_{(h)}r_{t+h} = \left(1 - \lambda^h\right)\Delta_{(h)}q_{t+h}$$

where $\lambda^h = \phi_s^h \Big/ \left(\phi_s^h + \phi_r^h\right)$. As $\left(\phi_s^h + \phi_r^h\right)$ is the response of q to mispricing d, λ^h is the share of this response that is brought about via the nominal rate, whereas $(1 - \lambda^h)$ is the share for prices.

The least-squares estimator automatically satisfies the aggregation constraints [equation (2.24)], and Table 2.9 presents the results using the twenty-four-country Big Mac data for horizons $h = 1, \ldots, 14$. As most of the parameters are insignificant, the split between the nominal rate and inflation cannot be precisely estimated. The χ^2 values in this table test the independence between (1) $-\Delta_{(h)}s_{t+h}$ and d_t and (2)

---

[10] Model (2.23) also can be viewed as part of the reduced form of a system of simultaneous equations. The structural equations comprise [(2.17) and using an obvious notation]

$$-\Delta_{(h)}s_{t+h} = \alpha_s^h + \beta_s^h \Delta_{(h)}q_{t+h} + \varepsilon_{st}^h, \quad \Delta_{(h)}r_{t+h} = \alpha_r^h + \beta_r^h \Delta_{(h)}q_{t+h} + \varepsilon_{rt}^h \quad (2.23')$$

where the endogenous variables are $-\Delta_{(h)}s_{t+h}, \Delta_{(h)}q_{t+h}$, and $\Delta_{(h)}r_{t+h}$, whereas d_t is exogenous. Substituting the right-hand side of equation (2.17) for $\Delta_{(h)}q_{t+h}$ in equation (2.23') then yields the reduced form, model (2.23), with

$$\eta_x^h = \alpha_x^h + \phi_x^h \eta^h, \quad \phi_x^h = \beta_x^h \phi^h, \quad u_{xt}^h = \varepsilon_{xt}^h + \beta_x^h u_t^h, \quad x = s, r$$

Table 2.9 *More predictive regressions, twenty-four countries, 1994–2008 (standard errors in parentheses)*

	(1) Negative change in nominal exchange rate $-(s_{c,t+h} - s_{c,t}) = \eta_s^b + \phi_s^b d_{ct} + u_{s,ct}^b$					(2) Inflation differential $r_{c,t+h} - r_{c,t} = \eta_r^b + \phi_r^b d_{ct} + u_{r,ct}^b$				
Horizon h (1)	Intercept $\eta_s^b \times 100$ (2)	Slope ϕ_s^b (3)	No. of observations (4)	R^2 (5)	χ^2 (6)	Intercept $\eta_r^b \times 100$ (7)	Slope ϕ_r^b (8)	No. of observations (9)	R^2 (10)	χ^2 (11)
				A. With overlapping observations						
1	5.85 (3.87)	-0.15 (0.22)	336	0.00	8.46*	-5.91 (3.80)	-0.16 (0.21)	336	0.00	7.91*
		-0.16 (0.22)	336				-0.14 (0.21)	336		
2	6.75 (4.54)	-0.21 (0.25)	312	0.00	12.15*	-8.43 (4.40)	-0.39 (0.25)	312	0.01	7.04*
		-0.23 (0.25)	312				-0.36 (0.25)	312		
3	7.68 (5.25)	-0.26 (0.29)	288	0.00	32.91*	-11.05 (5.17)	-0.62 (0.28)	288	0.01	1.49
		-0.29 (0.29)	288				-0.59 (0.28)	288		
4	9.26 (6.07)	-0.39 (0.32)	264	0.01	57.87*	-13.96 (5.96)	-0.73 (0.32)	264	0.02	0.000
		-0.41 (0.33)	264				-0.70 (0.32)	264		
5	12.07 (6.79)	-0.46 (0.36)	240	0.01	68.70*	-16.52 (6.77)	-0.77 (0.36)	240	0.02	1.57
		-0.46 (0.36)	240				-0.77 (0.36)	240		
6	13.01 (7.53)	-0.68 (0.39)	216	0.01	66.62*	-17.35 (7.57)	-0.72 (0.40)	216	0.02	1.27
		-0.65 (0.39)	216				-0.76 (0.40)	216		
7	14.95 (8.50)	-0.93 (0.46)	192	0.02	55.81*	-17.81 (8.59)	-0.59 (0.46)	192	0.01	3.15
		-0.82 (0.46)	192				-0.72 (0.46)	192		
8	19.15 (9.90)	-1.00 (0.54)	168	0.02	43.28*	-19.14 (10.03)	-0.61 (0.55)	168	0.01	0.00
		-0.73 (0.52)	168				-0.88 (0.53)	168		
9	25.30 (11.86)	-0.95 (0.63)	144	0.02	32.31*	-23.37 (12.09)	-0.53 (0.65)	144	0.01	0.02
		-0.45 (0.60)	144				-0.99 (0.61)	144		
10	32.90 (14.69)	-0.98 (0.74)	120	0.02	13.73*	-29.05 (14.96)	-0.45 (0.75)	120	0.00	0.96
		-0.24 (0.67)	120				-1.10 (0.68)	120		

11	47.17 (19.49)	−1.65 (0.90)	96	0.03	3.49	−39.15 (19.72)	0.18 (0.95)	96	0.00	2.92
		−0.26 (0.76)	96				−0.97 (0.76)	96	0.01	
12	62.87 (24.25)	−2.21 (1.08)	72	0.06	4.14*	−52.56 (24.44)	0.80 (1.09)	72		0.90
		−0.46 (0.88)	72				−0.66 (0.87)	72	0.03	
13	86.55 (31.94)	−2.98 (1.35)	48	0.10	0.97	−73.48 (31.98)	1.55 (1.36)	48		0.17
		−0.83 (1.17)	48				−0.27 (1.15)	48	0.08	
14	135.62 (53.16)	−4.94 (2.49)	24	0.15	2.06	−115.26 (51.96)	3.32 (2.43)	24		0.08
		−1.83 (2.41)	24				0.68 (2.29)	24		

B. Without overlapping observations

1	5.85 (3.87)	−0.15 (0.22)	336	0.00	8.46*	−5.91 (3.79)	−0.16 (0.21)	336	0.00	7.91*
		−0.16 (0.22)	336				−0.14 (0.21)	336		
2	11.55 (7.66)	−0.30 (0.42)	168	0.00	4.92*	−11.91 (7.46)	−0.28 (0.41)	168	0.00	9.00*
		−0.35 (0.42)	168				−0.23 (0.41)	168		
3	17.24 (13.14)	−0.71 (0.76)	96	0.01	15.02*	−19.45 (12.96)	−0.16 (0.75)	96	0.00	0.74
		−0.68 (0.76)	96				−0.20 (0.75)	96		
4	21.06 (17.56)	−0.54 (0.85)	72	0.01	15.47*	−27.52 (17.29)	−0.56 (0.84)	72	0.01	0.16
		−0.66 (0.84)	72				−0.40 (0.84)	72		
5	36.34 (24.78)	−1.79 (1.46)	48	0.03	15.97*	−42.28 (24.85)	0.92 (1.47)	48	0.01	0.01
		−1.31 (1.44)	48				0.35 (1.46)	48		
6	35.33 (23.92)	−1.43 (1.25)	48	0.03	18.55*	−39.56 (24.38)	0.40 (1.28)	48	0.00	0.17
		−1.32 (1.27)	48				0.27 (1.30)	48		

Table 2.9 (cont.)

Horizon b (1)	(1) Negative change in nominal exchange rate $-(s_{c,t+h} - s_{c,t}) = \eta_s^b + \phi_s^b d_{ct} + u_{s,ct}^b$					(2) Inflation differential $r_{c,t+b} - r_{c,t} = \eta_r^b + \phi_r^b d_{ct} + u_{r,ct}^b$				
	Intercept $\eta_s^b \times 100$ (2)	Slope ϕ_s^b (3)	No. of observations (4)	R^2 (5)	χ^2 (6)	Intercept $\eta_r^b \times 100$ (7)	Slope ϕ_r^b (8)	No. of observations (9)	R^2 (10)	χ^2 (11)
7	39.73 (23.72)	−1.72 (1.17)	48	0.05	30.08*	−39.87 (24.25)	0.30 (1.20)	48	0.00	8.07*
		−1.85 (1.19)	48				0.43 (1.22)	48		
8	92.91 (52.50)	−4.31 (2.45)	24	0.12	6.40*	−99.61 (53.62)	2.80 (2.51)	24	0.05	0.00
		−2.18 (2.24)	24				0.52 (2.30)	24		
9	99.31 (51.33)	−4.31 (2.40)	24	0.13	5.45*	−105.24 (52.74)	3.05 (2.47)	24	0.07	0.06
		−2.03 (2.22)	24				0.64 (2.29)	24		
10	104.54 (51.01)	−4.36 (2.37)	24	0.13	3.56	−108.70 (52.58)	2.98 (2.46)	24	0.06	0.00
		−1.97 (2.22)	24				0.49 (2.29)	24		
11	112.15 (51.65)	−4.49 (2.42)	24	0.14	2.74	−111.93 (52.49)	2.94 (2.46)	24	0.06	0.08
		−1.92 (2.27)	24				0.38 (2.30)	24		
12	115.14 (51.97)	−4.57 (2.43)	24	0.14	2.74	−111.09 (52.18)	3.14 (2.44)	24	0.07	0.30
		−1.93 (2.29)	24				0.60 (2.29)	24		
13	123.58 (52.21)	−4.79 (2.44)	24	0.15	2.06	−117.64 (51.79)	3.27 (2.42)	24	0.08	0.08
		−1.96 (2.33)	24				0.57 (2.30)	24		
14	135.62 (53.16)	−4.94 (2.49)	24	0.15	2.06	−115.26 (51.96)	3.32 (2.43)	24	0.08	0.08
		−1.83 (2.41)	24				0.68 (2.29)	24		

Notes:
1. The χ^2 statistics in columns 6 and 11 test the hypotheses of the independence between $-(s_{c,t+h} - s_{c,t})$ and d_{ct} and $r_{c,t+b} - r_{c,t}$ and d_{ct}, respectively. Under the null, χ^2 has one degree of freedom.
2. An asterisk (*) indicates significance at the 5 per cent level.

$\Delta_{(h)} r_{t+h}$ and d_t. Since for most horizons the χ^2 values for the nominal rate are considerably higher than those for inflation, we can possibly conclude that future changes in the real rate are mainly bought about by nominal exchange rates but recognise the uncertainty in the split. Looking at panel B of the table, which refers to the nonoverlapping case, it can be seen that the χ^2 value for the nominal rate is maximised for a horizon of four to seven years, which is not too different from the pattern for the real rate (see Table 2.8).

There are four countries that experienced considerable monetary turmoil associated with currency redenominations or a sudden switch from a fixed to a floating regime. These are Argentina, Brazil, Poland and Russia. When analysing nominal magnitudes such as exchange rates and prices, it is possible that this type of disruption could substantially affect the results. When model (2.23) is reestimated with these countries omitted, two major changes occur. First, the tendency for changes in the real exchange rate to be brought about by variations in the nominal rate is substantially more pronounced. Second, the estimates are now much more precisely estimated. For details, see Appendix 2A.4. The possible explanation for these changes is that most, if not all, of the changes in the exchange rates and prices that accompany monetary turmoil are unexpected. As these changes are only weakly related to past currency mispricing, including the experience of these four countries with the others skews the results and blurs the role of the nominal rate in doing most of the 'heavy lifting' in the adjustment process.

Next, suppose that at some horizon H there is complete adjustment of the real rate to mispricing so that

$$\Delta_{(H)} q_{t+H} = -d_t \tag{2.25}$$

According to this equation, if, for example, the currency is today undervalued by 10 per cent ($d_t = -0.10$), then over the next H years it appreciates by the same amount, $q_{t+H} - q_t = 0.10$. The complete adjustment restriction [equation (2.19)] then takes the form $\eta^H = 0$, $\phi^H = -1$, so equation (2.24) becomes

$$\eta_s^H + \eta_r^H = 0, \quad \phi_s^H + \phi_r^H = -1 \tag{2.24'}$$

Table 2.10 *Seemingly unrelated regressions under full adjustment, twenty-four countries, 1994–2008* $[-(s_{c,t+H} - s_{c,t}) = \eta_s^H + \phi_s^H d_{ct} + u_{s,ct}^H$ *and* $r_{c,t+H} - r_{c,t} = \eta_r^H + \phi_r^H d_{ct} + u_{r,ct}^H$, *with* $\eta_s^H + \eta_r^H = 0$ *and* $\phi_s^H + \phi_r^H = -1$ *(standard errors in parentheses)]*

	With overlapping observations			Without overlapping observations		
Horizon H (1)	Intercept $\eta_s^H \times 100$ (2)	Slope ϕ_s^H (3)	No. of observations (4)	Intercept $\eta_s^H \times 100$ (5)	Slope ϕ_s^H (6)	No. of observations (7)
1	5.90 (3.79)	−0.72 (0.21)	336	5.90 (3.79)	−0.72 (0.21)	336
		−0.74 (0.21)	336		−0.74 (0.21)	336
2	8.38 (4.42)	−0.60 (0.25)	312	11.97 (7.42)	−0.78 (0.40)	168
		−0.61 (0.25)	312		−0.83 (0.41)	168
3	10.79 (5.15)	−0.37 (0.28)	288	20.66 (12.80)	−0.91 (0.74)	96
		−0.39 (0.28)	288		−0.84 (0.75)	96
4	14.09 (5.94)	−0.27 (0.32)	264	30.79 (17.02)	−0.39 (0.82)	72
		−0.32 (0.32)	264		−0.60 (0.83)	72
5	14.80 (6.73)	−0.32 (0.36)	240	36.95 (24.26)	−1.81 (1.43)	48
		−0.37 (0.36)	240		−1.26 (1.41)	48
6	14.36 (7.49)	−0.56 (0.39)	216	26.54 (23.04)	−1.51 (1.21)	48
		−0.61 (0.39)	216		−1.46 (1.21)	48
7	15.14 (8.46)	−0.90 (0.46)	192	39.65 (23.15)	−1.97 (1.14)	48
		−0.86 (0.46)	192		−2.10 (1.17)	48
8	19.16 (9.83)	−1.11 (0.53)	168	84.01 (49.70)	−4.99 (2.13)	24
		−0.84 (0.52)	168		−3.64 (2.33)	24
9	26.48 (11.75)	−1.25 (0.63)	144	74.44 (46.53)	−5.41 (2.18)	24
		−0.66 (0.59)	144		−4.41 (1.96)	24
10	35.57 (14.52)	−1.28 (0.73)	120	85.92 (45.67)	−6.07 (2.14)	24
		−0.38 (0.67)	120		−4.68 (1.98)	24
11	49.86 (19.27)	−1.81 (0.93)	96	112.76 (48.49)	−6.05 (2.27)	24
		−0.18 (0.76)	96		−3.43 (2.19)	24
12	63.46 (23.92)	−2.23 (1.07)	72	119.41 (49.67)	−5.01 (2.32)	24
		−0.34 (0.87)	72		−1.30 (2.24)	24
13	81.25 (31.24)	−2.81 (1.33)	48	111.47 (49.46)	−3.72 (2.31)	24
		−0.64 (1.13)	48		−0.27 (2.19)	24
14	94.84 (49.41)	−3.69 (2.32)	24	94.84 (49.41)	−3.69 (2.31)	24
		−1.09 (2.03)	24		−1.09 (2.03)	24

The hypothesis of complete adjustment restricts the equations for the nominal rate and inflation according to equation (2.24′). We use the seemingly unrelated estimator (SURE) to estimate the two equations in model (2.23) as a system with the cross-equation restriction [equation (2.24′)] imposed and interpret the full adjustment horizon H as being successively equal to 1, ..., 14 years. Table 2.10 contains the results.

While many of the estimates are again imprecisely determined, for the nonoverlapping case, most of the estimates of ϕ_s^H for two- to four-year horizons are less than one standard error away from –1, which points to the nominal rate doing the bulk of the adjusting. Since the standard errors are still high, though, we conclude that precise measurement of the nominal/inflation split remains elusive. However, when the four high-inflation countries are omitted from the analysis, the results become more informative, with the nominal rate more clearly playing the role of the dominant adjuster to mispricing (see Appendix 2A.4 for details).

2.7 The geometry of adjustment

In this section we consider further the adjustment process by developing a simple geometric framework that highlights the relative flexibility of the exchange rate and prices. Consider model (2.23) for the complete-adjustment horizon H. Restriction (2.24′) means that the model then becomes

$$-\Delta_{(H)}s_{t+H} = \phi_s^H d_t, \quad \Delta_{(H)}r_{t+H} = -\left(1 + \phi_s^H\right)d_t$$

where for simplicity we have suppressed the intercepts and set the disturbances at their expected values of zero. The preceding equations can be written as

$$\Delta_{(H)}s_{t+H} = \gamma d_t, \quad \Delta_{(H)}r_{t+H} = -(1 - \gamma)d_t \tag{2.26}$$

where $\gamma = -\phi_s^H$. If the currency is undervalued ($d_t < 0$), then prices at home are too low relative to those abroad, that is, $p_t < s_t + p_t^* + \bar{q}$. Thus we expect $d_t < 0$ to be associated with (1) a future nominal appreciation, $\Delta_{(H)}s_{t+H} \leq 0$, implying that $\gamma \geq 0$, and/or (2) a rise in relative inflation, $\Delta_{(H)}r_{t+H} \geq 0$, implying $-(1 - \gamma) \leq 0$. Accordingly, $0 \leq \gamma \leq 1$, which means that the nominal rate changes by a fraction γ of the mispricing, whereas relative inflation changes by the remainder $1 - \gamma$. When the nominal rate does most of the adjusting, the parameter $\gamma > 0.5$, and we have the ranking of changes

$$\left|\Delta_{(H)}r_{t+H}\right| < \left|\Delta_{(H)}s_{t+H}\right| < \left|d_t\right|$$

In words, the change in the rate is bracketed by the change in relative inflation and the initial mispricing.

Combining the two equations in (2.26) to eliminate d_t yields

$$\Delta_{(H)} s_{t+H} = -\left(\frac{\gamma}{1-\gamma}\right) \Delta_{(H)} r_{t+H} \tag{2.27}$$

As the parameter γ is a positive fraction, the ratio $-\gamma/(1-\gamma)$ on the right-hand side of the preceding falls in the range $[-\infty, 0]$. Equation (2.27) describes the simultaneous adjustment of the exchange rate and prices in the future to current mispricing, with $-\gamma/(1-\gamma)$ the elasticity of the rate with respect to the price ratio P/P^* along the adjustment path. It is to be noted that as equation (2.27) deals with the equilibrating adjustments to mispricing, or a deviation from parity, this equation does not describe a PPP type of relation, whereby the rate and prices move proportionally. A deviation of either sign results in equilibrating adjustments in the nominal rate and inflation that are negatively correlated, which is why the elasticity in equation (2.27), $-\gamma/(1-\gamma)$, is negative. This elasticity characterises the tradeoff between a higher nominal rate and a lower price level, and vice versa, required to return the real rate back to its equilibrium value $\bar{q}$.

The schedule FF in Figure 2.17 corresponds to equation (2.27). This schedule passes through the origin and has slope $-\gamma/(1-\gamma) < 0$, which reflects the nature of the flexibility of the monetary side of the economy, that is, the relative flexibility of the rate as compared with prices. Going back to equation (2.26), when the nominal rate bears all adjustment to mispricing and relative inflation remains unchanged, $\gamma = 1$ and $1 - \gamma = 0$, and the FF schedule is vertical. In the opposite extreme, where the rate is fixed, $\gamma = 0$, $1 - \gamma = 1$, and FF coincides with the horizontal axis. In a fundamental sense, the slope of FF reflects the relative cost of changes in the exchange rate as compared with price changes. Related considerations include whether or not the country pursues inflation targeting as the objective of monetary policy and the extent to which the value of the currency is 'managed' by the monetary authorities.

One way to obtain some additional information regarding the split between the nominal rate and inflation is to employ signal-extraction theory (Lucas, 1973). Write the real exchange rate as the sum of its two components as

$$q = r + x \tag{2.28}$$

where $r = p - p^*$ is the relative price, and $x = -s = q - r$ is the reciprocal nominal rate, the (logarithmic) foreign-currency cost of a unit of

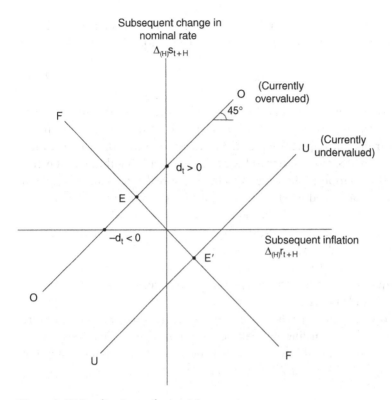

Figure 2.17 Implications of mispricing.

domestic currency.[11] Assume that (1) r is normally distributed with mean $\bar{r}$ and variance σ_r^2; (2) x is normal with mean $\bar{x}$ and variance σ_x^2; and (3) r and x are orthogonal. Our objective is to forecast x given q. We start with a linear conditional forecast of r,

$$r_f = \theta + \kappa q \tag{2.29}$$

where the subscript f denotes the forecast. Minimisation of the mean squared error, defined as $E(r_f - r)^2$, gives

$$\theta = (1 - \kappa)\bar{r} - \kappa\bar{x}, \quad \kappa = \frac{\sigma_r^2}{\sigma_x^2 + \sigma_r^2} \tag{2.30}$$

---

[11] In this paragraph, for notational simplicity we suppress subscript t for q, r and x (or s).

Substituting the first member of equation (2.30) into equation (2.29) yields $r_f = (1 - \kappa)\bar{r} + \kappa(q - \bar{x})$. Based on equation (2.28), we then have

$$E(x_f|r_f) = q - r_f = (1 - \kappa)(q - \bar{r}) + \kappa\bar{x} \tag{2.31}$$

This equation shows that the conditional forecast of the nominal rate is a weighted average of (1) the deviation of the real rate from the long-run relative price and (2) the historical mean of the nominal rate. If $\sigma_x^2 = \sigma_s^2 \gg \sigma_r^2$ (as seems to be the case empirically), the second member of equation (2.30) gives $\kappa \approx 0$, so the real rate term in equation (2.31) is accorded most of the weight in forecasting the nominal rate. That is, equation (2.31) becomes $E(x_f|r_f) \approx q - \bar{r}$, which implies that $E(\Delta x_f|r_f) \approx \Delta q$. In words, the future change in the real rate is almost entirely brought about by the nominal rate adjusting. In the context of the full-adjustment horizon H, we then can write equation (2.25) as $\Delta_{(H)}s_{t+H} \approx d_t$, which from equation (2.26) means that $\gamma \approx 1$, and the FF schedule in Figure 2.17 is near vertical in this case.

To be able to say where the economy locates on FF, we need more information regarding the link between mispricing, the change in the exchange rate, and inflation. This is provided by combining equation (2.25) and identity (2.22) for $h = H$:

$$\Delta_{(H)}s_{t+H} = d_t + \Delta_{(H)}r_{t+H} \tag{2.32}$$

To interpret this equation, first consider the overvaluation case so that $d_t > 0$. Equation (2.32) then gives the combinations of the future nominal depreciation and higher inflation at home required to eliminate the overvaluation. These combinations are represented by the schedule OO (for overvaluation) in Figure 2.17. This schedule has a slope of 45 degrees and an intercept on the vertical axis of $d_t > 0$. As the schedule indicates, the initial overvaluation could lead to (1) an equiproportional nominal depreciation with inflation unchanged $(\Delta_{(H)}s_{t+H} = d_t, \Delta_{(H)}r_{t+H} = 0)$; (2) no change in the nominal rate, with all the adjustment falling on inflation $(\Delta_{(H)}s_{t+H} = 0, \Delta_{(H)}r_{t+H} = -d_t)$; or (3) any combination thereof. The overall equilibrium is given by point E in Figure 2.17, the intersection of the OO and FF schedules. As can be seen, the overvaluation leads to a sharing of the adjustment between a depreciation and a slowing of inflation. It is to be noted that point E is uniquely determined by (1) the initial overvaluation, which gives the location of OO, and (2) the degree of relative flexibility of the exchange rate, as measured by the slope of FF.[12]

The preceding discussion refers to the situation in which the currency is initially overvalued. The undervaluation case is represented in Figure 2.17 by the schedule UU, so the overall equilibrium is now given by the point E'. Here the undervaluation leads to a subsequent appreciation and higher inflation.

2.8 Is there a dollar effect?

In the preceding discussion, currency mispricing is identified with the excess of the real exchange rate q over its mean $\bar{q}$. This reflects the preponderance of nonzero means in Figure 2.6, but Figure 2.8 also reveals that the corresponding mean for the US dollar is also far away from zero, and importantly, there are large swings in the dollar below and above the mean. As the twenty-four other currencies are all expressed in terms of the dollar, they thus could be subject to common shocks owing to dollar fluctuations. In this section we investigate this possibility.

Equation (2.16) defines mispricing as $d_t = q_t - \bar{q}$. We extend this to allow for a shock that hits all currencies simultaneously at time t, x_t, by redefining mispricing as $d'_t = d_t - x_t$. Since it is desirable for mispricing to have a zero expectation, we need $\sum_t x_t = 0$ so that $E(d'_t) = 0$. Replacing d_t on the right-hand side of the predictive regression [equation (2.17)] with d'_t, we then obtain

$$\Delta_{(h)}q_{t+h} = \Sigma_\tau \alpha_{\tau,\tau+h} D_{\tau,t} + \phi^h d_t + u_t^h \tag{2.33}$$

where $\alpha_{\tau,\tau+h} = \eta^h - \phi^h x_\tau$ is the coefficient of the time dummy variable $D_{\tau,t}$, which takes the value of 1 if $\tau = t$ and 0 otherwise. Note that

---

[12] The intercepts in the two equations in (2.23), η_s^h and η_r^h, represent the changes in the rate and relative inflation that occur for reasons other than mispricing. For simplicity of exposition, in the preceding we set the intercepts to zero. When these terms are nonzero, equation (2.27) becomes
$$\Delta_{(H)}s_{t+H} = -\frac{\eta_s^H}{1-\gamma} - \left(\frac{\gamma}{1-\gamma}\right)\Delta_{(H)}r_{t+H}$$
Thus, if $\eta_s^H < 0$, which amounts to an 'autonomous' depreciation in the rate, the term $-\eta_s^H/(1-\gamma) > 0$ and the FF schedule in Figure 2.17 now have a positive intercept on the vertical axis rather than passing through the origin. Accordingly, a given initial overvaluation is now associated with a larger subsequent depreciation of the rate and a smaller decrease in relative inflation. Vice versa when $\eta_s^H > 0$.

$\sum_t x_t = 0$ implies $\left(1/N^h\right) \Sigma_\tau \alpha_{\tau,\tau+h} = \eta^h$, where N^h is the number of year coefficients for horizon h, so the time effects 'wash out' over the whole period.

Table 2.11 contains the estimates of equation (2.33) for $h = 1, ..., 14$. To further allow for common shocks across countries, we use robust standard errors involving a cluster correction whereby the disturbances are equicorrelated (Kleok, 1981). The coefficients of the time dummies are cross-currency averages of the change in q over the relevant horizons after adjusting for the initial mispricing, as measured by the term $\phi^h d_t$; averaging over all nondollar currencies in this manner extracts the common dollar effect. Many of these year coefficients are significant, and for a given horizon, they vary substantially, which points to the importance of the dollar effect. It can be seen from the first row of the table (which refers to $h = 1$) that the year coefficients are initially positive, then negative, and end up positive. This pattern is the mirror image of the path of the US dollar given in Figure 2.8. The year 2008 plays a prominent role as the time effects involving this year, $\alpha_{\tau,2008}$, $\tau = 1994, ..., 2007$, are always among the largest in Table 2.11; these coefficients are the last entries of columns 2 through 15 of panel A. Depending on the base year for the comparison, these estimates range from about 8 to 23 per cent and are always highly significant. These values reflect the sharp depreciation of the dollar or the appreciation of other currencies in 2008 (see Figure 2.8). The importance of the dollar effects is also underscored by the increase in all relevant values of R^2 in going from Table 2.8 (where the year effects are excluded) to Table 2.11. The estimates of η^h and the slope coefficients given in columns 16 and 17 of Table 2.11 are close to what they were before in Table 2.8. Additionally, in the nonoverlapping case, the F-statistics for the hypothesis of full adjustment are not significant for three- and six-year horizons, as before.[13]

Next, we add time effects to the analysis of the split between the nominal rate and prices. In broad outline, this extension reveals little change from the results of Section 2.6, where the time effects were omitted. In particular, we continue to find that it is difficult to quantify the split in a precise manner. The detailed results are contained in Tables 2A.4 through 2A.6 in Appendix 2A.3. But, as before, when the four

---

[13] The F-statistic for $h = 7$ is now insignificant as well.

Table 2.11 *Predictive regressions for real exchange rates with time dummies, twenty-four countries, 1994–2008*

$[q_{c,t+b} - q_{c,t} = \sum_\tau \alpha_{\tau,\tau+b} D_{\tau,t} + \phi^b d_{c,t} + u_{c,t}^b$ (standard errors in parentheses)]

b	\multicolumn{14}{c}{Year dummies $\alpha_{\tau,\tau+b}$ (×100)}														$\eta^b = (1/N^b)\sum_\tau \alpha_{\tau,\tau+b}$ (×100)	Slope ϕ^b	No. of obs.	R^2	F
	94,94+b	95,95+b	96,96+b	97,97+b	98,98+b	99,99+b	00,00+b	01,01+b	02,02+b	03,03+b	04,04+b	05,05+b	06,06+b	07,07+b					
(1)	(2)	(3)	(4)	(5)	(6)	(7)	(8)	(9)	(10)	(11)	(12)	(13)	(14)	(15)	(16)	(17)	(18)	(19)	(20)
								\multicolumn{6}{c}{A. With overlapping observations}										
1	10.30	3.12	-0.80	-11.86	1.28	-6.33	-7.69	-3.50	-0.78	-2.44	-0.19	3.25	0.69	13.56	-0.10	-0.34	336	0.33	111.96*
	(3.05)	(2.78)	(1.72)	(2.73)	(2.34)	(1.77)	(1.79)	(5.26)	(2.36)	(1.84)	(1.87)	(1.50)	(2.07)	(3.10)	(0.45)	(0.06)			
2	10.41	2.12	-11.66	-6.06	-5.80	-11.99	-8.96	-3.73	-3.56	-2.23	2.71	2.54	13.99		-1.71	-0.62	312	0.47	28.23*
	(2.94)	(2.56)	(3.16)	(2.42)	(2.76)	(2.31)	(4.68)	(3.79)	(2.94)	(2.52)	(2.21)	(2.75)	(3.92)		(0.73)	(0.07)			
3	7.34	-8.32	-4.57	-9.28	-12.27	-11.71	-7.68	-6.52	-4.03	0.70	1.45	14.53			-3.36	-0.88	288	0.59	9.69*
	(2.70)	(3.77)	(2.56)	(3.11)	(2.77)	(4.30)	(3.24)	(3.64)	(2.97)	(2.43)	(3.25)	(4.59)			(0.85)	(0.07)			
4	-5.47	-1.60	-7.16	-12.45	-12.48	-8.88	-8.70	-6.43	-1.21	-0.16	13.29				-4.66	-1.07	264	0.67	11.93*
	(3.48)	(2.72)	(3.28)	(2.95)	(4.18)	(2.82)	(3.12)	(2.98)	(2.56)	(3.25)	(4.75)				(0.91)	(0.07)			
5	-1.21	-5.59	-10.89	-10.77	-9.62	-8.56	-6.75	-2.33	-1.37	12.54					-4.45	-1.15	240	0.71	12.34*
	(2.40)	(3.01)	(2.89)	(4.29)	(2.47)	(2.80)	(2.43)	(1.97)	(2.99)	(4.59)					(1.01)	(0.07)			
6	-4.83	-7.60	-7.50	-5.95	-10.10	-6.42	-2.97	-3.70	10.02						-4.35	-1.32	216	0.77	20.76*
	(3.51)	(2.81)	(4.10)	(2.50)	(2.27)	(2.32)	(1.31)	(2.45)	(4.19)						(1.02)	(0.07)			
7	-8.37	-4.40	-2.27	-4.29	-8.30	-1.62	-3.20	8.02							-3.05	-1.45	192	0.79	26.35*
	(3.84)	(3.60)	(2.42)	(2.69)	(2.41)	(1.61)	(2.12)	(3.56)							(1.07)	(0.08)			
8	-6.03	1.19	0.14	-0.56	-3.94	-1.16	9.15								-0.17	-1.58	168	0.81	34.52*
	(3.20)	(3.06)	(2.78)	(2.52)	(2.54)	(2.3)	(2.95)								(1.30)	(0.14)			
9	-4.29	-0.92	0.52	3.25	-2.17	12.68									1.51	-1.42	144	0.78	14.44*
	(3.49)	(3.94)	(3.04)	(2.72)	(3.24)	(3.87)									(2.27)	(0.16)			
10	-4.75	0.03	4.28	3.24	11.84										2.93	-1.32	120	0.75	6.68*
	(3.79)	(3.84)	(3.33)	(3.52)	(4.65)										(2.86)	(0.17)			
11	-0.87	7.26	6.84	17.69											7.73	-1.45	96	0.75	11.93*
	(2.98)	(3.34)	(3.71)	(4.69)											(3.15)	(0.15)			

Table 2.11 (cont.)

b (1)	Year dummies $\alpha_{\tau,\tau+b}$ (×100)														$\eta^b = (1/N^b)\sum_\tau \alpha_{\tau,\tau+b}$ (×100) (16)	Slope ϕ^b (17)	No. of obs. (18)	R^2 (19)	F (20)
	94,94+b (2)	95,95+b (3)	96,96+b (4)	97,97+b (5)	98,98+b (6)	99,99+b (7)	00,00+b (8)	01,01+b (9)	02,02+b (10)	03,03+b (11)	04,04+b (12)	05,05+b (13)	06,06+b (14)	07,07+b (15)					
12	4.06 (2.59)	7.72 (4.00)	19.95 (4.83)												10.58 (3.49)	−1.42 (0.16)	72	0.74	10.92*
13	5.74 (3.02)	22.54 (5.22)													14.14 (3.91)	−1.51 (0.15)	48	0.74	11.33*
14	20.37 (4.45)														20.38 (4.45)	−1.62 (0.27)	24	0.71	9.61*
B. Without overlapping observations																			
1	10.30 (3.05)	3.12 (2.78)	−0.80 (1.72)	−11.86 (2.73)	1.28 (2.34)	−6.33 (1.77)	−7.69 (1.79)	−3.50 (5.26)	−0.78 (2.36)	−2.44 (1.84)	−0.19 (1.87)	3.25 (1.50)	0.69 (2.07)	13.56 (3.10)	−0.10 (0.45)	−0.34 (0.06)	336	0.33	111.96*
2	10.29 (3.05)		−11.83 (3.29)		−5.73 (2.79)		−8.86 (4.77)		−3.42 (3.05)		2.81 (2.16)		13.99 (3.90)		−0.392 (0.84)	−0.61 (0.07)	168	0.46	13.39*
3	7.99 (2.64)			−8.69 (3.04)			−8.18 (3.15)			0.16 (2.38)					−2.18 (0.48)	−0.94 (0.07)	96	0.63	1.54
4	−5.23 (3.16)				−12.62 (3.92)				−1.48 (2.52)						−6.45 (1.57)	−1.09 (0.07)	72	0.68	5.54*
5	−3.52 (2.25)					−7.94 (2.89)									−5.73 (1.57)	−0.93 (0.10)	48	0.57	4.41*
6	−9.02 (2.56)						0.29 (2.29)								−4.36 (0.70)	−0.92 (0.08)	48	0.72	2.78

7	-12.48 (2.80)	13.14 (4.93)	0.33 (2.06)	-1.05 (0.17)	48	0.73	0.06
8	-6.71 (3.88)		-6.71 (3.88)	-1.51 (0.40)	24	0.70	7.80*
9	-5.94 (3.85)		-5.94 (3.85)	-1.26 (0.22)	24	0.77	6.75*
10	-4.13 (3.80)		-4.16 (3.76)	-1.38 (0.21)	24	0.81	8.17*
11	0.22 (2.49)		0.22 (2.49)	-1.55 (0.12)	24	0.91	18.01*
12	4.05 (1.88)		4.05 (1.88)	-1.42 (0.09)	24	0.92	11.55*
13	5.94 (2.86)		5.94 (2.86)	-1.53 (0.16)	24	0.85	7.58*
14	20.37 (4.44)		20.37 (4.45)	-1.62 (0.27)	24	0.71	9.61*

Notes:
1. The F-statistics of column 20 test the joint hypothesis of $\eta^b = 0$ and $\phi^b = -1$ for various values of b.
2. An asterisk (*) indicates significance at the 5 per cent level.
3. Standard errors are robust, based on a cluster correction (Kleok, 1981).

high-inflation countries are omitted, the nominal rate bears a larger burden of the adjustment than does inflation. However, this finding is somewhat less pronounced than before when the time effects (and the high-inflation countries) were omitted. See Tables 2A.9 through 2A.11 in Appendix 2A.4 for details.

To summarise, the persistent swings of the dollar play a role in the adjustment to mispricing of nondollar currencies. Even when these effects are allowed for, though, in broad outline the results of Sections 2.5 and 2.6 continue to hold: Within a period of three to six years, currency mispricing is more or less eliminated.

2.9 The 'burgernomics' literature

This section reviews the literature on the BMI. Cumby (1996) is widely known as the first 'burgernomics' paper and was originally a 1995 Georgetown University working paper. Almost at the same time, however, the paper by Ong (1995) was presented at the Australian National University (ANU)/University of Western Australia (UWA) PhD Conference in Economics and Business held in Perth, Australia, in November of 1995 and later published as Ong (1997). As far as we are aware, there are in total twenty-three academic papers and one book on the BMI/'burgernomics'. Table 2.12 lists these publications in chronological order. These papers can be broadly grouped into two categories: (1) the basic foundations and (2) 'adventurous' applications.

Regarding basic foundations, Cumby (1996) found out that the half-life of deviations from Big Mac parity is about one year, and these deviations provide significant information for forecasting exchange rates and Big Mac prices. Lutz (2001) applied Cumby's methodology to twelve price series published by the bank UBS as well as aggregate Consumer Price Index (CPI) data. Click (1996), Fujiki and Kitamura (2003), and Caetano et al. (2004) found country incomes to be important in explaining deviations from Big Mac PPP. Yang (2004) used the BMI to evaluate the Chinese yuan and found that currencies of low-income countries are overvalued due to the insufficient weight accorded to nontradables. Ong (1997) found that Big Macs are surprisingly accurate in tracking exchange rates over the long run. She also proposed the 'no-frills index' by excluding nontradable components from the BMI and established that this performs better than the BMI. Using Big Mac prices, Ong (1998a) analysed the Asian currency crisis, whereas Ong

Table 2.12 *The 'burgernomics' literature*

	Author	Key results
1.	Cumby (1996)	Deviations from Big Mac PPP tend to die out; half-life is about 1 year; the Big Mac is a useful exchange-rate predictor.
2.	Click (1996)	PPP holds in time-series dimension; departure is due to the productivity bias.
3.	Pakko and Pollard (1996)	Deviations from absolute PPP are persistent, and those from relative PPP are transitory; Big Macs are a useful but flawed PPP measure.
4.	Annaert and Ceuster (1997)	Relative Big Mac PPP is a valuable international asset allocator.
5.	Ong (1997)	BMI is surprisingly accurate in tracking exchange rates over the long term (revision of Ong, 1995).
6.	Ong (1998a)	BMI is a good indicator of currency devaluations.
7.	Ong (1998b)	Significant relationship between Big Mac real wages and the productivity bias, market status, and location.
8.	Ong and Mitchell (2000)	Big Mac academic real wages and quality-of-life indices are useful for relocation decisions.
9.	Ashenfelter and Jurajda (2001)	McWages highly correlated with other wage measures.
10.	Lutz (2001)	Results similar to Cumby (1996) obtained using UBS price series and aggregate consumer price index (CPI) data but are not robust.
11.	Fujiki and Kitamura (2003)	Big Mac PPP is sensitive to different models, sample periods, and countries.
12.	Pakko and Pollard (2003)	BMI is a useful but imperfect PPP measure.
13.	Ong (2003)	Long-run PPP is supported by BMI; BMI works as well as other board price indices.

Table 2.12 (*cont.*)

Author	Key results
14. Caetano et al. (2004)	Income and trade openness explain failure of Big Mac PPP.
15. Yang (2004)	Big Mac PPP overestimates currency values of low-income countries.
16. Lan (2006)	BMI is used to construct entire distribution of future exchange rates.
17. Monson (undated)	Adjustment towards parity is slower than that in Cumby (1996) and Ong (1997); the local price, rather than the nominal exchange rate, does most of the adjusting.
18. Chen et al. (2007)	BMI supports PPP more than does CPI.
19. Parsley and Wei (2007)	Speed of adjustment for Big Mac PPP is slower than that for tradable inputs but faster than that for nontradable inputs.
20. Parsley and Wei (2008)	Introduction of the euro did not raise prices nor decrease price dispersion.
21. Fukumoto (2009)	Big Mac prices suggest that regional price dispersion has diminished within regions, but global price dispersion has not decreased.
22. Winkels (2009)	Absolute PPP has predictive value for the performance of an international currency portfolio in the long run.
23. Clementi et al. (2010)	Inflation has increased, and there has been no significant reduction in price dispersion since introduction of the euro.
24. Clements and Lan (2010)	Real-time exchange-rate forecasts are derived from the BMI; these beat random walk over medium and longer horizons.

(1998b), Ong and Mitchell (2000), and Ashenfelter and Jurajda (2001) compared wages in different countries. Ong (2003) is the only book on 'burgernomics', and this comprises a series of papers by her and her coauthors. Pakko and Pollard (1996, 2003) concluded that Big Macs are a useful but flawed PPP measure as deviations from absolute PPP are persistent, whereas those from relative PPP are transitory. Chen et al. (2007) compared the behaviour of Big Mac prices with CPIs and found that the BMI supports the validity of PPP better than the CPI does. Parsley and Wei (2007), discussed previously in Section 2.3, related the price of a Big Mac to the costs of its ingredients and found that the speed of convergence of the overall Big Mac real exchange rate is bracketed by that for its tradable and nontradable inputs.

Annaert and Ceuster (1997) pursued a different line of research in one of the first adventurous applications of 'burgernomics'. They constructed currency portfolios selected on the basis of the BMI whereby undervalued currencies were bought and undervalued ones sold, and their results showed that Big Macs can serve as a useful international asset allocator. Given their volatility, exchange rates are notoriously difficult to forecast. As previous US Federal Reserve Bank Chairman Alan Greenspan (2004), put it, 'Despite extensive efforts on the part of analysts, to my knowledge, no model projecting directional movements in exchange rates is significantly superior to tossing a coin.' There is now an emerging stream of 'burgernomics' that investigates whether the BMI can be used to forecast exchange rates. Lan (2006) used Big Mac prices to forecast the whole distribution of future exchange rates, employing a novel iterative approach to adjust for econometric problems associated with estimation of dynamic panel models where the number of observations is not large. The provision of the whole distribution emphasises forecast uncertainty that enables users to make financial decisions in an informed manner with the appropriate degree of caution. Clements and Lan (2010) extended Lan (2006) and use Monte Carlo simulations to provide real-time exchange-rate forecasts using Big Mac prices for any horizon into the future. The final application of 'burgernomics' is by Parsley and Wei (2008), who employed Big Mac prices to examine aspects of the impact of introduction of the euro.

2.10 Concluding comments

The Economist magazine advocates as a currency-pricing rule the formula $S = P/P^*$, where S is the exchange rate (the domestic currency cost of one US dollar), P is the price of a Big Mac hamburger in the country in question, and P^* is the price in the United States. Thus an increase in the domestic price relative to the US price leads to a depreciation of the domestic currency. The rule is a precise, numerical relationship between the exchange rate and the relative price that can be used to identify mispricing of the currency in a quick and convenient way. This is a novel and controversial application of the PPP theory of exchange rates that is known as the 'BMI' and is published annually by *The Economist* for a large number of currencies.

The cost of a full-page advertisement in *The Economist* must be something like $50,000. For the magazine to continue to publish an annual article on the BMI for more than two decades means that it is worth this opportunity cost, at least in the mind of the editor. This chapter assessed the broader value of the BMI by analysing its properties and ability to track exchange rates. The major findings of the chapter are

- The index is a biased predictor of currency values.
- Once the bias is allowed for, the index tracks exchange rates reasonably well over the medium to longer term in accordance with relative PPP theory.
- The index is at least as good as the industry standard, the random-walk model, in predicting future currency values for all but short-term horizons.
- Future nominal exchange rates are more responsive than prices to currency mispricing.

Thus, while it is not perfect, as the cost of the magazine is less than $10, the BMI seems to provide good value for money. In showing that relative prices act as an 'attractor' or 'anchor' for exchange rates over the longer term, our results also have implications for exchange-rate economics: As currencies of high-inflation (low-inflation) countries depreciate (appreciate), over longer horizons, economic fundamentals tend to dominate currency pricing.

Appendix 2A
2A.1 The Big Mac Data

The Economist magazine has been publishing the BMI on an annual basis since 1986. The data presented in Tables 2A.1, 2A.2 and 2A.3 are compiled from a number of issues of the magazine from 1986 to 2008.

Table 2A.1 *Implied PPP exchange rates, 1996–2008*

Country	Year																						
	1986	1987	1988	1989	1990	1991	1992	1993	1994	1995	1996	1997	1998	1999	2000	2001	2002	2003	2004	2005	2006	2007	2008
Argentina							1.51	1.58	1.57	1.29	1.27	1.03	0.98	1.03	1.00	0.98	1.00	1.51	1.50	1.55	2.26	2.42	3.08
Aruba																	0.94	1.51	1.41	1.62	1.60		
Australia	1.09		0.82	1.04	1.05	1.09	1.16	1.08	1.07	1.06	1.06	1.03	1.04	1.09	1.03	1.18	1.21	1.11	1.12	1.06	1.05	1.01	0.97
Austria									14.8	16.8	15.3	14.1	13.3										
Bahrain																	0.34	0.31					
Belarus																	916	904	1021				
Belgium	56.3	56.3	37.7	44.6	44.1	44.4	49.3	47.8	47.4	47.0	46.2	45.0	42.6										
Brazil	7.80						1735	33772	652	1.04	1.25	1.23	1.21	1.21	1.18	1.42	1.45	1.68	1.86	1.93	2.07	2.02	2.10
Britain	0.69	0.71	0.50	0.62	0.64	0.74	0.80	0.79	0.79	0.75	0.76	0.75	0.72	0.78	0.76	0.78	0.80	0.73	0.65	0.61	0.63	0.58	0.64
Bulgaria																		1.10	1.03	0.98	0.97		
Canada	1.18		0.86	1.06	1.00	1.04	1.26	1.21	1.24	1.19	1.21	1.20	1.09	1.23	1.14	1.31	1.34	1.18	1.10	1.07	1.14	1.14	1.15
Chile									412	410	403	496	488	518	502	496	562	517	483	490	503	459	434
China							2.88	3.73	3.91	3.88	4.07	4.01	3.87	4.07	3.94	3.90	4.22	3.65	3.59	3.43	3.39	3.23	3.50
Colombia																	2289	2288	2241	2124	2097	2023	1961
Costa Rica																	351	417	390	369	365	331	504
Croatia																	5.98	5.50	5.14	4.87	4.84		
Czech Republic									21.7	21.6	21.6	21.9	21.1		21.7	22.1	22.6	20.9	19.5	18.4	19.1	15.5	18.5
Denmark	13.4		9.52	12.3	11.6	11.9	12.4	11.3	11.2	11.5	10.9	10.6	9.30	10.2	9.86	9.74	9.94	10.2	9.57	9.07	8.95	8.14	7.84
Dominican Rep																	20.1	22.1	20.7	19.6	19.4		
Egypt																		2.95	3.45	2.94	3.07	2.80	3.64
Estonia																	11.5	10.9	10.2	9.64	9.52	8.80	8.96
Euro area														1.04	1.02	1.01	1.07	1.00	0.94	0.95	0.95	0.90	0.94
Fiji																		1.47	1.39		1.50		
France	10.3	10.9	7.24	8.76	8.05	8.00	8.27	8.11	8.04	7.97	7.42	7.23	6.84	7.20	7.37	7.28							

Table 2A.1 (*cont.*)

Country	Year																						
	1986	1987	1988	1989	1990	1991	1992	1993	1994	1995	1996	1997	1998	1999	2000	2001	2002	2003	2004	2005	2006	2007	2008
Georgia																		1.35	1.26	1.19	1.34		
Germany						1.91	2.01	2.02	2.00	2.07	2.08	2.03	1.93	2.04	1.99	2.01							
Greece									270														
Guatemala																	6.43	5.90	5.52	5.47	5.57		
Holland	2.72	2.81	2.03	2.53	2.39	2.33	2.44	2.39	2.37	2.35	2.31	2.25	2.13	2.24									
Honduras																		9.58	12.4	11.7	11.6		
Hong Kong	4.75		3.18	3.76	3.91	3.96	4.06	3.95	4.00	4.10	4.20	4.09	3.98	4.20	4.06	4.21	4.50	4.24	4.14	3.92	3.87	3.52	3.73
Hungary						51	61	69	74	82	91	112	101	123	135	157	184	181	183	173	181	176	188
Iceland																	160	162	151	143	148	138	131
Indonesia										1681			3867	5967	5777	5787	6426	5941	5552	4771	4710	4663	5238
Ireland	0.74	0.74	0.51	0.64	0.59	0.62	0.66	0.65															
Israel										3.84	4.03	4.75	4.88	5.72	5.78		4.82						
Italy	2063	1381	1634	1773	1600	1872	1974	1978	1940	1907	1901	1901	1758	1852	1793	1693							
Jamaica																	48.2	41.7	39.0	53.9			
Japan	231		155		183	169	174	172	170	169	122	122	109	121	117	116	105	96.7	90	81.7	81	82	78
Jordan																			0.89	0.85			
Kuwait																	0.26	0.24	0.74				
Latvia																				0.36	0.44	0.41	0.43
Lebanon																		1587	1483	1405			
Lithuania																		2.40	2.24	1.12	2.10	1.94	1.93
Macau																	4.50	4.13	3.86	3.66	3.58		
Macedonia																		35.1	32.8	31.0			
Malaysia								1.47	1.64	1.62	1.59	1.60	1.68	1.86	1.80	1.78	2.02	1.86	1.74	1.72	1.77	1.61	1.54
Mexico								3.11	3.52	4.70	6.31	6.16	6.99	8.19	8.33	8.62	8.80	8.49	8.28	9.15	9.36	8.50	8.96
Moldova																					7.93	7.52	7.42
Morocco																	9.24	8.45	0.82	8.02	7.90		

Note: This page is a rotated (landscape) continuation of a multi-column data table. Country names run down the side; numeric values for each country row are given in reading order. No column headers appear on this page.

Country	Values
New Zealand	1.27 1.25 1.34 1.348 1.40 1.36 1.42 1.59 1.46 1.50 1.45 1.44 1.35 1.37
Nicaragua	11.9 11.3
Norway	14.0 14.6 12.2 12.7 13.9 11.7 11.2
Oman	0.36 0.33
Pakistan	36.5 37.9 42.5 41.9 41.1 39.2
Paraguay	2941 2903 3079
Peru	3.41 2.92 3.10 2.94 3.07 2.79 2.66
Philippines	23.2 26.1 24.0 23.8 26.1 27.4 24.9 24.4
Poland	13478 1.47 1.61 1.78 2.07 2.26 2.19 2.32 2.37 2.33 2.17 2.12 2.10 2.02 1.96
Portugal	191
Qatar	3.61 3.32 0.85 0.81
Russia	26.5 342 1261 3491 4025 4545 4688 13.8 15.7 15.1 14.5 13.7 15.5 15.3 16.5
Saudi Arabia	3.62 3.32 0.83 2.94 2.90 2.64 2.80
Serbia and Montenegro	45.8
Singapore	1.75 1.17 1.39 1.18 1.24 2.17 1.30 1.27 1.29 1.24 1.17 1.32 1.28 1.30 1.33 1.22 1.14 1.18 1.16 1.16 1.11
Slovakia	25.3 24.4 22.8 21.6 18.7 18.0 21.6
Slovenia	172.7 177.1 166.0 163.0 167.7
South Africa	2.97 3.22 3.13 3.54 3.59 3.82 3.90 5.15 4.28 4.56 4.50 4.55 4.73
South Korea	1188 955 933 1050 1009 1000 991 975 950 1016 1235 1195 1181 1245 1218 1103 817 807 850 896
Soviet Union	1.71 4.44
Spain	163 139 156 143 153 155 149 50.0 57.2 61.6
Sri Lanka	119 134 144 150 155 147 156 48.3 61.3 58.8

Table 2A.1 (cont.)

Country	\																						
	1986	1987	1988	1989	1990	1991	1992	1993	1994	1995	1996	1997	1998	1999	2000	2001	2002	2003	2004	2005	2006	2007	2008
Suriname	10.3																2410	2952					
Sweden			7.74	10.4	10.9	11.6	11.6	11.2	11.1	11.2	11.0	10.7	9.38	9.88	9.56	9.45	10.4	11.1	10.3	10.1	10.7	9.68	10.6
Switzerland								2.50	2.48	2.54	2.50	2.44	2.31	2.43	2.35	2.48	2.53	2.33	2.17	2.06	2.03	1.85	1.82
Taiwan									27.0	28.0	27.5	28.1	26.6	28.8	27.9	27.6	28.1	25.8	25.9	24.5	24.2	22.0	21.0
Thailand								21.1	20.9	20.7	20.3	19.3	20.3	21.4	21.9	21.7	22.1	21.8	20.3	19.6	19.4	18.2	17.4
Turkey																	1606425	1383763	1362069	1.31	1.36	1.39	1.44
Ukraine																	3.53	2.58	2.5	2.37	2.74	2.71	3.08
UAE																	3.61	3.32	0.84	2.94	2.90	2.93	2.80
Uruguay																	11.3	11.0	10.3	14.4	13.7	18.2	17.1
Venezuela							77.6										1004	1365	1517	1830	1839	2170	
West Germany	2.66	2.56	1.72	2.13	1.96																		
Yugoslavia			962	3465	7.27	14.2																	

Note: The implied PPP exchange rate for country c in year t is defined as P_{ct}/P_t^*, where P_{ct} is the price of a Big Mac hamburger in country c during t, and P_t^* is the corresponding price in the United States.

Table 2A.2 *Nominal exchange rates, 1986–2008*

Country	Year																						
	1986	1987	1988	1989	1990	1991	1992	1993	1994	1995	1996	1997	1998	1999	2000	2001	2002	2003	2004	2005	2006	2007	2008
Argentina							0.99	1.00	1.00	1.00	1.00	1.00	1.00	1.00	1.00	1.00	3.13	2.88	2.94	2.89	3.06	3.09	3.02
Aruba																	1.79	1.79	1.79	1.79	1.79		
Australia	1.64		1.36	1.24	1.32	1.27	1.31	1.39	1.42	1.35	1.27	1.29	1.51	1.59	1.68	1.98	1.86	1.61	1.43	1.30	1.33	1.17	1.03
Austria									12.0	9.72	10.7	12.0	13.0										
Bahrain																	0.38	0.38					
Belarus																	1745	2018	2161				
Belgium	42.0	39.1	34.8	39.5	34.7	34.5	33.6	32.5	35.2	28.4	31.2	35.3	38.0										
Brazil							2153	27521	949	0.90	0.99	1.06	1.14	1.73	1.79	2.19	2.34	3.07	3.17	2.47	2.30	1.91	1.58
Britain	0.67	0.679	0.54	0.59	0.61	0.56	0.57	0.64	0.69	0.62	0.66	0.61	0.60	0.62	0.63	0.70	0.69	0.63	0.56	0.55	0.53	0.50	0.50
Bulgaria																		1.78	1.62	1.60	1.54		
Canada	1.39		1.24	1.19	1.16	1.15	1.19	1.26	1.39	1.39	1.36	1.39	1.42	1.51	1.47	1.56	1.57	1.45	1.37	1.25	1.12	1.05	1.00
Chile									414	395	408	417	455	484	514	601	655	716	643	593	530	527	494
China						5.44		5.68	8.70	8.54	8.35	8.33	8.28	8.28	8.28	8.28	8.28	8.28	8.26	8.26	8.03	7.60	6.83
Colombia																	2261	2914	2765	2330	2504	1956	1799
Costa Rica																	351	390	433	474	510	519	551
Croatia																	8.29	6.87	6.16	5.96	5.72		
Czech Republic										29.7	26.2	27.6	29.2	34.4	39.1	39.0	34.0	28.9	26.6	24.5	22.1	21.1	14.5
Denmark		7.19	6.36	7.33	6.39	6.42	6.32	6.06	6.69	5.43	5.85	6.52	7.02	6.91	8.04	8.46	8.38	6.78	6.22	6.06	5.82	5.46	4.70
Dominican Rep																	17.2	23.0	45.5	28.3	32.6		
Egypt																		5.92	6.18	5.80	5.77	5.69	5.31
Estonia																	17.6	14.3	13.0	12.8	12.3	11.5	9.87
Euro area														0.93	1.08	1.14	1.12	0.91	0.83	0.81	0.78	0.73	0.63

Table 2A.2 (cont.)

Country	1986	1987	1988	1989	1990	1991	1992	1993	1994	1995	1996	1997	1998	1999	2000	2001	2002	2003	2004	2005	2006	2007	2008
																							Year
Fiji																			1.81		1.70	1.73	
France	6.65	6.30	5.63	6.37	5.63	5.65	5.55	5.34	5.83	4.80	5.13	5.76	6.17	6.10	7.07	7.44							
Georgia																		2.21	1.92	1.82	1.80		
Germany						1.67	1.64	1.58	1.71	1.38	1.52	1.71	1.84	1.82	2.11								
Greece																2.22							
Guatemala																	7.90	7.87	7.96	7.61	7.59		
Holland	2.28	2.13	1.86	2.13	1.88	1.88	1.84	1.77	1.91	1.55	1.70	1.92	2.07	2.05									
Honduras																		17.2	18.2	18.7	18.9		
Hong Kong	7.80	7.80	7.78	7.79	7.79	7.73	7.73	7.73	7.73	7.73	7.74	7.75	7.75	7.75	7.79	7.80	7.80	7.80	7.80	7.79	7.75	7.82	7.80
Hungary						75	80	88	103	121	150	178	213	237	279	303	272	224	211	204	206	180	144
Iceland																96.3	75.8	72.9	65.6	72.0	61.7	78.6	
Indonesia										2231			8500	8725	7945	10855	9430	8740	9096	9542	9325	9015	9152
Ireland	0.74	0.70	0.62	0.71	0.63	0.62	0.61	0.65															
Israel										2.95	3.17	3.38	3.70	4.04	4.05		4.79						
Italy	1342	1229	1382	1230	1239	1233	1523	1641	1702	1551	1683	1818	1799	2088		2195							
Jamaica																	47.4	56.7	60.2	61.1			
Japan	154		124	133	159	135	133	113	104	84	107	126	135	120	106	124	130	120	112	107	112	122	107
Jordan																			0.71	0.71			
Kuwait																	0.31	0.30	0.29				
Latvia																			0.55	0.57	0.55	0.51	0.44
Lebanon																		1512	1514	1509			
Lithuania																		3.15	2.87	2.80	2.69	2.53	2.18
Macau																8.03	8.03	8.03	8.00	8.00	7.99		
Macedonia																	55.8	55.8	51.7	49.9			
Malaysia								2.58	2.69	2.49	2.49	2.50	3.72	3.80	3.80	3.80	3.80	3.80	3.79	3.81	3.63	3.43	3.20

Country	Values
Mexico	3.10 3.36 6.37 7.37 7.90 8.54 9.54 9.41 9.29 9.28 10.5 11.5 10.9 11.3 10.8 10.2
Moldova	11.9 12.5 13.2
Morocco	11.5 9.82 9.15 8.99 8.71
New Zealand	1.51 1.47 1.45 1.82 1.87 2.01 2.47 2.24 1.78 1.64 1.40 1.62 1.28 1.32
Nicaragua	15.8 16.4
Norway	8.56 7.16 6.83 6.41 6.10 5.81 5.08
Oman	0.39 0.39
Pakistan	57.8 57.9 59.7 60.1 60.4 70.9
Paraguay	6250 5505 5145
Peru	3.43 3.46 3.50 3.26 3.26 3.17 2.84
Philippines	50.3 51.0 52.5 56.1 54.3 52.6 45.9 44.5
Poland	22433 2.34 2.64 3.10 3.46 3.98 4.30 4.04 3.89 3.86 3.31 3.10 2.75 2.03
Portugal	174
Qatar	3.64 3.63 3.65
Russia	99.0 686 1775 4985 4918 5739 5999 24.7 28.5 28.9 31.2 31.1 29.0 28.3 27.1 25.6 23.2
Saudi Arabia	3.75 3.75 3.75 3.76 3.75 3.75 3.75 3.75
Serbia and Montenegro	67.4
Singapore	2.15 2.00 1.96 1.88 1.77 1.65 1.57 1.40 1.41 1.44 1.62 1.73 1.70 1.81 1.82 1.78 1.72 1.66 1.59 1.52 1.35
Slovakia	46.8 37.4 33.4 31.6 29.5 24.6 19.1
Slovenia	253 212 198 194 189
South Africa	4.26 4.43 5.04 6.22 6.72 8.13 10.9 7.56 6.67 6.65 6.60 6.97 7.56
South Korea	666 707 721 778 796 810 769 779 894 1474 1218 1108 1325 1304 1220 1176 1004 952 923 1018
Soviet Union	0.60 1.74

Table 2A.2 (cont.)

Country	Year																						
	1986	1987	1988	1989	1990	1991	1992	1993	1994	1995	1996	1997	1998	1999	2000	2001	2002	2003	2004	2005	2006	2007	2008
Spain	133																						
Sri Lanka			111	117	106	103	102	114	138	124	126	144	156	155	179	189			99	100	103	111	108
Suriname																	2179	2515					
Sweden	6.87		5.89	6.41	6.10	6.04	5.93	7.43	7.97	7.34	6.71	7.72	8.00	8.32	8.84	10.3	10.3	8.34	7.58	7.41	7.28	6.79	5.96
Switzerland								1.45	1.44	1.13	1.23	1.47	1.52	1.48	1.70	1.73	1.66	1.37	1.28	1.25	1.21	1.21	1.02
Taiwan									26.4	25.7	27.2	27.6	33.0	33.2	30.6	32.9	34.8	34.8	33.5	31.1	32.1	32.8	30.4
Thailand								25.1	25.3	24.6	25.3	26.1	40.0	37.6	38.0	45.5	43.3	42.7	40.6	40.5	38.4	34.5	33.4
Turkey																	1324500	160500	1531007				
Ukraine																	5.33	5.34	5.33	5.07	5.05	5.03	4.60
UAE																	3.67	3.67	3.64	3.67	3.67	3.67	3.67
Uruguay																	16.8	28.5	29.9	24.2	23.9	23.9	19.2
Venezuela							60.6										857	1598	2973	2629	2630	2147	
West Germany	2.02	1.89	1.66	1.89	1.68																		
Yugoslavia		1400	9001	11.7	15.1												67.8	59.2					

Note: The nominal exchange rate is the domestic currency cost of one US dollar. An increase thus implies a depreciation of the domestic currency and vice versa.

Table 2A.3 Real exchange rates, 1986–2008

Country	1986	1987	1988	1989	1990	1991	1992	1993	1994	1995	1996	1997	1998	1999	2000	2001	2002	2003	2004	2005	2006	2007	2008
Argentina							42.01	45.68	44.8	25.7	24	3.252	−2.372	2.84	−0.399	−1.587	−113.7	−64.38	−67.27	−62.37	−30.39	−24.47	2.007
Aruba																	−64.43	−16.82	−23.62	−9.957	−11.42		
Australia	−40.51		−51.09	−17.63	−23.32	−15.39	−12.18	−25.74	−28.75	−24.56	−18.14	−22.21	−37.76	−37.71	−48.74	−51.66	−43.42	−37.46	−24.49	−20.21	−23.79	−14.53	−6.375
Austria									20.85	54.78	35.46	15.77	2.449										
Bahrain																	−10.72	−19.19					
Belarus																	−64.49	−80.3	−74.99				
Belgium	29.21	36.29	7.89	12.04	24.1	25.33	38.52	38.75	29.74	50.34	39.23	24.37	11.38										
Brazil	−57.05						−21.58	20.47	−37.51	14.76	23.32	14.65	6.037	−35.42	−42.07	−43.51	−48.15	−60.35	−53.41	−24.71	−10.8	5.771	28.49
Britain	2.578	3.899	−8.115	5.565	4.231	28.17	33.21	20.27	13.89	18.86	13.57	19.81	17.66	23.02	17.9	11.36	14.74	14.86	15.02	11.71	16.26	15.96	24.91
Bulgaria																		−48.16	−44.95	−48.71	−46.79		
Canada	−16.27		−36.86	−11.16	−15.3	−9.628	5.738	−4.006	−11.14	−15.2	−11.53	−15.53	−26.46	−20.47	−25.82	−17.39	−16.04	−20.54	−21.88	−15.14	1.373	8.033	13.6
Chile									−0.442	3.601	−1.347	17.32	7.059	6.789	−2.364	−19.19	−15.27	−32.64	−28.54	−19.02	−5.184	−13.83	−12.91
China							−63.71	−42.11	−79.9	−78.91	−71.92	−73.15	−76.13	−70.92	−74.16	−75.35	−67.48	−81.83	−83.36	−87.94	−86.32	−85.7	−66.82
Colombia																	1.238	−24.19	−21.03	−9.237	−17.75	3.391	8.631
Costa Rica																	0.115	6.688	−10.54	−25.13	−33.58	−44.86	−8.879
Croatia																	−32.6	−22.28	−18.09	−20.21	−16.73		
Czech Republic									−31.2	−19.53	−24.47	−28.76	−48.91		−59.06	−57.04	−40.83	−32.53	−30.86	−28.55	−14.86	−30.76	24.45
Denmark		62.55	40.32	51.38	59.55	61.62	67.74	62.25	51.49	75.3	62.33	48.98	28.09	38.8	20.41	14.13	17.07	41.23	43.04	40.33	43.05	39.91	51.21
Dominican Rep																	15.48	−3.81	−78.71	−36.7	−52.14		
Egypt																		−69.58	−58.23	−68.02	−63.28	−70.99	−37.72
Estonia																	−43.03	−27.28	−24.49	−28.12	−25.66	−26.79	−9.633
Euro area														11.33	−5.285	−11.61	−4.674	9.531	12.31	15.69	19.39	20.58	40.61
Fiji																			−21.03	−20.21	−14.27		

Table 2A.3 (cont.)

Country	1986	1987	1988	1989	1990	1991	1992	1993	1994	1995	1996	1997	1998	1999	2000	2001	2002	2003	2004	2005	2006	2007	2008
France	43.75	54.56	25.13	31.89	35.7	34.78	39.82	41.84	32.18	50.76	36.84	22.75	10.25	16.58	4.163	-2.126							
Georgia																		-49.52	-42.29	-42.53	-29.61		
Germany						13.49	22.55	24.45	15.67	40.5	31.19	16.9	4.961	11.27	-5.953	-10.04							
Greece																							
Guatemala																	-20.66	-28.74	-36.66	-33	-31.04		
Holland	17.59	27.7	8.711	17	23.85	21.6	28.34	30.05	21.56	41.58	30.63	15.95	2.806	8.988									
Honduras																		-58.57	-38.16	-47.13	-48.84		
Hong Kong	-49.6		-89.73	-72.65	-68.95	-67.77	-64.3	-67.21	-65.88	-63.54	-61.25	-63.89	-66.53	-61.32	-65.07	-61.6	-55.05	-60.87	-63.29	-68.66	-69.42	-79.85	-73.89
Hungary						-38.51	-27.18	-24.73	-33.77	-38.51	-50.33	-46.34	-74.45	-65.55	-72.55	-65.69	-38.9	-21.42	-14.05	-16.29	-13.13	-2.274	26.28
Iceland																	50.92	75.95	72.87	77.92	72.1	80.16	51.4
Indonesia										-28.3			-78.75	-37.99	-31.87	-62.89	-38.36	-38.6	-49.37	161.1	-68.31	-65.93	-55.8
Ireland	-0.338	5.488	-19.44	-9.824	-6.406	0.358	8.196	-0.035															
Israel										26.27	23.89	34.07	27.74	34.78	35.51		0.609						
Italy		43.01	11.64	16.73	36.55	25.57	41.76	25.92	18.69	13.07	20.65	12.17	-3.367	2.896	-15.24	-25.97							
Jamaica																	1.659	-30.7	-43.34	-12.52			
Japan	40.65		22.19	32.01	5.614	22.4	26.59	41.71	49.14	69.39	13.15	-3.647	-21.05	0.82	9.986	-6.887	-21.15	-21.61	-21.88	-26.83	-32.84	-39.59	-30.87
Jordan																			23	17.9			
Kuwait																	-17.19	-22.38	92.73				
Latvia																			-37.20	-46.61	-23.35	-22.41	-1.333
Lebanon																		4.847	-2.091	-7.11			
Lithuania																		-27.25	-24.93	-91.93	-24.91	-26.79	-12.04
Macau																	-57.96	-66.42	-72.82	-78.19	-80.26		
Macedonia																		-46.48	-45.49	-47.66			
Malaysia								-56.3	-49.54	-42.94	-44.65	-44.68	-79.51	-71.44	-74.68	-75.87	-62.99	-71.45	-77.95	-79.63	-71.59	-75.45	-73.1
Mexico								0.311	4.701	-30.44	-15.47	-24.93	-20	-15.27	-12.23	-7.462	-5.366	-21.57	-33.23	-17.06	-18.89	-23.9	-12.92
Moldova																			-40.72	-50.86	-57.61		
Morocco																	-22.17	-14.59	-241.2	-11.41	-9.72		

New Zealand	−17.19	−16.21	−7.668	−30.05	−29.01	−39.46	−55.54	−34.5	−19.98	−9.015	3.532	−12.09	5.248	3.904
Nicaragua									−28.08		−37.17			
Norway							49.6	71.08	58.01	68.33	82.15	70.26	79.1	
Oman							−7.603	−16.07						
Pakistan							−45.88	−42.29	−33.91	−35.99	−38.61	−59.22		
Paraguay									−75.38	−63.98	−51.34			
Peru							−0.478	−17.14	−12.08	−10.32	−6.184	−12.92	−6.508	
Philippines						−77.26	−66.97	−78.34	−85.77	−73.32	−65.15	−61.05	−60.19	
Poland	−50.95	−46.79	−49.44	−55.66	−51.36	−56.44	−67.41	−55.1	−53.36	−51.48	−57.61	−44.55	−39.1	−30.68	−3.469
Portugal	9.481													
Qatar							−0.704	−9.171	−145	−150.4				
Russia	−131.8	−69.58	−34.2	−35.61	−20.03	−23.32	−24.67	−58.31	−59.39	−74.07	−68.91	−72.06	−69.31	−72.64	−55.97	−51.81	−33.92
Saudi Arabia							−3.681	−12.15	−151.1	−24.29	−25.59	−35.12	−29.17	
Serbia and Montenegro										−38.6				
Singapore	−20.59	−53.48	−34.64	−46.42	−35.23	27.35	−19.21	−9.623	−8.711	−14.98	−32.38	−27.29	−28.78	−33.16	−31.72	−37.96	−41.24	−34.37	−31.42	−27.17	−19.9
Slovakia							−61.5	−42.9	−38.16	−38.13	−45.53	−31.37	12	
Slovenia							−38.19	−17.97	−18.09	−17.84	−11.93			
South Africa	−36.2	−31.8	−47.8	−56.39	−62.81	−75.56	−102.9	−38.43	−44.41	−37.65	−38.3	−42.75	−46.81	

Table 2A.3 (cont.)

Country	1986	1987	1988	1989	1990	1991	1992	1993	1994	1995	1996	1997	1998	1999	2000	2001	2002	2003	2004	2005	2006	2007	2008
South Korea			57.88		30.02	25.81	30	23.69	21.07	25.4	22.4	6.119	−37.25	1.351	7.577	−11.5	−4.632	−0.188	−6.408	−20.61	−16.59	−8.188	−12.73
Soviet Union					104.4	93.78																	
Spain	20.03		7.167	16.95	23.51	41.23	34.37	22.35	8.338	21.03	20.5	7.335	−6.294	−0.439	−18.07	−19.5							
Sri Lanka																		−70.41	−72.11	−55.88	−51.91	−58.91	−60.34
Suriname																	10.06	16.02					
Sweden	40.62		27.32	48.36	58.13	64.88	67.48	40.9	33.01	42.32	49.58	33.05	15.86	17.15	7.848	−8.431	1.367	28.32	30.65	30.95	38	35.43	58
Switzerland								54.47	54.29	81.12	70.93	50.59	41.62	49.5	32.4	36.03	42.14	52.88	52.45	50.1	51.85	42.32	57.94
Taiwan								2.086		8.633	1.251	1.792	−21.7	−14.19	−9.279	−17.71	−21.34	−29.81	−25.82	−23.88	−28.28	−39.97	−36.95
Thailand								−17.82	−19.25	−17.31	−21.83	−30.2	−67.76	−56.37	−55.05	−74.25	−67.31	−67.36	−69.31	−72.64	−68.51	−64.05	−65.4
Turkey																	19.3	−14.55	−11.69	−4.683	−12.81	6.907	19.25
Ukraine																	−41.2	−72.63	−75.72	−76.07	−61.07	−61.75	−40.07
UAE																	−1.525	−9.992	−146.5	−22.23	−23.44	−22.43	−27.02
Uruguay																	−40.15	−95.23	−106.5	−51.96	−56.05	−27.35	−11.4
Venezuela							24.71										15.83	−15.74	−67.27	−36.23	−35.77	1.07	
West Germany	27.38	30.61	3.288	11.89	15.14																		
Yugoslavia			−37.49	−95.45	−47.72	−6.121											−68.62	−42.39					

Notes:
1. The real exchange rate for country c in year t is defined as $q_{ct} = \log[P_{ct}/(S_{ct}P_t^*)]$, where P_{ct} is the price of a Big Mac hamburger in country c during t, P_t^* is the corresponding price in the United States, and S_{ct} is the nominal exchange rate, defined as the domestic currency cost of US\$1. A positive value of $q_{c,t}$ implies that the domestic currency is overvalued in real terms and vice versa.
2. All entries are to be divided by 100.

They consist of, respectively, the implied PPP exchange rates, nominal exchange rates, and real exchange rates of all countries that have appeared at least once in *The Economist*. Note that the data for 2002–8 are also based on information contained in the online BMI articles found on *The Economist* website (www.economist.com/). Some of this information is not contained in the hard-copy versions of the articles.

In years when countries were not included in either the printed or online versions of the articles, the corresponding cells of Tables 2A.1, 2A.2 and 2A.3 have been left blank. Note also that to ensure internal consistency, the implied PPP (IPPP) exchange rates were calculated from the Big Mac prices. The only exceptions to this rule are for 2004 and 2005, when a slightly different layout was used for the BMI articles. As nominal exchange rates and prices were not quoted in these years, we used the IPPP values and prices to reverse engineer the nominal exchange rates. The majority of exchange rates in the BMI articles are expressed in terms of the domestic currency price of one US dollar. However, from 1993 onwards, the British pound, the euro and the Irish pound were quoted in reciprocal form, which we inverted.

We have made adjustments for five discrepancies found in the published data:

1. *Brazil 1986.* The price of a Big Mac is listed by *The Economist* as Cz\$2.5 in Brazil and \$1.6 in the United States. The IPPP is 2.5/1.6 = 1.5625. However, the article lists the IPPP as 7.80, suggesting that the Brazilian price should be 7.8 × 1.6 = 12.48. As the article proceeds to use 7.8 as the IPPP for the overvaluation calculation, it seems that the error lies in the price, so we use 12.48 for this price.
2. *Chile 1999.* The last digit of the Chilean Big Mac price is omitted from the article: The price is recorded as 1,25, whereas in all other years the price is around 1,250 pesos. Using $P = \text{IPPP} \times P^*$ with IPPP = 518 and $P^* = \$2.43$, we have 518 × 2.43 = 1258.74. Thus the omitted last digit is 9 (rounded up from 8.74), so we use 1,259 for this price.
3. *France 1999.* The prices are listed as 8.5 francs and 2.43 dollars, whereas the IPPP is 7.20. These values are not internally consistent. It seems that the price in France should be 7.20 × 2.43 = 17.496 francs. As this price is much more in line with previous values, we use 7.2 as the IPPP value.

4. *Denmark 1998.* The IPPP rate is listed as 9.28, whereas using the listed prices we computed it at 9.297. To keep things internally consistent, we use the latter rate.
5. *France 1986.* As with Denmark 1998, there is a small deviation between the listed IPPP and our internally consistent calculated value, 10.30 versus 10.25. Again, we use the internally consistent calculated value.[14]

In the text of the chapter we use the Big Mac data for twenty-four countries/areas over the period of 1994–2008, so the total number of observations is $24 \times 15 = 360$. Tables 2.1 through 2.3 show the respective implied PPP exchange rates, nominal exchange rates, and real exchange rates. In two instances, Big Mac prices and nominal exchange rates are missing: New Zealand 1994 and the Czech Republic 1999. In these cases, nominal exchange rates are taken from the International Monetary Fund's International Financial Statistics (IFS) database (www.imfstatistics.org/imf/). The Big Mac prices are computed on the basis of the one-year percentage change in the Consumer Price Index (CPI), again taken from IFS. For example, the IPPP for New Zealand in 1994 is computed as $[P/(1+\pi)]/P^*$, where P is the 1995 price of a Big Mac in New Zealand, π is the 1994 CPI rate of inflation in New Zealand and P^* is the 1994 US dollar price of a Big Mac in the United States.

As the euro was not introduced until 1999, official data are unavailable for this currency from 1994 to 1998. However, the Big Mac data for the six member countries included in our figures – Belgium, France, Germany, Italy, Holland and Spain – exist for the pre-euro period. For the years 1994–8, we estimated the euro exchange rate as follows. Let S_{ct} be the nominal exchange rate (the domestic-currency cost of \$1) for European country c ($c = 1, \ldots, 6$) in year t ($t = 1994, \ldots, 1998$), the values of which are listed in *The Economist*, and let E_{ct} be the corresponding exchange rate for the European currency unit (ECU, the currency basket that was the effective predecessor to the euro), which is available on Inforeuro (http://ec.europa.eu/budget/inforeuro/index.cfm?Language=en). Then

---

[14] Items 4 and 5 are the only instances where internally calculated IPPPs differ from *The Economist*'s-internally consistent calculations and yield more decimal places, but when rounded, the figures are identical.

S_{ct}/E_{ct} is the cost of the dollar in terms of ECUs. Using the April ECU rates, the resulting values of S_{ct}/E_{ct} are very nearly the same for each country. The small differences are likely to be the result of rounding errors or changes in the currency values that occurred between the end-of-month (April) exchange rates on Inforeuro and the days within the month of April to which the data contained in *The Economist* articles refer (9, 15, 27, 12 and 11 April 1994–8, respectively). These differences are eliminated by averaging, so the euro exchange rate is defined as $E_t = (1/6) \sum_{c=1}^{6} S_{ct}/E_{ct}$. As P_{ct} is the price of a Big Mac in country c in terms of domestic currency, P_{ct}/E_{ct} is the price in ECUs (euros). For the period 1994–8, we define 'the' price of a Big Mac in Europe as the average over the six countries, so the corresponding IPPP is the ratio of $(1/6) \sum_{c=1}^{6} P_{ct}/E_{ct}$ to the US price.

2A.2 More on stationarity

Conventional tests of the stationarity of real exchange rates are usually based on the equation $\Delta q_t = \alpha + \rho q_{t-1} + \sum_k \lambda_k \Delta q_{t-k} + \varepsilon_t$. The null hypothesis of a unit root is $\rho = 0$, whereas the alternative of stationarity corresponds to $-1 < \rho < 0$. To implement this approach with the Big Mac data, due to the limited sample size ($T = 15$, before lags), a parsimonious specification that omits Δq_{i-k} on the right-hand side has to be employed. Following Lan (2006), we can gain efficiency by exploiting the multicurrency ($N = 24$) nature of the data and take a panel/SUR approach to estimate the model $\Delta q_{ct} = \alpha_c + \rho q_{c,t-1} + \varepsilon_{ct}$, for $c = 1, \ldots, N$ currencies and $t = 2, \ldots, T$ years, where the parameter ρ takes a common value to conserve degrees of freedom.

To allow for common shocks, the disturbances ε_{ct} are correlated across currencies with $N \times N$ covariance matrix $E(\boldsymbol{\varepsilon}_t \boldsymbol{\varepsilon}_t') = \boldsymbol{\Sigma}$, where $\boldsymbol{\varepsilon}_t = [\varepsilon_{ct}]$. However, as the number of currencies exceeds the sample size ($N > T$), there is an undersized sample problem, and the conventional estimate of $\boldsymbol{\Sigma}$ is singular. To deal with the problem, Lan (2006) patterns $\boldsymbol{\Sigma}$ in two ways: (1) a type of block independence whereby countries are classified into three blocks: Asia Pacific, Europe, and other (since it is assumed that exchange-rate innovations between countries in different blocks are uncorrelated, this is called 'block-sectional independence') and (2) a process that summarises the cross-country dependence in one factor common to all countries. The common-factor approach uses as weights the shares in world trade and world gross domestic product

(GDP). Using Lan's (2006) iterative methodology, which involves bias adjustments, the results are

	Covariance matrix specified as		
	Block-sectional independence	Common factor model	
		Trade	GDP
Estimated ρ	–0.18	–0.11	–0.09
Half-life (years), $-\log 2/2\log(1+\rho)$	3.5	5.9	7.3
Test statistic for H_0: $\rho = 0$	–4.15	–4.84	–4.16
Critical value 1%	–6.50	–4.84	–5.19
5%	–4.17	–3.72	–4.22
10%	–3.35	–3.33	–3.37

Thus the unit root hypothesis is rejected at about the 5 per cent level for all three cases. The estimated half-lives indicate relatively slow adjustment, which is consistent with the other results of this section. We also test the assumption of a common ρ for all countries using a quasi-F-test (Lan, 2006). The test statistic is 2.35 under block-sectional independence (5 per cent critical value = 6.35), 0.24 under the trade-based common factor model (0.40), and 0.27 with the GDP-based common factor model (0.48), so we are unable to reject the hypothesis of a common value of ρ.

2A.3 Additional results with time effects

Tables 2.9 and 2.10 of the text give the results for the predictive regressions when the real rate is decomposed into the nominal rate and relative inflation components. Tables 2A.4 through 2A.6 of this appendix give the corresponding results when time effects are added. As mentioned in the text, the inclusion of the time effects has little impact on the results. When all twenty-four countries are considered, it remains difficult to split precisely the overall adjustment of the real exchange rate between the nominal rate and prices.

Table 2A.4 Predictive regressions with time dummies, changes in nominal exchange rates, twenty-four countries, 1994–2008

$$[-(s_{c,t+b} - s_{c,t}) = \sum_\tau \alpha_{s,\tau,\tau+b} D_{\tau,t} + \phi_s^b d_{c,t} + u_{s,c,t}^b \text{ (standard errors in parentheses)}]$$

b	Year dummies $\alpha_{s,\tau,\tau+h}$ ($\times 100$)														$\eta^b = (1/N^b) \sum_\tau \alpha_{s,\tau,\tau+b}$ ($\times 100$)	Slope ϕ_s^b	No. of obs.	R^2
	94,94+b	95,95+b	96,96+b	97,97+b	98,98+b	99,99+b	00,00+b	01,01+b	02,02+b	03,03+b	04,04+b	05,05+b	06,06+b	07,07+b				
(1)	(2)	(3)	(4)	(5)	(6)	(7)	(8)	(9)	(10)	(11)	(12)	(13)	(14)	(15)	(16)	(17)	(18)	(19)
								A. With overlapping observations										
1	69.84 (49.02)	0.86 (6.38)	-2.00 (5.75)	-9.89 (4.12)	17.82 (24.57)	-4.50 (2.09)	-10.14 (3.80)	-7.94 (6.57)	2.72 (6.03)	2.02 (4.08)	3.72 (2.86)	0.53 (2.22)	5.94 (1.84)	10.64 (2.55)	5.69 (3.25)	-0.31 (0.37)	336	0.07
2	65.28 (49.23)	-5.80 (9.06)	-14.74 (8.00)	9.72 (20.01)	14.26 (25.17)	-12.09 (2.68)	-13.95 (6.38)	-1.33 (9.02)	7.58 (7.95)	8.37 (4.59)	6.06 (3.93)	6.66 (3.16)	16.45 (3.07)		6.65 (4.57)	-0.29 (0.51)	312	0.06
3	58.78 (49.58)	-18.47 (11.52)	4.88 (15.93)	6.01 (18.48)	6.67 (26.38)	-15.99 (4.83)	-7.46 (8.23)	3.46 (11.08)	13.89 (8.85)	10.66 (5.81)	12.17 (5.20)	17.20 (4.52)			7.65 (6.56)	-0.29 (0.64)	288	0.05
4	47.67 (49.93)	3.62 (15.02)	3.21 (15.82)	-0.43 (18.79)	1.90 (26.82)	-9.95 (5.53)	-3.89 (8.98)	7.89 (11.01)	14.46 (9.45)	15.52 (6.36)	21.56 (6.08)				9.23 (8.80)	-0.43 (0.68)	264	0.03
5	67.69 (47.86)	0.45 (13.80)	-4.01 (15.07)	-4.11 (17.86)	8.16 (27.53)	-5.33 (6.23)	2.11 (9.27)	9.76 (12.33)	20.18 (10.70)	25.78 (7.61)					12.07 (11.39)	-0.45 (0.78)	240	0.05
6	66.00 (47.81)	-3.96 (13.95)	-5.24 (14.12)	3.94 (17.12)	11.69 (28.37)	0.38 (6.02)	2.82 (9.86)	13.37 (13.21)	28.43 (12.06)						13.05 (12.16)	-0.64 (0.86)	216	0.05
7	61.67 (48.63)	-2.48 (12.78)	5.72 (12.54)	11.35 (15.99)	15.97 (29.77)	1.74 (6.73)	6.31 (11.96)	19.77 (16.71)							15.01 (12.61)	-0.95 (1.11)	192	0.05
8	58.88 (48.69)	5.82 (12.81)	11.98 (12.58)	18.52 (15.33)	17.53 (30.83)	7.49 (7.06)	15.93 (13.4)								19.45 (13.23)	-1.06 (1.28)	168	0.04
9	63.98 (48.36)	8.32 (12.67)	16.37 (12.16)	19.64 (14.48)	24.37 (31.64)	18.35 (7.80)									25.17 (14.50)	-0.94 (1.43)	144	0.03

Table 2A.4 (cont.)

(1) b	Year dummies $\alpha_{s,\tau,\tau+b}$ (× 100)														$\eta^b = (1/N^b)\sum_\tau \alpha_{s,\tau,\tau+b}$ (× 100)	Slope ϕ_s^b	No. of obs.	R^2
	94,94+b (2)	95,95+b (3)	96,96+b (4)	97,97+b (5)	98,98+b (6)	99,99+b (7)	00,00+b (8)	01,01+b (9)	02,02+b (10)	03,03+b (11)	04,04+b (12)	05,05+b (13)	06,06+b (14)	07,07+b (15)	(16)	(17)	(18)	(19)
10	67.60 (48.56)	12.80 (13.30)	17.13 (12.11)	24.82 (13.89)	35.51 (32.21)										31.57 (17.30)	-0.83 (1.53)	120	0.03
11	80.74 (50.12)	26.35 (17.93)	32.67 (17.83)	41.02 (18.71)											45.20 (23.23)	-1.49 (1.26)	96	0.05
12	88.60 (51.43)	41.65 (22.65)	50.93 (23.17)												60.39 (29.96)	-2.03 (1.11)	72	0.07
13	102.82 (54.39)	65.55 (30.42)													84.19 (40.16)	-2.81 (1.25)	48	0.11
14	135.62 (62.56)														135.62 (62.56)	-4.94 (2.25)	24	0.15
B. Without overlapping observations																		
1	69.84 (49.02)	0.86 (6.38)	-2.00 (5.75)	-9.89 (4.12)	17.82 (24.57)	-4.50 (2.09)	-10.14 (3.80)	-7.94 (6.57)	2.72 (6.03)	2.02 (4.08)	3.72 (2.86)	0.53 (2.22)	5.94 (1.84)	10.64 (2.55)	5.69 (3.25)	-0.31 (0.37)	336	0.07
2	68.23 (50.96)		-10.69 (10.25)		12.52 (25.83)		-16.24 (6.99)		4.19 (10.12)		3.77 (5.32)		16.34 (3.58)		11.16 (6.41)	-0.58 (0.67)	168	0.07
3	71.96 (53.54)			16.89 (21.41)			-17.72 (11.18)			-0.28 (10.51)					17.71 (11.21)	-1.55 (1.03)	96	0.07
4	54.19 (54.93)				-1.95 (28.88)				6.96 (15.30)						19.73 (14.41)	-1.05 (1.22)	72	0.03
5	95.48 (58.57)					-12.69 (9.68)									41.39 (25.98)	-3.11 (1.69)	48	0.12

6	88.01 (56.44)	−14.31 (14.99)		36.85 (22.80)	−2.74 (1.42)	48	0.10
7	83.34 (56.70)	−7.22 (19.16)		38.06 (21.20)	−3.02 (1.47)	48	0.01
8	92.91 (62.24)			92.91 (62.24)	−4.31 (2.24)	24	0.12
9	99.31 (60.23)			99.31 (60.23)	−4.31 (2.15)	24	0.13
10	104.54 (59.56)			104.54 (59.56)	−4.36 (2.12)	24	0.13
11	112.14 (60.56)			112.15 (60.56)	−4.49 (2.18)	24	0.14
12	115.14 (61.07)			115.14 (61.07)	−4.57 (2.19)	24	0.14
13	123.58 (61.37)			123.58 (61.37)	−4.79 (2.20)	24	0.15
14	135.62 (62.56)			135.62 (62.56)	−4.94 (2.25)	24	0.15

Note: Standard errors are robust, based on a cluster correction (Kleok, 1981).

Table 2A.5 Predictive regressions with time dummies, inflation differentials, twenty-four countries, 1994–2008

$[r_{c,t+b} - r_{c,t} = \sum_\tau \alpha_{r,\tau,\tau+b} D_{\tau,t} + \phi_\tau^b d_{c,t} + u_{r,c,t}^b$ (standard errors in parentheses)]

b (1)	Year dummies $\alpha_{s,\tau,\tau+b}$ (×100)														$\eta^b = (1/N^b) \sum_\tau \alpha_{s,\tau,\tau+b}$ (×100) (16)	Slope ϕ_τ^b (17)	No. of obs. (18)	R^2 (19)
	94,94+b (2)	95,95+b (3)	96,96+b (4)	97,97+b (5)	98,98+b (6)	99,99+b (7)	00,00+b (8)	01,01+b (9)	02,02+b (10)	03,03+b (11)	04,04+b (12)	05,05+b (13)	06,06+b (14)	07,07+b (15)				
								A. With overlapping observations										
1	−59.54 (48.22)	2.26 (6.40)	1.20 (5.68)	−1.97 (3.25)	−16.54 (25.56)	−1.83 (0.91)	2.44 (3.93)	4.44 (4.49)	−3.50 (5.17)	−4.46 (3.56)	−3.92 (3.50)	2.72 (2.26)	−5.25 (1.14)	2.92 (1.60)	−5.79 (3.09)	−0.04 (0.37)	336	0.05
2	−54.86 (48.52)	7.91 (8.86)	3.08 (7.54)	−15.78 (20.49)	−20.06 (25.51)	0.10 (1.88)	4.99 (4.49)	−2.41 (6.95)	−11.14 (6.74)	−10.60 (4.95)	−3.35 (4.29)	−4.12 (3.16)	−2.46 (2.02)		−8.36 (4.43)	−0.33 (0.49)	312	0.05
3	−51.44 (49.30)	10.14 (11.39)	−9.45 (15.92)	−15.24 (18.40)	−18.95 (26.89)	4.28 (2.07)	−0.22 (6.50)	−9.98 (9.27)	−17.93 (8.69)	−9.96 (5.92)	−10.73 (5.23)	−2.67 (4.27)			−11.01 (6.51)	−0.59 (0.63)	288	0.05
4	−53.14 (49.06)	−5.22 (14.7)	−10.38 (15.33)	−12.02 (18.95)	−14.38 (26.56)	1.06 (3.49)	−4.81 (7.08)	−14.32 (10.06)	−15.67 (8.91)	−15.68 (6.04)	−8.27 (5.52)				−13.89 (8.82)	−0.64 (0.66)	264	0.04
5	−68.90 (48.41)	−6.04 (13.06)	−6.88 (14.71)	−6.66 (17.88)	−17.77 (27.45)	−3.23 (4.28)	−8.87 (8.56)	−12.09 (12.17)	−21.54 (10.38)	−13.23 (7.23)					−16.52 (11.56)	−0.70 (0.77)	240	0.05
6	−70.83 (48.74)	−3.64 (13.55)	−2.25 (14.49)	−9.89 (17.50)	−21.80 (27.97)	−6.79 (5.13)	−5.78 (9.79)	−17.07 (13.46)	−18.41 (11.49)						−17.38 (12.28)	−0.68 (0.85)	216	0.05
7	−70.04 (49.05)	−1.92 (14.49)	−7.99 (13.59)	−15.64 (16.42)	−24.27 (29.76)	−3.36 (6.79)	−9.51 (12.33)	−11.75 (17.36)							−18.06 (12.77)	−0.49 (1.12)	192	0.04
8	−64.92 (50.11)	−4.63 (13.93)	−11.84 (13.47)	−19.08 (15.96)	−21.47 (30.39)	−8.65 (7.44)	−6.77 (13.72)								−19.62 (13.47)	−0.51 (1.26)	168	0.03
9	−68.26 (50.38)	−9.24 (15.12)	−15.85 (13.77)	−16.39 (14.81)	−26.54 (31.49)	−5.67 (8.50)									−23.66 (15.00)	−0.49 (1.46)	144	0.03

10	−72.35 (50.83)	−12.77 (15.88)	−12.85 (13.56)	−21.58 (14.25)	−23.67 (32.11)										−28.64 (18.00)	−0.49 (1.57)	120	0.03
11	−81.61 (51.3)	−19.09 (18.93)	−25.83 (17.95)	−23.33 (18.19)											−37.47 (23.58)	0.05 (1.31)	96	0.03
12	−84.55 (51.98)	−33.93 (23.21)	−30.98 (22.74)												−49.82 (29.96)	0.61 (1.19)	72	0.03
13	−97.09 (53.93)	−43.01 (29.52)													−70.05 (39.26)	1.31 (1.30)	48	0.05
14	−115.26 (61.02)														−115.26 (61.02)	3.32 (2.18)	24	0.08

B. Without overlapping observations

1	−59.54 (48.22)	2.26 (6.40)	1.20 (5.68)	−1.97 (3.25)	−16.54 (25.56)	−1.83 (0.91)	2.44 (3.93)	4.44 (4.49)	−3.50 (5.17)	−4.46 (3.56)	−3.92 (3.50)	2.72 (2.26)	−5.25 (1.14)	2.92 (1.60)	−5.79 (3.09)	−0.04 (0.37)	336	0.05
2	−57.94 (50.12)		−1.14 (9.45)		−18.24 (26.12)		7.38 (5.87)		−7.60 (8.71)		−0.96 (5.62)		−2.35 (1.93)		−11.55 (6.10)	−0.03 (0.65)	168	0.05
3	−63.97 (53.21)				−25.58 (21.47)		9.54 (9.97)			0.44 (10.31)					−19.89 (11.33)	0.61 (1.00)	96	0.04
4	−59.41 (54.00)				−10.68 (28.85)				−8.45 (14.94)						−26.18 (14.02)	−0.05 (1.16)	72	0.03
5	−99.00 (59.57)					4.75 (9.46)	14.60 (16.26)								−47.13 (26.96)	2.17 (1.76)	48	0.09
6	−97.03 (57.11)														−41.21 (22.96)	1.82 (1.43)	48	0.09

Table 2A.5 (cont.)

h	Year dummies $\alpha_{s,\tau,\tau+b}(\times 100)$														$\eta^b = (1/N^b)\sum_\tau e_{s,\tau,\tau+b}(\times 100)$	Slope ϕ_t^b	No. of obs.	R^2
	94,94+b	95,95+b	96,96+b	97,97+b	98,98+b	99,99+b	00,00+b	01,01+b	02,02+b	03,03+b	04,04+b	05,05+b	06,06+b	07,07+b				
(1)	(2)	(3)	(4)	(5)	(6)	(7)	(8)	(9)	(10)	(11)	(12)	(13)	(14)	(15)	(16)	(17)	(18)	(19)
7	−95.81 (56.97)							20.35 (21.16)							−37.73 (20.56)	1.97 (1.46)	48	0.08
8	−99.61 (63.84)														−99.61 (63.84)	2.80 (2.39)	24	0.05
9	−105.24 (62.38)														−105.24 (62.38)	3.05 (2.29)	24	0.07
10	−108.69 (62.02)														−108.69 (62.02)	2.98 (2.25)	24	0.06
11	−111.93 (61.70)														−111.93 (61.70)	2.94 (2.23)	24	0.06
12	−111.07 (61.29)														−111.09 (61.29)	3.14 (2.20)	24	0.07
13	−117.64 (60.82)														−117.64 (60.82)	3.27 (2.17)	24	0.08
14	−115.26 (61.02)														−115.26 (61.02)	3.32 (2.18)	24	0.08

Note: Standard errors are robust, based on a cluster correction (Kleok, 1981).

Table 2A.6 *Seemingly unrelated regressions under full adjustment with time dummies, twenty-four countries, 1994–2008*

$[-(s_{c,t+H} - s_{c,t}) = \sum_\tau \alpha_{s,\tau,\tau+H} D_{\tau,t} + \phi_s^H d_{c,t} + u_{s,c,t}^H$ and $r_{c,t+H} - r_{c,t} = \sum_\tau \alpha_{r,\tau,\tau+H} D_{\tau,t} + \phi_r^H d_{c,t} + u_{r,c,t}^H$ with
$\eta_s^H + \eta_r^H = 0, \phi_s^H + \phi_r^H = -1$ (standard errors in parentheses)]

H	94,94+H	95,95+H	96,96+H	97,97+H	98,98+H	99,99+H	00,00+H	01,01+H	02,02+H	03,03+H	04,04+H	05,05+H	06,06+H	07,07+H	$\eta^H = (1/N^H)\sum_\tau \alpha_{s,\tau,\tau+H}$ (× 100)	Slope ϕ_s^H	No. of obs.
					Year dummies $\alpha_{s,\tau,\tau+H}$ (× 100)												
(1)	(2)	(3)	(4)	(5)	(6)	(7)	(8)	(9)	(10)	(11)	(12)	(13)	(14)	(15)	(16)	(17)	(18)
						A. With overlapping observations											
1	75.20	9.32	5.17	−5.37	15.49	−5.26	−13.37	−13.43	−2.32	−1.46	0.49	−1.50	6.29	11.37	5.76	−0.77	336
	(14.15)	(14.54)	(14.36)	(14.08)	(14.00)	(13.94)	(14.06)	(14.28)	(14.23)	(14.08)	(14.06)	(13.99)	(13.92)	(13.92)	(3.73)	(0.25)	
2	70.22	1.21	−8.59	14.10	14.08	−11.22	−14.73	−3.62	5.59	7.42	5.28	6.67	18.05		8.03	−0.60	312
	(16.05)	(16.53)	(16.30)	(15.96)	(15.86)	(15.78)	(15.94)	(16.21)	(16.14)	(15.96)	(15.94)	(15.84)	(15.76)		(4.44)	(0.29)	
3	62.35	−14.27	8.82	9.41	8.71	−13.65	−5.61	4.86	15.38	12.46	14.03	19.29			10.15	−0.38	288
	(18.02)	(18.58)	(18.32)	(17.91)	(17.80)	(17.70)	(17.89)	(18.20)	(18.13)	(17.91)	(17.89)	(17.78)			(5.20)	(0.33)	
4	51.74	7.21	7.00	3.77	7.16	−4.93	1.52	13.65	20.15	20.96	26.96				14.11	−0.35	264
	(20.17)	(20.84)	(20.52)	(20.05)	(19.91)	(19.80)	(20.01)	(20.39)	(20.30)	(20.05)	(20.01)				(6.09)	(0.38)	
5	68.92	1.26	−3.03	−2.77	10.44	−3.26	4.53	12.48	22.84	28.22					13.96	−0.39	240
	(21.41)	(22.19)	(21.83)	(21.26)	(21.11)	(20.97)	(21.23)	(21.67)	(21.57)	(21.27)					(6.78)	(0.43)	
6	66.22	−4.10	−5.23	4.26	12.82	1.32	4.05	14.86	29.87						13.76	−0.59	216
	(22.59)	(23.48)	(23.07)	(22.42)	(22.24)	(22.09)	(22.38)	(22.89)	(22.77)						(7.55)	(0.47)	
7	61.63	−2.78	5.52	11.38	16.58	2.21	6.99	20.64							15.27	−0.92	192
	(24.08)	(25.24)	(24.70)	(23.86)	(23.62)	(23.42)	(23.80)	(24.47)							(8.54)	(0.56)	
8	59.40	6.97	12.86	18.86	16.46	6.74	14.66								19.42	−1.16	168
	(25.72)	(27.10)	(26.46)	(25.45)	(25.17)	(24.93)	(25.39)								(9.73)	(0.63)	
9	65.88	12.02	19.32	21.06	21.82	16.71									26.13	−1.20	144
	(27.56)	(29.23)	(28.46)	(27.24)	(26.89)	(26.60)									(11.29)	(0.72)	

Table 2A.6 (cont.)

H	94,94+H	95,95+H	96,96+H	97,97+H	98,98+H	99,99+H	00,00+H	01,01+H	02,02+H	03,03+H	04,04+H	05,05+H	06,06+H	07,07+H	$\eta^H = (1/N^H)\sum_\tau \alpha_{s,\tau,\tau+H}$ (×100)	Slope ϕ_s^H	No. of obs.
(1)	(2)	(3)	(4)	(5)	(6)	(7)	(8)	(9)	(10)	(11)	(12)	(13)	(14)	(15)	(16)	(17)	(18)
10	70.13 (30.09)	16.91 (32.05)	20.58 (31.13)	26.91 (29.7)	34.07 (29.29)										33.72 (13.62)	−1.07 (0.81)	120
11	81.44 (31.80)	27.37 (34.28)	33.57 (33.13)	41.65 (31.31)											46.01 (16.31)	−1.54 (0.94)	96
12	87.04 (34.00)	39.59 (36.99)	49.08 (35.60)												58.57 (20.51)	−1.96 (1.07)	72
13	92.43 (38.20)	52.32 (42.29)													72.38 (28.46)	−2.39 (1.33)	48
14	94.84 (49.41)														94.84 (49.41)	−3.69 (2.31)	24

B. Without overlapping observations

H	94,94+H	95,95+H	96,96+H	97,97+H	98,98+H	99,99+H	00,00+H	01,01+H	02,02+H	03,03+H	04,04+H	05,05+H	06,06+H	07,07+H	$\eta^H = (1/N^H)\sum_\tau \alpha_{s,\tau,\tau+H}$ (×100)	Slope ϕ_s^H	No. of obs.
(1)	(2)	(3)	(4)	(5)	(6)	(7)	(8)	(9)	(10)	(11)	(12)	(13)	(14)	(15)	(16)	(17)	(18)
1	75.20 (14.16)	9.32 (14.55)	5.17 (14.36)	−5.37 (14.08)	15.49 (14.00)	−5.26 (13.94)	−13.37 (14.06)	−13.43 (14.28)	−2.32 (14.23)	−1.46 (14.08)	0.49 (14.06)	−1.50 (13.99)	6.29 (13.92)	11.37 (13.92)	5.76 (3.77)	−0.77 (0.25)	336
2	73.05 (19.98)		−4.40 (20.49)		11.12 (19.59)		−18.38 (19.75)		0.59 (20.17)		1.64 (19.75)		17.11 (19.39)		11.53 (7.51)	−0.95 (0.46)	168
3	74.76 (26.73)			19.58 (26.26)			−16.09 (26.15)			1.32 (26.27)					19.89 (13.17)	−1.61 (0.85)	96
4	62.00 (30.80)				8.12 (29.80)				17.83 (31.28)						29.32 (17.68)	−0.91 (0.92)	72
5	92.78 (35.43)					−14.98 (32.10)									38.90 (15.92)	−3.08 (1.49)	48
6	81.57 (34.66)						−18.82 (33.52)								31.37 (24.11)	−2.64 (1.34)	48

7	83.23			38.03	−3.02	48
	(34.98)			(25.29)	(1.37)	
8	84.01			84.01	−4.99	24
	(49.70)			(49.70)	(2.33)	
9	74.44			74.44	−5.41	24
	(46.53)			(46.53)	(2.18)	
10	85.92			85.92	−6.07	24
	(45.67)			(45.67)	(2.14)	
11	112.76			112.76	−6.05	24
	(48.49)			(48.49)	(2.27)	
12	119.41	−7.18		119.41	−5.01	24
	(49.69)	(36.56)		(49.69)	(2.32)	
13	111.47			111.47	−3.72	24
	(49.46)			(49.46)	(2.31)	
14	94.84			94.84	−3.69	24
	(49.41)			(49.41)	(2.31)	

Table 2A.7 *More predictive regressions, twenty countries (Argentina, Brazil, Poland, Russia omitted), 1994–2008 (standard errors in parentheses)*

Horizon h (1)	(1) Negative change in nominal exchange rate $-(s_{c,t+h}-s_{c,t})=\eta_s^h+\phi_s^h d_{ct}+u_{s,ct}^h$					(2) Inflation differential $r_{c,t+h}-r_{c,t}=\eta_r^h+\phi_r^h d_{ct}^h+u_{r,ct}^h$				
	Intercept $\eta_s^h \times 100$ (2)	Slope ϕ_s^h (3)	No. of observations (4)	R^2 (5)	χ^2 (6)	Intercept $\eta_r^h \times 100$ (7)	Slope ϕ_r^h (8)	No. of observations (9)	R^2 (10)	χ^2 (11)
A. With overlapping observations										
1	0.31(0.66)	−0.15(0.04) −0.15(0.04)	280	0.04	6.54	−0.49(0.43)	−0.13(0.03) −0.13(0.03)	280	0.07	6.05
2	−0.47(0.97)	−0.43(0.06) −0.43(0.06)	260	0.15	8.57	−1.24(0.64)	−0.17(0.04) −0.16(0.04)	260	0.06	3.67
3	−1.47(1.19)	−0.72(0.08) −0.71(0.08)	240	0.26	29.53*	−1.58(0.84)	−0.16(0.06) −0.18(0.06)	240	0.04	0.09
4	−2.04(1.41)	−0.96(0.09) −0.95(0.09)	220	0.34	51.84*	−2.04(1.08)	−0.12(0.07) −0.12(0.07)	220	0.01	0.19
5	−1.57(1.60)	−1.13(0.10) −1.13(0.10)	200	0.39	65.20*	−1.86(1.31)	−0.06(0.08) −0.06(0.08)	200	0.00	2.81
6	−1.25(1.76)	−1.30(0.11) −1.30(0.11)	180	0.46	62.37*	−2.12(1.52)	−0.05(0.09) −0.05(0.09)	180	0.00	1.57
7	−1.08(1.83)	−1.33(0.11) −1.34(0.11)	160	0.49	52.64*	−1.33(1.73)	−0.09(0.10) −0.09(0.10)	160	0.01	3.39
8	0.78(2.00)	−1.16(0.12) −1.15(0.12)	140	0.40	41.05*	−0.72(2.00)	−0.28(0.12) −0.29(0.12)	140	0.04	0.00
9	2.72(2.30)	−1.00(0.14) −0.95(0.13)	120	0.31	28.27*	−1.09(2.28)	−0.41(0.14) −0.43(0.13)	120	0.07	0.03

10	3.38(2.65)	−0.90(0.15) −0.83(0.14)	100	0.27	10.52*	0.21(2.67)	−0.58(0.15) −0.57(0.14)	100	0.13	2.56	
11	3.12(3.66)	−0.66(0.20) −0.56(0.16)	80	0.12	1.92	4.82(3.59)	−0.92(0.20) −0.77(0.16)	80	0.22	4.03	
12	3.45(4.59)	−0.58(0.23) −0.47(0.18)	60	0.10	1.62	7.18(4.49)	−1.03(0.22) −0.81(0.18)	60	0.27	2.38	
13	6.57(5.96)	−0.59(0.27) −0.41(0.22)	40	0.11	0.23	5.21(5.99)	−0.97(0.27) −0.82(0.22)	40	0.25	1.91	
14	17.81(9.47)	−1.21(0.53) −0.66(0.47)	20	0.22	0.81	1.60(10.06)	−0.72(0.56) −0.67(0.46)	20	0.08	0.08	

B. Without overlapping observations

1	0.31(0.66)	−0.15(0.04) −0.15(0.04)	280	0.04	6.54	−0.49(0.43)	−0.13(0.03) −0.13(0.03)	280	0.07	6.05	
2	0.42(1.46)	−0.37(0.10) −0.37(0.10)	260	0.09	2.67	−1.01(0.91)	−0.20(0.06) −0.19(0.06)	260	0.07	7.68	
3	−1.54 (1.92)	−0.73(0.14) −0.74(0.13)	240	0.27	13.10*	−0.13(1.49)	−0.13(0.11) −0.13(0.10)	240	0.02	0.10	
4	−5.18 (3.01)	−0.86(0.19) −0.80(0.20)	220	0.25	11.29*	−1.08(2.52)	−0.29(0.16) −0.28(0.16)	220	0.05	0.52	
5	−4.87 (3.56)	−0.92(0.25) −1.00(0.24)	200	0.27	16.39*	1.68(3.40)	−0.12(0.23) −0.09(0.23)	200	0.01	0.02	
6	−3.56 (4.02)	−1.06(0.24) −1.07(0.23)	180	0.35	16.39*	−0.44(3.59)	−0.09(0.21) −0.09(0.21)	180	0.01	0.61	
7	−0.40 (4.92)	−1.79(0.27) −1.79(0.26)	160	0.54	25.89*	−2.36(3.96)	0.20(0.21) 0.21(0.21)	160	0.02	9.95*	

Table 2A.7 (*cont.*)

Horizon h (1)	(1) Negative change in nominal exchange rate $-(s_{c,t+h}-s_{c,t})=\eta_s^h+\phi_s^h d_{ct}+u_{s,ct}^h$						(2) Inflation differential $r_{c,t+h}-r_{c,t}=\eta_r^h+\phi_r^h d_{ct}+u_{r,ct}^h$				
	Intercept $\eta_s^b\times100$ (2)	Slope ϕ_s^b (3)	No. of observations (4)	R^2 (5)	χ^2 (6)		Intercept $\eta_r^b\times100$ (7)	Slope ϕ_r^b (8)	No. of observations (9)	R^2 (10)	χ^2 (11)
8	−24.96(7.36)	−0.55(0.41) −1.31(0.43)	140	0.09	4.21		18.64(8.31)	−0.51(0.46) 0.06 (0.43)	140	0.06	1.25
9	−14.16(8.17)	−0.79(0.46) −1.22(0.40)	120	0.14	2.81		11.82(8.64)	−0.45(0.48) −0.09(0.41)	120	0.05	0.00
10	−7.82(8.89)	−0.87(0.50) −1.11(0.41)	100	0.15	1.82		7.67(9.05)	−0.53(0.51) −0.29(0.42)	100	0.06	0.21
11	−2.24(8.86)	−0.91(0.50) −0.97(0.40)	80	0.16	1.25		4.30(9.68)	−0.62(0.54) −0.49(0.44)	80	0.07	0.000
12	−0.18(9.13)	−0.91(0.51) −0.91(0.42)	60	0.15	1.25		5.40(9.92)	−0.66(0.55) −0.49(0.45)	60	0.07	0.000
13	7.67 (8.78)	−1.15(0.49) −0.91(0.41)	40	0.23	0.81		−1.98(9.88)	−0.54(0.55) −0.60(0.45)	40	0.05	0.08
14	17.81(9.47)	−1.21(0.53) −0.66(0.47)	20	0.22	0.81		1.60(10.06)	−0.72(0.56) −0.67(0.46)	20	0.08	0.08

Notes:

1. The χ^2 statistics in columns 6 and 11 test the hypotheses of the independence between $-(s_{c,t+h}-s_{c,t})$ and d_{ct} and $r_{c,t+b}-r_{c,t}$ and d_{ct}, respectively. Under the null, χ^2 has one degree of freedom.
2. An asterisk (*) indicates significance at the 5 per cent level.

Table 2A.8 *Seemingly unrelated regressions under full adjustment, twenty countries (Argentina, Brazil, Poland, and Russia Omitted), 1994–2008* $[-(s_{c,t+H} - s_{c,t}) = \eta_s^H + \phi_s^H d_{ct} + u_{s,ct}^H$ *and* $r_{c,t+H} - r_{c,t} = \eta_r^H + \phi_r^H d_{ct} + u_{r,ct}^H$, *with* $\eta_s^H + \eta_r^H = 0$ *and* $\phi_s^H + \phi_r^H = -1$ (*standard errors in parentheses*)]

Horizon H (1)	With overlapping observations			Without overlapping observations		
	Intercept $\eta_s^H \times 100$ (2)	Slope ϕ_s^H (3)	No. of observations (4)	Intercept $\eta_s^H \times 100$ (5)	Slope ϕ_s^H (6)	No. of observations (7)
1	0.40 (0.45)	−0.51 (0.03) −0.51 (0.03)	280	0.40 (0.45)	−0.51 (0.03) −0.51 (0.03)	280
2	0.39 (0.60)	−0.63 (0.04) −0.63 (0.04)	260	0.72 (0.88)	−0.59 (0.06) −0.59 (0.06)	140
3	0.05 (0.73)	−0.78 (0.05) −0.78 (0.05)	240	−0.71 (1.21)	−0.80 (0.09) −0.80 (0.09)	80
4	0.00 (0.89)	−0.92 (0.06) −0.92 (0.06)	220	−2.05 (1.97)	−0.78 (0.13) −0.76 (0.13)	60
5	0.15 (1.04)	−1.04 (0.07) −1.04 (0.07)	200	−3.28 (2.44)	−0.90 (0.17) −0.96 (0.16)	40
6	0.44 (1.17)	−1.13 (0.07) −1.13 (0.07)	180	−1.56 (2.67)	−0.98 (0.16) −0.99 (0.16)	40
7	0.13 (1.27)	−1.12 (0.08) −1.12 (0.08)	160	0.98 (3.18)	−1.50 (0.17) −1.50 (0.17)	40

Table 2A.8 (cont.)

Horizon H (1)	With overlapping observations			Without overlapping observations		
	Intercept $\eta_s^H \times 100$ (2)	Slope ϕ_s^H (3)	No. of observations (4)	Intercept $\eta_s^H \times 100$ (5)	Slope ϕ_s^H (6)	No. of observations (7)
8	0.75 (1.43)	−0.94 (0.09) −0.93 (0.08)	140	−21.80 (5.44)	−0.52 (0.30) −1.19 (0.30)	20
9	1.90 (1.63)	−0.80 (0.10) −0.71 (0.02)	120	−12.99 (5.81)	−0.67 (0.33) −1.67 (0.29)	20
10	1.59 (1.90)	−0.66 (0.11) −0.63 (0.10)	100	−7.75 (6.21)	−0.67 (0.35) −0.91 (0.29)	20
11	−0.85 (2.59)	−0.37 (0.14) −0.40 (0.11)	80	−3.27 (6.44)	−0.64 (0.36) −0.74 (0.30)	20
12	−1.87 (3.24)	−0.27 (0.16) −0.33 (0.13)	60	−2.79 (6.61)	−0.63 (0.37) −0.71 (0.31)	20
13	0.68 (4.24)	−0.31 (0.20) −0.29 (0.16)	40	4.83 (6.51)	−0.80 (0.36) −0.65 (0.30)	20
14	8.10 (6.93)	−0.74 (0.39) −0.50 (0.33)	20	8.10 (6.93)	−0.74 (0.39) −0.50 (0.33)	20

Table 2A.9 Predictive regressions with time dummies, changes in nominal exchange rates, twenty countries (Argentina, Brazil, Poland, and Russia Omitted), 1994–2008 $[-(s_{c,t+h} - s_{c,t}) = \sum_\tau \alpha_{s,\tau,\tau+h} D_{\tau,t} + \phi_s^b d_{c,t} + u_{s,c,t}^b$ (standard errors in parentheses)]

b	94,94+h	95,95+h	96,96+h	97,97+h	98,98+h	99,99+h	00,00+h	01,01+h	02,02+h	03,03+h	04,04+h	05,05+h	06,06+h	07,07+h	$\eta^b = (1/N^b)$ $\sum_\tau \alpha_{s,\tau,\tau+h}$ (×100)	Slope ϕ_τ^b	No. of obs.	R^2
(1)	(2)	(3)	(4)	(5)	(6)	(7)	(8)	(9)	(10)	(11)	(12)	(13)	(14)	(15)	(16)	(17)	(18)	(19)
							A. With overlapping observations											
1	5.55	−2.52	−4.50	−13.17	−2.17	−3.39	−9.28	0.22	7.69	5.00	4.81	1.71	5.47	9.42	0.35	−0.11	280	0.36
	(4.15)	(2.52)	(2.04)	(3.14)	(1.43)	(1.89)	(1.63)	(1.53)	(2.30)	(1.20)	(1.12)	(1.22)	(1.62)	(2.30)	(0.59)	(0.07)		
2	2.99	−5.48	−16.35	−12.99	−7.12	−12.25	−8.96	6.28	11.98	9.43	6.14	6.67	14.95		−0.36	−0.29	260	0.49
	(5.09)	(4.01)	(3.98)	(3.00)	(2.46)	(2.38)	(1.92)	(3.41)	(2.99)	(1.84)	(1.54)	(2.03)	(3.09)		(0.95)	(0.12)		
3	−1.18	−16.73	−15.41	−14.96	−17.25	−10.96	−1.83	9.54	16.09	10.70	10.97	15.69			−1.28	−0.45	240	0.59
	(5.66)	(5.38)	(4.26)	(3.76)	(2.55)	(2.07)	(2.74)	(4.00)	(3.20)	(2.20)	(2.57)	(3.61)			(1.31)	(0.15)		
4	−14.08	−16.07	−17.29	−22.66	−16.62	−2.78	2.85	13.37	17.42	15.72	20.09				−1.82	−0.56	220	0.65
	(6.34)	(5.99)	(5.27)	(4.18)	(2.43)	(1.99)	(3.07)	(4.42)	(3.15)	(2.94)	(3.78)				(1.74)	(0.2)		
5	−14.48	−18.18	−24.96	−20.51	−8.81	2.57	7.61	14.58	22.49	24.96					−1.47	−0.62	200	0.68
	(6.65)	(6.70)	(5.85)	(3.65)	(3.27)	(2.31)	(3.34)	(4.59)	(3.81)	(4.05)					(2.14)	(0.24)		
6	−16.55	−24.88	−22.00	−11.34	−4.41	7.55	8.82	18.64	31.29						−1.43	−0.73	180	0.69
	(7.08)	(7.05)	(5.53)	(3.57)	(3.61)	(2.58)	(3.12)	(4.85)	(4.75)						(2.54)	(0.25)		
7	−24.49	−22.41	−13.00	−5.52	0.37	9.48	13.95	27.55							−1.76	−0.77	160	0.69
	(7.22)	(6.55)	(5.19)	(3.95)	(3.39)	(2.56)	(3.05)	(5.39)							(3.01)	(0.23)		
8	−23.17	−14.61	−7.97	−0.54	2.84	15.08	23.81								−0.65	−0.73	140	0.61
	(7.01)	(6.69)	(5.51)	(4.11)	(2.89)	(2.65)	(4.24)								(3.71)	(0.24)		
9	−15.63	−10.60	−3.81	0.88	9.32	24.86									0.84	−0.64	120	0.49
	(7.64)	(7.34)	(5.67)	(4.57)	(3.08)	(3.84)									(4.57)	(0.27)		

Table 2A.9 (cont.)

| (1) b | Year dummies $\alpha_{s,\tau,\tau+b}$ ($\times 100$) | | | | | | | | | | | | | | $\eta^b = (1/N^b) \sum_\tau \alpha_{s,\tau,\tau+b}$ ($\times 100$) | Slope ϕ_1^b | No. of obs. | R^2 |
	(2) 94,94+b	(3) 95,95+b	(4) 96,96+b	(5) 97,97+b	(6) 98,98+b	(7) 99,99+b	(8) 00,00+b	(9) 01,01+b	(10) 02,02+b	(11) 03,03+b	(12) 04,04+b	(13) 05,05+b	(14) 06,06+b	(15) 07,07+b	(16)	(17)	(18)	(19)
10	-10.71 (8.22)	-6.32 (7.30)	-2.47 (6.00)	5.97 (4.60)	19.49 (4.55)										1.19 (5.28)	-0.58 (0.27)	100	0.38
11	-5.56 (8.55)	-4.43 (8.13)	2.91 (6.43)	15.43 (5.55)											2.09 (6.81)	-0.57 (0.29)	80	0.21
12	-3.37 (8.60)	1.29 (7.69)	12.61 (6.45)												3.51 (7.33)	-0.58 (0.23)	60	0.15
13	2.65 (8.29)	11.67 (7.58)													7.16 (7.82)	-0.63 (0.21)	40	0.13
14	17.81 (7.26)														17.81 (7.26)	-1.21 (0.56)	20	0.22
B. Without overlapping observations																		
1	5.55 (4.15)	-2.52 (2.52)	-4.50 (2.04)	-13.17 (3.14)	-2.17 (1.43)	-3.39 (1.89)	-9.28 (1.63)	0.22 (1.53)	7.69 (2.30)	5.00 (1.20)	4.81 (1.12)	1.71 (1.22)	5.47 (1.62)	9.42 (2.30)	0.35 (0.59)	-0.11 (0.07)	280	0.36
2	2.96 (4.93)		-16.38 (4.11)		-7.09 (2.60)		-8.94 (2.04)		12.00 (3.24)		6.16 (1.57)		14.95 (3.09)		0.52 (1.16)	-0.28 (0.15)	140	0.45
3	0.22 (5.11)			-14.00 (3.55)			-2.97 (2.36)			10.04 (2.29)					-1.68 (1.89)	-0.60 (0.15)	80	0.45
4	-12.17 (5.73)				-18.66 (2.97)				16.07 (3.37)						-4.92 (2.46)	-0.75 (0.26)	60	0.58

					N	
5	−14.10 (6.05)	2.47 (2.57)		−5.82 (3.57)	−0.66 (0.35)	40	0.36
6	−17.35 (6.15)		9.47 (3.68)	−3.94 (3.66)	−0.64 (0.32)	40	0.49
7	−22.54 (6.17)			24.84 (6.38)	1.15 (3.81)	−0.97 (0.38)	40	0.71
8	−24.96 (6.67)				−24.96 (6.67)	−0.55 (0.42)	20	0.09
9	−14.16 (6.50)				−14.16 (6.50)	−0.79 (0.51)	20	0.14
10	−7.82 (6.74)				−7.82 (6.74)	−0.87 (0.57)	20	0.15
11	−2.24 (6.79)				−2.24 (6.79)	−0.91 (0.58)	20	0.16
12	−0.18 (7.00)				−0.18 (7.00)	−0.91 (0.53)	20	0.15
13	7.67 (6.62)				7.67 (6.62)	−1.15 (0.50)	20	0.23
14	17.81 (7.26)				17.81 (7.26)	−1.21 (0.56)	20	0.22

Note: Standard errors are robust, based on a cluster correction (Kleok, 1981).

Table 2A.10 *Predictive regressions with time dummies, inflation differentials, twenty countries, (Argentina, Brazil, Poland, and Russia Omitted), 1994–2008* $[r_{c,t+b} - r_{c,t} = \sum_\tau \alpha_{r,\tau,\tau+b} D_{\tau,t} + \phi_r^b d_{c,t} + u_{r,c,t}^b$ *(standard errors in parentheses)]*

b	94,94+b	95,95+b	96,96+b	97,97+b	98,98+b	99,99+b	00,00+b	01,01+b	02,02+b	03,03+b	04,04+b	05,05+b	06,06+b	07,07+b	$\eta^b = (1/N^b)$ $\sum_\tau \alpha_{s,\tau,\tau+b}$ $(\times 100)$	Slope ϕ_r^b	No. of obs.	R^2
(1)	(2)	(3)	(4)	(5)	(6)	(7)	(8)	(9)	(10)	(11)	(12)	(13)	(14)	(15)	(16)	(17)	(18)	(19)
									A. With overlapping observations									
1	3.23	2.34	2.57	−2.31	7.31	−2.64	1.60	2.94	−7.23	−5.58	−4.89	0.28	−6.32	1.68	−0.50	−0.15	280	0.39
	(1.88)	(1.83)	(1.50)	(1.58)	(0.76)	(0.64)	(1.04)	(1.32)	(0.92)	(0.96)	(1.60)	(0.76)	(1.13)	(1.65)	(0.57)	(0.03)		
2	4.58	5.43	0.91	7.49	3.59	−0.22	5.43	−5.17	−13.08	−10.52	−4.72	−6.43	−4.52		−1.33	−0.29	260	0.39
	(3.42)	(2.28)	(1.98)	(2.02)	(1.18)	(1.12)	(1.59)	(1.79)	(1.31)	(2.09)	(1.93)	(1.26)	(1.78)		(1.09)	(0.07)		
3	6.27	3.52	10.78	5.83	5.46	4.50	−1.46	−11.23	−17.98	−10.20	−11.35	−4.85			−1.73	−0.38	240	0.41
	(4.12)	(2.91)	(2.65)	(2.37)	(1.64)	(1.72)	(1.64)	(2.09)	(2.30)	(2.22)	(1.61)	(2.04)			(1.54)	(0.09)		
4	3.50	13.25	9.17	8.98	9.84	−1.85	−6.79	−16.27	−17.62	−16.73	−9.73				−2.20	−0.43	220	0.42
	(4.90)	(3.95)	(3.37)	(2.71)	(2.29)	(1.90)	(1.92)	(3.13)	(2.53)	(1.88)	(2.16)				(1.98)	(0.13)		
5	12.93	11.95	12.64	14.33	3.02	−6.89	−11.55	−16.34	−24.30	−15.16					−1.94	−0.49	200	0.43
	(5.81)	(5.14)	(4.17)	(3.50)	(2.42)	(2.16)	(2.75)	(3.66)	(2.33)	(2.40)					(2.42)	(0.18)		
6	11.41	15.92	18.46	8.63	−2.65	−11.38	−11.41	−23.62	−22.98						−1.96	−0.56	180	0.39
	(6.70)	(6.18)	(5.17)	(4.02)	(2.70)	(2.88)	(2.96)	(3.62)	(2.79)						(2.87)	(0.22)		
7	14.83	21.93	13.04	4.19	−7.63	−10.82	−18.21	−22.68							−0.67	−0.63	160	0.33
	(7.40)	(7.17)	(5.76)	(4.48)	(3.90)	(3.00)	(2.95)	(4.21)							(3.37)	(0.27)		
8	20.74	17.29	9.29	0.56	−7.92	−17.34	−17.14								0.78	−0.73	140	0.32
	(8.24)	(8.02)	(6.42)	(5.00)	(4.17)	(2.74)	(3.11)								(4.17)	(0.30)		
9	15.39	13.79	6.02	1.88	−15.10	−15.73									1.04	−0.81	120	0.26
	(8.90)	(8.86)	(6.87)	(5.30)	(4.03)	(2.84)									(5.10)	(0.33)		

10	11.10 (9.36)	10.49 (9.03)	7.47 (6.99)	−3.98 (5.39)	−13.90 (4.23)										2.24 (5.98)	−0.88 (0.33)	100	0.23
11	8.01 (9.72)	13.18 (8.94)	2.63 (6.97)	−1.31 (5.18)											5.63 (7.42)	−1.00 (0.32)	80	0.26
12	9.08 (9.66)	7.46 (8.92)	4.87 (6.63)												7.14 (8.14)	−1.03 (0.30)	60	0.27
13	2.48 (9.28)	8.77 (7.88)													5.63 (8.36)	−1.00 (0.25)	40	0.25
14	1.60 (8.12)														1.60 (8.12)	−0.72 (0.53)	20	0.08
B. Without overlapping observations																		
1	3.23 (1.89)	2.34 (1.83)	2.57 (1.50)	−2.31 (1.58)	7.31 (0.77)	−2.64 (0.64)	1.60 (1.04)	2.94 (1.32)	−7.23 (0.92)	−5.58 (0.96)	−4.89 (1.60)	0.28 (0.76)	−6.32 (1.13)	1.68 (1.65)	−0.50 (0.57)	−0.15 (0.03)	280	0.39
2	4.04 (3.14)		0.26 (2.05)		4.17 (1.42)		5.87 (1.62)		−12.70 (1.37)		−4.50 (1.96)		−4.50 (1.71)		−1.05 (1.19)	−0.23 (0.08)	140	0.37
3	5.68 (3.95)			5.43 (2.40)			−0.99 (1.88)			−9.92 (2.39)					0.05 (1.92)	−0.32 (0.13)	80	0.21
4	2.36 (4.18)				11.05 (3.31)				−16.82 (3.29)						−1.14 (2.99)	−0.31 (0.24)	60	0.41
5	12.22 (5.52)					−6.70 (2.42)									2.76 (3.50)	−0.42 (0.33)	40	0.18
6	9.78 (5.73)						−10.09 (4.10)								−0.15 (3.80)	−0.40 (0.29)	40	0.15

Table 2A.10 (*cont.*)

b (1)	Year dummies $\alpha_{s,\tau,\tau+b}$ (×100)														$\eta^b = (1/N^b) \sum_\tau \alpha_{s,\tau,\tau+b}$ (×100) (16)	Slope ϕ_η^b (17)	No. of obs. (18)	R^2 (19)
	94,94+b (2)	95,95+b (3)	96,96+b (4)	97,97+b (5)	98,98+b (6)	99,99+b (7)	00,00+b (8)	01,01+b (9)	02,02+b (10)	03,03+b (11)	04,04+b (12)	05,05+b (13)	06,06+b (14)	07,07+b (15)				
7	11.91 (5.70)							−18.63 (5.88)							−3.36 (4.35)	−0.33 (0.33)	40	0.25
8	18.64 (6.70)														18.64 (6.70)	−0.51 (0.48)	20	0.06
9	11.82 (7.09)														11.82 (7.09)	−0.45 (0.53)	20	0.05
10	7.67 (7.60)														7.67 (7.60)	−0.53 (0.53)	20	0.06
11	4.30 (7.72)														4.30 (7.72)	−0.62 (0.56)	20	0.07
12	5.40 (7.92)														5.40 (7.92)	−0.66 (0.57)	20	0.07
13	−1.98 (8.21)														−1.98 (8.21)	−0.54 (0.54)	20	0.05
14	1.60 (8.12)														1.60 (8.12)	−0.72 (0.53)	20	0.08

Note: Standard errors are robust, based on a cluster correction (Kleok, 1981).

Table 2A.11 *Seemingly unrelated regressions under full adjustment with time dummies, twenty countries, (Argentina, Brazil, Poland, and Russia Omitted), 1994–2008* $[-(s_{c,t+H} - s_{c,t}) = \sum_\tau \alpha_{s,\tau,\tau+H} D_{\tau,t} + \phi_s^H d_{c,t} + u_{s,c,t}$ *and* $r_{c,t+H} - r_{c,t} = \sum_\tau \alpha_{r,\tau,\tau+H} D_{\tau,t} + \phi_r^H d_{c,t} + u_{r,c,t}$, *with* $\eta_s^H + \eta_r^H = 0, \phi_s^H + \phi_r^H = -1$ *(standard errors in parentheses)]*

H	94,94+H	95,95+H	96,96+H	97,97+H	98,98+H	99,99+H	00,00+H	01,01+H	02,02+H	03,03+H	04,04+H	05,05+H	06,06+H	07,07+H	$\eta^H = (1/N^H)\sum_\tau \alpha_{s,\tau,\tau+H}\ (\times 100)$	Slope ϕ_s^H	No. of obs.
(1)	(2)	(3)	(4)	(5)	(6)	(7)	(8)	(9)	(10)	(11)	(12)	(13)	(14)	(15)	(16)	(17)	(18)
							A. With overlapping observations										
1	10.63	5.52	1.49	−9.52	−6.66	−4.18	−12.60	−5.75	4.87	3.24	3.34	0.70	5.77	9.36	0.44	−0.58	280
	(2.23)	(2.25)	(2.23)	(2.22)	(2.23)	(2.21)	(2.22)	(2.24)	(2.22)	(2.21)	(2.21)	(2.21)	(2.21)	(2.21)	(0.59)	(0.03)	
2	7.52	1.01	−11.21	−9.40	−8.92	−11.61	−9.99	3.49	11.28	9.43	6.35	7.17	16.32		0.88	−0.60	260
	(2.74)	(2.79)	(2.76)	(2.73)	(2.75)	(2.72)	(2.73)	(2.77)	(2.73)	(2.72)	(2.72)	(2.72)	(2.71)		(0.76)	(0.04)	
3	2.44	−12.30	−11.54	−11.74	−16.25	−8.95	−0.51	10.13	17.55	12.45	12.81	17.64			0.98	−0.58	240
	(3.08)	(3.15)	(3.10)	(3.06)	(3.09)	(3.05)	(3.07)	(3.12)	(3.06)	(3.05)	(3.05)	(3.05)			(0.89)	(0.05)	
4	−11.11	−13.04	−14.30	−19.72	−13.84	0.07	5.66	16.12	20.23	18.55	22.93				1.05	−0.57	220
	(3.40)	(3.49)	(3.42)	(3.37)	(3.40)	(3.34)	(3.38)	(3.45)	(3.37)	(3.35)	(3.35)				(1.02)	(0.06)	
5	−12.85	−17.02	−23.48	−18.66	−5.66	5.13	10.58	17.97	25.38	27.68					0.91	−0.54	200
	(3.71)	(3.83)	(3.74)	(3.67)	(3.72)	(3.64)	(3.68)	(3.78)	(3.67)	(3.65)					(1.17)	(0.08)	
6	−16.12	−25.63	−21.93	−10.34	−0.16	10.32	12.60	23.48	34.87						0.79	−0.54	180
	(4.01)	(4.16)	(4.05)	(3.96)	(4.03)	(3.93)	(3.98)	(4.10)	(3.97)						(1.34)	(0.09)	
7	−25.03	−24.28	−13.95	−5.41	4.14	11.58	17.19	31.99							−0.47	−0.56	160
	(4.17)	(4.36)	(4.22)	(4.11)	(4.19)	(4.06)	(4.13)	(4.28)							(1.48)	(0.10)	
8	−24.50	−17.17	−9.67	−1.27	5.49	16.19	25.97								−0.71	−0.53	140
	(4.36)	(4.59)	(4.42)	(4.28)	(4.38)	(4.22)	(4.31)								(1.65)	(0.12)	
9	−17.38	−13.60	−5.95	−0.27	11.62	25.59									0.00	−0.44	120
	(4.78)	(5.09)	(4.86)	(4.68)	(4.81)	(4.60)									(1.96)	(0.14)	

Table 2A.11 (cont.)

(1) H	Year dummies $\alpha_{s,\tau,\tau+H}$ (×100)														$\eta^H = (1/N^H)\sum_\tau \alpha_{s,\tau,\tau+H}$ (×100)	Slope ϕ_S^H	No. of obs.
	(2) 94,94+H	(3) 95,95+H	(4) 96,96+H	(5) 97,97+H	(6) 98,98+H	(7) 99,99+H	(8) 00,00+H	(9) 01,01+H	(10) 02,02+H	(11) 03,03+H	(12) 04,04+H	(13) 05,05+H	(14) 06,06+H	(15) 07,07+H	(16)	(17)	(18)
10	-12.84 (5.25)	-9.70 (5.62)	-4.99 (5.35)	4.45 (5.13)	21.42 (5.28)										-0.33 (2.38)	-0.38 (0.156)	100
11	-8.86 (5.77)	-9.40 (6.23)	-0.91 (5.89)	12.93 (5.62)											-1.56 (2.94)	-0.30 (0.19)	80
12	-7.72 (6.29)	-4.91 (6.85)	7.69 (6.44)												-1.65 (3.77)	-0.28 (0.21)	60
13	-2.51 (6.98)	4.64 (7.72)													1.06 (5.20)	-0.33 (0.26)	40
14	10.47 (8.94)														10.47 (8.94)	-0.86 (0.50)	20
B. With overlapping observations																	
1	10.63 (2.23)	5.52 (2.25)	1.49 (2.23)	-9.52 (2.22)	-6.66 (2.23)	-4.18 (2.21)	-12.60 (2.22)	-5.76 (2.24)	4.87 (2.22)	3.24 (2.21)	3.34 (2.21)	0.70 (2.21)	5.77 (2.21)	9.36 (2.21)	0.44 (0.59)	-0.58 (0.03)	280
2	7.45 (2.98)	-11.17 (3.01)			-10.14 (2.99)		-11.07 (2.96)		10.27 (2.95)		5.49 (2.93)		15.68 (2.92)		0.931 (1.12)	-0.66 (0.06)	140
3	2.18 (3.31)			-12.26 (3.22)			-2.30 (3.25)			10.95 (3.18)					-0.36 (1.62)	-0.67 (0.11)	80
4	-8.50 (3.96)				-14.05 (4.00)				20.51 (3.82)						-0.68 (2.27)	-0.71 (0.15)	60
5	-12.13 (4.85)					5.15 (4.33)									-3.49 (2.16)	-0.60 (0.23)	40
6	-14.82 (5.17)						12.49 (5.02)								-1.17 (3.60)	-0.62 (0.22)	40

7	−23.44		2.66	−0.76	40
	(5.50)		(4.03)	(0.23)	
8	−25.60		−25.60	−0.55	20
	(7.03)		(7.03)	(0.39)	
9	−14.30		−14.30	−0.80	20
	(7.79)		(7.79)	(0.44)	
10	−7.77	28.77	−7.77	−0.74	20
	(8.43)	(5.91)	(8.43)	(0.47)	
11	−1.79		−1.79	−1.02	20
	(8.45)		(8.45)	(0.47)	
12	0.96		0.96	−1.03	20
	(8.71)		(8.71)	(0.49)	
13	7.91		7.91	−1.17	20
	(8.45)		(8.45)	(0.47)	
14	10.47		10.47	−0.86	20
	(8.94)		(8.94)	(0.50)	

2A.4 High inflation and monetary turmoil

In 1994, 1995, and 1998, the Brazilian real, Polish zloty and Russian rouble, respectively, were redenominated. This can be seen from the prices and exchange rates for these countries in Tables 2.1 and 2.2, as well as in the volatility measures in Figure 2.5. Additionally, following the floating of its currency in 2002, there was considerable monetary turmoil in Argentina. What is the impact of these episodes on the performance of the BMI? As large increases in prices tend to be offset by corresponding depreciations of the currency that restore the real rate, at least as an approximation, the impact of high inflation and redenominations is likely to be less pronounced when the real rate is analysed. In what follows, we thus redo some of the analysis that involves the nominal exchange rate.

We start with the predictive regressions of Section 2.6 of this chapter:

$$-\Delta_{(h)}s_{t+h} = \eta_s^h + \phi_s^h d_t + u_{st}^h, \quad \Delta_{(h)}r_{t+h} = \eta_r^h + \phi_r^h d_t + u_{rt}^h \quad (2.34)$$

where, for horizon h, $\eta_s^h, \phi_s^h, \eta_r^h$ and ϕ_r^h are parameters; d_t is current mispricing, defined by equation (2.16); and u_{st}^h and u_{rt}^h are zero-mean error terms. Table 2A.7 presents the estimates of model (2.34) with the four high-inflation countries omitted. In comparison with the results when these four countries were included (Table 2.9), there is now a tendency for $\left|\phi_s^h\right|$ to be higher and $\left|\phi_r^h\right|$ lower, making $\phi_s^h / \left(\phi_s^h + \phi_r^h\right)$ closer to unity, so the nominal rate does more of the adjusting. Moreover, the estimates are more precisely determined, and intercepts (the autonomous changes in exchange rates and prices) are now considerably smaller.

As discussed in Section 2.6 of the text, when there is complete adjustment at horizon H, the intercepts and slopes of model (2.34) satisfy $\eta_s^H + \eta_r^H = 0$, $\phi_s^H + \phi_r^H = -1$. The two equations in (2.34) with this cross-equation restriction imposed can be estimated by SURE, and Table 2A.8 contains the results when the four countries are omitted. Comparing these results to those of Table 2.10, again, we see a substantially clearer picture, with the nominal rate doing the vast bulk of the adjustment, the values of the intercepts falling, and the parameters being better determined.

Tables A2.4 through A2.6 give the results, for all twenty-four countries, pertaining to the split between the nominal rate and prices when

Table 2A.12 *Summary of presentation of results, high-inflation countries included and excluded*

Impact of currency mispricing on future value of	High-inflation countries (number of table containing relevant results)	
	Included	Excluded
(1)	(2)	(3)
1. Nominal exchange rate, with time effects		
• Excluded	2.9	2A.7
• Included	2A.4	2A.9
2. Prices, with time effects		
• Excluded	2.9	2A.7
• Included	2A.5	2A.10
3. Nominal rate and prices jointly under full adjustment, with time effects		
• Excluded	2.10	2A.8
• Included	2A.6	2A.11

time effects are added. Tables 2A.9 through 2A.11 contain the corresponding results when the four high-inflation countries are omitted. Now there is a slight tendency for there to be a more equal sharing of the adjustment between the nominal rate and inflation, but still the exchange rate does the majority of the work.

The preceding discussion of the results when the high-inflation countries are excluded involves the additional dimension of time effects both included and excluded. To assist with an understanding of the presentation of these results, Table 2A.12 provides an analytical overview of the structure of the various pairwise comparisons. Thus, for example, the first entries of columns 2 and 3 of this table refer to Tables 2.9 and 2A.7. A comparison of these two tables reveals the impact of the high-inflation countries on the results pertaining to the effect of mispricing on the nominal exchange rate when time effects are excluded. Similarly, from the first two elements of column 3, Tables 2A.7 and 2A.9, the impact on the nominal-rate results of inclusion of time effects, when the high-inflation countries are excluded, is given by a comparison between Tables 2A.7 and 2A.9.

References

Annaert, J., and M. J. K. Ceuster (1997). 'The Big Mac: More than a Junk Asset Allocator?' *International Review of Financial Analysis* 6: 79–192.

Ashenfelter, O., and S. Jurajda (2001). 'Cross-country Comparison of Wage Rates: The Big Mac Index'. Unpublished paper, available at: http://economics.uchicago.edu/download/ bigmac.pdf.

Balassa, B. (1964). 'The Purchasing Power Parity Doctrine: A Reappraisal'. *Journal of Political Economy* 72: 584–96.

Caetano, S., G. Moura and S. Da Silva (2004). 'Big Mac Parity, Income and Trade'. *Economics Bulletin* 6: 1–8.

Chen, C.-F., C.-H. Shen and C.-A. Wang (2007). 'Does PPP hold for Big Mac Prices or the Consumer Price Index? Evidence from Panel Cointegration'. *Economics Bulletin* 6: 1–15.

Clementi, F., M. Gallegati and A. Palestrini (2010). 'A Big Mac Test of Price Dynamics and Dispersion Across Euro Area'. Available at: http://ssrn.com/abstract=1536700.

Clements, K. W., and Y. Lan (2010). 'A New Approach to Forecasting Exchange Rates'. *Journal of International Money and Finance* 29: 1424–37.

Click, R. W. (1996). 'Contrarian MacParity'. *Economics Letters* 53: 209–12.

Cumby, R. E. (1996). 'Forecasting Exchange Rates and Relative Prices with the Hamburger Standard: Is What You Want What You Get with McParity?' NBER Working Paper 5675.

Flood, R., and M. Taylor (1996). 'Exchange Rate Economics: What's Wrong with the Conventional Macro Approach?' In J. Frankel, G. Galli, and A. Giocannini (eds), *The Microstructure of Foreign Exchange Markets*. The University of Chicago Press. Pp. 261–94.

Frenkel, J. A., and M. L. Mussa (1980). 'The Efficiency of the Foreign Exchange Market and Measures of Turbulence'. *American Economic Review* 70: 374–81.

Froot, K. A., and K. Rogoff (1995). 'Perspectives on PPP and Long-Run Real Exchange Rates'. In G. Grossman and K. Rogoff (eds), *Handbook of International Economics*, Vol. 3. Amsterdam: North-Holland. Pp. 1647–88.

Fujiki, H., and Y. Kitamura (2003). 'The Big Mac Standard: The Statistical Illustration'. Discussion Paper 446, Institute of Economic Research, Hitotsubashi University.

Fukumoto, Y. (2009). 'International Price Dispersions of the Big Mac and Economic Integration'. Mimeo, Osaka University of Economics.

Greenspan, A. (2004). 'Remarks'. Panel discussion entitled, 'The Euro in Wider Circles', European Banking Congress 2004, Frankfurt, November 19.

Isard, P. (1995). *Exchange Rate Economics*. Cambridge University Press.

James, C. (2007a). 'The CommSec iPod Index: Global Comparisons'. *CommSec Economic Insight*, 18 January 2007.

James, C. (2007b). 'The CommSec iPod Index: Consumers Win as Prices Fall: Global Comparisons and Currency Changes'. *CommSec Economic Insight*, 18 May 2007. Available at: http://images.comsec.com.au/ipo/ UploadedImages/ipodindexe771774183 be45349abe6efea3d52610.pdf. Accessed 10 September 2007.

Kleok, T. (1981). 'OLS Estimation of a Model Where a Microvariable is Explained by Aggregates and Contemporaneous Disturbances are Equicorrelated'. *Econometrica* 49: 205–7.

Lan, Y. (2002). 'The Explosion of Purchasing Power Parity'. In M. Manzur (ed), *Exchange Rates, Interest Rates and Commodity Prices*. Cheltenham, UK: Elgar. Pp. 9–38.

Lan, Y. (2006). 'Equilibrium Exchange Rates and Currency Forecasts: A Big Mac Perspective'. *International Economics and Finance Journal* 1: 291–311.

Lan, Y., and L. L. Ong (2003). 'The Growing Evidence on Purchasing Power Parity'. In L. L. Ong (ed), *The Big Mac Index: Applications of Purchasing Power Parity*. London: Palgrave Macmillan. Pp. 29–50.

Lothian, J. R. (1985). 'Equilibrium Relationships Between Money and Other Economic Variables'. *American Economic Review* 75: 828–35.

Lucas, R. E. (1973). 'Some International Evidence on Output-Inflation Tradeoffs'. *American Economic Review* 63: 326–34.

Lutz, M. (2001). 'Beyond Burgernomics and MacParity: Exchange-Rate Forecasts Based on the Law of One Price'. Unpublished manuscript, University of St. Gallen.

MacDonald, R. (2007). *Exchange Rate Economics: Theories and Evidence*. Milton Park, UK: Routledge.

MacDonald, R., and J. L. Stein (1999). 'Introduction: Equilibrium Exchange Rates'. In R. MacDonald and J. L. Stein (eds), *Equilibrium Exchange Rates*. Boston: Kluwer.

Meese, R. A. and K. Rogoff (1983a). 'Empirical Exchange Rate Models of the Seventies: Do They Fit Out of Sample?' *Journal of International Economics* 14: 3–24.

Meese, R. A., and K. Rogoff (1983b). 'The Out-of-Sample Failure of Empirical Exchange Rates: Sampling Error or Misspecification?' In

J. A. Frenkel (ed), *Exchange Rates and International Macroeconomics.* The University of Chicago Press.

Monson, T. D. (undated). 'The Big Mac Index Revisited'. Mimeo, Michigan Technological University.

Obstfeld, M. (1995). 'International Currency Experience: New Lessons and Lessons Relearned'. *Brookings Papers on Economic Activity* 1: 119–220.

Ong, L. L. (1995). 'Burgernomics: the Economics of the Big Mac Standard'. Presented at the ANU/UWA PhD Conference in Economics and Business, University of Western Australia.

Ong, L. L. (1997). 'Burgernomics: the Economics of the Big Mac Standard'. *Journal of International Money and Finance* 16: 865–78.

Ong, L. L. (1998a). 'Burgernomics and the ASEAN Currency Crisis'. *Journal of the Australian Society of Security Analysts* 1: 15–16.

Ong, L. L. (1998b). 'Big Mac and Wages to Go, Please: Comparing the Purchasing Power of Earnings around the World'. *Australian Journal of Labour Economics* 2: 53–68.

Ong, L. L. (2003). *The Big Mac Index: Applications of Purchasing Power Parity.* Houndmills, UK: Palgrave Macmillan.

Ong, L. L., and J. D. Mitchell (2000). 'Professors and Hamburgers: An International Comparison of Real Academic Salaries'. *Applied Economics* 32: 869–76.

Pakko, M. R., and P. S. Pollard (1996). 'For Here to Go? Purchasing Power Parity and the Big Mac'. *Federal Reserve Bank of St. Louis Review* 78: 3–21.

Pakko, M. R., and P. S. Pollard (2003). 'Burgernomics: A Big Mac Guide to Purchasing Power Parity'. *Federal Reserve Bank of St. Louis Review* 85: 9–27.

Parsley, D., and S. Wei (2007). 'A Prism into the PPP Puzzles: The Micro-Foundations of Big Mac Real Exchange Rates'. *Economic Journal* 117: 1336–56.

Parsley, D., and S. Wei (2008). 'In Search of a Euro Effect: Big Lessons from a Big Mac Meal?' *Journal of International Money and Finance* 27: 260–76.

Rogoff, K. (1996). 'The Purchasing Power Parity Puzzle'. *Journal of Economic Literature* 34: 647–668.

Samuelson, P. A. (1964). 'Theoretical Notes on Trade Problems'. *Review of Economics and Statistics* 46: 145–54.

Sarno, L., and M. P. Taylor (2002). *The Economics of Exchange Rates.* Cambridge University Press.

Sjaastad, L. A. (1980). 'Commercial Policy "True Tariffs" and Relative Prices'. In J. Black and B. V. Hindley (eds), *Current Issues in Commercial Policy and Diplomacy*. London: Macmillan.

Taylor, A. M., and M. P. Taylor (2004). 'The Purchasing Power Parity Debate'. *Journal of Economic Perspectives* 18: 135–58.

Taylor, M. P. (2006). 'Real Exchange Rates and Purchasing Power Parity: Mean Reversion in Economic Thought'. *Applied Financial Economics* 16: 1–17.

Winkels, R. D. A. (2009). 'The Big Mac Portfolio'. Master's thesis, Tilburg University.

Yang, J. (2004). 'Nontradables and the Valuation of RMB: An Evaluation of the Big Mac Index'. *China Economic Review* 15: 353–59.

3 | Commodity currencies and currency commodities

KENNETH W. CLEMENTS AND RENÉE FRY

3.1 Introduction

When the value of the currency of a commodity-exporting country moves in parallel with world commodity prices, it is said to be a 'commodity currency'. Thus, when there is a commodity boom, appreciation of a commodity currency has the effect of dampening the impact of the boom as domestic-currency prices increase by less than world prices, profitability in the export sector increases by less than otherwise, and domestic consumers gain from the appreciation in the form of lower-priced imports. This automatic stabiliser has the effect of moving part of the required adjustment to the boom away from commodity producers and reduces the cyclical volatility of the economies of commodity-exporting countries. Australia, New Zealand, South Africa and Canada, as well as some other smaller developing countries, all possibly have commodity currencies to varying degrees.

What if, in addition to having a commodity currency, a country is a sufficiently large producer of a certain commodity that it can affect the world price? In other words, what if this country has some degree of power over the world market? A commodity boom appreciates the country's currency, and as this squeezes its exporters, the volume of exports falls. However, as the country is now large, reduced exports have the effect of increasing world prices further. Thus, as the appreciation leads to a still higher world price, the interaction of the commodity currency and pricing power leads to amplification of the initial commodity boom. To convey the symmetric relationship with commodity currencies, commodities whose prices are substantially affected by currency fluctuations can be called 'currency commodities'. This chapter explores in detail the implications of the phenomena of commodity currencies and currency commodities operating simultaneously. We establish the precise conditions for a country to have a commodity currency, as well as the requirements for a currency commodity. The

126

chapter also shows how the framework yields considerable insight into the impacts on commodity prices and exchange rates of (1) a currency fad in which there is sudden large shift in investor sentiment towards the home country's currency, (2) a technical change in the form of development of a new product that acts as a good substitute for the commodity, and (3) globalisation that exposes the home country to greater international competition and makes its economy more flexible. We also derive conditions under which the interactions between currency values and commodity prices form a stable process so that exchange rates and prices converge to well-defined equilibrium values. The chapter also provides preliminary empirical evidence on the extent to which exchange rates are affected by commodity prices and vice versa.

There is a fairly substantial body of literature devoted to commodity currencies; this literature is predominantly empirical and tends to start with observed correlation between the terms of trade and real exchange rates in a number of commodity-exporting countries. Prominent examples include Amano and van Norden (1995), Blundell-Wignall and Gregory (1990), Blundell-Wignall et al. (1993), Broda (2004), Cashin et al. (2004), Chen and Rogoff (2003), Freebairn (1990), Gruen and Kortian (1998), Gruen and Wilkinson (1994), McKenzie (1986) and Sjaastad (1990). For theory on the dependence of the real exchange rate on the terms of trade, see Connolly and Devereux (1992), Devereux and Connolly (1996), Edwards (1988, 1989), Edwards and van Wijnbergen (1987) and Neary (1988). Closely allied to commodity currencies is the concept of booming sector economics, which analyses the implications for other sectors of the economy of a surge in one form of exports (mostly taken to be commodities, and natural resources in particular). Here a surge in resource exports leads to real appreciation of the county's exchange rate, which has the effect of hurting other exporters and producers in the import-competing sector. This phenomenon is variously known as the 'Dutch disease', the 'Gregory effect' and 'de-industrialisation'. Important papers in this area include Corden (1984), Corden and Neary (1982), Gregory (1976) and Snape (1977).

While there is also a substantial body of literature on the implications of countries that are large in terms of international trade related to optimal trade taxes, there are much fewer studies on the related topic of the link between exchange rates and world prices of commodities.

The link is that if a commodity-producing country has some degree of market power, it can pass on increases in domestic costs to foreign buyers of its exports. Studies in this tradition include Clements and Manzur (2002), Dornbusch (1987), Gilbert (1989, 1991), Keyfitz (2004), Ridler and Yandle (1972), Sjaastad (1985, 1989, 1990, 1998a, 1998b, 1999, 2000, 2001), Sjaastad and Manzur (2003) and Sjaastad and Scacciavillani (1996).

The only previous paper that we are aware of that explicitly considers the implications of the joint operation of commodity currencies and currency commodities is by Swift (2004). The author starts with an analysis of Ridler and Yandle (1972), which deals with the dependence of the world price of a certain commodity on the N exchange rates in the world, and notes that if an individual exporting country is small in international trade terms, then a change in the value of its currency has no impact on the world price. Suppose that there is a boom that exogenously increases the world price of a certain commodity such that a number of small countries that produce the commodity are all hit simultaneously by a common shock that improves their terms of trade. If these countries all have commodity currencies, then their exchange rates appreciate, and the Ridler and Yandle framework implies that there is a subsequent increase in the world price of the commodity they export. Thus there is both an initial terms-of-trade shock and then a subsequent reinforcing move related to the commodity-currency mechanism. In this sense, the terms of trade are endogenous, even though the countries are all individually small. Swift analyses the processes by which these countries adjust to the terms-of-trade improvement and emphasises that the shocks are greater when the terms of trade are endogenous. While Swift describes and discusses these matters mostly, but not exclusively, in words, she does not formally model the processes involved.

The second part of this chapter provides some empirical evidence on some of the propositions of the theoretical model using a multivariate latent factor model. This approach leads to an assessment of the relative importance of various factors in explaining volatility in each market in a model in which commodity currency and price returns are endogenously determined. This class of model is used in the literature on finance and business cycles to explain time series as a function of a set of unobserved (latent) factors. For examples, see Diebold and Nerlove (1989), Dungey (1999), Mahieu and Schotman (1994) and Stock and Watson (1991). The model in this chapter is a three-factor model comprising a common factor, a commodity-currency factor and a commodity-price factor. The idea is that information that is specific to the complete data set is captured by the common factor, information specific to the commodity currencies is captured by the commodity-currency factor and information specific to the set of commodity-price returns in the model is captured by the commodity factor. Spillovers across the two markets can then be modelled by examining the impact of the asset-specific factors (the currency factor or the commodity factor) on the other asset type. The advantage of the approach is that observable variables do not have to be identified and modelled, which is particularly convenient as it implicitly takes into account shocks that affect all markets simultaneously.

There are several methods available to estimate this class of model, including the generalised method of moments (Hamilton, 1994; Hansen, 1982), the Kalman filter (Hamilton, 1994; Harvey, 1981, 1990; Kalman, 1960, 1963), and simulation-based techniques such as indirect estimation (Duffie and Singleton, 1993; Dungey et al., 2000; Gallant and Tauchen, 1996; Gourieroux et al., 1993). The Kalman filter is adopted here as it is assumed that the quarterly data series are not complicated by features such as nonnormal distributions. The other advantage is that it is simple to extract a time series of the factors when using the Kalman filter. This time series can then be used to examine how the relationship between commodity currencies and price returns has changed over time, which helps in assessing some of the propositions raised in the theoretical section of the chapter, particularly in relation to globalisation.

The results of the empirical model suggest that commodity returns are more affected by the currency factor than vice versa, although the importance of spillovers across the two market types is relatively small. This is in contrast to most papers, which do not even consider that commodity prices may be endogenous and only model exchange rates as a function of commodity prices. The implications of this result are that the commodity-currency countries appear to have some degree of market power, at least on a collective basis. The reverse link from the commodity factor to the currency returns is much weaker and is jointly insignificant. Over time, as markets have become more competitive and integrated, the role of the commodity-currency factor in determining the currency and commodity returns seems to have become more important.

The chapter is structured as follows: The next section sets out in considerable detail the analytical framework that merges the economics of commodity currencies with that of currency commodities. Section 3.3 provides an initial investigation into the data series that motivates the structure of the latent factor model developed and estimated in Section 3.4. Section 3.5 provides some concluding comments.

3.2 Analytical framework

As discussed earlier, the literature has tended to analyse only one part of the interaction between world commodity prices and exchange rates in isolation from the other; that is, it has focussed on either the causal link from commodity prices to currency values (the commodity-currency model) or the reciprocal link, the impact of exchange-rate changes on commodity prices, which involves pricing power in world markets (currency commodities). By contrast, our focus here is on joint determination of exchange rates and commodity prices or on the two-way interactions between exchange rates and commodity prices. The latent factor approach set out in Section 3.4 is a multivariate model that deals with the simultaneous determination of these two sets of variables.

Notwithstanding our simultaneous approach, it is convenient to discuss the major elements independently. Thus, in the first subsection below, we set out a model of the impacts of changes in exchange rates on world commodity prices under the assumption that the former are given exogenously. We then turn in the second part of Section 3.2 through the fourth part of Section 3.2 to the second arm, the effects of changes in commodity prices on exchange rates. The fifth part of Section 3.2 through the seventh part of Section 3.2 investigate joint working of the commodity and currency markets by considering the two arms simultaneously. In the final subsection, we consider as illustrative examples of the approach the general equilibrium impacts on commodity and currency markets of a fad that causes the currency to appreciate, a technological change that leads to the introduction of new substitute products and globalisation that enhances the flexibility of the economy.

3.2.1 *Market power and commodity pricing*

Consider a country that is a dominant exporter of a certain commodity in the sense that a larger volume of exports places downward pressure on the world price. Examples could include oil from Saudi Arabia, wool from Australia and several minerals from Australia, such as iron ore, tantalite and possibly coal. In such a case, the country is a price-maker or has market power. This situation is well known in international economics and is related to optimal export taxes, the formation of cartels among exporting nations and price-stabilisation schemes. We consider the somewhat different issue of what happens to the world price of such a commodity if there is a major depreciation in the currency of the dominant producing country. If costs do not increase equiproportionally so that it is a real depreciation, the enhanced revenue drops straight to the bottom line, and domestic producers of the commodity have an incentive to expand production and export more. However, such an expansion of exports would depress the world price as, by assumption, the country is large. Accordingly, for such a country, there is an immediate link between the value of its currency and the world price of the commodity. In a series of papers, Sjaastad and coauthors have elaborated this basic model and considered a number of implications of this rich framework.[1]

To fix the ideas, take the world gold market as an example, and suppose for simplicity that there are only two 'countries' in the world, the United States and Europe. If the price of an ounce of gold is p in dollars and p^* in euros, then we have as an arbitrage relation

$$p = Sp^* (1+x)$$

where S is the US dollar cost of one euro, and x represents the spread between American and European gold prices due to transaction costs, etc. (which are presumably small). If the factors determining the spread are constant over time, then this equation implies that

$$\hat{p} = \hat{S} + \hat{p}^* \tag{3.1}$$

where a hat denotes proportional change ($\hat{x} = dx/x$). This is the familiar purchasing power parity (PPP) equation that states that the change in the dollar price of gold equals the change in the euro price adjusted for the change in the exchange rate. To illustrate the working and

---

[1] See Sjaastad (1985, 1989, 1990, 1998a, 1998b, 1999, 2000, 2001), Sjaastad and Manzur (2003), Sjaastad and Scacciavillani (1996), Dornbusch (1987), Gilbert (1989, 1991) and Ridler and Yandle (1972). For an application, see Keyfitz (2004).

implications of equation (3.1), suppose that the dollar depreciates relative to the euro by 10 per cent, so $\hat{S} = 0.10$. Equation (3.1) then means that $\hat{p} - \hat{p}^* = 0.10$, so the dollar price relative to the euro price increases by 10 per cent. There are three possibilities:

1. The dollar price increases by the full 10 per cent, with the euro price constant.
2. The euro price decreases by 10 per cent, and the dollar price remains unchanged.
3. Any linear combination of cases 1 and 2.

Case 1 is the familiar small-country situation, and here the United States is a price-taker in the world gold market. The opposite extreme is when the United States completely dominates the pricing of gold and is an extremely large county, as in case 2. Case 3 pertains to various intermediate situations in which the United States has some market power but not complete dominance. Case 3 is possibly the most commonly experienced: Fears of inflation in the United States lead to depreciation of the dollar, and an increase in the dollar price of gold occurs with a simultaneous decrease in the euro price. These three cases are shown in Figure 3.1.

We develop a simple stylised model of the world market for a commodity in which PPP holds for the commodity but not for prices in

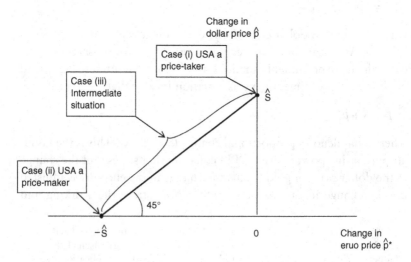

Figure 3.1 The world gold market.

general.[2] This model reveals considerable insights into the working of commodity markets in general and identifies the nature of 'small' and 'large' in a precise manner. The commodity is produced only in the home country according to the following supply equation:

$$q^s = q^s \left(\frac{p}{P} \right) \tag{3.2}$$

where q^s is the quantity supplied, p is the price in terms of domestic-currency units and P is an index of costs in general in the home country. All the output of the commodity is exported, and the foreign demand function is

$$q^d = q^d \left(\frac{p^*}{P^*} \right) \tag{3.3}$$

where an asterisk denotes a foreign-currency price, so p^*/P^* is the relative price faced by foreign consumers. Ignoring changes in stocks of the commodity, the world market equilibrium is given by

$$q^s = q^d \tag{3.4}$$

This model can be solved as follows: If we denote the price elasticity of supply by $\varepsilon \geq 0$ and the price elasticity of demand by $\eta \leq 0$, we can then express the supply and demand equations (3.2) and (3.3) in change form as

$$\hat{q}^s = \varepsilon \left(\hat{p} - \hat{P} \right), \quad \hat{q}^d = \eta \left(\hat{p}^* - \hat{P}^* \right) \tag{3.5}$$

Using the market-clearing equation (3.4) to equate the right-hand sides of both members of equation (3.5), we obtain $\varepsilon(\hat{p} - \hat{P}) = \eta(\hat{p}^* - \hat{P}^*)$ or, in view of the PPP relation (3.1), $\varepsilon(\hat{p}^* + \hat{S} - \hat{P}) = \eta(\hat{p}^* - \hat{P}^*)$. Subtracting $\varepsilon(\hat{p}^* - \hat{P}^*)$ from both sides of the last equation and rearranging, we obtain $\hat{p}^* - \hat{P}^* = [\varepsilon/(\eta - \varepsilon)](\hat{S} + \hat{P}^* - \hat{P})$ or

$$\hat{p}^* - \hat{P}^* = \frac{\varepsilon}{\varepsilon - \eta} \left(\hat{P} - \hat{S} - \hat{P}^* \right)$$

If we define the real exchange rate as $R = P/SP^*$, the preceding equation can be expressed more compactly as

$$\widehat{\frac{p^*}{P^*}} = \alpha \hat{R} \tag{3.6}$$

[2] For an earlier version of this model, see Clements and Manzur (2002).

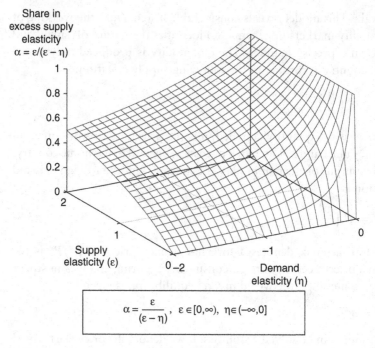

$$\alpha = \frac{\varepsilon}{(\varepsilon - \eta)}, \quad \varepsilon \in [0,\infty), \ \eta \in (-\infty,0]$$

Figure 3.2 Share of supply in excess supply elasticity.

where

$$\alpha = \frac{\varepsilon}{\varepsilon - \eta} \tag{3.7}$$

is the share of supply in the excess supply elasticity. As the supply elasticity $\varepsilon \geq 0$ and the demand elasticity $\eta \leq 0$, it follows that $0 \leq \alpha \leq 1$. Figure 3.2 provides a visualisation of the nature of α in a plot against ε and η. The real exchange rate R is the producer country's nominal exchange rate adjusted for relative price levels; this exchange rate is defined such that an increase in R represents a real appreciation of the currency of the producing country.

Equation (3.6) is the fundamental pricing rule for commodities. It states that a change in the world relative price of a commodity is a positive fraction α of the change in real value of the producing country's currency. Accordingly, a 10 per cent real appreciation ($\hat{R} = 0.10$) means that the world price increases, but by 10 per cent at most. The mechanism is that real appreciation squeezes firms that are producing

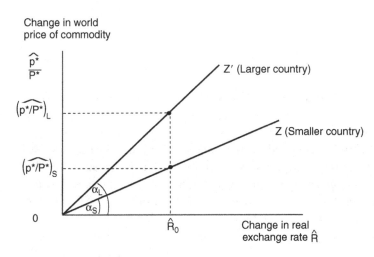

Figure 3.3 Country size, exchange rate and commodity price.

and exporting the commodity, so the lower volume of exports pushes up their price on the world market. In the case in which $\varepsilon = 1$ and $\eta = -1$, the value of the fraction α is $\frac{1}{2}$, so the 10 per cent appreciation leads to a 5 per cent increase in the commodity price.

A small country is unable to affect world prices. Thus, when a small country experiences real appreciation of its currency, for the world price to be constant, equation (3.6) implies that the value of α must be zero. This occurs when the excess supply elasticity $\varepsilon - \eta$ is large. Conversely, when the excess supply elasticity is small, α is near its upper limit of unity and the country is large. The implications of the distinction between larger and smaller countries are demonstrated in Figure 3.3. Consider first the case of a smaller country that has an α value of α_S so that $\widehat{p^*/P^*} = \alpha_S \hat{R}$. Line OZ from the origin with slope α_S represents this equation, so appreciation of $\hat{R}_0$ causes a modest increase in the world price of $(\widehat{p^*/P^*})_S = \alpha_S \hat{R}_0$.[3] The larger country has a larger α coefficient, $\alpha_L > \alpha_S$, and a steeper line from the origin OZ', so the same real appreciation causes the price to increase by more, $(\widehat{p^*/P^*})_L = \alpha_L \hat{R}_0$. This leads to an attractively simple result: The elasticity of the preceding differential change in the world price is just the difference in

---

[3] In the limit, for a trivially small country $\alpha_S = 0$, the line from the origin coincides with the horizontal axis, and the world price is constant.

value for the α coefficients:

$$\frac{\widehat{p_L^*/p_S^*}}{\hat{R}} = \alpha_L - \alpha_S$$

Figure 3.4 illustrates further the working of the commodity market in terms of levels (rather than changes). Quadrant I contains the supply curve and quadrant III the demand curve, whereas the market-clearing relationship is contained in quadrant II. The link between domestic and foreign nominal prices of the commodity is provided by the PPP relation $p = Sp^*$, where we have ignored the spread as it is not essential. Dividing both sides of this equation by P and using $R = P/SP^*$, we have $p^*/P^* = R(p/P)$. This equation provides a link between domestic and foreign *relative* prices, so it can be considered as a real version of PPP. This link closes the model and is represented in quadrant IV of the

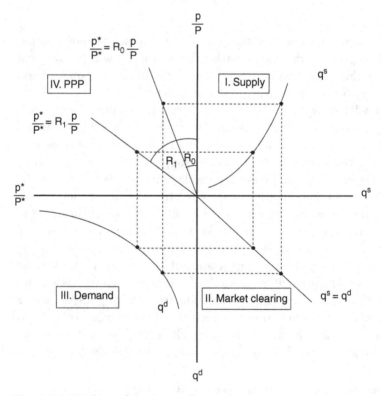

Figure 3.4 Working of the commodity market.

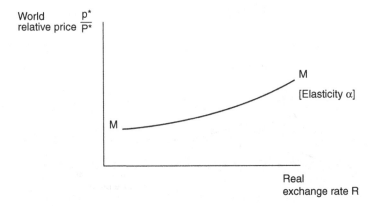

Figure 3.5 Market power, commodity price and exchange rate.

figure. Here the real exchange rate is given by the slope of the PPP line from the origin. Appreciation of the domestic currency causes this line to become steeper (with respect to the domestic price axis), and the equilibrium world price increases. Accordingly, we have an increasing relationship between the exchange rate and world prices, as represented by the curve labelled *MM* in Figure 3.5; the elasticity of *MM* is α.

An alternative representation of the interactions between the exchange rate and the commodity price is given in Figure 3.6. In panel *A*, curve WW shows the world and domestic prices for which the world market clears. It is downward-sloping because an increase in the domestic price stimulates production, and for the market to continue to clear, this has to be offset by a reduction in the world price to stimulate demand. Clearing of the commodity market implies $\varepsilon(\hat{p} - \hat{P}) = \eta(\hat{p}^* - \hat{P}^*)$, so

$$\frac{\widehat{p^*}}{P^*} = \left(\frac{\varepsilon}{\eta}\right)\frac{\hat{p}}{P} = -\left(\frac{\alpha}{1-\alpha}\right)\frac{\hat{p}}{P}$$

with α defined as in equation (3.7). This shows that $-\alpha/(1-\alpha) < 0$ is the elasticity of the WW curve. The link between domestic and foreign prices of the commodity is provided by the real PPP relationship discussed earlier, $p^*/P^* = R(p/P)$. This equation is represented in panel *A* of the figure by line OX from the origin with slope *R*. For overall equilibrium, the market must be simultaneously located on WW and OX, that is, at the point of intersection of the two curves E_0. Appreciation of the producer-country currency increases the steepness of the

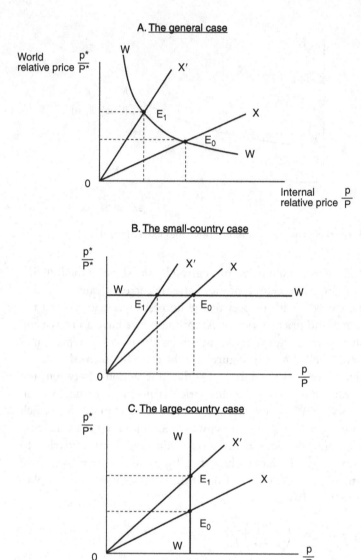

Figure 3.6 Impact of appreciation on commodity prices.

line, which moves from OX to OX', so the equilibrium point shifts from E_0 to E_1 as the world price increases and the domestic price decreases. In the small-country case (panel B), the WW curve is horizontal as $\alpha = 0$, appreciation has no impact on the world price, and

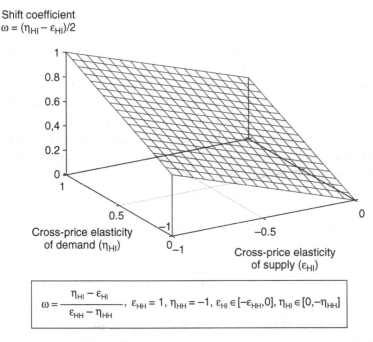

Shift coefficient
$\omega = (\eta_{HI} - \varepsilon_{HI})/2$

$$\omega = \frac{\eta_{HI} - \varepsilon_{HI}}{\varepsilon_{HH} - \eta_{HH}}, \ \varepsilon_{HH} = 1, \ \eta_{HH} = -1, \ \varepsilon_{HI} \in [-\varepsilon_{HH}, 0], \ \eta_{HI} \in [0, -\eta_{HH}]$$

Figure 3.7 The shift coefficient.

the domestic price decreases equiproportionally. Finally, for a large country in the extreme ($\alpha = 1$), the WW curve is vertical, the domestic relative price remains unchanged, and the world price increases by the full amount of the appreciation (Figure 3.7).

The model discussed in this subsection is a simple one that deals with the pricing of a single commodity in a two-country world. However, its predictions are robust as they carry over in a natural manner to a multicountry, multicommodity world in which there is domestic consumption of the commodity. For details, see, for example, Gilbert (1989), Sjaastad (1990) and Ridler and Yandle (1972).

3.2.2 Commodity currencies

In this subsection we consider the link between commodity prices and exchange rates. We again use a simple stylised model and show how a country's terms of trade are linked to its real exchange rate. This model starts with the sector approach introduced by Sjaastad (1980) for analysis of the impact of protection.[4]

We divide the whole economy into three broad sectors: importables (denoted by the subscript I), exportables (X) and everything else, goods that do not and cannot enter into international trade because of prohibitively high transport costs, which are called 'home goods' (H). For our purposes, we can focus on the market for home goods. If q_H^s and q_H^d represent the quantity demanded and supplied, respectively, of home goods, and p_i is the price of good $i (i = I, X, H)$, we can write the supply and demand functions as

$$q_H^s = q_H^s (p_I, p_X, p_H), \quad q_H^d = q_H^d (p_I, p_X, p_H)$$

We define the own- and cross-price elasticities of supply and demand as

$$\varepsilon_{Hj} = \frac{\partial \left(\log q_H^s \right)}{\partial \left(\log p_j \right)}, \quad \eta_{Hj} = \frac{\partial \left(\log q_H^d \right)}{\partial \left(\log p_j \right)}$$

which satisfy the homogeneity constraints $\sum_j \varepsilon_{Hj} = \sum_j \eta_{Hj} = 0$. The supply and demand functions for home goods can then be expressed in change form as

$$\hat{q}_H^s = \sum_j \varepsilon_{Hj} \hat{p}_j, \quad \hat{q}_H^d = \sum_j \eta_{Hj} \hat{p}_j \tag{3.8}$$

Market clearing for home goods implies that $\hat{q}_H^s = \hat{q}_H^d$ or, from equation (3.8), that $\sum_j \varepsilon_{Hj} \hat{p}_j = \sum_j \eta_{Hj} \hat{p}_j$. Solving for $\hat{p}_H$, we obtain

$$\hat{p}_H = \left(\frac{\eta_{HI} - \varepsilon_{HI}}{\varepsilon_{HH} - \eta_{HH}} \right) \hat{p}_I + \left(\frac{\eta_{HX} - \varepsilon_{HX}}{\varepsilon_{HH} - \eta_{HH}} \right) \hat{p}_X$$

or, more compactly,

$$\hat{p}_H = \omega \hat{p}_I + (1 - \omega) \hat{p}_X \tag{3.9}$$

where

$$\omega = \frac{\eta_{HI} - \varepsilon_{HI}}{\varepsilon_{HH} - \eta_{HH}} \tag{3.10}$$

[4] For extensions and elaborations of Sjaastad's model, see Clague and Greenaway (1994), Clements and Sjaastad (1981, 1984), Greenaway (1989) and Greenaway and Milner (1988). See Choi and Cumming (1986) for early work on measurement of the transfers across sectors implied by the approach.

When complementarity is ruled out, which does not seem unreasonable at this level of aggregation, the value of the coefficient ω lies between 0 and 1.[5] Equation (3.9) shows that the change in price of home goods is a weighted average of the changes in prices of importables and exportables. The weights in this equation reflect the substitutability in both production and consumption between home goods on the one hand and the two traded goods on the other. When home goods and importables are good substitutes, then the weight ω is near its upper value of unity, the prices of these two goods move together closely, and their relative price p_H/p_I is more or less constant. Alternatively, when home goods and exportables are good substitutes, then $(1 - \omega)$, the second weight in equation (3.9), is close to unity, and the relative price p_H/p_X is approximately constant.

Equation (3.9) is known as the 'incidence equation' as it has been used extensively to measure the degree to which protection acts as a tax on the country's own exporters. To illustrate, suppose a small country imposes an import duty of 10 per cent so that $\hat{p}_I = 0.10$ and has no export taxes or subsidies so that $\hat{p}_X = 0$. Equation (3.9) then implies that the price of home goods increases by a fraction ω of 0.10. This can be interpreted as an increase in costs in general, an increase that has to be paid by producers in all sectors of the economy. However, as exporters cannot pass on the higher costs (the small-country assumption), this fraction of import protection acts as a tax on exporters. As the incidence of the import protection is shifted onto exporters, ω is known as the 'shift coefficient'.[6]

---

[5] *Proof*: It follows from the demand homogeneity constraint $\Sigma_j \eta_{Hj} = 0$ that $\eta_{HI} = -\eta_{HH} - \eta_{HH}$. The law of demand implies that $\eta_{HH} < 0$, and the assumption of no complementarity means that $\eta_{Hj} = 0$ $(j = I, X)$. It then follows that the maximum value of $\eta_{HI} = -\eta_{HH} > 0$, which occurs when home goods and exportables are independent in consumption, that is, when $\eta_{HX} = 0$. A parallel argument on the supply side establishes that the minimum algebraic value of $\varepsilon_{HI} = -\varepsilon_{HH} < 0$. Substituting these extreme values into the definition of ω given by equation (3.10) yields $\omega = 1$. The minimum value of $\eta_{HI} = 0$ occurs when home goods and importables are independent in consumption, whereas the maximum value is $\varepsilon_{HI} = 0$ (the two goods are independent in production); these values jointly imply that $\omega = 0$. As $\eta_{HI}(\varepsilon_{HI})$ decreases (increases) from its maximum (minimum) value and moves towards it minimum (maximum), ω moves monotonically from 1 to 0. For a geometric representation, see Figure 3.7.

[6] There have been a number of applications of this framework; see Clements and Sjaastad (1984) for an early survey of estimates of the shift coefficient and

Next, let the overall index of prices in the country be a weighted geometric mean of the three sectoral prices so that

$$\hat{P} = \alpha_H \hat{p}_H + \alpha_I \hat{p}_I + \alpha_X \hat{p}_X \tag{3.11}$$

where α_i is a weight for sector i ($i = H, I, X$). The weights α_i are all positive fractions, with $\Sigma_i \alpha_i = 1$. Substituting the right-hand side of equation (3.9) for $\hat{p}_H$ in equation (3.11) and defining $\beta = \alpha_H(1 - \omega) + \alpha_I$, we obtain an equation that expresses the rate of inflation in terms of the prices of the two traded goods:

$$\hat{P} = \hat{p}_X - \beta \left(\hat{p}_X - \hat{p}_I \right) \tag{3.12}$$

The coefficient β in this equation is positive and is most likely to be less than 1. A similar equation describes inflation in the rest of the world (denoted by an asterisk):

$$\hat{P}^* = \hat{p}_X^* - \beta^* \left(\hat{p}_X^* - \hat{p}_I^* \right) \tag{3.13}$$

Using the definition of the change in the real exchange rate, $\hat{R} = \hat{P} - \hat{P}^* - \hat{S}$, together with equations (3.12) and (3.13), we obtain

$$\hat{R} = \gamma \widehat{\frac{p_X}{p_I}} \tag{3.14}$$

The coefficient in this equation is defined as $\gamma = 1 - (\beta + \beta^*)$ or

$$\gamma = 1 - \left\{ [\alpha_H (1 - \omega) + \alpha_I] + [\alpha_H^* (1 - \omega^*) + \alpha_I^*] \right\} \tag{3.15}$$

Clague and Greenaway (1994) for a subsequent survey. The methodology has been applied to Malawi (Zgovu, 2003), Spain 1879–1913 (Pardos and Serrano-Sanz, 2002), Spain 1978–93 (Asensio and Pardos, 2002), South Asia (Panday, 2003) and the United States for the late nineteenth century (Irwin, 2006), among others. Note that in the absence of any additional information, the value of $\omega = 1/2$ has some attractions for the following reasons: Recall that the shift coefficient is defined as $\omega = (\eta_{HI} - \varepsilon_{HI})/(\varepsilon_{HH} - \eta_{HH})$ and that the price elasticities of supply and demand are subject to the homogeneity constraints $\Sigma_j \varepsilon_{Hj} = \Sigma_j \eta_{Hj} = 0$. As demand homogeneity implies that the sum of the two cross-elasticities, $\eta_{HI} + \eta_{HX}$, equals the negative of the own-price elasticity, $-\eta_{HH}$, if we know nothing about the nature of the substitutability among goods, a neutral approach is to distribute $-\eta_{HH}$ equally to both goods by setting $\eta_{HI} = \eta_{HX} = -(1/2)\eta_{HH}$. This approach, together with a similar argument on the supply side, yields $\omega = 1/2$. A related approach is to regard the shift coefficient as a uniformly distributed random variable with range $[0, 1]$. Then the expected value of the coefficient is exactly midway between the upper and lower values, that is, $E(\omega) = 1/2$.

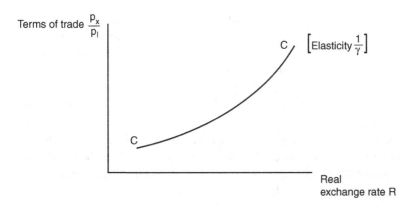

Figure 3.8 The reciprocal commodity-currency relationship.

which is the elasticity of the home country's real exchange rate with respect to its terms of trade.[7]. On the basis of equation (3.15), the following can be said about the possible values of γ. In both countries, the shares for home goods and importables are positive fractions, whereas the shift coefficient lies between 0 and 1. This implies that the lower bound for γ, associated with $\omega = \omega^* = 0$, can be negative, whereas the upper bound ($\omega = \omega^* = 1$) is $1 - (\alpha_I + \alpha_I^*)$, which is likely to be a positive fraction.[8]

Figure 3.8 gives the commodity-currency relationship. For convenience, this is presented in reciprocal form so that, from equation (3.14), the elasticity of CC in the figure is $1/\gamma$.

3.2.3 Income effects of terms-of-trade changes

In the preceding discussion, we moved freely between changes in world prices and changes in domestic prices. This, however, ignores an important point regarding the source of the price changes: While changes in domestic relative prices brought about by, say, domestic protection policies have no first-order income effects (when starting from

---

[7] In deriving equation (3.14), we used the PPP relationship for the two traded goods and the reciprocal nature of trade in a two-region world. That is, the exports of the home country represent imports by the rest of the world and vice versa for home-country imports, so $\hat{p}_X = \hat{p}_I^* + \hat{S}$ and $\hat{p}_I = \hat{p}_X^* + \hat{S}$.

[8] For a related analysis, see Milner et al. (1995).

an undistorted equilibrium), this is not true for changes in world prices. If domestic prices change because of worsening of the country's terms of trade, for example, this makes the country as a whole worse off, which has implications for the working of the market for home goods. Accordingly, the preceding framework needs some modification or reinterpretation to deal with the first-order income effects of changes in the terms of trade. Let η_H be the income elasticity of demand for home goods, which is taken to be positive as these goods can be reasonably expected to be normal, and let α_I', α_X' be the shares of imports and exports, respectively (*not* importables and exportables) in gross domestic product (GDP). Then an increase in the domestic price of importables of $\hat{p}_I$, brought about by a world price rise, decreases real income in proportionate terms by $\alpha_I' \hat{p}_I$, which in turn causes the demand for home goods to decrease by $\eta_H \alpha_I' \hat{p}_I$. Similarly, an increase in the price of exportables arising from a world price increase leads to an increase in the demand for home goods of $\eta_H \alpha_X' \hat{p}_X$. Thus the demand equation for home goods, the second member of equation (3.8), becomes

$$\hat{q}_H^d = \sum_j \eta_{Hj} \hat{p}_j - \eta_H \alpha_I' \hat{p}_I + \eta_H \alpha_X' \hat{p}_X$$

Retracing our steps, the incidence equation (3.9) is then modified to

$$\hat{p}_H = [\omega + \phi_I] \hat{p}_I + [(1 - \omega) + \phi_X] \hat{p}_X$$

where $\phi_I = -\eta_H \alpha_I' / (\varepsilon_{HH} - \eta_{HH}) < 0$ and $\phi_X = \eta_H \alpha_X' / (\varepsilon_{HH} - \eta_{HH}) > 0$. Relative to equation (3.9), the coefficient for $\hat{p}_I$ is now lower, whereas that for $\hat{p}_X$ is higher. When trade is balanced, $\alpha_X' = \alpha_I' = \alpha_T'$, the share of trade in GDP, and $\phi_I = -\phi_X = \phi_T < 0$. Under this condition, the preceding equation simplifies to

$$\hat{p}_H = \omega' \hat{p}_I + (1 - \omega') \hat{p}_X \tag{3.16}$$

where $\omega' = \omega + \phi_T$ is the modified shift coefficient.

To illustrate the working of equation (3.16), consider the case in which the income elasticity of demand for home goods is unity, trade accounts for 30 per cent of the economy, the price elasticity of the supply for home goods is unity, and the price elasticity of demand for these goods is minus unity. Then $\phi_T = -\eta_H \alpha_T' / (\varepsilon_{HH} - \eta_{HH}) = -1 \times 0.3 / (1 + 1) = -0.15$, so the value of the conventional shift

A. An import tariff

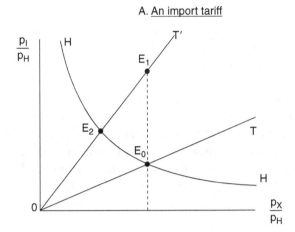

B. Worsening of the terms of trade

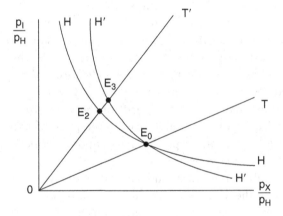

Figure 3.9 Relative prices, import tariffs and the terms of trade.

coefficient has to be reduced by 15 percentage points to allow for income effects associated with terms-of-trade changes. Figure 3.9 presents the geometry of the differential effects on internal prices of the imposition of an import tariff and worsening of the country's terms of trade.[9] In panel *A*, *HH* is the locus of relative prices for which the market for home goods clears; it follows from equation (3.9) that the

[9] Panel *A* of Figure 3.9 is due to Dornbusch (1974).

elasticity of this curve is $-[(1 - \omega)/\omega] < 0$. The slope of line OT from the origin is the internal price of importables in terms of exportables p_I/p_x, which under free trade is equal to world prices, p_I^*/p_X^*, and the initial overall equilibrium is at the point E_0. Imposition of an import tariff causes the line from the origin to become steeper and shift to OT', with slope $(1 + t)p_I^*/p_X^*$, where t is the tariff rate. With the relative price of exportables held constant, equilibrium then moves from E_0 to E_1, and the relative price of importables increases by the full amount of the tariff. However, at E_1 there is excess demand for home goods, which causes their price to increase in terms of both traded goods, and the economy moves from E_1 to E_2, which has the dual effect of eroding some of the protection afforded to the domestic importables sector and taxing the production of exportables. It is in this sense that import protection is a tax on exporters.

Panel B of Figure 3.9 considers the implications of worsening of the country's terms of trade by $t \times 100$ per cent, so the shift from OT to OT' is exactly the same as that in panel A. Along $H'H'$, the home-goods market clears when the income effects of changes in the terms of trade are allowed for. The elasticity of $H'H'$ is $-[(1 - \omega')/\omega'] < 0$, which for $\omega' < \omega$ is larger in absolute value than $-[(1 - \omega)/\omega]$. Accordingly, where the two schedules intersect, such as at point E_0, $H'H'$ is steeper than HH.[10] This means that relative to a tariff of the same size, an increase in the world price of importables causes the price of home goods to increase by less, so domestic producers of importables benefit by more and exporters are taxed by less.

The results of this subsection can be summarised as follows: equation (3.16) has exactly the same form as equation (3.9), so we can continue to use the commodity-currency framework, as summarised by equations (3.14) and (3.15), for changes in world prices. All that is required is reinterpretation of the shift coefficient ω to refer to its modified version ω'. In what follows, we continue to refer to the role of the shift coefficient ω in equations (3.14) and (3.15), but as we discuss changes in world prices, it should be understood that these references are, strictly speaking, to its modified counterpart ω'.

---

[10] Recall that the elasticity at a point on a curve is the ratio of the slope of the curve to the slope of a line from the origin to the point. When two curves intersect, the two lines from the origin coincide, as do their slopes. Accordingly, when two curves intersect, the relative slopes reflect relative elasticities.

3.2.4 When does a country have a commodity currency?

As the value of a commodity currency moves in parallel with a country's terms of trade, equations (3.14) and (3.15) provide a framework for identification of such a currency. For a commodity currency, its elasticity with respect to prices γ is a substantial positive number but less than unity (so that the domestic-currency price of the commodity increases with the world price). However, as β and β^* are both positive fractions, it is evident that γ will not always be substantially different from zero. In fact, as $\beta = \alpha_H(1 - \omega) + \alpha_I$ and $\beta^* = \alpha_H^*(1 - \omega^*) + \alpha_I^*$, there is a presumption that both these coefficients would be of the order of 0.5, which implies $\gamma \approx 0$. The value of 0.5 is based on the following considerations: The share of home goods in the overall economy could be something like 60 per cent in both regions, so $\alpha_H = \alpha_H^* = 0.6$; on the basis of the preceding discussion on the possible value of the shift coefficient, $\omega = 1/2$, and a not unreasonable value for the share of importables in both regions is 20 per cent, so $\alpha_I = \alpha_I^* = 0.2$. These values mean that $\beta = \beta^* = 0.5$, so the elasticity $\gamma = 0$, and the home country does *not* have a commodity currency in this case. This is, of course, reassuring as in most cases we would not expect the currency to be a commodity one; that is to say, commodity currencies are the exception to the rule.

Under what conditions does a country have a commodity currency? It follows from equation (3.15) that the elasticity γ will be further away from zero and closer to unity when

- Home goods occupy a smaller fraction of the economy (i.e., when α_H, α_H^* are both small).
- Home goods and importables are good substitutes in consumption and production (i.e., when the shift coefficients ω, ω^* are both large).
- Importables are relatively less important (i.e., when α_I, α_I^* are both small).

Note that the first and last conditions jointly imply that γ will be greater when exportables account for a larger share of the economy. We thus obtain the following simple rule: *A country is more likely to have a commodity currency when (1) exportables are relatively important in the economy and (2) the shift coefficient ω is large (nearer unity).*

3.2.5 Interactions between commodity and currency markets

In this subsection we combine the results of the preceding discussion to consider the joint implications of market power and commodity currencies. To simplify matters, in what follows, we assume that the home country's terms of trade p_X/p_I coincide with the relative commodity price p^*/P^*.[11] This means that the country under consideration is a commodity exporter, and as P^*, the index of prices in the rest of the world, now also plays the role of the price index of the country's imports, these imports are a representative market basket of goods from the rest of the world. Thus the country is specialised in its exports and diversified in imports, a pattern of trade not dissimilar to that of many developing economies.

Curve MM in Figure 3.10 is from Figure 3.5 and shows the relation between the world price of a commodity and the country's real exchange rate on account of its market power. The upward slope of the curve implies that the country has some degree of market power as real appreciation increases the world price. The elasticity of MM is the coefficient α in equation (3.6). When the country has no market power, $\alpha = 0$, and MM is horizontal. Curve CC in Figure 3.10 is the commodity-currency relationship from Figure 3.8. The elasticity of CC is $1/\gamma > 0$, so when the country does not have a commodity currency, $1/\gamma \to \infty$, and the curve is vertical. The elasticity of MM lies between 0 and 1, whereas that of CC is always greater than 1. This means that where the two curves intersect, CC is unambiguously steeper than MM; in other words, the CC schedule always cuts MM from below. It is evident that the initial overall equilibrium in the commodity and currency markets pertains at point E_0.

Next, we analyse the general equilibrium effects on prices and the exchange rate of a commodity boom resulting from an exogenous increase in world demand for the commodity. To do this, we need to extend the initial demand equation (3.3) to include foreign real income y^*:

---

[11] Note that as p_X/p_I and p^*/P^* are both relative prices that reflect real factors independent of currency units of measurement, we are not mixing currencies in taking these prices to be the same.

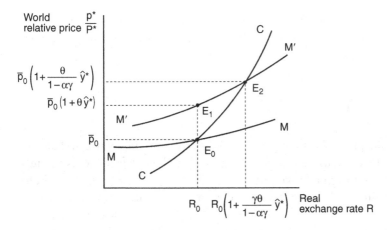

Figure 3.10 Impact of a commodity boom.

$$q^d = q^d\left(\frac{p^*}{P^*}, y^*\right), \quad \text{with} \quad \lambda = \frac{\partial\left(\log q^d\right)}{\partial\left(\log y^*\right)} > 0$$

so that λ is the income elasticity of demand for the commodity. Retracing our steps, we find that the extended version of the fundamental pricing rule [equation (3.6)] is

$$\widehat{\frac{p^*}{P^*}} = \alpha\hat{R} + \theta\hat{y}^* \tag{3.17}$$

where $\theta = \lambda/(\varepsilon - \eta) > 0$ is the elasticity of the world price with respect to income. The term $\theta\hat{y}^*$ is the initial increase in prices resulting from the income increase $\hat{y}^*$, with the real exchange rate held constant. In the case in which the income elasticity is unity and $\varepsilon = -\eta = 1/4$, which are not unreasonable values for the short term, the coefficient θ in equation (3.17) takes a value of 2. Thus, as the elasticity of commodity prices with respect to world income is 2, prices exhibit a form of excess volatility.

In terms of Figure 3.10, the effect of the increase in income is to shift MM up equiproportionally to $M'M'$ so that at the preexisting exchange rate R_0 the price increases by the full initial amount $\theta\hat{y}^*$, and the market moves from point E_0 to E_1. However, as we are dealing with a commodity currency, this price increase leads to appreciation, which causes the price to increase further with the move from E_1 to E_2. It is thus evident that the interaction between market power and a commodity currency has the effect of amplifying the initial increase in prices. That is, setting $\widehat{p_X/p_I} = \widehat{p^*/P^*}$, we can combine equations (3.14) and (3.17) to yield

$$\frac{\widehat{p^*}}{P^*} = \left(\frac{\theta}{1-\alpha\gamma}\right)\hat{y}^* \geq \theta\hat{y}^* \qquad (3.18)$$

The inequality in this equation follows from α lying between 0 and 1, and $0 < \gamma < 1$ for a commodity currency. Thus, if $\bar{p}_0$ denotes the initial equilibrium relative price associated with point E_0, and if we hold the value of the exchange rate constant at R_0, it follows from equation (3.17) that the new price at E_1 is $\bar{p}_0(1 + \theta\hat{y}^*)$. When the exchange rate is allowed to appreciate, equation (3.18) implies that the commodity price further increases to $\bar{p}_0\{1 + [\theta/(1-\alpha\gamma)]\hat{y}^*\}$ at the equilibrium point E_2. Continuing with the numerical example of the preceding paragraph, whereby $\theta = 2$ and the market power elasticity $\alpha = 1/2$, suppose in addition that the commodity-currency elasticity $\gamma = 1/2$. These values imply that the coefficient of income in equation (3.18) is

$$\left(\frac{\theta}{1-\alpha\gamma}\right) = \frac{2}{1 - \frac{1}{2}\times\frac{1}{2}} \approx 2.7$$

Thus, relative to the partial equilibrium effect of equation (3.17), the general equilibrium interaction between the commodity and currency markets adds another $0.7/2 = 35$ per cent to the volatility of prices.

On combining equations (3.18) and (3.14), it is evident that the commodity boom also results in currency appreciation:

$$\hat{R} = \left(\frac{\gamma\theta}{1-\alpha\gamma}\right)\hat{y}^* \qquad (3.19)$$

Thus, in terms of Figure 3.10, the exchange rate increases from R_0 to $R_0\{1 + [\gamma\theta/(1-\alpha\gamma)]\hat{y}^*\}$. The result is that the world price increases, and the currency appreciates; however, as the proportionate appreciation is less than the price increase, domestic producers benefit as the internal relative price also increases. That is, from the definition of the real exchange rate R, $p/P = (1/R)(p^*/P^*)$, and equations (3.18) and (3.19), we have

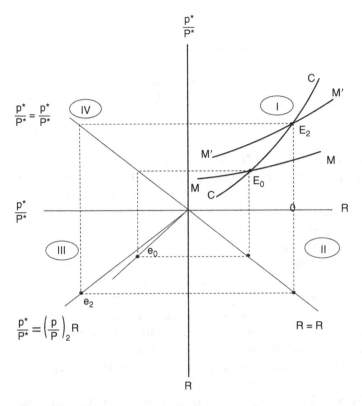

Figure 3.11 More on a commodity boom.

$$\frac{\widehat{p}}{P} = \frac{\widehat{p^*}}{P^*} - \widehat{R} = \left(\frac{(1-\gamma)\theta}{1-\alpha\gamma}\right)\hat{y}^* > 0$$

This increase in domestic prices is illustrated in Figure 3.11. This figure starts in quadrant I with the essential features of the commodity boom from Figure 3.10. Quadrant III contains the real version of the PPP relationship, $p^*/P^* = (p/P)R$. Point e_0 in this quadrant coincides with E_0 in quadrant I, so the slope of the line from the origin passing through e_0 is the equilibrium internal relative price $(p/P)_0$. The boom causes the economy to move to point e_2, which corresponds to E_2, and as the slope of the new line from the origin is steeper (with reference to the R axis) than before, the net effect of the increase in the world price and the appreciation is that the internal price increases to $(p/P)_2 > (p/P)_0$.

3.2.6 Stability

We discussed earlier the relative slopes of the MM and CC curves and why the latter always intersects the former from below. This amounts to the elasticity of the CC curve, $1/\gamma$, exceeding that of the MM curve, α, or, as both schedules are positively sloped,

$$0 < \alpha\gamma < 1 \tag{3.20}$$

As defined by equation (3.7), the elasticity α always lies between 0 and 1. The elasticity γ is defined by equation (3.15) and, as discussed earlier, can range from a negative value to a positive fraction. Given that $0 \le \alpha \le 1$, if we ignore the boundary case when $\alpha = 0$, condition (3.20) further restricts γ by ruling out negative values, so this elasticity is confined to the range [0, 1]. To further clarify the implications of this condition, suppose that it is not satisfied so that CC intersects MM from above, as in Figure 3.12. It is evident that the impact of the commodity boom in moving the economy from the initial equilibrium E_0 to E_2 is to *decrease* the world price and *depreciate* the currency, which clearly makes no sense. If we again ignore boundary values, it should also be noted that condition (3.20) implies the inequality in equation (3.18), that the full impact of the boom on prices is never less than its initial effect.

Condition (3.20) can also be interpreted as a stability condition. To see this, let $\bar{p}$ denote the world relative price of the commodity p^*/P^*, and write a levels version of the reciprocal of the market-power

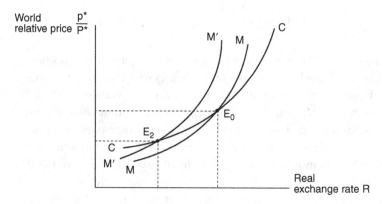

Figure 3.12 The unstable case.

relation [equation (3.6)] in logarithmic form as $\log R = f(\log \bar{p})$, with elasticity $f' = 1/\alpha$, where the prime denotes the derivative, and α is as defined in equation (3.7). The commodity-currency relation, analogous to equation (3.14), is $\log R = g(\log \bar{p})$, with $g' = \gamma$, defined by equation (3.15). Consider a situation in which the value of $\bar{p}$ is initially away from equilibrium so that the exchange rate required to clear the currency market, $g(\log \bar{p})$, differs from that needed to equilibrate the commodity market, $f(\log \bar{p})$. Suppose that the forces of the currency market prevail in the sense that $\bar{p}$ increases when $g(\log \bar{p}) > f(\log \bar{p})$ and decreases when $g(\log \bar{p}) < f(\log \bar{p})$. This behaviour can be expressed in the form of the following price-adjustment rule: $d(\log \bar{p})/dt = H[g(\log \bar{p}) - f(\log \bar{p})]$, where $H(\cdot)$ is a speed of adjustment function, with $H(0) = 0$ and $H' > 0$. Linearising around the equilibrium price $\bar{p}_0$ so that $g(\log \bar{p}_0) = f(\log \bar{p}_0)$, and defining $H' = \psi$ as the speed of adjustment coefficient, we have

$$d\left(\log \bar{p}\right)\big/dt = \psi\left(g' - f'\right)\left(\log \bar{p} - \log \bar{p}_0\right)$$

or

$$\frac{d\left(\log \bar{p}\right)}{dt} = \psi\left(\gamma - \frac{1}{\alpha}\right)\left(\log \bar{p} - \log \bar{p}_0\right)$$

The solution to this differential equation for the initial price at time zero, $\log \bar{p}$, is

$$\log \bar{p}\left(t\right) = \log \bar{p}_0 + \left(\log \bar{p} - \log \bar{p}_0\right) e^{\psi[\gamma - (1/\alpha)]t}$$

which is stable and converges to $\log \bar{p}_0$ when $(\gamma - 1/\alpha) < 0$. This amounts to $\alpha\gamma < 1$, which is part of condition (3.20). Exactly the same stability condition emerges if, alternatively, the dynamics of the exchange rate is formulated as $d(\log R)/dt = H_R[f^{-1}(\log R) - g^{-1}(\log R)]$, where $H_R(\cdot)$ is a new adjustment function with $H_R(0) = 0$ and $H_R' > 0$. In what follows, we assume that condition (3.20) is satisfied.

3.2.7 A typology of commodities and currencies

Figure 3.10 considered the implications of a commodity boom when the country (1) has a commodity currency ($\gamma > 0$) and (2) is a price-maker ($\alpha > 0$). Figure 3.13 elaborates the 2×2 possible combinations.

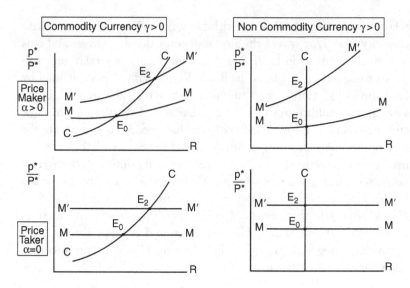

Figure 3.13 Interactions between market power and commodity currency: the four possibilities.

The top left-hand panel is a stripped-down version of Figure 3.10, which is the general case of a commodity currency and some degree of market power. Immediately below this is the situation for a price-taker ($\alpha = 0$) and a commodity currency ($\gamma > 0$). In this case, the boom causes the price to increase by less than previously; the price increases by just the vertical distance between the two curves MM and $M'M'$, which in proportionate terms is $\theta \hat{y}^*$. The currency appreciates, but by less than before. In the general case, the boom initially increases the price, and owing to the commodity currency, the exchange rate then appreciates. When the country is a price-maker, this appreciation serves to push up the world price further (as profitability in the export sector is squeezed), which, in turn, leads to a further appreciation. But when the country is a price-taker, there are no 'second round' effects, so the initial effect of the boom is the end of the story. Accordingly, when the country is a price-taker and has a commodity currency, the boom causes the world price to increase by less, and the currency appreciation is dampened.

The top right-hand panel of Figure 3.13 represents the price-maker and non-commodity-currency case. Here the price increases by the same amount as in the previous case, by $\theta \hat{y}^*$, but now there is no change in the exchange rate as the country does not have a commodity currency. The final case of a price-taker and non-commodity currency is given in the bottom panel on the right, and the outcome is identical to the previous case: The price increases by $\theta \hat{y}^*$, and the exchange rate remains unchanged.

3.2.8 Further applications

We now illustrate the approach by considering three further examples, the effects on prices and exchange rates of (1) a shift in investor sentiment towards the currency of the home country, (2) technological change that creates new alternatives for the commodity, and (3) globalisation that injects an added degree of flexibility into the domestic economy.

A currency fad

The notorious volatility of exchange rates is sometimes attributed to sudden large shifts in the portfolio preferences of international investors. It is instructive to analyse the impact of such a currency fad within our framework. Suppose that commodity prices are constant and that the onset of a fad causes the country's real exchange rate to appreciate in proportionate terms by $\rho > 0$ so that the commodity-currency relationship [equation (3.14)] becomes $\hat{R} = \gamma \widehat{(p^*/P^*)} + \rho$. Combining this with the market-power relationship [equation (3.6)] yields

$$\hat{R} = \left(\frac{1}{1 - \alpha\gamma} \right) \rho, \quad \widehat{\frac{p^*}{P^*}} = \left(\frac{\alpha}{1 - \alpha\gamma} \right) \rho \tag{3.21}$$

In view of the stability condition [equation (3.20)], the interactions between markets lead to appreciation of the exchange rate by more than the initial effect of the fad, $\hat{R} = \rho$. The explanation for this is that the initial appreciation leads to a higher commodity price, and this leads to further appreciation via the commodity-currency link, which causes a total increase in the rate of $\hat{R} = \rho/(1 - \alpha\gamma) > \rho$. This is illustrated in panel A of Figure 3.14, where point E_0 is the initial equilibrium associated with the price $\bar{p}_0$ and exchange rate R_0. The currency fad shifts CC to the right, in proportionate terms by ρ, to $C'C'$. At the initial price $\bar{p}_0$, the fad results in a move to E_1, at which point

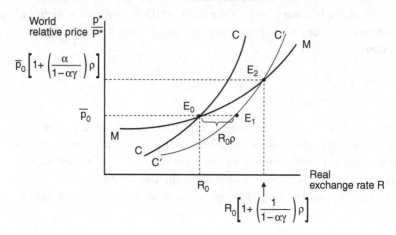

A. A currency fad

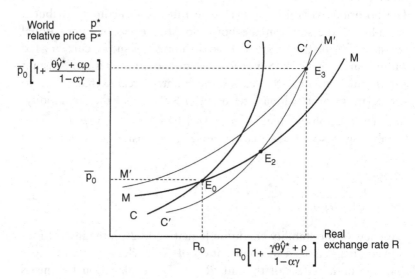

B. A currency fad plus commodity boom

Figure 3.14 Impact of a currency fad and a commodity boom.

there is excess demand for the commodity. The price has to increase accordingly, and the new overall equilibrium is given by point E_2. Note also that equation (3.21) implies that even though the world price increases, a currency fad hurts domestic producers as the internal price decreases:

$$\frac{\widehat{p}}{P} = \frac{\widehat{p^*}}{P^*} - \hat{R} = -\left(\frac{1-\alpha}{1-\alpha\gamma}\right)\rho < 0$$

It may be more realistic to think of a commodity boom that prompts investors to reevaluate future prospects for the relevant commodity currency. In such a case, the boom occurs simultaneously with the currency fad, and we can obtain the overall impact on the exchange rate and prices simply by adding the individual effects derived earlier. Thus, for the exchange rate, we add the right-hand side of equation (3.19) and the first member of equation (3.21) and proceed analogously for prices. This yields

$$\widehat{R} = \frac{\gamma\theta\hat{y}^* + \rho}{1-\alpha\gamma}, \frac{\widehat{p^*}}{P^*} = \frac{\theta\hat{y}^* + \alpha\rho}{1-\alpha\gamma}$$

Here the CC and MM curves both shift, as in panel *B* of Figure 3.14, and the equilibrium moves from the initial point E_0 to E_3. The change in internal prices is

$$\frac{\widehat{p}}{P} = \frac{\widehat{p^*}}{P^*} - \widehat{R} = \frac{(1-\gamma)\theta\hat{y}^* - (1-\alpha)\rho}{1-\alpha\gamma} \tag{3.22}$$

which has an ambiguous sign as γ and α both lie in the range [0, 1]. However, we can state that for given boom and fad sizes, that is, for fixed values of $\theta\hat{y}^*$ and ρ, the internal relative price is more likely to decrease under two conditions. First, when there is a stronger commodity-currency relationship (i.e., when γ is larger), the internal price is more likely to decrease because of the direct currency translation effect. Second, the price is also more likely to decrease when the country has less pricing power (lower α) as then there is a more limited offsetting increase in world prices following appreciation. More definitively, suppose that the magnitude of the two shocks coincide in the sense that the initial increase in the world price on account of the commodity boom ($\theta\hat{y}^*$) is exactly equal to the initial appreciation due to the currency fad (ρ). Thus, with $\theta\hat{y}^* = \rho = z$ (say), equation (3.22) becomes

$$\frac{\widehat{p}}{P} = \left(\frac{\alpha-\gamma}{1-\alpha\gamma}\right)z$$

As $z > 0$, this shows that the internal price decreases when $\alpha < \gamma$ or when the country has less market power than the extent to which it has a commodity currency.

A technological change

Suppose that a continued high price for the commodity stimulates a search for alternatives and that an endogenous technical-change process results in invention of a new substitute product. An example could be successful use of hydrogen as a substitute fuel for petroleum in cars. We show that this type of technical change has a stabilising effect as the volatility of commodity prices and the exchange rate of the dominant producing country both decrease. It is convenient to analyse these effects within the context of the commodity-boom framework discussed earlier. In what follows, some elasticities and variables change on introduction of the new product, whereas others remain unchanged. We indicate those which change by adding a subscript 0 for the old value and 1 for the new value. The elasticities that remain unchanged have no subscript.

We treat the new product as an additional substitute for the commodity so that demand becomes more price elastic and the elasticity increases (in absolute value) to $\eta_1 < \eta_0 < 0$. Accordingly, the new value of the market-power elasticity in equation (3.6) is

$$\left(\alpha_1 = \frac{\varepsilon}{\varepsilon - \eta_1}\right) < \left(\alpha_0 = \frac{\varepsilon}{\varepsilon - \eta_0}\right)$$

Thus availability of the new product reduces the country's market power. Equation (3.17), when representing the impact of the commodity boom, becomes

$$\left(\frac{\widehat{p^*}}{P*}\right)_1 = \alpha_1 \hat{R} + \theta_1 \hat{y}^*$$

where $\theta_1 = \lambda/(\varepsilon - \eta_1) < \theta_0 = \lambda/(\varepsilon - \eta_0)$. The relevant part of equation (3.18) is then modified to $(\widehat{p^*/P^*})_1 = [\theta_1/(1 - \alpha_1\gamma)]\hat{y}^*$ so that

$$\left[\left(\frac{\widehat{p^*}}{P*}\right)_1 = \left(\frac{\theta_1}{1 - \alpha_1\gamma}\right)\hat{y}^*\right] < \left[\left(\frac{\widehat{p^*}}{P*}\right)_0 = \left(\frac{\theta_0}{1 - \alpha_0\gamma}\right)\hat{y}^*\right]$$

As the same increase in foreign income ($\hat{y}^*$) causes the world price to increase by less when the new substitute product is available, the volatility of prices decreases. Similarly, the volatility of the country's exchange rate will now be lower, as

$$\left[\hat{R}_1 = \left(\frac{\gamma\theta_1}{1 - \alpha_1\gamma} \right) \hat{y}^* \right] < \left[\hat{R}_0 = \left(\frac{\gamma\theta_0}{1 - \alpha_0\gamma} \right) \hat{y}^* \right]$$

which follows from equation (3.19). It thus can be concluded that this type of technological change stabilises markets.

Globalisation

It is often observed that highly protected economies are characterised by a low degree of resource mobility across sectors or a lack of over-all flexibility. The postwar Australian economy up to the 1980s is an example. Suppose now that this all changes as the economy becomes more exposed to the discipline of international trade because of reduced protection and/or transport costs. This could reasonably be taken to mean that as the domestic economy is now more integrated with the world economy and more exposed to the competitive pressures of inter-national trade, resources flow more easily between the home-goods sector on the one hand and importables on the other. In other words, home goods and importables become more substitutable in both pro-duction and consumption with this form of globalisation. Thus we consider the effects of an increase in the shift coefficient ω. From equation (3.15), this increase in ω increases the elasticity γ in the commodity-currency relationship [equation (3.14)] from γ_0 to γ_1 so that the country's currency behaves more like a commodity currency. Proceeding with the effects of the commodity boom as before, we obtain

$$\left[\left(\widehat{\frac{p^*}{P^*}} \right)_1 = \left(\frac{\theta}{1 - \alpha\gamma_1} \right) \hat{y}^* \right] > \left[\left(\widehat{\frac{p^*}{P^*}} \right)_0 = \left(\frac{\theta}{1 - \alpha\gamma_0} \right) \hat{y}^* \right],$$

$$\left[\hat{R}_1 = \left(\frac{\gamma_1\theta}{1 - \alpha\gamma_1} \right) \hat{y}^* \right] > \left[\hat{R}_0 = \left(\frac{\gamma_0\theta}{1 - \alpha\gamma_0} \right) \hat{y}^* \right]$$

This result states that the greater flexibility of the economy leads to higher volatility for the commodity price and the exchange rate. Usu-ally, enhanced flexibility tends to be associated with more stable prices, so this result is somewhat surprising. The key to understanding what is taking place here is that enhanced flexibility in this case means that a given change in the world price, brought about by an increase in world economic activity, now leads to a larger appreciation of the domestic currency. This leads to lower exports and, as the country has market power, a still higher world price. The interaction between the flexibility of the economy and the commodity-currency nature of its exchange rate is the mechanism that gives rise to the result of globalisation generating greater volatility.

3.3 A first look at the data

Section 3.2 outlined the conditions necessary for a commodity currency and market power in commodity markets. Section 3.4 addresses these issues by specifying and estimating a multivariate latent factor model that can examine the joint determinants of currency and commodity prices. However, as a precursor, this section provides a preliminary analysis of the data set, the results of which will be used to motivate the multivariate model of Section 3.4.

The data set consists of $m = 3$ commodity-currency exchange-rate variables, $n = 1$ additional currencies and $v = 5$ commodity-price variables. The commodity currencies considered include the Australian dollar (AUD_t), the Canadian dollar (CND_t) and the New Zealand dollar (NZD_t). The British pound (GBP_t) represents an additional currency. The ith nominal exchange rate $S_{i,t}$ is transformed to a real rate $R_{i,t}$ which is expressed in terms of US dollars (USD_t) per unit of national currency, $R_{i,t} = P_{i,t}/S_{i,t}P_t^*$, where $P_{i,t}$ and P_t^* represent the national and US consumer price indices, respectively. Demeaned continuously compounding percentage returns of the commodity currencies ($CE_{i,t}$) are computed by taking the quarterly difference of the natural logarithm of the real exchange rates, subtracting the sample mean and multiplying by 100. The additional currency, denoted E_t, is similarly transformed.

The International Monetary Fund (IMF) publishes an overall index of commodity prices, as well as five subindices that capture the major commodity groups. These subindices include agricultural materials, beverages, food, metals and energy. The choice of commodity-price indices is motivated by the IMF subclassifications, and data were in fact sourced from the IMF International Financial Statistics database. The exception is the oil price index, which is used to proxy the IMF energy index because the latter is only reported from 1992. The oil price index was obtained from Datastream. The five commodity-price variables thus include indices of agricultural materials (AGR_t), beverages (BEV_t),

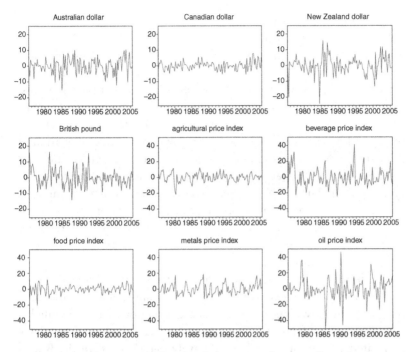

Figure 3.15 Real percentage demeaned currency and commodity-price returns.

food (FOO_t), metals (MET_t) and oil prices (OIL_t). The kth nominal commodity-price index is also expressed in real terms by deflating by the US consumer price index. Real demeaned commodity-price percentage returns, denoted $PC_{k,t}$, are determined analogously to those for the commodity-currency returns. The vector Y_t

$$Y_t = \left\{ CE_{i,t}, E_t, PC_{k,t} \right\} \tag{3.23}$$

summarises the data.

The sample period for the model extends from quarter 1 of 1975 to quarter 3 of 2005 for $T = 123$ observations. Quarter 1 of 1975 represents the beginning of the construction of the commodity-price indices by the IMF. The data are expressed in quarterly terms as the Australian consumer price index used to deflate the Australian exchange rate into real terms is only available on a quarterly basis. Table 3A.1 in Appendix 3A at the end of this chapter contains details on variable sources and codes.

The complete data set is contained in Figure 3.15, and Tables 3.1 and 3.2 present a selection of descriptive statistics.[12] Table 3.1 indicates that the commodity-price returns are generally more volatile than the currency returns. The standard deviations for commodities range between 5.0 per cent for food returns and 13.3 per cent for oil returns. The returns for the oil index also show the smallest minimum and the greatest maximum over the sample period. Of the currency returns, the Canadian dollar is the least volatile, with a standard deviation of 2.7, and the New Zealand dollar is the most volatile, with a standard deviation of 5.8. The Jarque–Bera tests indicate mixed evidence of normality for the data series. The null hypothesis of normality cannot be rejected for Australian and Canadian dollar returns or for the metal price index but is rejected for the remaining currency and commodity returns. For simplicity, normality is assumed for convenience of estimation in Section 3.4.

The upper triangle of the correlation matrix is given above the diagonal in Table 3.2, whereas the elements on and below the diagonal represent the covariance matrix. The correlation matrix highlights some interesting features. The commodity currencies are positively correlated with each other but negatively correlated with the British pound, which indicates the different structures of the respective types of economies. Commodity returns are mostly positively correlated. As expected, commodity-currency returns (expressed in terms of US dollars per national currency) are generally positively correlated with commodity-price returns. The exceptions for which correlations are negative (albeit comparatively small) are the Australian dollar and oil (−0.005), the Canadian dollar and food (−0.092) and the New Zealand dollar and beverages (−0.001).

To form a view on the lag structure of the factor model, correlograms of the currency and commodity-price returns are presented in Table 3.3. To examine further the possible lag structure of the system as a whole, Table 3.4 contains the lag-length criteria of the modified likelihood ratio (LR), Akaike (AIC), Schwarz (SC) and Hannan-Quinn (HQ) for a vector autoregression (VAR) of the data. The correlograms indicate that there is some temporal dependence among the individual variables, with the exception of the Australian dollar. The

---

[12] All calculations for Section 3.3 were performed in Eviews 5.

Table 3.1 *Descriptive statistics for currency and commodity returns*

	Currency				Commodity				
	AUD	CND	NZD	GBP	AGR	BEV	FOO	MET	OIL
Mean	0.000	0.000	0.000	0.000	0.000	0.000	0.000	0.000	0.000
Median	0.179	−0.147	0.197	0.029	0.821	−2.542	0.261	−0.863	−0.661
Max.	10.420	7.672	15.902	16.267	12.245	41.167	12.307	18.925	46.437
Min.	−15.145	−5.643	−24.213	−14.294	−21.757	−24.784	−20.342	−13.432	−49.693
SD	4.896	2.656	5.778	5.402	5.674	10.940	5.014	6.700	13.322
Skewness	−0.342	0.429	−0.660	0.458	−0.623	0.908	−0.533	0.443	−0.164
Kurtosis	3.088	3.349	5.977	3.670	4.404	4.463	4.492	2.852	6.226
Jarq.-Bera	2.420	4.360	53.897	6.551	17.929	27.632	17.081	4.092	53.450
Probability	0.298	0.113	0.000	0.038	0.000	0.000	0.000	0.129	0.000

Table 3.2 *Correlation, variance and covariance for currency and commodity returns*

	Currency				Commodity				
	AUD	CND	NZD	GBP	AGR	BEV	FOO	MET	OIL
Currency									
AUD	23.777	0.503	0.655	−0.271	0.066	0.032	0.020	0.232	−0.005
CND	6.488	6.994	0.298	−0.116	0.079	0.008	−0.092	0.115	0.075
NZD	18.380	4.540	33.112	−0.454	0.203	−0.001	0.062	0.247	0.044
GBP	−7.098	−1.645	−14.046	28.938	0.003	0.029	−0.143	−0.179	−0.224
Commodity									
AGR	1.808	1.178	6.612	0.085	31.932	0.143	0.308	0.298	0.027
BEV	−1.686	0.230	−0.041	1.709	8.829	118.712	0.142	0.226	−0.044
FOO	−0.487	1.178	1.775	−3.850	8.688	7.703	24.933	0.298	0.027
MET	7.558	2.036	9.501	−6.407	8.897	16.442	9.939	44.518	0.165
OIL	−0.326	2.628	3.339	−16.004	16.920	−6.326	1.810	14.587	176.034

Note: Variances are the shaded diagonals; correlations (covariances) are above (below) the diagonal.

Table 3.3 *Correlograms of currency and commodity returns*

Lag	Currency			Commodity		
	Autocorr. coeffic.	Ljung-Box Q statistic	p-value	Autocorr. coeffic.	Ljung-Box Q statistic	p-value
	Australia			*Agricultural materials*		
1	−0.014	0.023	0.879	0.385	18.550	0.000
2	0.049	0.324	0.850	0.083	19.425	0.000
3	0.121	2.174	0.537	−0.108	20.907	0.000
4	0.028	2.273	0.686	−0.003	20.908	0.000
	Canada			*Beverages*		
1	0.069	0.592	0.442	0.307	11.746	0.001
2	0.005	0.595	0.743	−0.007	11.752	0.003
3	0.222	6.884	0.076	0.125	13.736	0.003
4	0.112	8.504	0.075	0.025	13.815	0.008
	New Zealand			*Food*		
1	0.080	0.796	0.372	0.079	0.786	0.375
2	0.149	3.586	0.166	−0.239	8.008	0.018
3	0.182	7.774	0.051	0.022	8.069	0.045
4	−0.032	7.903	0.095	0.124	10.033	0.040
	Great Britain			*Metals*		
1	0.180	4.056	0.044	0.318	12.646	0.000
2	−0.077	4.802	0.091	0.175	16.519	0.000
3	0.199	9.814	0.020	0.126	18.527	0.000
4	0.116	11.550	0.021	0.000	18.527	0.001
				Oil		
1				0.208	5.389	0.020
2				−0.130	7.533	0.023
3				0.062	8.014	0.046
4				−0.033	8.157	0.086

commodity-price returns tend to exhibit the strongest autocorrelation. The AIC, SC and HQ statistics show that a structure of one lag is sufficient to characterise the system as a whole, although the LR test indicates an optimal structure of four lags.

To add support to the model developed in Section 3.4, the results of simple bivariate Granger causality tests are presented in Table 3.5. The

Table 3.4 *Lag selection criteria for a VAR of currency and commodity returns*

Lag	Log L	LR	AIC	SC	HQ
1	−3228.064	n.a.	56.086*	57.988*	56.858*
2	−3170.768	97.112	56.488	60.291	58.032
3	−3111.125	91.992	56.850	62.555	59.166
4	−3032.124	109.797*	56.883	64.491	59.972

Notes: An asterisk indicates lag order selected by the criterion. LR = sequential modified LR test statistic (each test at 5 per cent level); AIC = Akaike information criterion; SC = Schwarz information criterion; HQ = Hannan-Quinn information criterion.

results suggest that currencies Granger-cause commodity prices rather than the other way around. The null hypotheses that the Australian dollar does not Granger-cause agricultural returns, food returns, metal returns and oil returns is rejected at the 0.05 level of significance. The same is true for the Canadian dollar for food and metals and for the New Zealand dollar for agricultural materials, food and metals. Conversely, the null hypothesis that commodity prices do not Granger-cause currencies is not rejected in all cases. Finally, the British pound Granger-causes the New Zealand dollar, food prices and metal price returns. In summary, these preliminary tests suggest that commodity prices are perhaps driven by currency movements rather than the other way around. The next section explores whether or not this is true when the system is modelled jointly rather than on a bivariate basis.

3.4 A latent factor model

Although there are many empirically based papers on commodity currencies, there is usually an implicit assumption that either commodity prices are exogenous and currency commodities are a function of these prices (Cashin et al., 2004; Freebairn, 1990; Gruen and Kortian, 1998) or, to a lesser degree, vice versa (Amano and van Norden, 1995) consider the possibility for Canada but find that causality runs from the terms of trade to the Canadian dollar.] Chen and Rogoff (2003) highlight the possibility that commodity prices may be endogenous in simple exchange-rate models for Australia, Canada and

Table 3.5 *Bivariate Granger causality between currency and commodity returns (p-values for H₀: Variable x does not cause y)*

y / x	Currency				Commodity				
	AUD	CND	NZD	GBP	AGR	BEV	FOO	MET	OIL
Currency									
AUD	–	0.556	0.522	0.306	0.028*	0.555	0.001*	0.031*	0.022*
CND	0.114	–	0.982	0.970	0.137	0.223	0.042*	0.012*	0.295
NZD	0.830	0.825	–	0.095	0.027*	0.435	0.000*	0.030*	0.113
GBP	0.433	0.187	0.042*	–	0.163	0.475	0.000*	0.004*	0.753
Commodity									
AGR	0.930	0.978	0.826	0.331	–	0.003*	0.137	0.190	0.043*
BEV	0.721	0.976	0.316	0.100	0.589	–	0.666	0.084	0.363
FOO	0.886	0.412	0.537	0.984	0.274	0.255	–	0.561	0.411
MET	0.881	0.430	0.416	0.380	0.432	0.510	0.011*	–	0.007*
OIL	0.738	0.878	0.841	0.646	0.777	0.172	0.189	0.916	–

Note: An asterisk denotes significance at the 5 per cent level.

New Zealand. However, they control for endogeneity using the IMF world commodity-price index as an instrument for country-specific commodity prices. They do not go on to estimate a multivariate model. Broda (2004) also considers the potential endogeneity of the terms of trade but finds that it is rare for such commodity-exporting countries to have market power. The only empirical papers that attempt to model the case in which the two effects operate simultaneously are those which use a VAR framework, which allows for feedback mechanisms between the variables. Examples of such papers include Hatzinikolaou and Polasek (2005) and Fisher (1996). Despite the feedback effects in such models, the analysis is generally focussed on the effects of commodity prices or the terms of trade on exchange rates and not the other way around, although Fisher (1996) provides some brief comments on the effects of shocks (real and nominal) on terms of trade.

The model specified in this chapter examines the concepts in Section 3.2 and addresses this gap in the empirical literature by jointly examining the determinants of currency and commodity-price returns as a function of a set of independent latent factors. Influences that are common to each subset of variables are captured by a single time series (factor), which is intuitively likely to be a function of more than one observable variable. The advantage is that these observable variables do not have to be identified and modelled. It is particularly convenient to adopt such a specification as it can implicitly take into account shocks that simultaneously affect each type of market, such as business-cycle shocks or shocks to the US economy, without formally modelling such linkages (see Chen and Rogoff, 2003 and Freebairn, 1990 for discussions of the difficulties in accounting for the many possible influences on the exchange rate). This class of model is common in the financial literature, high-frequency-data exchange-rate models and the literature on business cycles (Diebold and Nerlove, 1989; Dungey, 1999; Mahieu and Schotman, 1994; Stock and Watson, 1991). One of the key advantages of this framework is its parsimony. The model can provide an understanding of the underlying importance of linkages across markets while controlling the number of parameters to be estimated.

There are three key factors in the model: a common factor, which captures information that is common to the complete data set; a currency factor, which is specific to exchange rates; and a commodity factor, which captures information specific to commodity prices. The joint impact of (commodity) currencies on commodities and the symmetric impact of commodities on currencies can then be assessed by examining spillovers across markets. The model allows an assessment of (1) the importance of the currency factor in determining currency values, (2) the importance of the commodity factor in determining commodity prices, and (3) the importance of spillovers across each type of market. The factor model describing the data in equation (3.23) can be separated into three components: the commodity currency $(CE_{i,t})$ returns, the additional currency (E_t) returns and the commodity-price returns $(PC_{k,t})$. The following provides a specification for each component of the model.

3.4.1 Commodity-currency returns

The following equation is the model for the commodity-currency returns:

$$CE_{i,t} = \lambda_i V_t + \varphi_i CF_t + \gamma_i PCF_{t-1} + \sigma_i U_{i,t}, \quad i = 1, \ldots, m \qquad (3.24)$$

The commodity-currency returns are a function of a common factor V_t, which is included in all equations for the system; a commodity-currency returns factor CF_t, hereafter referred to as the 'currency factor'; and an idiosyncratic term $U_{i,t}$ with loadings λ_i, φ_i and σ_i, respectively. Inclusion of the pound (E_t) in the model (described below) and implicit inclusion of the US dollar as the numeraire currency should provide sufficient information to identify the factor V_t common to all variables. The existence of the commodity-currency returns factor is supported by the correlations reported in Table 3.2, which show that the commodity currencies are positively correlated with each other but negatively correlated with the British pound. To examine the extent to which commodity-currency returns are a function of commodity-price returns and vice versa, cross-market linkages are modelled through spillover factors. In the case of commodity currencies, spillovers from the commodity-returns series are modelled through the lagged commodity-price factor PCF_{t-1}, with loading γ_i. The commodity-price factor at time t is specific only to the commodity-returns series for the model and is described in more detail in equations (3.28) and (3.29) below.

The common and currency returns factors are modelled as $AR(1)$ processes with loadings ρ_V and ρ_{CF} such that

$$V_t = \rho_V V_{t-1} + \eta_{V,t} \tag{3.25}$$

$$CF_t = \rho_{CF} CF_{t-1} + \eta_{CF,t} \tag{3.26}$$

Given that the data set is of short duration and expressed in terms of returns, it is reasonable to impose a lag structure of one lag on the common, commodity currency and commodity-price factors in equations (3.24), (3.25) and (3.29). This specification is supported by the correlograms and the lag-length criteria reported in Section 3.3. It is assumed that the idiosyncratic factors that capture the component of each return series not explained by the other factors do not exhibit autocorrelation.

3.4.2 Additional currency returns

The additional currency return variable, which is not considered a commodity currency, is included in the model to help identify the global or common influences V_t and to separate movements in the commodity currencies from currency markets in general. This is particularly important as all the currency returns are expressed in terms of US dollars per unit of national currency, and the commodity-price indices are constructed from US dollar prices. Exclusion of a common factor may result in the detection of spurious linkages owing to these US dollar effects.[13] The following equation presents the model for additional currency returns:

$$E_{j,t} = \lambda_j V_t + \sigma_j U_{j,t}, \quad j = 1,\ldots,n \tag{3.27}$$

These returns are a function of the world factor and the idiosyncratic factor with loadings λ_j and σ_j, respectively.

---

[13] A version of this model was estimated excluding the additional currency (i.e., without the common factor V_t), and it was found that the currency factor had a substantial impact on the commodity price returns. Some factor models for currency markets include an additional numeraire factor where a parameter is held fixed across all equations (Dungey, 1999; Dungey et al., 2003; Mahieu and Schotman, 1994). As the contribution of this factor to overall asset market volatility is minimal in most applications, it is excluded here.

3.4.3 Commodity returns

The commodity-price returns equation is similar in nature to the commodity-currency returns specification:

$$PC_{k,t} = \lambda_k V_t + \delta_k PCF_t + \beta_k CF_{t-1} + \sigma_k U_{k,t}, \quad k = 1, \dots, v \quad (3.28)$$

Commodity returns are a function of the common factor V_t, the commodity-price returns factor PCF_t, spillovers from the previous period's currency returns factor CF_{t-1} and an idiosyncratic factor $U_{k,t}$. The parameter loadings on these factors are λ_k, δ_k, β_k and σ_k. Like the common and currency factors, the commodity factor is an $AR(1)$ process:

$$PCF_t = \rho_{PCF} PCF_{t-1} + \eta_{PCF,t} \quad (3.29)$$

3.4.4 The complete model

For convenience, the preceding model can be expressed in matrix form as

$$Y_t = \Lambda F_t + \Delta F_{t-1} + W_t \quad (3.30)$$

$$F_{t+1} = \Psi F_t + V_t \quad (3.31)$$

where Y_t is a function of the latent factors contained in F_t (namely, V_t, CF_t and PCF_t and the idiosyncratics) with parameter loading Λ and spillovers, which are modelled through the lag of the latent factors F_{t-1} with parameter loading Δ. The state equation (3.31) shows that factor F_{t+1} is an autoregressive process with loading Ψ. The error matrices V_t and W_t are vector white-noise processes such that

$$E\left(V_t V_\tau'\right) = \begin{cases} Q & \text{for } t = \tau \\ 0 & \text{otherwise} \end{cases} \quad (3.32)$$

and

$$E\left(W_t W_\tau'\right) = \begin{cases} R & \text{for } t = \tau \\ 0 & \text{otherwise} \end{cases} \quad (3.33)$$

Here $W_t = 0$, and hence $R = 0$.

The model in equations (3.30) through (3.33) is estimated using maximum likelihood and the Kalman filter. The likelihood function is maximised using the MAXLIK procedure in Gauss 5.0 with the Broyden-Fletcher-Goldfarb-Shanno (BFGS) iterative gradient algorithm and numerical derivatives. For details on the Kalman filter algorithm, see Harvey (1981, 1990), Hamilton (1994, chap. 13) and Lütkepohl (1993, chap. 13).

3.4.5 Variance decompositions

The assumption of independence of the factors means that the results can be interpreted in terms of the contribution of each factor to the overall volatility of each asset. The volatility of currency and commodity returns can be decomposed in terms of the factors by squaring both sides of equations (3.24), (3.27) and (3.28) and taking expectations. The decomposition of the variances for commodity currencies is

$$E\left(CE_{i,t}^2\right) = \frac{\lambda_i^2}{1 - \rho_V^2} + \frac{\varphi_i^2}{1 - \rho_{CF}^2} + \frac{\gamma_i^2}{1 - \rho_{PCF}^2} + \sigma_i^2, \quad i = 1, \ldots, m \quad (3.34)$$

where $\lambda_i^2 / 1 - \rho_v^2$ represents the contribution of the world factor to volatility in commodity currency i, $\varphi_i^2 / 1 - \rho_{CF}^2$ represents the contribution of the currency factor, $\gamma_i^2 / 1 - \rho_{PCF}^2$ represents the contribution of spillovers from the commodity factor and σ_i^2 represents the contribution of the idiosyncratic factor. Analogous to equation (3.34), the decomposition for additional currencies is

$$E\left(E_{j,t}^2\right) = \frac{\lambda_j^2}{1 - \rho_V^2} + \sigma_j^2, \quad j = 1, \ldots, n \quad (3.35)$$

whereas that for the commodity-price series is

$$E\left(PC_{k,t}^2\right) = \frac{\lambda_k^2}{1 - \rho_V^2} + \frac{\delta_k^2}{1 - \rho_{PCF}^2} + \frac{\beta_k^2}{1 - \rho_{CF}^2} + \sigma_k^2, \quad k = 1, \ldots, v \quad (3.36)$$

These percentage contributions to overall volatility provide a convenient mechanism for interpretation of the results.

3.4.6 Empirical results

Table 3.6 presents the volatility decompositions expressed in equations (3.34) through (3.36), and Table 3.7 presents the parameter estimates of the model [equations (3.24) through (3.29)]. For all variables except for the Australian dollar, the idiosyncratic factors are most important in explaining the volatility of the returns. The large contribution of the idiosyncratic factors is as expected as returns are less predictable than levels. The common factor is most important to the British pound and the New Zealand dollar, contributing 44.0 and 33.0 per cent of the volatility, respectively. It is not surprising that these two currencies are similar as they seem to be related according to the causality results in Table 3.5. The common factor contributes about 6 per cent to the volatility of the Australian dollar and 0.03 per cent to that of the Canadian dollar. Among the commodity returns, metals are most affected by the common factor (7.6 per cent), with the other commodities affected by less than 4 per cent. These results are reflected in the parameter estimates reported in Table 3.7, which shows that the common factor is significant for the Australian, New Zealand and British currencies, as well as for metal prices. It is also of interest to note that for the commodity currencies the signs for the common-factor parameter estimates are the same (negative). For the commodity prices, the common-factor parameters are also negative, with the exception of beverages; thus all markets (other than those for the pound and beverages) are affected in the same way by the common factor.

The (commodity) currency-market factor has an important role in the volatility of the commodity currencies (Table 3.6). The contribution to volatility for Canada and New Zealand is just under 30 per cent and is approximately 81 per cent for the Australian dollar. The Australian dollar thus seems to dominate movements among the commodity-currency markets, although the contribution of the factor for all three series is quite large. The commodity factor plays a mixed role in explaining volatility in the commodity markets. Agricultural materials, beverages and metals are most affected by the commodity factor, with a contribution of between 20 and 30 per cent to volatility. Food and oil are least affected, although the parameter loading on the parameter for food is significant at the 5 per cent level. Oil is the only commodity for which the commodity factor is not significant, possibly because of the special role that OPEC can play in controlling supply

Table 3.6 *Volatility decomposition of currency and commodity returns* (*percentages*)

Variable	Common factor	Currency factor	Commodity factor	Spillovers from		Idiosync.
				Commodities	Currencies	
A. Currency						
Australian dollar	6.49	80.93		0.44		12.14
Canadian dollar	0.03	29.78		0.69		69.50
New Zealand dollar	32.93	28.67		0.83		37.56
British pound	43.95					56.05
B. Commodity						
Agriculture	1.91		28.64		2.08	67.37
Beverages	2.03		23.54		0.01	74.42
Food	3.92		7.21		5.23	83.64
Metals	7.64		21.09		2.34	68.93
Oil	3.62		2.51		2.71	91.16

and pricing in that market. Similar to the case for the currency factor in relation to currencies, the parameter loadings on the commodity factor for all commodities have the same sign.

Commodity currencies or currency commodities?
The volatility decompositions in Table 3.6 show that commodities are more affected by spillovers from the currency factor than currencies are affected by the commodity factor.[14] This suggests that commodity-exporting nations perhaps do exhibit a small degree of market power. The commodity factor is not significant for the currency of any country, and the contribution of commodity-price movements to the exchange-rate volatilities is close to zero. These results are reinforced by the LR results in Table 3.8. The joint test of the hypothesis that the loadings for the commodity factor in the currency equations are zero [H_0: $\gamma_i =$

---

[14] An additional parameterisation was also estimated whereby a factor common to the commodity currencies and commodity prices was specified to control for joint contemporaneous movements across the two types of markets. The volatility decompositions of this model were quite similar to the ones presented here and the spillover effects much the same.

Table 3.7 *Parameter estimates for currency and commodity returns (p-values in parentheses)*

Variable	Common	Currency	Commodity	Spillovers from Commodities	Spillovers from Currencies	Idiosync.
A. Currency						
Australian dollar	−1.076	−4.337		−0.247		1.682
	(0.031)	(0.000)		(0.579)		(0.108)
Canadian dollar	−0.042	−1.444		−0.169		2.209
	(0.872)	(0.000)		(0.487)		(0.000)
New Zealand dollar	−2.847	−3.033		−0.398		3.478
	(0.000)	(0.000)		(0.417)		(0.000)
British pound	3.023					3.905
	(0.000)					(0.000)
B. Commodity						
Agriculture	−0.676		−2.298		−0.804	4.590
	(0.359)		(0.001)		(0.143)	(0.000)
Beverages	1.359		−4.063		0.113	9.407
	(0.268)		(0.002)		(0.927)	(0.000)
Food	−0.840		−1.001		−1.109	4.439
	(0.142)		(0.042)		(0.030)	(0.000)
Metals	−1.593		−2.325		−1.007	5.474
	(0.030)		(0.000)		(0.118)	(0.000)
Oil	−2.205		−1.613		−2.178	12.660
	(0.124)		(0.215)		(0.092)	(0.000)
ρ_V	0.486					
	(0.008)					
ρ_{CF}		−0.058				
		(0.599)				
ρ_{PCF}			0.641			
			(0.000)			
Log likelihood	−3,390.90					

$0, i = 1,\ldots,m$ in equation (3.24)] cannot be rejected, with a *p*-value of 0.808. Table 3.7 shows that the estimates of these loadings [γ_i in equation (3.24)] have the same sign as those for the commodity-factor loadings for the commodity prices [δ_k in equation (3.28)]. This confirms

Table 3.8 *Likelihood ratio tests of spillover factors*

Hypothesis	LR statistic	p-value
1. Commodity factor in Commodity-currency returns ($H_0 : \gamma_i = 0, \quad \forall i = 1,\ldots,m$)	0.969	0.808
2. Currency factor in commodities returns ($H_0 : \beta_k = 0, \quad \forall k = 1,\ldots,v$)	9.463	0.092*

Note: An asterisk denotes significance at the 10 per cent level.

prior expectations as commodity currencies and commodity prices tend to move in the same direction. The same is generally true for the signs for the currency factor in currency equations and their spillovers into commodities [compare φ_i in equation (3.24) and β_k in equation (3.28)].

The impact of the currency-market factor on commodities is slightly more important but accounts for less than 5.5 per cent of the volatility for all markets. Spillovers to beverages are the least important, with almost no contribution to volatility from the currency factor. This probably reflects the fact that Australia, New Zealand and Canada do not produce the commodities included in the beverages index and have no market power.[15] Spillovers from currency returns to commodities are most important for the returns for food (5.2 per cent), followed by oil (2.7 per cent), metals (2.3 per cent) and agricultural materials (2.1 per cent). The parameter estimates are only significant in the case of food and oil; however, the LR results in Table 3.8 show that the hypothesis that the parameter loadings for the currency factor in the commodity equations are jointly zero [$H_0 : \beta_k = 0$, $k = 1,\ldots,v$ in equation (3.28)] is rejected, with a p-value of 0.092. It is peculiar that the spillovers from currencies to oil prices are significant. However, it should be acknowledged that this result possibly reflects the special nature of oil, including (1) its complementarity in production with many other goods, including other commodities, and (2) the above-mentioned role of OPEC in the operation of the oil market.

[15] For a summary of the commodity-producing countries and their principal exports, see Cashin et al. (2004).

Globalisation and latent factors

The advantage of using the Kalman filter as the estimation methodology is that it provides a time series of each of the factors in the model. This facilitates an analysis of changes in the importance of each factor over time, which is particularly relevant in light of the discussion of Section 3.2 on the effects of globalisation. Section 3.2 concluded that increases in volatility over time may be due to the interaction between the enhanced flexibility of the economy and the commodity-currency nature of its exchange rate. The times series for each factor are not presented here as the factors seem to be quite noisy owing to the returns nature of the data. However, Table 3.9 presents the contribution of each factor over subperiods. The first subperiod is from the beginning of the sample (excluding three observations, one due to construction of the returns data and two due to the initialisation of the factors in the Kalman filter) to quarter 4 of 1982. This breakdown was chosen to coincide with the period prior to deregulation in the financial systems of Australia and New Zealand. The second subperiod extends from quarter 1 of 1983 to quarter 4 of 1990, followed by five-year periods.

Certain patterns are evident in the subperiod decompositions, although the results are quite stable over time. The exchange rates are all more affected by the currency factor over time, and spillovers from the commodity market to currencies become marginally less important. A possible reason for the increasing importance of the currency factor is that commodity-type economies have become more closely linked as globalisation proceeds. That this is reflected more in the currency factor than in the common factor may be because the economies considered compete in the same markets. For commodity returns, the commodity factor is marginally less important over time. Spillovers from currency markets are increasingly important, although again the effects are small relative to the impact of other factors.

3.5 Summary and conclusions

Much research, both theoretical and empirical, into the determination of exchange rates of commodity producers highlights the role of commodity prices. Countries that are commonly thought to

Table 3.9 *Volatility decomposition of currency and commodity-price returns over time (percentages)*

Variable	Common factor	Currency factor	Commodity factor	Spillovers from Commodity	Spillovers from Currency	Idiosync.
A. 1975:Q3 to 1982:Q4						
Australian dollar	13.94	79.38		2.55		4.13
Canadian dollar	0.03	13.80		1.88		84.28
New Zealand dollar	54.80	21.79		3.71		19.69
British pound	49.69					50.31
Agriculture	0.97		34.47		0.45	64.11
Beverages	1.41		38.93		0.00	59.66
Food	1.74		7.61		1.01	89.65
Metals	5.52		36.29		0.73	57.46
Oil	4.09		6.75		1.32	87.84
B. 1983:Q1 to 1990:Q4						
Australian dollar	9.79	84.50		0.88		4.83
Canadian dollar	0.04	28.82		1.28		69.86
New Zealand dollar	39.12	23.59		1.31		35.98
British pound	53.43					46.57
Agriculture	1.74		31.57		1.33	65.36
Beverages	2.31		32.37		0.01	65.32
Food	3.87		8.64		3.65	83.84
Metals	7.49		25.08		1.62	65.81
Oil	3.41		2.87		1.80	91.91
C. 1991:Q1 to 1995:Q4						
Australian dollar	9.26	84.73		0.86		5.15
Canadian dollar	0.04	24.60		1.06		74.31
New Zealand dollar	38.29	24.48		1.32		35.91
British pound	47.05					52.95
Agriculture	1.65		30.64		1.35	66.36
Beverages	1.92		27.68		0.01	70.39
Food	3.85		8.80		3.87	83.48
Metals	7.25		24.89		1.68	66.18
Oil	3.31		2.85		1.87	91.97
D. 1996:Q1 to 2000:Q4						
Australian dollar	8.13	86.47		0.78		4.62
Canadian dollar	0.04	27.63		1.06		71.27

Table 3.9 (*cont.*)

Variable	Common factor	Currency factor	Commodity factor	Spillovers from Commodity	Spillovers from Currency	Idiosync.
New Zealand dollar	35.67	26.50		1.27		36.56
British pound	46.17					53.83
Agriculture	1.64		31.38	1.56		65.42
Beverages	1.77		26.13	0.01		72.10
Food	3.54		8.31	4.13		84.03
Metals	6.96		24.54	1.86		66.63
Oil	2.99		2.65	1.96		92.40
E. 2001:Q1 to 2005:Q3						
Australian dollar	6.65	88.92		0.63		3.80
Canadian dollar	0.03	27.70		0.84		71.44
New Zealand dollar	33.62	31.41		1.18		33.79
British pound	47.22					52.78
Agriculture	1.65		31.53	1.96		64.86
Beverages	1.80		26.53	0.01		71.66
Food	3.41		8.00	4.97		83.62
Metals	6.87		24.17	2.30		66.67
Oil	2.96		2.62	2.42		92.00

have 'commodity currencies' include Australia, Canada and New Zealand, as well as many developing countries that are rich in natural resources. Few previous papers consider the reciprocal case of 'currency commodities', whereby the value of the exchange rate for a commodity-exporting country can have an impact on world commodity prices. This situation can arise if a country (or a group of countries) is a large producer of a commodity and is thus able to influence world prices. This chapter considered issues related to the joint determination of exchange rates and commodity prices. The theoretical framework provided conditions necessary for the existence of a commodity currency and market power in commodity markets, as well as an analysis of the simultaneous working of both effects. Three scenarios were analysed to illustrate the workings of this approach. These were (1) a shift in investor sentiment towards the currency of a commodity-producing country, (2) technological change that created new substitute products for the commodity in question, and

(3) globalisation that injected an added degree of flexibility into the domestic economy.

The empirical section of the chapter examined quarterly real exchange rates and commodity prices since the mid-1970s to reveal evidence of the existence of commodity currencies and currency commodities. The currencies considered were the Australian dollar, the Canadian dollar and the New Zealand dollar, and the commodities were agricultural materials, beverages, food, metals and oil. To identify simultaneous relationships between the two types of assets, a multivariate latent factor model was used. This model allows volatility of the asset returns to be decomposed into a common factor, a currency factor, a commodity factor and spillovers across each type of market. Spillovers from currencies (commodities) to commodities (currencies) were modelled by the lagged impact of the currency (commodity) factor. This approach provided an interesting set of results that seem to challenge conventional thinking regarding the determinants of currency values of commodity-producing countries. The results suggest that there is less evidence that currencies are affected by commodities than commodities are affected by currencies. Spillovers from commodities to currencies contributed less than 1 per cent to the volatility of the currencies, whereas spillovers from currencies to commodities generally contributed between 2 and 5 per cent for commodities. Commodity-currency models that fail to account for the endogeneity between currency values and prices may mislead.

The empirical part of the chapter is an initial exploration of the issues and as such is subject to a set of caveats. First, the commodity-price data were obtained (mostly) from broad indexes complied by the IMF. These price indexes were not specifically tailored to the economies considered in the model. In subsequent research it might be worthwhile to use commodity prices that are more relevant to Australia, Canada and New Zealand (perhaps while also controlling for movements in commodity markets in general through the inclusion of some generic commodity price index). Presumably, the results for the joint impact of currency markets would be stronger, and there may be more spillovers from commodities to the currencies.

Second, rather than examining the joint determination of currencies and commodities in a general framework with a number of currencies and commodities as adopted here, an alternative would be to assess the endogenous determination of a currency and commodity pairing. For example, one hypothesis could be that Australia is a price-maker in the market for iron ore. Our model could be extended to examine this hypothesis in conjunction with the hypothesis that the price of iron ore has an impact on the Australian dollar by examining spillovers from the idiosyncratic factor specific to the exchange rate to the commodity price and vice versa. This framework may indicate evidence of more specific sources of market power.

Third, little attention has been devoted to the role of the terms of trade. The role of the terms of trade is probably an important element in the endogenous determination of exchange rates and commodity prices. Some of the commodities considered are representative of the exports of the countries in the model, and others are imports. Thus, while it would be possible to establish the impact of each commodity on the terms of trade of each country, it would be better to have a series of commodities that are less generic in nature and to also consider the role of other imports that are not commodity-based, such as manufactured goods, to comprehensively analyse this issue.

Future research may explore these matters. Caveats aside, the research has broad implications in a number of areas. The results suggest that it is important for commodity exporters (both producers and countries) to consider the comovement of prices and currency values, which may help to gain a better understanding of the notorious volatility of currency values and commodity prices. Although the majority of volatility in these asset markets results from idiosyncratic factors, common and market-specific factors are also important. The results also suggest that in an increasingly integrated world, the use of the assumption of a small country may need to be reassessed. Apart from the United States, most countries are traditionally assumed to be small. The advantage of our framework is that it provides an indirect method of identifying countries that are large in terms of international trade, that is, those possessing hidden market power in the global pricing of commodities. If volatility in a set of markets has spillover effects on another set of markets, then there is collective evidence of large-country effects. This was the case here with the currency factor jointly specific to Australia, Canada and New Zealand affecting commodity prices.

The results also have implications for risk management by producers and consumers. Within our framework with bidirectional causality, the links between exchange rates and currency prices are stronger than those implied by traditional unidirectional commodity-currency models. With spillovers from one market to another, commodity-price risk cannot be assessed independently of foreign-exchange risk and vice versa. In this context, hedging of these risks is an even more important part of the risk-management strategies of producers and consumers.

The use of factor models in examining the determinants of more than one asset market is a new area of research in the literature on financial market contagion (Dungey and Martin, 2007) and also in the joint determination of bond and equity markets or other macro variables during noncrisis times. The emphasis on the latter style of model is usually on determination of the term structure in conjunction with some other market (Bekaert and Grenadier, 2001; Rudebusch and Wu, 2004; Diebold et al., 2005). This chapter provides another example of the importance of accounting for cross-market linkages. Although the factors derived from the latent factor models cannot be specifically mapped back to observable fundamentals (such as macroeconomic conditions, industry policies, trade agreements, etc.), the advantage is that a sense of the relative importance of each factor can be gleaned. The model also has the advantage of parsimony as the impact of the common factor in each equation (which could be a composite of many common variables) can be measured by just one parameter. This parsimony also has benefits for forecasting of the factors and hence the exchange rates and commodity returns, although this avenue was not pursued here.

Appendix 3A
3A.1 Data sources and codes

Table 3A.1 lists the data sources and codes used for the model.

Table 3A.1 *Data sources and codes*

Variable	Source	Code .
Australian dollar AUD/USD	IMF IFS	193..AG.ZF...
Canadian dollar CND/USD	IMF IFS	156..AE.ZF...
New Zealand dollar NZD/USD	IMF IFS	196..AG.ZF...
British Pound GBP/USD	IMF IFS	112..AG.ZF...
Australian consumer price index	IMF IFS	19364...ZF...
Canadian consumer price index	IMF IFS	15664...ZF...
New Zealand consumer price index	IMF IFS	19664...ZF...
United Kingdom consumer price index	IMF IFS	11264...ZF...
US consumer price index	IMF IFS	11164...ZF...
Agricultural raw materials index	IMF IFS	00176BXDZF...
Beverages index	IMF IFS	00176DWDZF...
Food index	IMF IFS	00176EXDZF...
Metals index	IMF IFS	00176AYDZF...
Oil price index	Datastream	WDI76AADF

References

Amano, R. A., and S. van Norden (1995). 'Terms of Trade and Real Exchange Rates: The Canadian Evidence'. *Journal of International Money and Finance* 14: 83–104.

Asensio, M.-J., and E. Pardos (2002). 'Trade Policy and Spanish Specialisation, 1978–93'. *Journal of International Trade and Economic Development* 11: 163–87.

Bekaert, G., and S. Grenadier (2001). 'Stock and Bond Pricing in an Affine Economy'. NBER Working Paper No. 7346.

Blundell-Wignall, A., J. Fahrer and A. J. Heath (1993). 'Major Influences on the Australian Dollar Exchange Rate'. In A. Blundell-Wignall (ed), *The Exchange Rate, International Trade and the Balance of Payments*. Sydney: Reserve Bank of Australia. pp. 30–78.

Blundell-Wignall, A., and R. G. Gregory (1990). 'Exchange Rate Policy in Advanced Commodity Exporting Countries: Australia and New Zealand'. In V. Argy and P. de Grauwe (eds), *Choosing an Exchange Rate Regime: The Challenge for Smaller Industrial Countries*. Washington, DC: International Monetary Fund. pp. 224–71.

Broda, C. (2004). 'Terms of Trade and Exchange Rate Regimes in Developing Countries'. *Journal of International Economics* 63: 31–58.

Cashin, P., L. F. Céspedes and R. Sahay (2004). 'Commodity Currencies and the Real Exchange Rate'. *Journal of Development Economics* 75: 239–68.

Chen, Y.-C., and K. Rogoff (2003). 'Commodity Currencies'. *Journal of International Economics* 60: 133–60.

Choi, K.-H., and T. Cumming (1986). 'Who Pays for Protection in Australia?' *Economic Record* 62: 490–6.

Clague, C., and D. Greenaway (1994). 'Incidence Theory, Specific Factors and the Augmented Heckscher-Ohlin Model'. *Economic Record* 70: 36–43.

Clements, K. W., and M. Manzur (2002). 'Notes on Exchange Rates and Commodity Prices'. In M. Manzur (ed), *Exchange Rates, Interest Rates and Commodity Prices*. Cheltenham, UK: Elgar. pp. 145–56.

Clements, K. W., and L. A. Sjaastad (1981). 'The Incidence of Protection: Theory and Measurement'. Discussion Paper No. 81.04. Department of Economics, The University of Western Australia, Perth.

(1984). 'How Protection Taxes Exporters'. Thames Essay No. 39. Trade Policy Research Centre, London.

Connolly, M., and J. Devereux (1992). 'Commercial Policy, the Terms of Trade and Real Exchange Rates'. *Oxford Economic Papers* 44: 507–12.

Corden, W. M. (1984). 'Booming Sector and Dutch Disease Economics: Survey and Consolidation'. *Oxford Economic Papers* 36: 359–80.

Corden, W. M., and J. P. Neary (1982). 'Booming Sector and De-Industrialisation in a Small Open Economy'. *Economic Journal* 92: 825–48.

Diebold, F. X., and M. Nerlove (1989). 'The Dynamics of Exchange Rate Volatility: A Multivariate Latent-Factor ARCH Model'. *Journal of Applied Econometrics* 4: 1–22.

Diebold, F. X., M. Piazzesi and G. Rudebusch (2005). 'Modelling Bond Yields in Finance and Macroeconomics'. *American Economic Review*, May: 415–20.

Devereux, J., and M. Connolly (1996). 'Commercial Policy, the Terms of Trade and the Real Exchange Rate Revisited'. Journal of Development Economics 50: 81–99.

Dornbusch, R. (1974). 'Tariffs and Nontraded Goods'. *Journal of International Economics* 4: 177–85.

(1987). 'Exchange Rate Economics'. *Economic Journal* 97: 1–18.

Duffie, D., and K. Singleton. (1993). 'Simulated Moments Estimator of Markov Models of Asset Prices'. *Econometrica* 61: 929–62.

Dungey, M. (1999). 'Decomposing Exchange Rate Volatility Around the Pacific Rim'. *Journal of Asian Economics* 10: 525–35.

Dungey, M., R. A. Fry and V. L. Martin (2003). 'Equity Transmission Mechanisms from Asia to Australia: Interdependence or Contagion?' *Australian Journal of Management* 28: 157–82.

Dungey, M., V. L. Martin and A. R. Pagan (2000). 'A Multivariate Latent Factor Decomposition of International Bond Yield Spreads'. *Journal of Applied Econometrics* 15: 697–715.

Dungey, M., and V. L. Martin (2007). 'Unravelling Financial Market Linkages During Crises'. *Journal of Applied Econometrics* 22: 89–119.

Edwards, S. (1988). *Exchange Rate Misalignment in Developing Countries.* Baltimore, MD: Johns Hopkins University Press.

(1989). *Real Exchange Rates, Devaluation and Adjustment: Exchange Rate Policy in Developing Countries.* Cambridge, MA: MIT Press.

Edwards, S., and S. van Wijnbergen (1987). 'Tariffs, the Real Exchange Rate and the Terms of Trade: On Two Popular Propositions in International Economics'. *Oxford Economic Papers* 39: 458–64.

Fisher, L. (1996). 'Sources of Exchange Rates and Price Level Fluctuations in Two Commodity Exporting Countries: Australia and New Zealand'. *Economic Record* 72: 345–58.

Freebairn, J. (1990). 'Is the $A a Commodity Currency?' In K. W. Clements and J. Freebairn (eds), *Exchange Rates and Australian Commodity Exports.* Perth: Centre of Policy Studies, Monash University, and Economic Research Centre, The University of Western Australia. pp. 180–207.

Gallant, A. R., and G. Tauchen (1996). 'Which Moments to Match?' *Econometric Theory* 12: 657–81.

Gilbert, C. L. (1989). 'The Impact of Exchange Rates and Developing Country Debt on Commodity Prices'. *Economic Journal* 99: 773–84.

(1991). 'The Response of Primary Commodity Prices to Exchange Rate Changes'. In L. Phlips (ed), *Commodity, Futures and Financial Markets.* Dordrecht: Kluwer. pp. 87–124.

Gourieroux, C., A. Monfort and E. Renault (1993). 'Indirect Inference'. *Journal of Applied Econometrics* 8: S85–118.

Greenaway, D. (1989). 'Commercial Policy and Policy Conflict: An Evaluation of the Incidence of the Protection in a Non-Industrialised Economy'. *The Manchester School* 52: 125–41.

Greenaway, D., and C. Milner (1988). 'Intra-Industry Trade and the Shifting of Protection Across Sectors'. *European Economic Review* 32: 927–45.

Gregory, R. G. (1976). 'Some Implications of Growth in the Minerals Sector'. *Australian Journal of Agricultural Economics* 20: 71–91.

Gruen, D. W. R., and T. Kortian (1998). 'Why Does the Australian Dollar Move So Closely with the Terms of Trade?' Discussion Paper 98.26. Department of Economics, The University of Western Australia, Perth.

Gruen, D. W. R., and J. Wilkinson (1994). 'Australia's Real Exchange Rate – Is it Explained by the Terms of Trade or by Real Interest Differentials?' *Economic Record* 70: 204–19.

Hamilton, J. (1994). *Time Series Analysis*. Princeton University Press.

Hansen, L. P. (1982). 'Large Sample Properties of Generalised Method of Moments Estimators'. *Econometrica* 50: 1029–54.

Harvey, A. C. (1981). *The Econometric Analysis of Time Series*. Oxford, UK: Philip Allan.

   (1990). *Forecasting Structural Time Series Models and the Kalman Filter*. Cambridge University Press.

Hatzinikolaou, D., and M. Polasek (2005). 'The Commodity-Currency View of the Australian Dollar'. *Journal of Applied Economics* 8: 81–99.

Irwin, D. (2006). 'Tariff Incidence in America's Gilded Age'. Working Paper. Department of Economics, Dartmouth College, Hanover, NH.

Kalman, R. E. (1960). 'A New Approach to Linear Filtering and Prediction Problems'. *Journal of Basic Engineering, Transactions of the ASE Series D* 82: 35–45.

   (1963). 'New Methods in Weiner Filtering Theory'. In J. L. Bogdanoff and F. Kozin (eds), *Proceedings of the First Symposium of Engineering Applications of Random Function Theory and Probability*. New York: Wiley. pp. 270–88.

Keyfitz, R. (2004). 'Currencies and Commodities: Modelling the Impact of Exchange Rates on Commodity Prices in the World Market'. Working Paper. Development Prospects Group, World Bank, Washington, DC.

Lütkepohl, H. (1993). *Introduction to Multiple Time Series Analysis*, 2nd edn. Heidelberg: Springer-Verlag.

McKenzie, I. M. (1986). 'Australia's Real Exchange Rate During the Twentieth Century'. *Economic Record*. 62 (suppl.): 69–78.

Mahieu, R., and P. Schotman (1994). 'Neglected Common Factors in Exchange Rate Volatility'. *Journal of Empirical Finance* 1: 279–311.

Milner, C., J. Presley and T. Westaway (1995). 'True Protection and the Real Exchange Rate in a Capital-Rich Developing Country: Some Evidence for Saudi Arabia'. *Applied Economics* 27: 623–30.

Neary, J. P. (1988). 'Determinants of the Equilibrium Real Exchange Rate'. *American Economic Review* 78: 210–15.

Panday, P. (2003). 'Incidence Theory and the Shifting of Protection Across Sectors: The South Asian Experience'. *Applied Economics* 35: 125–32.

Pardos, E., and J.-M. Serrano-Sanz (2002). 'The Incidence of Protection on Exports: The Case of Spain, 1870–1913'. *Open Economy Review* 19: 183–203.

Ridler, D., and C. A. Yandle (1972). 'A Simplified Method for Analysing the Effects of Exchange Rate Changes on Exports of a Primary Commodity'. *IMF Staff Papers* 19: 550–78.

Rudebusch, G. D., and T. Wu (2004). 'A Macro-Finance Model of the Term Structure, Monetary Policy, and the Economy'. Working Paper No. 2003–17. Federal Reserve Bank of San Francisco.

Sjaastad, L. A. (1980). 'Commercial Policy "True Tariffs" and Relative Prices'. In J. Black and B. V. Hindley (eds), *Current Issues in Commercial Policy and Diplomacy*. London: Macmillan.

(1985). 'Exchange Rate Regimes and the Real Rate of Interest'. In M. Connolly and J. McDermott (eds), *The Economics of the Caribbean Basin*. New York: Praeger.

(1989). 'Debt, Depression, and Real Rates of Interest in Latin America'. In P. L. Brock, M. Connolly and C. Gonzalez-Vega (eds), Latin American Debt and Adjustment. New York: Praeger.

(1990). 'Exchange Rates and Commodity Prices: The Australian Case'. In K. W. Clements and J. Freebairn (eds), *Exchange Rates and Australian Commodity Exports*. Clayton, Victoria: Center for Policy Studies, Monash University.

(1998a). 'On Exchange Rates, Nominal and Real'. *Journal of International Money and Finance* 17: 407–39.

(1998b). 'Why PPP Real Exchange Rates Mislead'. *Journal of Applied Economics* 1: 179–207.

(1999). 'Exchange Rate Management Under the Current Tri-Polar Regime'. *Singapore Economic Review* 43: 1–9.

(2000). 'Exchange Rate Strategies for Small Countries'. *Zagreb Journal of Economics* 4: 3–33.

(2001). 'Some Pitfalls of Regionalisation'. *The Journal of the Korean Economy* 2(2): 201–9.

Sjaastad, L. A., and M. Manzur. (2003). 'Import Protection, Capital Inflows and Real Exchange Rate Dynamics'. *Journal of Applied Economics* 6: 177–203.

Sjaastad, L. A., and F. Scacciavillani (1996). 'The Price of Gold and the Exchange Rates'. *Journal of International Money and Finance* 15: 879–97.

Snape, R. H. (1977). 'The Effects of Mineral Development on the Economy'. *Australian Journal of Agricultural Economics* 21: 147–56.

Stock, J. H., and M. W. Watson (1991). 'A Probability Model of the Coincident Economic Indicators'. In K. Lahiri and G. H. Moore (eds),

Leading Economic Indicators: New Approaches and Forecasting Records: Cambridge University Press.

Swift, R. (2004). 'Exchange Rate Changes and Endogenous Terms of Trade Effects in a Small Open Economy'. *Journal of Macroeconomics* 26: 737–45.

Zgovu, E. (2003). 'The Implications of Trade Policy and "Natural" Barriers Induced Protection for Aggregate Demand for Imports: Evidence for Malawi'. CREDIT Research Paper No. 03/17. University of Nottingham.

PART II

Commodity prices

4 | *Three facts about marijuana prices*

KENNETH W. CLEMENTS

4.1 Introduction

Over the longer term, higher productivity has led to average annual price decreases for many agricultural products of the order of 1 to 2 per cent. In this chapter, analysis reveals that a similar process seems to have occurred for marijuana, with one important difference. Marijuana prices have decreased much more rapidly than those of most other agricultural products, by approximately 5 per cent per annum in real terms, over the past decade. Research on the behaviour of marijuana prices is of interest owing to widespread use of the product. Surveys indicate that in some countries up to one-third of the adult population have used marijuana, and in Australia, one of the world's greatest consumers, over 40 per cent of people favour its decriminalisation. It has been estimated that expenditure on marijuana by Australians is approximately twice what they spend on wine.[1]

Why have marijuana prices decreased so much? What is the nature of the marijuana market in Australia? To what extent has the decline in marijuana prices been responsible for the high level of consumption? This chapter addresses these issues and argues that there are three defining characteristics of the behaviour of marijuana prices, referred to here as three facts:

- Regional markets seem to exist for marijuana rather than one national market. Prices are substantially more expensive in the Sydney market, followed by Melbourne and Canberra, and then the rest of Australia.

---

[1] For details, see Clements and Daryal (2005). Due to marijuana's illicit status, these are unofficial estimates that are subject to more than the usual degree of uncertainty. Australian marijuana prices have been analysed in the context of the demand for marijuana, tobacco and alcohol by Cameron and Williams (2001) and Zhao and Harris (2003).

- The real price of marijuana has decreased by almost 40 per cent over the 1990s in Australia. As indicated earlier, this decrease is much more than that for most agricultural products. One explanation is the widespread adoption of hydroponic production techniques, which has enhanced productivity and lowered costs. Another explanation is that because of changing community attitudes, laws have become softer and penalties have been reduced, which have thus decreased part of the expected full cost for transacting marijuana.
- Lower prices have stimulated marijuana consumption and reduced alcohol consumption. As marijuana and alcohol both seem to satisfy a similar consumer want, they are probably consumption substitutes. Under reasonable assumptions, lower marijuana prices would have resulted in a substantial increase in marijuana consumption and a corresponding decrease in alcohol consumption.

Section 4.2 provides information regarding data on marijuana prices. Section 4.3 identifies regional markets for marijuana in Australia. The substantial decrease in prices is analysed in depth in Section 4.4 and compared to the price behaviour for other commodities. Section 4.5 provides an exploratory analysis of the extent to which lower prices have encouraged marijuana usage and discouraged the consumption of a substitute product, alcohol. Section 4.6 contains some concluding comments.

4.2 Prices

Data on Australian marijuana prices were obtained from Mark Hazell of the Australian Bureau of Criminal Intelligence (ABCI).[2] These prices were collected by law enforcement agencies in the various states and territories during undercover purchases. In general, the data are quarterly and refer to the period 1990–9 for each state and territory. The different types of marijuana identified separately are leaf, heads, hydroponics, skunk, hash resin and hash oil. However, we focus on prices for only leaf and heads as these products are the most popular. The ABCI (1996) discusses difficulties with such data regarding different recording practices used by the various agencies and missing observations. While it is unlikely that these data constitute a random sample, a

---

[2] This section draws on Clements and Daryal (2001).

common problem when studying the prices of almost any illicit good, it is not clear that they would be biased either upwards or downwards. In any event, they are the only data available.

Prices are usually recorded in the form of ranges, and the basic data are listed in Clements and Daryal (2001). The data were consolidated by (1) using the midpoint of each price range, (2) converting all gram prices to ounce prices by multiplying by twenty-eight, and (3) annualising the data by averaging quarterly or semiannual observations. Annualisation reduces the considerable noise in the quarterly/semiannual data. Plots of the data revealed several outliers that probably reflect some of the above-mentioned recording problems. Observations were treated as outliers if they were either less than half the mean or greater than twice the mean for the corresponding state. This rule led to five outlying observations, which are omitted and replaced with relevant means based on the remaining observations. After consolidation and editing, the data for each state and territory are given in Tables 4.1 and 4.2 for leaf and heads, respectively, purchased in either grams or ounces. Columns 2–5 of Table 4.3 give the corresponding Australian prices (defined as population-weighted means of the state prices), and column 6 gives a weighted mean of the four prices defined as $\exp\left\{\sum_{i=1}^{4} w_i \log p_{it}\right\}$, where p_{it} is the price of product i in year t, and w_i is the market share of product i, 'guestimated' to be 0.06 for leaf/gram, 0.24 for leaf/ounce, 0.14 for head/gram and 0.56 for head/ounce. This is Stone's (1953) weighted geometric mean, with weights reflecting the relative importance of the products in consumption (see Clements, 2002 for full details). Column 6 of Table 4.3 shows that the marijuana price index exhibited a substantial decrease over the 1990s, starting at \$577 per ounce in 1990 and ending some 23 per cent lower nine years later at \$442. This decrease is further addressed in Section 4.4.[3]

A further aspect of the prices in Table 4.3 is the substantial quantity discounts available when buying in bulk. In 1999, for example, the price of heads purchased in grams was \$841 per ounce, whereas

---

[3] Note that the internal relative prices of the four types of marijuana changed quite substantially over the period. On average, the relative price of leaf/gram increased by 4 per cent per annum, head/gram decreased by 1 per cent, leaf/ounce increased by 1 per cent and head/ounce declined by 1 per cent. For details, see Clements (2002).

Table 4.1 *Marijuana prices: leaf (AU$ per ounce)*

Year	NSW	VIC	QLD	WA	SA	NT	TAS	ACT	Weighted mean
				A. Purchased in grams					
1990	770	735	700	802	700	700	910	630	747
1991	1,050	770	700	770	700	700	1,050	642	852
1992	1,060	700	630	700	560	700	700	630	798
1993	583	711	683	653	630	665	613	595	645
1994	998	698	648	700	630	665	443	753	779
1995	1,085	700	560	700	630	735	560	753	797
1996	1,400	793	665	753	630	788	508	700	949
1997	1,400	490	560	653	630	718	525	613	843
1998	1,097	735	630	467	653	683	467	723	798
1999	1,155	636	700	556	630	700	642	700	816
Mean	1,060	697	648	675	639	705	642	674	802
				B. Purchased in ounces					
1990	438	513	225	210	388	275	313	413	390
1991	475	450	215	170	400	275	350	325	381
1992	362	363	188	340	225	300	188	350	313
1993	383	409	168	200	388	281	175	250	326
1994	419	394	181	288	325	244	170	400	341
1995	319	400	400	308	347	294	163	256	350
1996	325	383	350	283	350	263	200	408	339
1997	288	285	431	263	350	288	375	386	320
1998	333	363	375	250	350	300	375	450	344
1999	275	313	444	250	350	300	262	450	322
Mean	362	387	298	256	347	282	257	369	343

the same quantity purchased in ounces was $403 per ounce, a discount of approximately 52 per cent. Such quantity discounts have been observed in other illicit drug markets (Brown and Silverman, 1974; Caulkins and Padman, 1993). One explanation for these discounts involves the pricing of risk (e.g., Brown and Silverman, 1974). It is argued that when drugs are sold in smaller lots, the risk of being caught is not proportionally less than when dealing with larger lots. This leads to an expected penalty that increases with lot size, but less than proportionately, and thus to quantity discounts. Another explanation is that the discounts are simply a reflection of value added as

Table 4.2 *Marijuana prices: heads (AU$ per ounce)*

Year	NSW	VIC	QLD	WA	SA	NT	TAS	ACT	Weighted mean
			A. *Purchased in grams*						
1990	1,120	1,050	1,400	1,120	1,400	700	910	840	1,159
1991	1,120	1,120	1,400	962	1,400	700	1,120	840	1,168
1992	1,400	1,120	910	770	700	700	1,225	770	1,103
1993	863	665	858	840	1,173	700	927	747	834
1994	1,155	770	1,068	840	1,120	770	735	980	992
1995	1,190	793	843	749	1,138	793	1,155	1,033	974
1996	1,171	840	771	704	910	840	963	1,400	944
1997	1,400	858	630	700	840	863	700	793	977
1998	1,120	840	723	630	840	823	723	840	889
1999	1,224	630	589	560	840	840	630	1,006	841
Mean	1,176	869	919	788	1,036	773	909	925	988
			B. *Purchased in ounces*						
1990	600	650	413	600	400	325	525	463	557
1991	600	550	425	502	200	325	450	375	504
1992	375	450	388	390	363	450	425	500	401
1993	500	348	363	431	450	363	344	383	419
1994	550	367	328	400	425	325	363	550	432
1995	538	400	320	354	438	358	350	438	430
1996	550	400	398	325	406	283	388	525	444
1997	550	400	538	300	400	358	383	442	466
1998	488	388	550	275	340	325	367	450	437
1999	513	400	300	250	400	300	325	479	403
Mean	526	435	402	383	382	341	392	461	449

drugs flow through the distribution chain, which operates in exactly the same way as those for licit goods (Brown and Silverman, 1974). Thus, for example, as groceries move from wholesale to retail levels, lots sizes typically decrease, and unit costs increase, which reflects the costs of the retail services provided. For a further discussion, see Clements (2006).

4.3 Fact 1: Marijuana is expensive in New South Wales (NSW)

Is the market for marijuana a nationally organised activity, or is it merely a cottage industry that just satisfies local demand? In other words, is marijuana a (nationally) traded good, or is it nontraded?

Table 4.3 *Marijuana prices in Australia (AU$ per ounce)*

Year	Purchase form				Total (weighted mean)
	Gram		Ounce		
	Leaf	Heads	Leaf	Heads	
(1)	(2)	(3)	(4)	(5)	(6)
1990	747	1,159	390	557	577
1991	852	1,168	381	504	547
1992	798	1,103	313	401	454
1993	645	834	326	419	446
1994	779	992	341	432	475
1995	797	974	350	430	476
1996	949	944	339	444	484
1997	843	977	320	466	489
1998	798	889	344	437	473
1999	816	841	322	403	442
Mean	802	988	343	449	486

If there were a national market for marijuana, then after appropriate allowance for transport costs, etc., marijuana prices should be more or less equalised across states and territories. This section investigates these issues.

South Australia decriminalised marijuana in 1987, and media reports have focussed on Adelaide as the centre of the marijuana industry. Radio National (1999) noted that

Cannabis is by far and away the illicit drug of choice for Australians. There is a multi-billion dollar industry to supply it, and increasingly, the centre of action is the city of churches.

That program quoted a person called 'David' as saying

Say five, ten years ago, everyone spoke of the country towns of New South Wales and the north coast. Now you never hear of it; those towns have died in this regard I'd say, because they've lost out to the indoor variety, the hydro, and everyone was just saying South Australia, Adelaide, Adelaide, Adelaide, and that's where it all seems to be coming from.

In a similar vein, the ABCI (1999, p. 18) commented on marijuana being exported from South Australia to other states as follows:

New South Wales Police reported that cannabis has been found secreted in the body parts of motor vehicles from South Australia.... It is reported that cannabis originating in South Australia is transported to neighbouring jurisdictions. South Australia Police reported that large amounts of cannabis are transported from South Australia by air, truck, hire vehicles, buses and private motor vehicles.

Queensland Police reported that South Australian cannabis is sold on the Gold Coast. New South Wales Police reported South Australian vehicles returning to that state have been found carrying large amounts of cash or amphetamines, or both. It also considers that the decrease in the amount of locally grown cannabis is the result of an increase in the quantity of South Australian cannabis in New South Wales.

The Australian Federal Police in Canberra reported that the majority of cannabis transported to the Australian Capital Territory is from the Murray Bridge area of South Australia.

As the preceding comments point to Adelaide as a major exporter of marijuana to other parts of Australia, this seems to imply that the market is a national and not a local one. In turn, this would mean that marijuana prices would tend to be equalised across Australia if differences in transport and other distribution costs were relatively minor. The validity of this hypothesis can be examined using our regional-level data, and panel A of Table 4.4 gives the results of regressing prices on dummy variables for each state and territory. In this panel, the dependent variable is log p_{rt}, where p_{rt} is the price of the relevant type of marijuana in region r ($r=1, ..., 8$) and year t ($t=1990, ..., 1999$). As the data are pooled over time and regions, the total number of observations for each equation is $8 \times 10 = 80$. Given the use of the logarithm of the price and NSW as the base, when multiplied by 100, the coefficient of a given dummy variable is interpreted as the approximate percentage difference between the price in a region and that in NSW.

In panel A of Table 4.4 there are seven dummy-variable coefficients for each of the four products. Only two of these twenty-eight coefficients are positive, leaf/ounce in Victoria and the Australian Capital Territory (ACT), but neither of these is significantly different from zero. The vast majority of the other coefficients are significantly negative,

Table 4.4 *Estimated regional effects for marijuana prices, income and house prices* $[\log y_{rt} = \alpha + \sum_{u=2}^{8} \beta_u z_{urt}$ *(t-values in parentheses)]*

Dependent variable y_{rt}	Intercept α	Coefficients of dummy variables, $\beta_u \times 100$							$\bar{R}^2$	Regional dispersion $\left[(1/7)\sum_{u=1}^{7}\beta_u^2\right]^{1/2} \times 100$
		VIC	QLD	WA	SA	NT	TAS	ACT		
A. Marijuana prices										
1. Leaf gram	6.94	−39.80	−46.70	−43.40	−47.70	−38.00	−51.20	−42.90	0.44	44.45
	(134.60)	(−5.46)	(−6.41)	(−5.95)	(−6.54)	(−5.21)	(−7.02)	(−5.89)		
2. Leaf ounce	5.88	7.00	−24.60	−34.90	−3.60	−23.70	−37.90	1.40	0.28	23.56
	(77.70)	(0.65)	(−2.30)	(−3.26)	(−0.34)	(−2.22)	(−3.54)	(0.13)		
3. Head gram	7.06	−31.10	−28.00	−40.90	−14.40	−41.40	−27.40	−24.80	0.23	30.96
	(108.30)	(−3.37)	(−3.04)	(−4.44)	(−1.56)	(−4.49)	(−2.97)	(−2.69)		
4. Head ounce	6.26	−20.10	−28.20	−34.50	−33.50	−43.60	−29.80	−13.40	0.28	30.43
	(106.00)	(−2.41)	(−3.37)	(−4.13)	(−4.01)	(−5.22)	(−3.57)	(−1.60)		
B. Income										
5. Gross household	10.11	−2.78	−15.12	−6.98	−13.09	−9.25	−22.06	28.54	0.68	16.23
	(312.47)	(−0.61)	(−3.31)	(−1.52)	(−2.86)	(−2.02)	(−4.82)	(6.24)		
6. Gross house disposable	9.84	−2.41	−14.56	−7.69	−12.24	−4.96	−21.42	30.34	0.67	16.17
	(289.02)	(−0.50)	(−3.03)	(−1.60)	(−2.54)	(−1.03)	(−4.45)	(6.30)		
C. Housing prices										
7. Houses	5.33	−26.94	−47.24	−55.03	−60.63	−33.36	−70.02	−31.72	0.68	48.82
	(120.30)	(−4.30)	(−7.54)	(−8.78)	(−9.68)	(−5.32)	(−11.18)	(−5.06)		
8. Units	5.11	−30.80	−38.95	−65.50	−61.85	−37.39	−72.48	−31.42	0.71	51.02
	(115.40)	(−4.92)	(−6.22)	(−10.46)	(−9.87)	(−5.97)	(−11.57)	(−5.02)		

Notes:

1. The regional dummy variable $z_{urt} = 1$ if $u = r$, 0 otherwise.
2. In all cases the data are annual for the period 1990–9, pooled over the eight regions.
3. Gross household income and gross household disposable income are in terms of nominal dollars per capita.

Sources:

1. Marijuana prices, Tables 4.1 and 4.2.
2. Income, Australian Bureau of Statistics, *Australian National Accounts: State Accounts* (Cat. No. 5220.0, 13 November 2002), Table 27.
3. Housing prices, David Wesney, Manager, Research and Statistics, REIA, Canberra. The data refer to quarterly median sale prices for established houses and units (flats, units and townhouses) in capital cities. The quarterly data are annualised by averaging.

which indicates that marijuana prices are significantly lower in all regions relative to NSW. Although the $\bar{R}^2$ values for these equations are low, this is not necessarily a problem given that the purpose is to test for regional price differences rather than to explain how prices are determined. As the market share is greatest for head ounces (see Section 4.2), we concentrate on the results for this product. Row 4 of Table 4.4 reveals that for this product, the Northern Territory (NT) is the cheapest region, with marijuana costing approximately 44 per cent less here than in NSW. NT is followed by Western Australia (WA; 35 per cent less), South Australia (SA; 34 per cent), Tasmania (30 per cent), Queensland (28 per cent), Victoria (20 per cent) and, finally, the ACT (13 per cent). The last column of Table 4.4 gives a measure of the dispersion of prices around those in NSW, $\{(1/7)\sum_{u=1}^{7}\beta_u^2\}^{1/2} \times 100$, where β_u is the coefficient of the dummy variable for region u. This measure is approximately the percentage standard deviation of prices around NSW prices. If prices are equalised across regions, then this measure is zero. However, the standard deviation ranges from 24 to 44 per cent.

It is clear from the significance of the regional dummies in panel *A* of Table 4.4 that marijuana prices are not equalised nationally. However, this conclusion raises the question as to what possible barriers to interregional trade would prevent prices from being equalised. In other words, what prevents an entrepreneur from buying marijuana in NT and selling it in NSW to realise a (gross) profit of more than 40 per cent for head ounces? Although such a transaction is certainly not risk-free, is a risk premium of more than 40 per cent plausible? Are there other substantial costs to be paid that would rule out arbitraging away the price differential? To what extent do the regional differences in marijuana prices reflect the cost of living in the location where it is sold? Panels *B* and *C* of Table 4.4 explore this issue using per-capita incomes and housing prices as proxies for regional living costs.[4] In panel *B*, we regress the logarithm of income on seven regional dummies. All the coefficients are negative, except those for the ACT. The last column of panel *B* shows that regional dispersion of income is considerably less

---

[4] Although the Australian Bureau of Statistics publishes a consumer price index for each of the six capital cities, these indexes are not harmonised. Accordingly, the levels of the CPI cannot be compared across cities to provide information on the level of regional living costs.

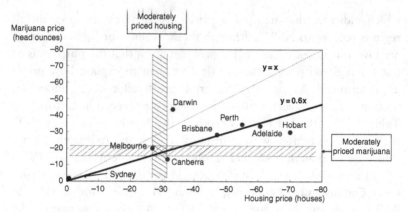

Figure 4.1 Marijuana and housing prices (logarithmic ratio to Sydney ×100; inverted scales).

than that of marijuana prices (approximately half), which could reflect the fiscal equalisation feature of the federal system. Panel C repeats the analysis for housing prices, and the results in the last column show that regional dispersion of housing prices is of the same order of magnitude as for marijuana prices.

Figure 4.1 compares prices for marijuana and housing relative to NSW/Sydney using the regional dummy-variable coefficients for head ounces (row 4 of Table 4.4) and houses (row 7 of Table 4.4). As housing prices refer to the capital city in each region, whereas marijuana prices refer to regions as a whole, for simplicity, we refer to just capital cities rather than regions for marijuana prices and the corresponding capital city for housing prices simultaneously. The broken line from the origin has a slope of 45 degrees, and as the scales of both axes are inverted, the vertical distance between this line and any point is a measure of the difference in the relative housing/marijuana price between the city in question and that in Sydney. This relative price is thus higher for Darwin and lower for the rest of the capital cities. An equivalent way of interpreting the figure is to note that as the two price differences relative to Sydney are equal along the 45-degree line, all points on the line correspond to an elasticity of unity for marijuana prices with respect to housing prices; for the points above (below) the line, the elasticity is greater than (less than) unity. Accordingly, in all cities apart from Darwin, this elasticity is less than unity. The solid line in Figure 4.1 is the least-squares regression line, constrained to pass through the origin.[5] The slope of this line is positive but substantially less than unity. The estimated elasticity is 0.59 and has a standard error of 0.09, so the elasticity is significantly different from both unity and zero. Since the observation for Darwin lies substantially above the regression line, we can say that marijuana prices in that city are cheap given its housing prices or that housing is expensive in view of the cost of marijuana. Among the seven cities other than Sydney, given its housing prices, marijuana would seem to be most overpriced or housing most underpriced in Hobart.[6] The final interesting feature of the figure is that it can be used to naturally divide up Australia into three superregions/cities: (1) NSW/Sydney, with expensive marijuana and housing, (2) Victoria/Melbourne and ACT/Canberra, with moderately priced marijuana and housing, and (3) the rest, with cheap marijuana and housing.

The preceding discussion shows that to the extent that housing costs are a good proxy for living costs, marijuana prices are at least partly related to costs in general. As a substantial part of the overall price of marijuana is likely to reflect local distribution activities, which differ significantly across different regions, this could explain the finding that the market is not a national one but a series of regional markets that are not very closely linked. Our understanding of marijuana pricing can be enhanced if we split the product into (1) a (nationally) traded component comprising mainly the raw product, whose price is likely to be approximately equalised in different regions, and (2) a nontraded component associated with packaging and local distribution, the price of which is less likely to be equalised. As such services are likely to be labour-intensive, their prices will mainly reflect local wages, which, in turn, would partly reflect local living costs. The results of this section point to the importance of the nontraded component of marijuana prices.

[5] As prices are all expressed in terms of logarithmic ratios to Sydney, any fixed effects drop out.
[6] The slope of a line from the origin to any of the seven cities in Figure 4.1 is the elasticity of marijuana prices with respect to housing prices for the city in question. Visually, it is evident that this elasticity is slightly lower for Canberra than for Hobart. However, as this elasticity is the percentage change in marijuana prices for a *unit* percentage change in housing prices, it should not be confused with using the regression line to identify anomalies in marijuana pricing. The *vertical distance* between any observation and the regression line represents the extent of mispricing.

4.4 Fact 2: Marijuana has become substantially cheaper

This section documents the decrease in marijuana prices and explores some possible explanations.[7] Table 4.5 shows that over the 1990s, marijuana prices decreased by approximately 23 per cent in nominal terms (column 2) and by 35 per cent relative to the consumer price index (CPI; column 5). The last entries in columns 10 and 11 of this table reveal that, on average, over the decade, marijuana prices decreased by 4.9 per cent per annum relative to consumer prices and by 5.7 per cent per annum relative to alcohol prices. Regardless of whether the CPI or alcohol prices are used as the deflator, the result is the same: The relative price of marijuana substantially decreased over the period.

How do marijuana prices compare with those of other commodities? In an influential article, Grilli and Yang (1988) analyse the prices of twenty-four internationally traded commodities. We convert these to relative prices (using the US CPI) and then compute the average annual log changes over the period 1914–86. Figure 4.2 gives the price changes for the twenty-four commodities plus marijuana. The striking feature of this graph is that marijuana prices have decreased the most by far. The only commodity to come close is rubber, but its average price decrease is one percentage point less than that for marijuana (−3.9 versus −4.9 per cent per annum). There is a substantial drop-off in the price decreases after rubber (palm oil −2.3 per cent, rice −2.2 per cent, cotton −2.0 per cent, etc.). Surprisingly, the price of tobacco, which might be considered to be related to marijuana in both consumption and production, increased by 0.9 per cent per annum. The price decreases for most of the commodities reflect the impact of productivity enhancement coupled with low income elasticity of demand. In addition, in earlier parts of the twentieth century, the area devoted to agriculture was still increasing in some countries, which would have contributed to the downward pressure on commodity prices.[8]

---

[7] The first part of this section is based on Clements and Daryal (2001), except that here we use population-weighted marijuana prices.

[8] For a further comparison of the evolution of marijuana prices with that of the prices of thirty goods that are not traded (from *The Economist*, 2000–1), the price of light over the past 200 years (Nordhaus, 1997) and the price of personal computers (Berndt and Rappaport, 2001), see Clements (2002). This comparison shows that, on average, only the price of phone calls and PCs fell by more than marijuana prices.

Table 4.5 Marijuana, consumer and alcohol price indexes

Year	Levels					Log change (×100)				
	Nominal prices			Relative prices		Nominal prices			Relative prices	
	MPI	CPI	API	$\frac{MPI}{CPI}$	$\frac{MPI}{API}$	MPI	CPI	API	$\frac{MPI}{CPI}$	$\frac{MPI}{API}$
(1)	(2)	(3)	(4)	(5)	(6)	(7)	(8)	(9)	(10)	(11)
1990	100.00	100.00	100.00	100.00	100.00					
1991	94.80	103.20	104.50	91.90	90.70	-5.34	3.17	4.39	-8.49	-9.73
1992	78.70	104.20	107.50	75.50	73.20	-18.64	0.98	2.85	-19.60	-21.49
1993	77.30	106.10	111.10	72.90	69.60	-1.78	1.80	3.28	-3.58	-5.06
1994	82.30	108.10	114.80	76.20	71.70	6.30	1.88	3.25	4.43	3.05
1995	82.50	113.20	119.30	72.90	69.20	0.21	4.53	3.86	-4.40	-3.65
1996	83.90	116.10	124.20	72.20	67.50	1.67	2.58	4.02	-0.86	-2.36
1997	84.70	116.40	127.30	72.80	66.60	1.03	0.25	2.44	0.77	-1.41
1998	82.00	117.40	128.90	69.80	63.60	-3.33	0.85	1.24	-4.18	-4.57
1999	76.60	118.70	–	64.50	–	-6.78	1.13	–	-7.88	–
Mean	–	–	–	–	–	-2.96	1.91	3.17	-4.87	-5.65

Note: MPI = marijuana price index; CPI = consumer price index; and API = alcohol price index.
Sources: The MPI is from column 6 of Table 4.3 with 1990 = 100; the CPI is from the DX database, rebased such that 1990 = 100; and the API is a levels version of a Divisia index of the prices of beer, wine and spirits from Clements and Daryal (2005).

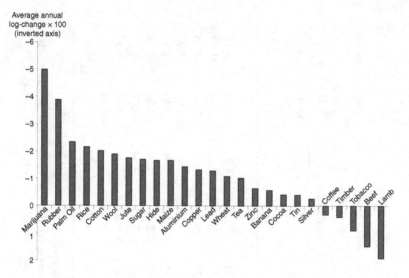

Figure 4.2 Relative price changes for marijuana and other commodities. *Sources:* Marijuana prices, Table 4.5; commodity prices, Grilli and Yang (1998). See Clements (2002) for further details of commodity prices.

Why did marijuana prices fall by so much? One reason is that marijuana growing experienced productivity enhancements on the adoption of hydroponic techniques,[9] which yield a higher-quality product containing higher Δ-9-tetrahydrocannabinol (THC) levels.[10] For example, analyses revealed that hydroponically grown marijuana from northern Tasmania contained 16 per cent THC, whereas that grown outdoors in the south of the state contained 12.8 per cent (ABCI, 1996). The ease of concealment and near-ideal growing conditions that produce good-quality plants are the main reasons for the shift to hydroponic systems. According to the ABCI (1996),

Hydroponic systems are being used to grow cannabis on a relatively large scale. Unlike external plantations, hydroponic cultivation can be used in

---

[9] The word 'hydroponic' means water working. For details of hydroponic techniques, see, e.g., Asher and Edwards (1981) and Ashley's Sister (1997).

[10] The content of the main psychoactive chemical, Δ-9-tetrahydrocannabinol (THC), determines the potency and quality of marijuana. This is evidenced by the fact that flowers (so-called heads or buds), which contain more THC than leaves, are considerably more expensive.

any region and is not regulated by growing seasons. Both residential and industrial areas are used to establish these indoor sites. Cellars and concealed rooms in existing residential and commercial properties are also used.... The use of shipping containers to grow cannabis with hydroponic equipment has been seen in many cases. The containers are sometimes buried on rural properties to reduce chances of detection.

Other anecdotal evidence also points to an increase in hydroponic activity over this period. For example, according to the *Yellow Pages* telephone directory, in 1999, Victoria had 149 hydroponics suppliers, NSW had 115, SA had 69, Queensland had 59 and WA had 58. It is likely that many of these operations supply marijuana growers. For a further discussion of this anecdotal evidence, see Clements (2002).

A second possible reason for the decrease in marijuana prices is that because of changing community attitudes, laws have become softer and penalties have been reduced. Information on the enforcement of marijuana laws distinguishes between (1) infringement notices issued for minor offences and (2) arrests. Table 4.6 presents the available data on infringement notices for the three states/territories that use them, SA, NT and the ACT. It is evident that per-capita infringement notices declined substantially in SA since 1996, increased in NT, and first increased and then declined in the ACT, and declined notably for Australia as a whole, where they decreased by almost 50 per cent. This information points to a lower policing effort. Data on arrests and prosecutions for marijuana offences are given in Table 4.7. Panel A shows that the arrest rate for NSW was more or less stable over the six-year period, whereas that for Victoria decreased substantially due to a 'redirection of police resources away from minor cannabis offences' (ABCI, 1998). For Queensland, the arrest rate increased by more than 50 per cent in 1997 and then fell back to a more or less stable value, but in WA the rate decreased markedly in 1999 with the introduction of a trial scheme of cautioning and mandatory education to 'reduce the resources previously used to pursue prosecutions for simple cannabis offences' (ABCI, 2000). For Australia, the arrest rate decreased from 342 (per 100,000 population) in 1996 to 232 in 2001, a decline of 32 per cent. Data on successful prosecution of marijuana cases for three states are given in panel B of Table 4.7 (data for the other states/territories are not available). For both NSW and SA, the prosecution rate substantially decreased, and lighter sentences became

Table 4.6 *Infringement notices for minor cannabis offences (rate per 100,000 population)*

Year	SA	NT	ACT	Australia
1996	1114	–	96	92
1997	857	124	103	72
1998	725	115	76	60
1999	631	179	49	53
2000	579	401	–	50
2001	580	208	59	48
Mean	748	205	77	63

Sources:
1. Australian Bureau of Criminal Intelligence, *Australian Illicit Drug Report 2001–02*.
2. Australian Bureau of Statistics, *Australian Historical Population Statistics, 2002*.
3. Australian Bureau of Statistics, *Year Book of Australia* (various issues).

much more common. Interestingly, in the early 1990s, the prosecution rate was much higher in SA than in NSW, but by the end of the decade, the rate was approximately the same in the two states. In WA, the prosecution rate was fairly stable, but the period was much shorter. No clear pattern emerges from the information on the percentage of arrests resulting in a successful prosecution, as shown in panel *C* of Table 4.7.

To understand further the evolution of enforcement of marijuana laws, it is useful to consider a simple model. Let p_{it}^r be a penalty of type i ($i=1, 2$ for an infringement notice and an arrest, respectively) in region r ($r=1, ..., 8$) and year t ($t=1996, ..., 2001$). A simple logarithm decomposition of penalties takes the form $\log p_{it}^r = \alpha_r + \beta_i + \gamma_t + \varepsilon_{it}^r$, where α_r is a regional effect, β_i is a penalty effect, γ_t is a time effect and ε_{it}^r is a disturbance term. If we suppose that the time effect is exponential, so that $\gamma_t = \lambda t$, we can then implement this model as a regression equation:

$$\log p_{it}^r = \delta + \sum_{s=2}^{8} \alpha_s z_{sit}^r + \beta x_{it}^r + \lambda t + \varepsilon_{it}^r \qquad (4.1)$$

where $z_{sit}^r = 1$ if $r=s$ and 0 otherwise, $x_{sit}^r = 1$ if $i=$ an infringement and 0 otherwise, and δ, α_s, β and λ are parameters. The value of the regional

Table 4.7 *Arrests and prosecutions for marijuana offences*

Year	NSW	VIC	QLD	WA	SA	NT	TAS	ACT	AUST
			A. Arrests (per 100,000 population)						
1996	238	421	286	795	141	210	531	47	342
1997	227	199	441	713	232	245	228	54	304
1998	245	195	380	633	182	222	253	45	287
1999	247	198	385	330	172	183	156	28	256
2000	220	157	386	363	210	62	170	–	242
2001	211	136	366	389	151	224	223	48	232
Mean	231	218	374	537	181	191	260	37	277
			B. Successful prosecutions (per 100,000 population)						
1991	112	–	–	–	–	–	–	–	–
1992	123	–	–	–	273	–	–	–	–
1993	113	–	–	–	315	–	–	–	–
1994	94	–	–	–	350	–	–	–	–
1995	83	–	–	–	326	–	–	–	–
1996	90	–	–	–	304	–	–	–	–
1997	81	–	–	–	205	–	–	–	–
1998	85	–	–	222	46	–	–	–	–
1999	92	–	–	234	38	–	–	–	–
2000	77	–	–	251	59	–	–	–	–
2001	73	–	–	238	76	–	–	–	–
Mean	93	–	–	236	199	–	–	–	–
			C. Prosecutions/arrests (percentage)						
1996	38	–	–	–	215	–	–	–	–
1997	36	–	–	–	88	–	–	–	–
1998	35	–	–	35	25	–	–	–	–
1999	37	–	–	71	22	–	–	–	–
2000	35	–	–	69	28	–	–	–	–
2001	35	–	–	61	51	–	–	–	–
Mean	36	–	–	59	72	–	–	–	–

Notes:
1. Arrests exclude the issuing of Cannabis Expiation Notices, Simple Cannabis Offence Notices and Infringement Notices, which are used in SA, NT and ACT. For details of these, see Table 4.6.
2. The arrests data for 1996 for SA seem to be problematic and need to be treated with caution. According to the *Australian Illicit Drug Report 2000–2001*, there were 2,076 arrests, which, when divided by the SA population of 1,474,253, yields 141 per 100,000, as reported earlier. However, according to the 2001–2 edition of the above-mentioned publication, arrests for the same state in the same year were 18,477, or 1,253 per 100,000. We used the 141 figure as it seems to be more consistent with data for adjacent years; however, use of this figure leads to a prosecution/arrest rate of 215 per cent, as reported in panel C of this table.

Sources:
1. Australian Bureau of Criminal Intelligence, *Australian Illicit Drug Report 2000–2001*.
2. NSW Bureau of Crime Statistics and Research, *NSW Criminal Courts Statistics, 1991–2001*.
3. Office of Crime Statistics and Research, *Crime and Justice in South Australia, 1992–2001*.
4. The University of WA Crime Research Centre, *Crime and Justice Statistics for Western Australia, 1996–2001*.
5. Australian Bureau of Statistics, *Australian Historical Population Statistics, 2002*.

Table 4.8 *Estimates for the penalty model*
$$[\log p_{it}^r = \delta + \sum_{s=2}^{8} \alpha_s z_{sit}^r + \beta x_{it}^r + \lambda t]$$

Parameter	Estimate	(Standard error)
Intercept δ	165.36	(60.89)
Regional dummies α_s		
VIC	−0.13	(0.12)
QLD	0.47	(0.11)
WA	0.78	(0.12)
SA	0.09	(0.16)
NT	−0.55	(0.20)
TAS	0.03	(0.15)
ACT	−1.78	(0.13)
Infringement dummy β	0.70	(0.16)
Exponential time trend λ	−0.08	(0.03)
R^2	0.81	
Number of observations	63	

Note: The standard errors are White heteroskedasticity-adjusted.

parameter α_s indicates the severity of penalties in region s relative to NSW (the base case); the parameter β denotes the infringement rate in comparison with that of arrests; and λ is the residual exponential trend for all enforcement types in all regions.

Table 4.8 gives estimates of model (4.1) obtained using the data in Tables 4.6 and 4.7. Compared with NSW, Victoria, NT and ACT are all low-penalty regions, whereas the other four regions have higher penalties on average. In Section 4.3 we ranked regions in terms of the cost of marijuana, which can be compared with the severity of penalties as follows:

Cost (cheapest to most expensive):	NT	WA	SA	TAS	QLD	VIC	ACT	NSW
Penalties (weakest to most severe):	ACT	NT	VIC	NSW	TAS	SA	QLD	WA

As the relationship between the two rankings is obviously weak, with major differences for most states, regional disparities in penalties do not seem to be systematically associated with regional price differences. Controlling for regional and time effects, the estimated coefficient for the infringement dummy indicates that these are significantly higher than arrests. The estimated trend term shows that

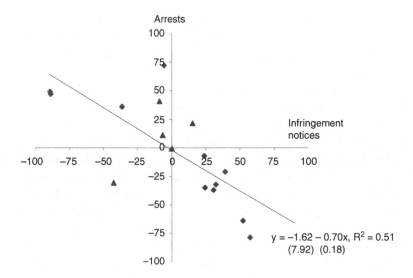

Figure 4.3 Relationship between unexpected arrests and infringement notices (logarithmic ratio of actual to expected ×100).

all penalties decreased on average by approximately 8 per cent per annum, a decrease that is significantly different from zero. Consider the three regions that have infringement notices. To what extent have infringement notices partly displaced arrests? In other words, are the two forms of penalties substitutes for one another? For example, in NT the infringement rate increased from 179 in 1999 to 401 in 2000, whereas over the same period the arrest rate decreased from 183 to 62. This seems to support the idea that the two types of penalties are substitutes. However, to proceed more systematically, we need to control for all the effects of factors determining penalties in model (4.1) by using the residuals and examine the comovement of infringements and arrests in the three regions over the six years. Figure 4.3 is a scatter plot of these residuals, and a significant negative relationship between arrests and infringements is evident. This means that more infringement notices are associated with fewer arrests, with other factors remaining unchanged. This, of course, must have been one of the key objectives for introduction of the infringement regime.

Taken as a whole, the preceding analysis seems to support the idea that participants in the marijuana industry have faced a declining probability of being arrested or successfully prosecuted; even if they are arrested and successfully prosecuted, the expected penalty is now lower. In other words, both the effort devoted to enforcement of existing laws and the penalties seem to have decreased. Accordingly, the expected value of this component of the full cost of marijuana use has decreased. During the period considered, NSW, Victoria, WA and Tasmania all introduced marijuana cautioning programs (ABCI, 2000), and SA, NT and ACT all issued marijuana offence notices. This seems to indicate changing community attitudes towards marijuana associated with the reduced policing effort. It is plausible that this has also led to lower marijuana prices. As the riskiness of buying and selling marijuana has decreased, so may have any risk premium built into prices. This explanation of lower prices has been challenged, however, by Basov et al. (2001), who analyse illicit drug prices in the United States. They show that while drug prohibition enforcement costs have increased substantially over the past twenty-five years, the relative prices of drugs have nonetheless declined. These authors suggest four possible reasons for the decrease in prices: (1) Production costs for drugs have declined, (2) tax and regulatory cost increases have raised the prices of legal goods but not illicit goods such as drugs, (3) the market power of the illicit drug industry has fallen, and (4) technologies to evade enforcement have improved. Although hard evidence is necessarily difficult to obtain, Basov et al. argue against explanations 1 and 2 and favour explanations 3 and 4 as realistic possibilities.[11]

---

[11] Miron (1999) studies the impact of prohibition on alcohol consumption in the United States during 1920–33. Using the death rate from liver cirrhosis as a proxy for alcohol consumption, he finds that prohibition 'exerted a modest and possibly even positive effect on consumption'. This could be because prices fell for reasons given above. However, there are other possibilities, including a highly inelastic demand for alcohol and/or prohibition giving alcohol the status of a 'forbidden fruit', which some consumers might find attractive (Miron, 1999). To shed further light on the impact of prohibition on prices, Miron (2003) also compares the markup from farmgate to retail for cocaine and heroin with that for several legal products. He finds that while the markup for cocaine is high, it is of the same order of magnitude as that for chocolate, coffee, tea and barley/beer. While there are other factors that determine markups, this evidence suggests that illegality per se may not increase drug prices by as much as people might think. On the basis of this and other evidence, Miron (2003, p. 529) concludes that 'the black market price of cocaine is 2–4 times the price that would obtain in a legal market, and of heroin 6–19 times. In contrast, prior research has suggested that cocaine sells at 10 to 40 times its legal price and heroin at hundreds of times its legal price'. Consistent with this line of thinking is research showing that increased

We can summarise this section as follows: First, the relative price of marijuana has decreased substantially, by more than that of many other commodities. Second, two possible explanations for this decline are (1) productivity improvements in marijuana production associated with the adoption of hydroponic techniques and (2) lower expected penalties for buying and selling marijuana. On the basis of the evidence currently available, both explanations seem to be equally plausible.

4.5 Fact 3: Lower prices have boosted marijuana consumption and reduced alcohol consumption

This section explores the likely impact of lower marijuana prices on usage and their role in determining the consumption of a product that shares important common characteristics, alcohol. It should be acknowledged that our price and quantity data for marijuana are imperfect and are subject to more than the usual uncertainties. Moreover, as we have data for only a decade, we are severely constrained in carrying out an econometric analysis of the price responsiveness of consumption. Although Clements and Daryal (2005) attempted such an analysis, in this section we explore the alternative approach of drawing on the literature and putting sufficient structure on the problem to be able to derive numerical values of the price elasticity of demand. This approach is used extensively in the literature on computable general equilibrium (CGE) and equilibrium displacement modelling.

We assume that alcohol and marijuana as a group is weakly separable from all other goods in the consumer's utility function. While this rules out any specific substitutability or complementarity relationships between groups, it is a fairly mild assumption. This assumption means that we can proceed conditionally and analyse consumption within the group independently of the prices of other goods (Clements, 1987). Next, we make the simplifying assumption that tastes with respect to alcohol and marijuana can be characterised by a utility function of the preference-independent form. This means that if there are n goods in the group, the utility function is the sum of n subutility functions, one for each good, $u(q_1, ..., q_n) = \sum_{i=1}^{n} u_i(q_i)$, where q_i is the quantity of good i consumed. 'Preference independence' (PI)

enforcement of drug laws does not seem to result in higher prices (DiNardo, 1993; Weatherburn and Lind, 1997; Yuan and Caulkins, 1998).

means that the marginal utility of each good is independent of the consumption of all others. The implications of PI are that all income elasticities are positive, so inferior goods are ruled out, and all pairs of goods are Slutsky substitutes. The PI hypothesis has been tested using alcohol data for seven countries by Clements et al. (1997). Using a variety of tests, they find that the hypothesis cannot be rejected.[12] There have been nine prior studies of the relationship between alcohol and marijuana consumption, eight for the United States and one for Australia (Cameron and Williams, 2001). Four of the nine studies find substitutability between alcohol and marijuana (Cameron and Williams, 2001; Chaloupka and Laixuthai, 1997; DiNardo and Lemieux, 1992; Model, 1993), two find complementarity (Pacula, 1997, 1998), one finds the relationship to be mostly complementarity (Saffer and Chaloupka, 1998), and two are inconclusive (Saffer and Chaloupka, 1995; Thies and Register, 1993). Thus, while these studies do not give a completely unambiguous picture, the weight of evidence seems to point to alcohol and marijuana being substitutes, which is not inconsistent with the PI assumption.

The further implications of PI are as follows: Let p_i be the price of good i ($i = 1, ..., n$), q_i be the corresponding quantity demanded, $M = \sum_{i=1}^{n} p_i q_i$ be total expenditure ('income' for short), and $w_i = p_i w_i / M$ be the budget share of good i. Furthermore, let $\eta_{ij} = \partial \left(\log q_i \right) / \partial (\log p_j)$ be the compensated elasticity of demand for good i with respect to the price of good j, let ϕ be the price elasticity of demand for the group of goods as a whole, and let η_i be the income elasticity of demand for good i. We then have the fundamental relationship linking the price and income elasticities under PI:

$$\eta_{ij} = \phi \eta_i (\delta_{ij} - w_j \eta_j) \tag{4.2}$$

where δ_{ij} is the Kronecker delta ($\delta_{ij} = 1$ if $1 = j$, 0 otherwise). For the derivation of equation (4.2) and more details, see Clements et al. (1995). We now obtain numerical price elasticity values using equation (4.2) in conjunction with values of ϕ and η_i published in the literature.

Table 4.9 presents income elasticity estimates for three alcoholic beverages, beer, wine and spirits, for several countries, as well as the

---

[12] Earlier studies tended to reject PI [see Barten (1977) for a survey], but it is now understood that the source of many of these rejections was the use of asymptotic tests, which were biased against the null (Selvanathan, 1987, 1993).

Table 4.9 *Demand elasticities for alcoholic beverages*

Country	Sample Period	Income elasticity			Price elasticity of alcohol as a whole
		Beer	Wine	Spirits	
(1)	(2)	(3)	(4)	(5)	(6)
Australia	1955–85	0.81	1.00	1.83	−0.50
Canada	1953–82	0.74	1.05	1.25	−0.42
Finland	1970–83	0.45	1.32	1.32	−1.35
New Zealand	1965–82	0.84	0.88	1.45	−0.44
Norway	1960–86	0.34	1.48	1.55	−0.08
Sweden	1967–84	0.21	0.69	1.52	−1.43
United Kingdom	1955–85	0.82	1.06	1.34	−0.54
Mean		0.60	1.07	1.47	−0.68

Source: Clements et al. (1997).

price elasticity of alcohol as a whole. These elasticity values are derived from estimates of the Rotterdam model under PI. We use them as a guide to income elasticity values for members of the broader group alcohol and marijuana, as set out in Table 4.10. From column 2 of Table 4.10, beer is taken to have an income elasticity of 0.5 (so it is a necessity), wine 1.0 (a borderline case) and spirits 2.0 (a strong luxury). We will return to the elasticity for marijuana. Column 3 gives the four budget shares, which are based on the means given in the last row of Table 4.11. We derive the income elasticity of marijuana from the constraint $\Sigma_{i=1}^{4} w_i \eta_i = 1$. This yields $\eta_4 = 1.2$, as indicated by the last entry of column 2 in Table 4.10, which implies that marijuana is a mild luxury.[13]

---

[13] It is appropriate to say a few words about the consumption data in Table 4.11. The quantity of marijuana consumed is estimated on the basis of the National Drug Strategy Household Survey (various issues), together with some plausible assumptions that link intensity of use to frequency of use; see Clements and Daryal (2005) for details. Although all care was taken in preparing these estimates, and they are not inconsistent with independent estimates, it must be acknowledged that they are likely to be subject to a substantial margin of error. Panel A of Table 4.11 reveals that over the 1990s, per-capita beer consumption decreased from 140 to 117 litres, wine increased from 22.9 to 24.6 litres, spirits increased from 3.87 to 4.32 litres and marijuana consumption increased from 0.765 to 0.788 ounce per capita. In what follows, we analyse the extent

Table 4.10 *Income elasticities and budget shares*

Good (1)	Income elasticity η_i (2)	Budget share w_i (3)
Beer	0.50	0.40
Wine	1.00	0.15
Spirits	2.00	0.15
Marijuana	1.20	0.30

The only remaining parameter on the right-hand side of equation (4.2) to discuss is ϕ, the own-price elasticity of demand for the group (alcohol and marijuana) as a whole. It is evident from equation (4.2) that ϕ acts as a scaling parameter. Prior estimates of ϕ for alcohol are given in column 6 of Table 4.9, and these average -0.7. As marijuana is likely to be a substitute for alcohol, the effect of expanding the group of goods in question from alcoholic beverages to alcohol plus marijuana would be a decrease in absolute value for price elasticity. This means that we should use a $|\phi|$ value of less than 0.7 for the alcohol and marijuana group. Clements and Daryal (2005) estimate ϕ for Australia for alcohol or marijuana to be -0.4; while going in the right direction, this estimate is subject to some qualifications owing to the uncertainties associated with the limited data available. It would thus seem sensible to use several values of ϕ to reflect the genuine uncertainties surrounding the values of this parameter. This approach is pursued in Table 4.12, where we apply equation (4.2) with four values of ϕ. It is evident that the own-price elasticity of marijuana, for example, decreases (in absolute value) from -0.8 (when $\phi = -1.0$) to -0.5 (when $\phi = -0.6$) to -0.2 (when $\phi = -0.3$) to -0.1 (when $\phi = -0.1$).

We now use the cross-price elasticities to simulate consumption under the counterfactual assumption that marijuana prices did not decrease by as much as they did. As alcohol and marijuana are substitutes, this would stimulate consumption of the three beverages and

to which the decrease in marijuana prices caused alcohol consumption to increase at a slower rate than would otherwise be the case. The final thing to note about Table 4.11 is that from panel *D*, the average budget shares are approximately 0.40, 0.15, 0.15 and 0.30 for beer, wine, spirits and marijuana, respectively. Accordingly, expenditure on marijuana is approximately equal to the sum of that on wine and spirits or twice the expenditure on wine.

Table 4.11 *Quantity consumed, price, expenditure and budget share for alcoholic beverages and marijuana*

Year	Beer	Wine	Spirits	Marijuana
A. Quantity (litres or ounces per capita)				
1990	139.9	22.85	3.870	0.7652
1991	134.9	23.01	3.614	0.8278
1992	127.8	23.23	3.595	0.7695
1993	123.8	23.14	3.982	0.7090
1994	122.1	23.19	4.168	0.7120
1995	120.2	22.96	4.130	0.6913
1996	118.7	23.29	4.106	0.7442
1997	117.6	24.18	4.158	0.7575
1998	116.9	24.63	4.318	0.7875
Mean	124.7	23.39	3.990	0.7516
B. Price (AU$ per litre or per ounce)				
1990	3.12	6.80	36.60	577
1991	3.27	6.88	39.06	547
1992	3.36	7.06	40.53	454
1993	3.48	7.27	41.85	446
1994	3.58	7.60	43.04	475
1995	3.72	7.98	44.25	476
1996	3.89	8.31	45.69	484
1997	3.98	8.56	46.71	489
1998	4.02	8.75	47.09	473
Mean	3.60	7.69	42.76	491
C. Expenditure (AU$ per capita)				
1990	435.93	155.40	141.65	441.52
1991	441.26	158.38	141.18	452.81
1992	429.54	163.91	145.71	349.35
1993	430.58	168.25	166.63	316.21
1994	437.48	176.17	179.41	338.20
1995	447.62	183.29	182.77	329.06
1996	461.86	193.45	187.59	360.19
1997	468.17	206.96	194.24	370.42
1998	469.94	215.64	203.33	372.49
Mean	446.93	180.16	171.39	370.03

Table 4.11 (*cont.*)

Year	Beer	Wine	Spirits	Marijuana
		D. Budget share (percentage)		
1990	37.12	13.23	12.06	37.59
1991	36.97	13.27	11.83	37.94
1992	39.46	15.06	13.39	32.09
1993	39.81	15.55	15.41	29.23
1994	38.67	15.57	15.86	29.90
1995	39.17	16.04	15.99	28.80
1996	38.39	16.08	15.59	29.94
1997	37.76	16.69	15.67	29.88
1998	37.26	17.10	16.12	29.53
Mean	38.29	15.40	14.66	31.65

Note: Per capita refers to those fourteen years of age and over.
Sources: The marijuana prices are from column 6 of Table 4.3. All other data are from Clements and Daryal (2005).

cause marijuana usage to increase by a lesser amount. Let q_{it} be the per-capita consumption of good i ($i = 1, 2, 3, 4$, for beer, wine, spirits and marijuana) in year t ($t = 1, ..., T$), and let $Dq_i = \log q_{iT} - \log q_{i,1}$ be the corresponding log change from the first year in the period (1990) to the last (1998). Then, if $\eta_{ij} = \partial(\log q_i)/\partial(\log p_j)$ is the elasticity of consumption of good i with respect to the price of good j, as an approximation, it follows that $Dq_i = \eta_{ij} \times Dp_j$, where Dp_j is the log change in the jth price over the nine years. In the simulation, let all determinants of consumption be unchanged except the price of marijuana, which is specified to take the value $D\hat{p}_4$. The associated simulated value of the change in consumption of good i is then $\eta_{i4}D\hat{p}_4$. This change in consumption holds everything else constant. The impact on consumption of the observed changes in all factors, including the price of marijuana, is incorporated in the observed log change Dq_i. We allow these factors to vary, as in fact they did, but we need to exclude the impact of the observed changes in marijuana prices. Let the observed log change in marijuana prices over the whole period be α. If marijuana prices were constant and the other determinants took their observed values, then the change in consumption of good i would be $Dq_i - \eta_{i4}\alpha$. Adding back the effect due to the simulated price change $D\hat{p}_4$, the simulated change

Table 4.12 *Own- and cross-price elasticity for alcoholic beverages and marijuana*

Good	Beer	Wine	Spirits	Marijuana
	A. $\phi = -1.0$			
Beer	−0.40	0.08	0.15	0.18
Wine	0.20	−0.85	0.30	0.36
Spirits	0.40	0.30	−1.40	0.72
Marijuana	0.24	0.18	0.36	−0.77
	B. $\phi = -0.6$			
Beer	−0.24	0.05	0.09	0.11
Wine	0.12	−0.51	0.18	0.22
Spirits	0.24	0.18	−0.84	0.43
Marijuana	0.14	0.11	0.22	−0.46
	C. $\phi = -0.3$			
Beer	−0.12	0.02	0.05	0.05
Wine	0.06	−0.26	0.09	0.11
Spirits	0.12	0.09	−0.42	0.22
Marijuana	0.07	0.05	0.11	−0.23
	D. $\phi = -0.1$			
Beer	−0.04	0.01	0.02	0.02
Wine	0.02	−0.09	0.03	0.04
Spirits	0.04	0.03	−0.14	0.07
Marijuana	0.02	0.02	0.04	−0.08

Note: The parameter ϕ is the own-price elasticity of demand for alcohol and marijuana as a group. The (i, j)th element in a given panel is η_{ij}, the compensated elasticity of demand for good i with respect to the price of good j.

in consumption of good i over the whole period is

$$D\hat{q}_i = Dq_i + \eta_{i4}(D\hat{p}_4 - \alpha) \qquad (4.3a)$$

As $D\hat{q}_i = \log \hat{q}_{iT} - \log q_{i,1}$ and $Dq_i = \log q_{iT} - \log q_{i,1}$, where $\hat{q}_{iT}$ is simulated consumption of good i in year T, it follows that equation (4.3a) simplifies to

$$\log\left(\frac{\hat{q}_{iT}}{q_{iT}}\right) = \eta_{i4}(D\hat{p}_4 - \alpha) \qquad (4.3b)$$

In words, simulated consumption in the last year relative to actual consumption in that year is equal to the relevant price elasticity applied to the counterfactual change in the price of marijuana, adjusted for the observed change.

To implement equation (4.3b), we go back to Table 4.11, which shows the observed quantities and prices in terms of levels in panels A and B. Columns 2 through 5 of Table 4.13 convert these data to annual log changes. Column 7 contains the Divisia volume and price indexes for alcohol and marijuana as a group, defined as

$$DQ_t = \sum_{i=1}^{4} \bar{w}_{it} Dq_{it}, \quad DP_t = \sum_{i=1}^{4} \bar{w}_{it} Dp_{it} \qquad (4.4a)$$

where $\bar{w}_{it} = (w_{it} + w_{i,t-1})/2$ is the arithmetic average of the ith budget share in years t and $t - 1$, and $Dq_{it} = \log q_{it} - \log q_{i,t-1}$ and $Dp_{it} = \log p_{it} - \log p_{i,t-1}$ are the annual quantity and price log changes. It is evident from the second-last entry in column 7 of panel A that, on average, per-capita consumption of the group decreases by approximately 0.4 per cent per annum. From column 7 of panel B, the price index of the group increases by approximately 1.2 per cent per annum on average, whereas over the whole period 1990–8 the price index increases by 10.0 per cent. Denoting the alcohol group by the subscript A, the within-alcohol version of equation (4.4a) is

$$DQ_{At} = \sum_{i=1}^{3} \left(\frac{\bar{w}_{it}}{1 - \bar{w}_{4t}} \right) Dq_{it}, \quad DP_{At} = \sum_{i=1}^{3} \left(\frac{\bar{w}_{it}}{1 - \bar{w}_{4t}} \right) Dp_{it} \quad (4.4b)$$

It follows from equations (4.4a) and (4.4b) that the two sets of indexes are related according to $DQ_t = (1 - \bar{w}_{4t})DQ_{At} + \bar{w}_{4t}Dq_{4t}$, $DP_t = (1 - \bar{w}_{4t})DP_{At} + \bar{w}_{4t}Dp_{4t}$. The alcohol indexes are presented in column 6 of Table 4.13. According to the price index for alcohol (panel B, column 6), on average, the price of this group increases more rapidly than that of alcohol plus marijuana (column 7) as marijuana prices increase much more slowly (in fact, they decrease on average). Exactly the opposite situation occurs with the volume indexes for the two groups, given in panel A.

We are now in a position to evaluate equation (4.3b) for $i =$ beer, wine, spirits and marijuana. From the last entry in column 5 of Table 4.13, the log change in the price of marijuana α over the whole period 1990–8 is -19.87×10^{-2}. Regarding the counterfactual trajectory of

Table 4.13 *Log changes in quantity consumed and price for alcoholic beverages and marijuana*

Year	Beer	Wine	Spirits	Marijuana	Divisia indexes	
					Alcohol	Alcohol + marijuana
(1)	(2)	(3)	(4)	(5)	(6)	(7)
A. Quantities						
1991	−3.64	0.70	−6.84	7.86	−3.33	0.90
1992	−5.41	0.95	−0.53	−7.30	−3.07	−4.55
1993	−3.18	−0.39	10.22	−8.19	0.22	−2.36
1994	−1.38	0.22	4.57	0.42	0.29	0.33
1995	−1.57	−1.00	−0.92	−2.95	−1.29	−1.78
1996	−1.26	1.43	−0.58	7.37	−0.50	1.82
1997	−0.93	3.75	1.26	1.77	0.65	0.99
1998	−0.60	1.84	3.78	3.88	0.98	1.84
Mean	−2.25	0.94	1.37	0.36	−0.76	−0.35
Sum	−17.96	7.50	10.95	2.87	−6.05	−2.82
B. Prices						
1991	4.85	1.20	6.51	−5.34	4.39	0.72
1992	2.71	2.48	3.69	−18.64	2.85	−4.67
1993	3.42	3.00	3.19	−1.78	3.28	1.73
1994	2.97	4.39	2.82	6.30	3.25	4.15
1995	3.86	4.96	2.77	0.21	3.86	2.79
1996	4.39	3.97	3.19	1.67	4.02	3.33
1997	2.29	3.00	2.22	1.03	2.44	2.02
1998	0.97	2.26	0.80	−3.33	1.24	−0.11
Mean	3.18	3.16	3.15	−2.48	3.17	1.24
Sum	25.47	25.26	25.19	−19.87	25.35	9.95

Note: All entries are to be divided by 100.

marijuana prices, we first assume that they were constant over the period, so $D\hat{p}_4 = 0$. Using these values, together with the elasticities involving marijuana prices η_{i4} given in the last column of Table 4.12, we obtain the counterfactual quantity changes.

Panel *A* of Table 4.14 contains the results. According to the first row of this panel, which is based on the group price elasticity ϕ taking a value of −1.0 , if marijuana prices had been constant over the

Table 4.14 *Counterfactual log changes in quantity consumed for alcoholic beverages and marijuana*

Own-price elasticity of demand for alcohol and marijuana as a group ϕ (1)	Beer (2)	Wine (3)	Spirits (4)	Marijuana (5)
A. Marijuana prices constant ($D\hat{p}_4 = 0$)				
−1.00	3.58	7.15	14.31	−15.26
−0.60	2.15	4.29	8.59	−9.16
−0.30	1.07	2.15	4.29	−4.58
−0.10	0.36	0.72	1.43	−1.53
B. Marijuana and alcohol prices increase at the same rate ($D\hat{p}_4 = 25.35 \times 10^{-2}$)				
−1.00	8.14	16.28	32.56	−34.73
−0.60	4.88	9.77	19.54	−20.84
−0.30	2.44	4.88	9.77	−10.42
−0.10	0.81	1.63	3.26	−3.47

Note: The elements in this table are 100 times the logarithmic ratios of simulated consumption ($\hat{q}_{iT}$) to actual consumption (q_{it}) in year $T = 1998$. They are thus interpreted as approximately equal to the percentage differences between simulated and actual consumption in that year, with the differences attributable to counterfactual marijuana prices, whereby prices are (1) held constant over the period 1990–8 (panel A) and (2) increase at the same rate as alcohol prices over this period (panel B).

whole period, rather than falling by approximately 20 per cent, simulated consumption in 1998 would be approximately 3.6 per cent higher than actual for beer, 7.2 per cent higher than for wine, 14.3 per cent higher than for spirits, and 15.3 per cent lower than for marijuana. The differences among the three alcoholic beverages reflect the values of their elasticities with respect to the price of marijuana. Spirits consumption increases the most as it has the largest cross-price elasticities, with $\eta_{34} = 0.72$ (from the last column of panel A of Table 4.12), followed by wine ($\eta_{24} = 0.36$) and beer ($\eta_{14} = 0.18$). The second, third and fourth rows of panel A of Table 4.14 contain the same results for different values of ϕ. As there are uncertainties about the precise value of this elasticity, as discussed earlier, we adopt the conservative approach of focussing on a $|\phi|$ value that is likely to be on the low side, namely, 0.3. According to this value, beer consumption is higher by 1.1 per cent when marijuana prices are held constant, wine consumption is 2.2 per cent higher, spirits consumption is 4.3 per cent higher, and marijuana consumption is 4.6 per cent lower.

In the second simulation, it was assumed that marijuana prices increased at the same rate as alcohol prices during 1990–8. The last entry in column 6 of Table 4.13 shows that the log change in the alcohol price index over this period was 25.35×10^{-2}, so on the right-hand side of equation (4.3b) we set $D\hat{p}_4 = 25.35 \times 10^{-2}$ and $\alpha = -19.87 \times 10^{-2}$, as before. The results are given in panel B of Table 4.14. Focussing again on the case when $\phi = -0.3$, it is evident that when the relative price of alcohol/marijuana is held constant, beer consumption would be 2.4 per cent higher, wine consumption 4.9 per cent higher, spirits consumption 9.8 per cent higher and marijuana consumption 10.4 per cent lower than actual consumption in 1998. Although these differences are not huge, they are still far from trivial and clearly demonstrate the interrelationships between alcohol and marijuana prices.[14]

4.6 Conclusion

This chapter identified a substantial decrease in the relative price of marijuana over the 1990s and discussed the possible causes and analysed some of the implications. Some regional aspects of the market for marijuana were also investigated. Rather than reiterating the findings, we comment briefly on some of their broader implications:

- By their very nature, illicit goods and services are excluded from official statistics. If the prices of other illicit activities have decreased by as much as marijuana prices, the CPI will be overstated, and real incomes and productivity measures will be understated.
- Further studies of illicit sectors of the economy could be rewarding to gain an understanding of how incentives operate to encourage the adoption of new technology. This might provide some guidance

[14] Note that it follows from equations (4.3a) and (4.3b) that the elements of Table 4.14 are also interpreted as $D\hat{q} - Dq_i$, the difference between $\log(\hat{q}_{iT}/q_{il})$ and $\log(q_{iT}/q_{il})$. Accordingly, we can compute $D\hat{q}_i$ by simply adding the relevant entry in Table 4.14 to Dq_i.

regarding appropriate policies for boosting productivity in legal activities and the identification of impediments to the introduction of technological improvements.

- Our analysis indicates that lower marijuana prices are likely to lead to reduced consumption of a substitute product, alcohol. In some scenarios, this reduction is substantial. Producers of beer, wine and spirits might be tempted to argue that on the basis of considerations of competitive neutrality, marijuana production should be legalised and subject to the same hefty taxes as alcohol products are.
- Suppose that marijuana were legalised and its production taxed. Who would bear most of the burden of this tax, growers or consumers? In view of the apparent ease with which marijuana can now be grown using hydroponic techniques, and because demand is almost surely price-inelastic, it would be consumers who would bear the bulk of the incidence of the tax, not growers. Would this mean that incentives for growers to continue to innovate would remain more or less unchanged in a legalised regime?

References

Asher, C. J., and D. G. Edwards (1981). *Hydroponics for Beginners*. St Lucia: Department of Agriculture, University of Queensland.

Ashley's Sister (1997). *The Marijuana Hydroponic Handbook*. Carlton South: Waterfall.

Australian Bureau of Criminal Intelligence (ABCI) (1996). Australian Illicit *Drug Report 1995–1996*. Canberra: ABCI.

(1998). *Australian Illicit Drug Report 1997–1998*. Canberra: ABCI.

(1999). *Australian Illicit Drug Report 1998–1999*. Canberra: ABCI.

(2000). *Australian Illicit Drug Report 1999–2000*. Canberra: ABCI.

Barten, A. P. (1977). 'The Systems of Consumer Demand Functions Approach: A Review'. *Econometrica* 45: 23–51.

Basov, S., M. Jacobson and J. Miron (2001). 'Prohibition and the Market for Illegal Drugs: An Overview of Recent History'. *World Economics* 2: 133–57.

Berndt, E. R., and N. J. Rappaport (2001). 'Price and Quality of Desktop and Mobile Personal Computers: A Quarter-Century Historical Overview'. *American Economic Review* 91: 268–73.

Brown, G. F., and L. P. Silverman (1974). 'The Retail Price of Heroin: Estimation and Applications'. *Journal of the American Statistical Association* 69: 595–606.

Cameron, L., and J. Williams (2001). 'Cannabis, Alcohol and Cigarettes: Substitutes or Complements?' *Economic Record* 77: 19–34.

Caulkins, J. P., and R. Padman (1993). 'Quantity Discounts and Quality Premia for Illicit Drugs'. *Journal of the American Statistical Association* 88: 748–57.

Chaloupka, F., and A. Laixuthai (1997). 'Do Youths Substitute Alcohol and Marijuana? Some Econometric Evidence'. *Eastern Economic Journal* 23: 253–76.

Clements, K. W. (1987). 'The Demand for Groups of Goods and Conditional Demand'. In H. Theil and K. W. Clements (eds), *Applied Demand Analysis: Results from System-Wide Approaches*. Cambridge, MA: Ballinger. Pp. 163–84.

(2002). 'Three Facts about Marijuana Prices'. Discussion Paper No. 02.10, Department of Economics, The University of Western Australia.

(2006). 'Price and Packaging: The Case of Marijuana'. *The Journal of Business* 79: 2019–44.

Clements, K. W., and M. Daryal (2001). 'Marijuana Prices in Australia in the 1990s'. Discussion Paper No. 01.01, Department of Economics, The University of Western Australia.

(2005). 'The Economics of Marijuana Consumption'. In E. A. Selvanathan and S. Selvanathan (eds), *The Demand for Alcohol, Tobacco, Marijuana: International Evidence*. London: Ashgate. Pp. 243–68.

Clements, K. W., S. Selvanathan and E. A. Selvanathan (1995). 'The Economic Theory of the Consumer'. In E. A. Selvanathan and K. W. Clements (eds), *Recent Developments in Applied Demand Analysis: Alcohol, Advertising and Global Consumption*. Berlin: Springer Verlag. Pp. 1–72.

Clements, K. W., W. Yang and S. W. Zheng (1997). 'Is Utility Additive? The Case of Alcohol'. *Applied Economics* 29: 1163–67.

DiNardo, J. (1993). 'Law Enforcement, the Price of Cocaine and Cocaine Use'. *Mathematical and Computer Modelling* 17: 53–64.

DiNardo, J., and T. Lemieux (1992). 'Alcohol, Marijuana and American Youth: The Unintended Effects of Government Regulation'. Working Paper No. 4212, National Bureau of Economic Research.

Grilli, E. R., and M. C. Yang (1988). 'Primary Commodity Prices, Manufactured Goods Prices, and the Terms of Trade of Developing Countries: What the Long Run Shows'. *World Bank Economic Review* 2: 1–47.

Miron, J. A. (1999). 'The Effect of Alcohol Prohibition on Alcohol Consumption'. Unpublished paper, Department of Economics, Boston University.

(2003). 'The Effects of Drug Prohibition on Drug Prices: Evidence from the Markets for Cocaine and Heroin'. *Review of Economics and Statistics* 85: 522–30.

Model, K. (1993). 'The Effect of Marijuana Decriminalisation on Hospital Emergency Drug Episodes: 1975–1980'. *Journal of the American Statistical Association* 88: 737–47.

National Drug Strategy Household Survey. Computer file, various issues. Social Data Archives, The Australian National University, Canberra.

Nordhaus, W. D. (1997). 'Do Real-Output and Real-Wage Measures Capture Reality? The History of Lighting Suggests Not'. In T. F. Bresnahan and R. J. Gordon (eds), *The Economics of New Goods*. Chicago: The University of Chicago Press. Pp. 29–66.

Pacula, R. L. (1997). 'Does Increasing the Beer Tax Reduce Marijuana Consumption?' *Journal of Health Economics* 17: 577–85.

(1998). 'Adolescent Alcohol and Marijuana Consumption: Is There Really a Gateway Effect?' Working Paper No. 6348, National Bureau of Economic Research.

Radio National (1999). 'Adelaide – Cannabis Capital'. Background Briefing, 28 November. Transcript available at: www.abc.net.au/rn/talks/bbing/stories/s69754.htm. Accessed 7 February 2000.

Saffer, H., and F. Chaloupka (1995). 'The Demand for Illicit Drugs'. Working Paper No. 5238, National Bureau of Economic Research.

(1998). 'Demographic Differentials in the Demand for Alcohol and Illicit Drugs'. Working Paper No. 6432, National Bureau of Economic Research.

Selvanathan, S. (1987). 'A Monte Carlo Test of Preference Independence'. *Economics Letters* 25: 259–61.

(1993). *A System-Wide Analysis of International Consumption Patterns*. Dordrecht: Kluwer.

Stone, J. R. N. (1953). *The Measurement of Consumer Expenditure and Behaviour in the United Kingdom, 1920–1938*, Vol. 1. Cambridge University Press.

The Economist (2000–1). 'The Price of Age'. *The Economist*, 23 December 2000 to 5 January 2001. Pp. 91–94.

Thies, C., and F. Register (1993). 'Decriminalisation of Marijuana and the Demand for Alcohol, Marijuana and Cocaine'. *Social Science Journal* 30: 385–99.

Weatherburn, D., and B. Lind (1997). 'The Impact of Law Enforcement Activity on a Heroin Market'. *Addiction* 92: 557–69.

Yuan, Y., and J. P. Caulkins (1998). 'The Effect of Variation in High-Level Domestic Drug Enforcement on Variation in Drug Prices'. *Socio-Economic Planning Sciences* 32: 265–76.

Zhao, X., and M. N. Harris (2003). 'Demand for Marijuana, Alcohol and Tobacco: Participation, Frequency and Cross-Equation Correlations'. Unpublished paper, Department of Econometrics and Business Statistics, Monash University.

5 | Patterns in world metal prices

MEI-HSIU CHEN AND KENNETH W. CLEMENTS

5.1 Introduction

In recent years, major fluctuations in international commodity markets have once again focussed attention on the nature and functioning of these markets. Major issues include the following questions: How long can high prices be sustained? Is there excessive price volatility? Do prices reflect underlying fundamentals? To what extent has the role of commodities as financial assets changed the way in which they are priced? What is the role of speculators? Do they smooth or amplify price fluctuations? These issues are of direct importance to commodity producers and consumers, as well as to governments in large producing countries that rely on commodities for a substantial part of their revenue. In addition, those who consume food, energy and metal products – that is, everyone – are also indirectly affected by developments in international commodity markets.

These issues can only be properly addressed once there is a clear understanding of exactly what has occurred in commodity markets. In this chapter we make an initial attempt to gain such an understanding using a descriptive statistical approach to identify longer-term patterns, or empirical regularities, in commodity data. In particular, we consider the price behaviour of metals, an important class of commodities, from 1950 to 2010; to avoid being overwhelmed with detail, we confine attention to the sixteen metals that comprise the bulk of global mineral trade. Of these sixteen metals, ten are traded on the London Metal Exchange, a well-organised, deep market. We also examine some related aspects of the behaviour of the corresponding volumes. Our approach is to summarise the data in the form of price and volume indexes and comparison matrices that provide a convenient way of making pairwise comparisons of different metals. Finally, we also present some evidence on the sensitivity of metal prices to variations in supplies.

226

5.2 Sixteen important metals

We consider the sixteen metals listed in column 1 of Table 5.1. The price/volume data are annual for the sixty-one-year period 1950–2010 from the US Geological Survey (USGS).[1] These metals represent the most valuable among the thirty-eight metal commodities included in the USGS data in 2010.[2] Prices are expressed in terms of US dollars per metric tonne (which is equivalent to 1,000 kilograms), whereas volumes are in metric tonnes. Plots of the data are given in Appendix 5A.1.

We define $Dx_t = \log x_t - \log x_{t-1} = \log(x_t/x_{t-1})$ as the log change in any variable $x_t > 0$ from year $t - 1$ to t, which, for small changes, is approximately the annual percentage change when multiplied by 100. Then, if p_{it} and q_{it} are the price and volume of metal i ($i = 1$, ..., 16) in year t ($t = 1$, ..., 61), Dp_{it} and Dq_{it} are the corresponding log changes. These changes over the whole period are summarised in Table 5.1, and several patterns are evident. First, for the majority of the metals, the average rate of price increases is the same order of magnitude as that for volumes; for all the metals, prices increase by an average of approximately 4.4 per cent per annum and volumes by 3.4 per cent (last entries of columns 2 and 7, respectively). Second, the distributions of price changes tend to be skewed to the right as the mean exceeds the median in all but three cases. This pattern does not apply to volumes. Third, the standard deviations in columns 6 and 11 indicate that except for one instance (magnesium), price changes are more volatile than volumes; averaging over all metals, the standard deviation for price changes is approximately 18.0 per cent, whereas that for volumes is 4.8 per cent.

The economic importance of metal i in year t is its value $p_{it}q_{it}$. If $M_t = \Sigma_{i=1}^{16} p_{it}q_{it}$ is the total value of the sixteen metals, then the

---

[1] The USGS provides time-series data for approximately 90 minerals from more than 18,000 mineral producers and consumers around the world. Prices are annual averages of apparent consumption prices, obtained from international trade statistics, whereas volumes refer to world production. See http://minerals.usgs.gov/ds/2005/140/.

[2] The term 'most valuable' refers to volumes multiplied by prices $p_{it}q_{it}$ for $t =$ 2010 in the notation introduced below. There are altogether forty-three metals commodities listed on the USGS online database. However, due to missing price or volume data in the beginning or ending of the period, five metals (boron, bromine, columbium, silicon and tellurium) are discarded, leaving thirty-eight.

Table 5.1 *Summary of logarithmic changes in prices and volumes for sixteen metals, 1950–2010*

	Metal (1)	Prices						Volumes				
		Mean (2)	Median (3)	Minimum (4)	Maximum (5)	SD (6)	Mean (7)	Median (8)	Minimum (9)	Maximum (10)	SD (11)	
1.	Aluminium	2.96	2.86	−41.87	49.00	17.44	5.52	5.91	−11.94	18.90	5.76	
2.	Chromium	5.96	4.99	−54.19	60.36	23.73	3.86	5.85	−23.91	38.26	12.15	
3.	Cobalt	3.97	1.39	−69.31	88.49	29.19	4.21	5.36	−36.41	43.22	14.60	
4.	Copper	4.63	3.59	−33.11	59.44	18.15	3.19	2.84	−5.20	13.86	3.62	
5.	Gold	5.94	0.46	−28.60	68.91	18.27	1.78	1.71	−7.70	11.91	3.84	
6.	Iron ore	5.03	4.57	−15.20	22.92	9.26	3.89	3.90	−9.40	18.08	6.67	
7.	Lead	3.51	3.82	−35.93	48.91	18.26	1.54	0.68	−9.84	17.73	5.07	
8.	Magnesium	3.79	0.00	−31.40	67.16	14.66	4.68	3.06	−61.31	59.66	19.81	
9.	Manganese	5.09	4.98	−55.23	69.31	20.23	2.85	3.59	−18.54	33.38	9.90	
10.	Molybdenum	4.65	2.55	−90.17	113.47	35.04	4.69	4.51	−39.81	42.61	14.23	
11.	Nickel	5.15	4.48	−56.70	104.78	24.72	3.99	4.51	−24.43	30.47	9.82	
12.	Platinum	3.93	4.65	−72.18	53.90	23.49	5.36	4.24	−39.46	22.75	9.80	
13.	Silver	5.49	0.75	−67.36	71.99	23.09	2.16	2.70	−7.26	10.18	3.79	
14.	Sulphur	2.29	0.60	−504.53	372.50	89.31	3.07	2.91	−7.41	31.10	5.77	
15.	Tin	3.83	1.38	−43.84	55.45	19.54	0.79	1.51	−26.83	14.41	7.41	
16.	Zinc	3.33	4.43	−55.08	86.07	21.54	2.87	2.45	−6.56	12.17	3.79	
	All metals	4.35	3.22	−504.53	372.50	18.03	3.40	3.32	−61.31	59.66	4.75	

Note: All entries are to be divided by 100.

relative value of i is the share $w_{it} = p_{it}q_{it}/M_t$, which we shall refer to as the 'value share of i'. The sixteen value shares at the beginning and end of the period are given in columns 2 and 3 of Table 5.2, where, for convenience, metals are now ordered in terms of their shares in 2010. Thus we see that the most important are iron ore, copper, gold and aluminium and that the value of iron ore is now more than twice that of copper. Furthermore, column 4 of the table reveals some rather substantial changes in the value shares over the sixty-one years: For example, zinc accounted for 10.5 per cent of the total in 1950, but this share decreased to 3.6 per cent over the ensuing six decades. Sulphur, tin and lead also experienced similar large decreases. The largest increase was for iron ore, for which the value share increased by 15.5 percentage points to 35.2 per cent in 2010. The last three columns of Table 5.2, which deal with a decomposition of the changes in shares, will be discussed later in this chapter.

5.3 Indexes of prices and volumes

If there are n metals, then $M = \sum_{i=1}^{n} p_i q_i$ is their value, and the value share of i is $w_i = p_i q_i / M$. The differential of the value identity is $dM = \sum_{i=1}^{n} p_i dq_i + \sum_{i=1}^{n} q_i dp_i$ or, using $d(\log x) = dx/x, d(\log M) = \sum_{i=1}^{n} w_i d(\log p_i) + \sum_{i=1}^{n} w_i d(\log q_i)$. We write this as

$$d(\log M) = d(\log P) + d(\log Q) \tag{5.1}$$

where

$$d(\log P) = \sum_{i=1}^{n} w_i d(\log p_i), \qquad d(\log Q) = \sum_{i=1}^{n} w_i d(\log q_i) \tag{5.2}$$

are price and volume indexes. Thus the logarithmic change in value can be conveniently decomposed into price and volume indexes. The price (volume) index is a share-weighted average of the n price (volume) changes and is of the Divisia form. These indexes have an attractively simple sampling interpretation (Theil, 1967, pp. 136–7). We write the price change of metal i, $d(\log p_i)$ as x_i and consider a discrete random

Table 5.2 *Value shares for sixteen metals, 1950–2010*

Metal (1)	Share			Component of change		
	1950 (2)	2010 (3)	Change (4)	Price (5)	Volume (6)	Approximation error (7) = (4) − (5) − (6)
1. Cobalt	0.42	0.48	0.06	−0.17	0.24	−0.02
2. Magnesium	0.40	0.55	0.15	−0.23	0.39	−0.02
3. Sulphur	3.07	0.65	−2.42	−2.57	−0.26	0.41
4. Tin	5.79	0.78	−5.01	−1.52	−4.94	1.45
5. Molybdenum	0.50	1.14	0.64	0.02	0.68	−0.06
6. Platinum	0.52	1.16	0.64	−0.34	1.04	−0.06
7. Lead	7.67	1.34	−6.33	−2.95	−4.75	1.38
8. Silver	2.40	2.00	−0.40	1.18	−1.51	−0.07
9. Chromium	0.85	2.60	1.75	1.41	0.58	−0.24
10. Manganese	2.85	2.83	−0.02	0.84	−0.77	−0.10
11. Zinc	10.50	3.64	−6.86	−5.40	−1.85	0.39
12. Nickel	2.29	4.67	2.38	1.15	1.44	−0.22
13. Aluminium	9.27	12.65	3.38	−10.79	14.57	−0.40
14. Gold	15.71	13.63	−2.08	11.79	−13.37	−0.49
15. Copper	18.07	16.66	−1.41	0.38	−1.20	−0.59
16. Iron ore	19.70	35.22	15.52	7.18	9.70	−1.36
Total	100.00	100.00	0.00	0.00	0.00	0.00

Note: All entries are to be divided by 100.

variable X that can take the n possible values $x_1,\ldots,x_n$. To derive the probabilities for these n realisations, suppose that the names of the metals are drawn at random from this distribution such that each dollar of the total value has an equal chance of being selected. This means that the probability of drawing x_i is w_i, the value share of i. Accordingly, the expected value of the random variable X is $E(X) = \sum_{i=1}^{n} w_i x_i$, which coincides with $d(\log P)$, so the index can be interpreted as the expected value of the distribution of price changes. The volume index $d(\log Q)$ has a similar interpretation.

To apply the indexes to discrete data, we replace (1) the value share w_i with its arithmetic average over years $t-1$ and t, $\bar{w}_{it} = 1/2(w_{it} + w_{i,t-1})$, and (2) $d(\log p_i)$ with the corresponding log change Dp_{it} and similarly for volumes. Thus the discrete versions of the continuous-time indexes (5.2) for the $n=16$ metals are

$$DP_t = \sum_{i=1}^{16} \bar{w}_{it} Dp_{it}, \qquad DQ_t = \sum_{i=1}^{16} \bar{w}_{it} Dq_{it} \qquad (5.3)$$

The results are contained in the top panel of Figure 5.1. The same information is also displayed in panel A of Figure 5.2 and columns 3 and 4 of panel A of Table 5.3 in the form of decade averages. It is evident from Figure 5.2 that prices surged in the 1970s, slumped in the 1990s and accelerated again in the 2000s, whereas volumes exhibited smoother growth.[3] Fisher's factor reversal test requires that the product of the price and volume indexes equal the observed value. In the context of the log-change formulation, this becomes $DM_t = DP_t + DQ_t$, where $DM_t = \log(M_t/M_{t-1})$. It is evident from column 5 of Table 5.3 that while the indexes (5.3) do not satisfy this test exactly, the approximation errors are on the whole modest. Finally, Figure 5.3 presents the indexes (5.3) in level form, obtained by setting them to 100 in the first year and then accumulating the changes, as well as the corresponding level of value. This shows that over the six-decade period, average volumes increased by a factor of approximately 9, prices by a factor of 13, and values by 120 ($\approx 9 \times 13$).

---

[3] The bottom panel of Figure 5.1 and panel B of Figure 5.2 are discussed later in this chapter.

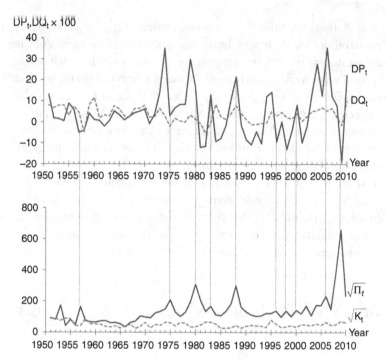

Figure 5.1 Price and volume indexes and dispersion for metals, 1950–2010, changes.

5.4 A decomposition of value shares and volatilities

This section considers a decomposition of the value shares into price and volume components and the volatilities of the prices and volumes.

Using $w_i = p_i q_i / M$, we have $d(\log w_i) = d(\log p_i) + d(\log q_i) - d(\log M)$ or $dw_i = w_i[d(\log p_i) + d(\log q_i) - d(\log M)]$. In view of equation (5.1), $dw_i = w_i[d(\log p_i) - d(\log P) + d(\log q_i) - d(\log Q)]$. This shows that the change in the value share is made up of the sum of two terms, a relative price component and a relative volume component, which can be written as

$$dw_i = w_i d\left(\log \frac{p_i}{P}\right) + w_i d\left(\log \frac{q_i}{Q}\right) \tag{5.4}$$

Using the relative price in this way has the advantage of avoiding monetary units so that both terms on the right-hand side of equation (5.4) are pure numbers, as is the change in the share.

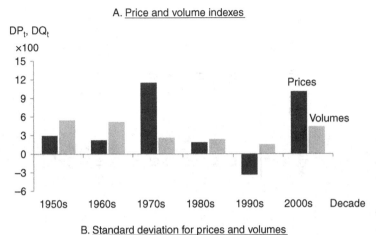

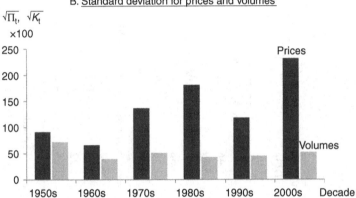

Figure 5.2 Summary of price and volume indexes and dispersion for metals, 1950–2010.

Using the same approach, finite-change data can be applied to decomposition (5.4):

$$\Delta w_{it} = \bar{w}_{it} D\left(\frac{p_{it}}{P_t}\right) + \bar{w}_{it} D\left(\frac{q_{it}}{Q_t}\right) + \text{approximation error}_{it} \quad (5.5)$$

where $\Delta w_{it} = w_{it} - w_{i,t-1}$ and $D(p_{it}/P_t) = Dp_{it} - DP_t$ and similarly for the volume term. The approximation error in equation (5.5) is analogous to that discussed previously. Each element in equation (5.5),

Table 5.3 *Summary of price and volume indexes and volatilities for metals, 1950–2010 (logarithmic change)*

Period (1)	Index of			Approximation error $(2) - (3) - (4)$ (5)	Second-order moment		Price–volume correlation (8)
	Values DM_t (2)	Prices DP_t (3)	Volumes DQ_t (4)		Prices $\sqrt{\Pi_t}$ (6)	Volumes $\sqrt{K_t}$ (7)	
A. Average by decade							
1950–9	8.43	2.96	5.46	0.01	91.48	72.26	0.04
1960–9	7.40	2.22	5.19	0.00	66.37	39.86	0.02
1970–9	14.12	11.51	2.63	−0.02	136.99	51.54	−0.04
1980–9	4.23	1.86	2.38	−0.01	181.43	43.13	0.01
1990–9	−1.84	−3.38	1.54	0.00	118.29	45.52	0.08
2000–10	14.76	10.07	4.41	0.29	231.71	52.63	−0.02
B. Summary statistics over 1950–2010							
Mean	7.96	4.32	3.58	0.05	140.05	50.49	0.02
Median	8.56	3.24	3.13	0.00	123.39	46.81	0.04
Minimum	−16.84	−19.02	−5.22	−0.52	35.05	25.29	−0.62
Maximum	41.06	35.58	11.58	4.24	659.77	89.76	0.63

Note: All entries except those in column 8 are to be divided by 100.

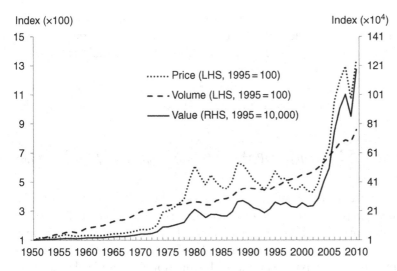

Figure 5.3 Value, price and volume indexes for metals, 1950–2010.

when summed over the n metals, is zero:

$$\sum_{i=1}^{n} \Delta w_{it} = \sum_{i=1}^{n} \bar{w}_{it} D\left(\frac{p_{it}}{P_t}\right) = \sum_{i=1}^{n} \bar{w}_{it} D\left(\frac{q_{it}}{Q_t}\right)$$

$$= \sum_{i=1}^{n} \text{approximation error}_{it} = 0$$

which reflects the "within metals" nature of the decomposition.

To apply equation (5.5) to the sixteen metals, we now measure time in sixty-one-year units so that all changes in this equation are to be interpreted as referring to the transition from 1950 to 2010; the arithmetic average of the value share $\bar{w}_{it}$ now becomes ½($w_{i, 2010} + w_{i, 1950}$). The results are given in columns 5 through 7 of Table 5.2. Consider the case of iron ore (row 16), the share of which increased by 15.5 percentage points over the whole period. This is made up of an increase in its relative price, accounting for a 7.2 percentage point increase, a relative volume growth component of 9.7 points and an approximation error of −1.4 points. The largest decrease in the volume component is for gold (−13.4 points), which is partially offset by its price growth of 11.8 points. Interestingly, this price term for gold is by far the largest among the sixteen metals, whereas the volume term is by far the smallest (or the largest decline). There is a weak tendency for the price and volume components to move in opposite directions, and this is further discussed later in this chapter.

Indexes (5.3) are weighted first-order moments of the distributions of the price and volume log changes. The corresponding second-order moments are

$$\Pi_t = \sum_{i=1}^{16} \bar{w}_{it}(Dp_{it} - DP_t)^2, \qquad K_t = \sum_{i=1}^{16} \bar{w}_{it}(Dq_{it} - DQ_t)^2 \qquad (5.6)$$

These are measures of dispersion in that if each of the sixteen prices move proportionately; for example, then $\Pi_t = 0$; otherwise, $\Pi_t > 0$. As before, prices and volumes are weighted by value shares to recognise the relative economic importance of different metals. These measures are known as 'Divisia variances'. In equation (5.6) and subsequently, the average of the value share $\bar{w}_{it}$ should be interpreted as the arithmetic average of the share in years $t-1$ and t, whereas the price and volume log changes refer to one-year transitions.

Columns 6 and 7 of Table 5.3 give a summary of the square roots of the variances (5.6). This shows that prices are substantially more variable than volumes; on average over the whole period, the standard deviation is approximately 140 per cent per annum for prices and 50 per cent for volumes. This reflects the well-known volatility of prices. The decade averages of the standard deviations are also plotted in panel *B* of Figure 5.2, which shows a substantial increase in price volatility in the 2000s. In addition to the variances (5.6), there is also the corresponding price–volume correlation:

$$\frac{\Gamma_t}{\sqrt{\Pi_t K_t}}, \text{ with } \Gamma_t = \sum_{i=1}^{16} \bar{w}_{it}(Dp_{it} - DP_t)(Dq_{it} - DQ_t)$$

The last column of Table 5.3 reveals that at most times the correlation is close to zero. While prices and volumes are more or less uncorrelated in terms of growth rates, as established in Section 5.6, there is a striking negative relationship between the levels of the two variables.

As mentioned earlier, the upper panel of Figure 5.1 plots the price and volume indexes against time. The lower panel of this figure gives the corresponding volatilities $\sqrt{\Pi_t}$ and $\sqrt{K_t}$. The interesting pattern that emerges is that when there is a large change in the price index DP_t

in either direction, the dispersion of prices increases. This pattern is illustrated by the vertical lines in the figure that identify years of large price changes. This comovement, which does not occur at all times of large changes but does in the majority of cases, is real in that it is not simply an artefact of the way in which the indexes and volatilities are constructed.[4]

5.5 Multimetal matrix (MMM) comparisons

This section systematically compares one metal with another. For n metals, there are $\frac{1}{2} \times n(n-1)$ distinct pairwise comparisons, which can be conveniently arranged in the form of an $n \times n$ matrix $X = [x_{ij}]$. We thus term these 'multimetal matrix' (MMM) comparisons. One specific way to formulate these comparisons would be the dollar value of metal i minus that of metal j, $p_i q_i - p_j q_j$. Obviously, when a metal is compared with itself, the comparison yields zero, so $x_{ii} = 0$, $i = 1$, ..., n. Furthermore, as i compared to j is identical to the comparison of j with i, except for the sign, all pairwise comparisons satisfy a skew-symmetric property; that is, $x_{ij} = -x_{ji}$, $i, j = 1,\ldots,n$. This means that the comparison matrix X is skew symmetric, $X = -X'$.[5]

It is more convenient to use a logarithmic formulation, which yields a comparison matrix X_t for year t that has $x_{ijt} = \log(p_{it}q_{it}) - \log(p_{jt}q_{jt})$ as the (i,j)th element, or

$$x_{ijt} = \log\left(\frac{p_{it}q_{it}}{p_{jt}q_{jt}}\right) = \log\left(\frac{p_{it}}{p_{jt}}\right) + \log\left(\frac{q_{it}}{q_{jt}}\right) \tag{5.7}$$

This shows that each value comparison can be decomposed into corresponding price and volume components. As we have a comparison matrix for each of the sixty-one years, to keep things manageable, we average them to give the average comparison matrix $\overline{X} = 1/61 \cdot \left[\Sigma_{t=1}^{61} x_{ijt}\right]$. For convenience, the sixteen metals are ordered from the most to the least valuable, where, as before, value is interpreted as

---

[4] A similar pattern has been found in consumer prices whereby higher inflation is associated with increased price dispersion. See, for example, Balk (1978), Clements and Nguyen (1981), Foster (1978), Glejser (1965), Parks (1978) and Vining and Eltwertowski (1976).

[5] Clements and Izan (2012) use an analogous matrix comparison approach to analyse the structure of pay schedules. See Appendix 5A.2 for some details of the comparison matrix approach.

the product of price and volume. Table 5.4 contains the upper triangle of this matrix, bordered by an additional row and column. The diagonal elements are suppressed as they are all zero, whereas the elements below the diagonal are to be interpreted as the negative of those above the diagonal. The first row of the table refers to iron ore, and the elements are 31, 39, 72, ..., 379. These numbers are all positive and increasing, which reflects the ordering and the fact that iron ore is the most valuable metal. As the elements are logarithmic differences multiplied by 100, the first number in the row, 31, means that iron ore is approximately 31 per cent more valuable than aluminium (the second most valuable metal), 39 per cent more valuable than copper, 72 per cent more valuable than gold and so on.

The last element in the first row of Table 5.4, 204, is the average of all elements in the row, including the suppressed zero first element. To interpret this row average, average equation (5.7) over $j = 1, ..., 16$:

$$x_{i \cdot t} = \frac{1}{16} \sum_{j=1}^{16} \log \left(\frac{p_{it} q_{it}}{p_{jt} q_{jt}} \right) = \log (p_{it} q_{it}) - \frac{1}{16} \sum_{j=1}^{16} \log (p_{jt} q_{jt}) \qquad (5.8)$$

This $x_{i \cdot t}$ is the logarithmic difference between the value of metal i and the log of the geometric mean of the sixteen values; equivalently, $\exp(x_{i \cdot t})$ is the ratio of the value of i to the geometric mean of the value of all metals. The differences $x_{i \cdot t}$ have a zero sum over the sixteen metals, $\Sigma_{i=1}^{16} x_{i \cdot t} = 0$. The last column of Table 5.4 presents the sixty-one-year averages of these differences for each of the sixteen metals, $\bar{x}_{i \cdot} = 1/61 \cdot \Sigma_{t=1}^{61} x_{i \cdot t}$. Thus the first entry in this column, for example, states that on average for the period the value of iron ore is approximately 204 per cent greater than average for all metals, that of aluminium is 173 per cent greater, that of copper is 165 per cent greater and so on. Since the metals are ordered from the most to the least valuable, the elements in column 18 always decrease as we move down the column and are positive (negative) for above-average (below-average) metals. Manganese and lead are located near the average. The elements in the last column of Table 5.4 are plotted in Figure 5.4. Finally, the last row of Table 5.4 contains the column averages, which are the negatives of the row averages because of the skew symmetry.

We use a similar procedure to construct comparison matrices for prices and volumes, and these are summarised in Table 5.5. This table

Table 5.4 Comparison of average metal values, 1950–2010 (logarithmic difference ×100)

Metal (1)	Iron ore (2)	Aluminium (3)	Copper (4)	Gold (5)	Zinc (6)	Nickel (7)	Manganese (8)	Lead (9)	Tin (10)	Sulphur (11)	Silver (12)	Chromium (13)	Platinum (14)	Molybdenum (15)	Magnesium (16)	Cobalt (17)	Row average (18)
1. Iron ore		31	39	72	140	172	206	219	244	246	253	276	298	334	357	379	204
2. Aluminium			8	41	109	141	175	188	214	215	222	245	268	303	326	348	173
3. Copper				32	101	133	167	180	205	207	214	237	259	295	318	340	165
4. Gold					68	100	135	147	173	174	181	205	227	263	285	307	133
5. Zinc						32	66	79	105	106	113	137	159	195	217	239	64
6. Nickel							35	47	73	74	81	105	127	163	185	207	32
7. Manganese								13	38	40	47	70	92	128	150	173	−2
8. Lead									26	27	34	57	80	115	138	160	−15
9. Tin										1	8	32	54	90	112	135	−40
10. Sulphur											7	30	53	88	111	133	−42
11. Silver												23	46	81	104	126	−49
12. Chromium													22	58	80	103	−72
13. Platinum														36	58	81	−94
14. Molybdenum															22	45	−130
15. Magnesium																22	−153
16. Cobalt																	−175
Column average	−204	−173	−165	−133	−64	−32	2	15	40	42	49	72	94	130	153	175	0

239

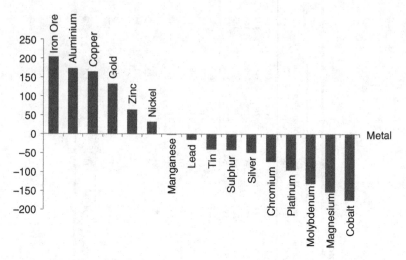

Figure 5.4 Differences in average metal values, 1950–2010 (logarithmic deviation from mean ×100).

has three panels that refer to values, prices and volumes. The last row of panel *A* reproduces the row averages from the last column of Table 5.4. The corresponding decade averages are given in the other six rows of that panel. The value of iron ore, for example, was 226 per cent greater than average in the 1960s and 180 per cent greater than in the 1990s. The values are reasonably stable for the more valuable metals but are more variable for some of the others, such as tin, sulphur and platinum. The standard deviation of these values, given in column 18, decreased modestly over the whole period, from approximately 126 per cent at the beginning to 123 per cent at the end.

Panels *B* and *C* of Table 5.5 compare prices and volumes and are interpreted analogously to panel *A*. As everything is in logs, the elements in the three panels satisfy the identity value = price + volume, which is a reflection of equation (5.7). In the vast majority of cases, for a given metal, prices and volumes have opposite signs, with magnesium the major exception to the rule. Thus a metal with an above-average price has a below-average volume. This negative correlation refers to levels of prices and volumes and is different from the preceding finding for changes over time, for which there was little or no relationship.

Table 5.5 *Summary of average values, prices and volume comparisons, 1950–2010 (logarithmic difference ×100)*

Decade (1)	Metal																SD (18)
	Iron ore (2)	Aluminium (3)	Copper (4)	Gold (5)	Zinc (6)	Nickel (7)	Manganese (8)	Lead (9)	Tin (10)	Sulphur (11)	Silver (12)	Chromium (13)	Platinum (14)	Molybdenum (15)	Magnesium (16)	Cobalt (17)	
A. Values																	
1950–9	205	142	176	122	88	−11	28	71	26	−2	−51	−115	−193	−153	−157	−175	126
1960–9	226	178	182	102	75	24	2	29	9	5	−53	−129	−145	−128	−157	−220	128
1970–9	211	174	169	93	63	45	−22	−4	−5	−18	−48	−88	−104	−101	−169	−195	116
1980–9	199	171	126	158	45	15	−16	−65	−49	22	−21	−58	−64	−156	−143	−163	111
1990–9	180	188	162	172	65	41	1	−54	−97	−71	−66	−32	−42	−164	−137	−146	118
2000–10	203	187	174	147	52	76	−4	−61	−118	−173	−54	−17	−25	−83	−152	−152	123
Average	204	173	165	133	64	32	−2	−15	−40	−42	−49	−72	−94	−130	−153	−175	115
B. Prices																	
1950–9	−522	−97	−69	678	−152	8	−264	−139	56	−405	309	−258	717	70	−64	130	329
1960–9	−505	−97	−63	669	−160	23	−289	−163	75	−408	337	−253	715	88	−60	90	329
1970–9	−515	−128	−74	707	−162	28	−295	−180	89	−458	363	−222	713	92	−75	118	342
1980–9	−513	−141	−117	771	−178	1	−268	−223	74	−414	378	−207	734	38	−62	128	351
1990–9	−534	−138	−96	755	−158	13	−224	−189	35	−496	326	−192	742	23	−53	186	351
2000–10	−523	−148	−84	757	−170	50	−225	−175	22	−581	346	−178	755	103	−86	136	361
Average	−519	−125	−84	723	−164	21	−260	−178	58	−462	343	−218	730	70	−67	131	343
C. Volumes																	
1950–9	727	238	244	−556	240	−19	291	210	−31	403	−359	142	−910	−223	−93	−306	390
1960–9	731	275	244	−567	235	1	291	192	−66	413	−390	124	−860	−217	−98	−310	387
1970–9	725	302	243	−614	226	17	273	176	−94	440	−412	135	−818	−193	−94	−313	388
1980–9	712	312	243	−613	223	13	252	158	−123	435	−399	149	−798	−194	−81	−290	382
1990–9	715	326	258	−583	223	28	225	135	−132	424	−392	160	−784	−186	−84	−332	378
2000–10	726	335	258	−611	221	27	221	114	−140	407	−400	161	−780	−186	−66	−288	378
Average	723	299	249	−591	228	11	258	163	−98	420	−392	146	−824	−200	−86	−306	383

241

Commodity prices

5.6 A simple metals pricing model

Expression (5.8) gives for year t the average of the ith row of the comparison matrix $\mathbf{X}_t$ in terms of values; this is the logarithmic deviation of the value of metal i from the average value of all sixteen metals. We define the analogous price and volume concepts as

$$x^p_{i\cdot t} = \log p_{it} - \frac{1}{16}\sum_{j=1}^{16}\log p_{jt}, \qquad x^q_{i\cdot t} = \log q_{it} - \frac{1}{16}\sum_{j=1}^{16}\log q_{jt} \quad (5.9)$$

which satisfy $x^p_{i\cdot t} + x^q_{i\cdot t} = x_{i\cdot t}$, where $x_{i\cdot t}$ is the value concept defined by equation (5.8).

Next, consider a regression of prices on volumes

$$x^p_{i\cdot t} = \beta x^q_{i\cdot t} + \varepsilon_{it}, \qquad i = 1,\ldots,16; \qquad t = 1,\ldots,T \qquad (5.10)$$

where ε_{it} is a disturbance term, and T is the number of observations. This equation has no intercept as prices and volumes are expressed as deviations from the mean. The logarithmic formulation means that the slope β is the elasticity of price with respect to volume, $\beta = d(\log p_i)/d(\log q_i)$, which is also known as the 'price flexibility'. The least-squares estimator of this flexibility is $\hat{\beta} = \sigma_{p,q}/\sigma^2_q$, where

$$\sigma_{p,q} = \frac{1}{16 \times T}\sum_{i=1}^{16}\sum_{t=1}^{T}\left(\log p_{it} - \frac{1}{16}\sum_{j=1}^{16}\log p_{jt}\right)$$

$$\left(\log q_{it} - \frac{1}{16}\sum_{j=1}^{16}\log q_{jt}\right),$$

$$\sigma^2_q = \frac{1}{16 \times T}\sum_{i=1}^{16}\sum_{t=1}^{T}\left(\log q_{it} - \frac{1}{16}\sum_{j=1}^{16}\log q_{jt}\right)^2$$

are the price–volume covariance and volume variance, respectively.

Figure 5.5 is a scatter plot of $x^p_{i\cdot t}$ against $x^q_{i\cdot t}$ for $i = 1, \ldots, 16, t = 1, \ldots, 61$. The vast majority of the points are scattered around a downward-sloping line with slope of approximately -0.9. Rather than pooling the data over the sixty-one years, we can also estimate the model (5.10) separately for each year, and Table 5.6 summarises these results. It is evident that the estimated slope is reasonably stable and tends to fall

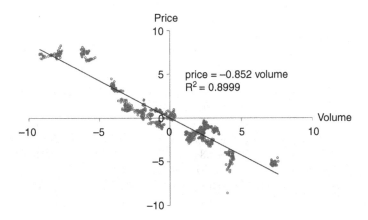

Figure 5.5 Prices and volumes of sixteen metals, 1950–2010.
Notes: This is a scatter plot of prices against volumes for sixteen metals in each of sixty-one years, with both variables measured as the logarithmic difference from the mean. That is, the variable on the vertical axis is $\log p_{it} - 1/16 \cdot \Sigma_{j=1}^{16} \log p_{jt}$, whereas that on the horizontal axis is $\log q_{it} - 1/16 \cdot \Sigma_{j=1}^{16} \log q_{jt}$, for $i = 1, \ldots, 16$, $t = 1, \ldots, 61$.

in the range between -0.8 and -0.9. Thus, if as an approximation we set the price flexibility to -1 and the random disturbance ε_{it} to its expected value of zero, then the model (5.10) takes a very simple form:

$$\log p_{it} = \log \overline{M}_t - \log q_{it} \qquad (5.11)$$

where

$$\log \overline{M}_t = \frac{1}{16} \sum_{i=1}^{16} \log (p_{it} q_{it}) = \log P_t + \log Q_t.$$

The terms $\log P_t$ and $\log Q_t$ are price and volume indexes, defined as $\log P_t = 1/16 \cdot \sum_{i=1}^{16} \log p_{it}$ and $\log Q_t = 1/16 \cdot \sum_{i=1}^{16} \log q_{it}$. Thus $\log \overline{M}_t$ is the log of the geometric mean of values in year t and the sum of (logarithmic) price and volume indexes.

According to equation (5.11), the price of metal i depends on two factors. The first is $\log \overline{M}_t$, which reflects the overall state of the metals market, as measured by values; this indicator of the state of the market contains both aggregate price and volume components. The elasticity of each price with respect to the market is unity, so prices move in

Table 5.6 *Price flexibility for metals, 1950–2010*
$(x_{i \cdot t}^p = \beta_t x_{i \cdot t}^q + \varepsilon_{it}, i = 1, \dots, 16)$

Period (1)	Price flexibility β (2)	R^2 (3)
A. Average by decade		
1950–9	−0.80	0.91
1960–9	−0.81	0.90
1970–9	−0.84	0.91
1980–9	−0.88	0.91
1990–9	−0.88	0.90
2000–10	−0.90	0.89
B. Summary statistics over 1950–2010		
Mean	−0.85	0.90
Median	−0.86	0.90
Minimum	−0.94	0.81
Maximum	−0.77	0.94

Note: The regression equation given at the top of the table is estimated separately for each year. Panel A gives the decade averages of the estimated slope coefficients and R^2 values, whereas panel B summarises the sixty-one estimates of the slopes and R^2 values. For estimates when the data are pooled over the sixty-one years, see Figure 5.5.

proportion to the market. The second term is $-\log q_{it}$, which measures the impact of changes in the volume of metal i on its price; as the corresponding elasticity is −1, the price of a metal is inversely proportional to its volume. If, for example, the overall metals market grows by 10 per cent in a year and the volume of metal i also increases by 10 per cent, then the price of i will remain unchanged. It will increase (decrease) if its volume increases at a slower (faster) rate than that of the overall market. In other words, according to equation (5.11), the price of a metal is a simple sum of a marketwide factor and a metal-specific factor. Alternatively, equation (5.11) can be written as

$$\log p_{it} - \log P_t = -(\log q_{it} - \log Q_t)$$

which expresses the relative price of metal i, $\log p_{it} - \log P_t$, in terms of the corresponding relative volume, $\log q_{it} - \log Q_t$. This shows that the relative price of i decreases (increases) if the relative volume increases (decreases).

Nutting (1977) used the following metal-pricing model:

$$\log p_{it} = \alpha_t + \beta' \log q_{it} + \varepsilon'_{it} \tag{5.12}$$

where ε'_{it} is a disturbance term. Using data for fourteen metals, he obtained an estimated slope coefficient of approximately -0.7. Nutting's work occupies a reasonably prominent place in the literature on metals pricing, and the log-linear model (5.12) is known as 'Nutting's law'. In view of definition (5.9), models (5.10) and (5.12) are the same, with

$$\alpha_t = \frac{1}{16} \sum_{i=1}^{16} \log p_{jt} + \beta \frac{1}{16} \sum_{j=1}^{16} \log q_{jt}, \qquad \beta = \beta', \qquad \varepsilon_{it} = \varepsilon'_{it}$$

This accounts for the similarity between Nutting's result of $\hat{\beta}' \approx -0.7$ and ours of $\hat{\beta}$ falling in the range -0.8 to -0.9.

Returning to Figure 5.5, one notable pattern is the clustering of observations for each metal. This suggests that model (5.10) should be extended by adding a dummy variable for each metal to account for fixed effects:

$$x^p_{i \cdot t} = \alpha_i + \beta x^q_{i \cdot t} + \varepsilon_{it}, \qquad i = 1, \ldots, 16; \qquad t = 1, \ldots, T \tag{5.13}$$

where α_i is the metal-specific intercept. As $\Sigma_{i=1}^{16} x^p_{i \cdot t} = \Sigma_{i=1}^{16} x^q_{i \cdot t} = 0$, the intercepts and disturbances of equation (5.13) satisfy $\sum_{i=1}^{16} \alpha_i = \sum_{i=1}^{16} \varepsilon_{it} = 0.$[6] Table 5.7 contains the results for the whole

---

[6] The least-squares estimates of α_i sum over metals to zero. To show this, it is convenient to write equation (5.13) as $y_{it} = \alpha_i + \beta x_{it} + \varepsilon_{it}, i = 1, \ldots n, t = 1, \ldots T$. Defining $\mathbf{y} = [y_{11}, \ldots, y_{1T}, \ldots, y_{n1}, \ldots, y_{nT}]', \boldsymbol{\alpha} = [\alpha_1, \ldots, \alpha_n], \mathbf{x} = [x_{11}, \ldots, x_{1T}, \ldots, x_{n1}, \ldots, x_{nT}]',$ and $\boldsymbol{\varepsilon} = [\varepsilon_{11}, \ldots, \varepsilon_{1T}, \ldots, \varepsilon_{n1}, \ldots, \varepsilon_{nT}]'$, we have $\mathbf{y} = \mathbf{D}\boldsymbol{\alpha} + \mathbf{x}\beta + \boldsymbol{\varepsilon}$, where $\mathbf{D} = \iota_T \otimes \mathbf{I}_n$ is an $nT \times n$ matrix, ι_T is a $T \times 1$ column vector of unit elements, and $\mathbf{I}_n$ is an $n \times n$ identity matrix. The LS estimators are (Greene, 2008, p. 195) $\hat{\boldsymbol{\alpha}} = [\mathbf{D}'\mathbf{D}]^{-1}\mathbf{D}' \left(\mathbf{y} - \mathbf{x}\hat{\beta} \right)$ and $\hat{\beta} = [\mathbf{x}'\mathbf{M}\mathbf{x}]^{-1}\mathbf{x}'\mathbf{M}\mathbf{y}$, where $\mathbf{M} = \mathbf{I}_{nT} - \mathbf{D}(\mathbf{D}'\mathbf{D})^{-1}\mathbf{D}'$. As $\mathbf{D}'\mathbf{D} = T \cdot \mathbf{I}_n$, we have $\hat{\boldsymbol{\alpha}} = T^{-1}\mathbf{D}'(\mathbf{y} - \mathbf{x}\hat{\beta})$. In scalar terms,

$$\hat{\alpha}_i = T^{-1} \sum_{t=1}^{T} \left(y_{it} - \hat{\beta} x_{it} \right) = \bar{y}_i - \hat{\beta}\bar{x}_i, \quad i = 1, \ldots, n$$

where $\bar{y}_i$ and $\bar{x}_i$ are means over time. As $\sum_{i=1}^{n} y_{it} = \sum_{i=1}^{n} x_{it} = 0$, the estimated fixed effects have a zero sum:

$$\sum_{i=1}^{n} \hat{\alpha}_i = T^{-1} \left[\sum_{i=1}^{n} \sum_{t=1}^{T} y_{it} - \hat{\beta} \sum_{i=1}^{n} \sum_{t=1}^{T} x_{it} \right] = 0.$$

Table 5.7 *Price flexibility for metals and metal-specific intercepts,*
1950–2010 $(x^p_{i \cdot t} = \alpha_i + \beta x^q_{i \cdot t} + \varepsilon_{it}, i = 1, \ldots, 16; t = 1, \ldots, 61)$

Variable (1)	Coefficient (2)	Standard error (3)	t-value (4)	p-value (5)
Volume β	−0.07	0.05	−1.45	0.15
Intercept α_i				
Aluminium	−1.06	0.14	−7.37	0.00
Chromium	−2.08	0.08	−25.78	0.00
Cobalt	1.11	0.15	7.59	0.00
Copper	−0.67	0.12	−5.52	0.00
Gold	6.84	0.27	25.13	0.00
Iron ore	−4.71	0.33	−14.21	0.00
Lead	−1.67	0.09	−19.14	0.00
Magnesium	−0.73	0.06	−12.02	0.00
Manganese	−2.43	0.13	−19.29	0.00
Molybdenum	0.56	0.10	5.54	0.00
Nickel	0.22	0.05	4.67	0.00
Platinum	6.76	0.38	17.91	0.00
Silver	3.17	0.18	17.25	0.00
Sulphur	−4.34	0.20	−22.11	0.00
Tin	0.51	0.06	7.99	0.00
Zinc	−1.49	0.11	−13.10	0.00
R^2	0.99			

period. It is evident that adding the fixed effects causes the estimated
slope coefficient to become nearly zero and insignificant. Owing to the
relatively limited variability of the data over time for each metal (which
is evident in the clustering), the fixed effects act as a substitute for the
volume variable, so when both sets of variables are included, volumes
play little or no role in price determination.

Before concluding this section, some additional comments are appropriate. Regressing prices on volumes treats volumes as exogenous. This
is usually thought to be to a satisfactory approach for agricultural
products with lengthy gestation periods so that current supplies on the
market are more or less unrelated to current prices. For a sampling
interval of one year, a similar argument is also possibly applicable to
metals. In such a case, equations (5.10) through (5.13) are interpreted
as inverse demand models that give the price needed to sell a given

volume of metal. However, they are a special type of inverse demand function as the slope (the price flexibility) is the same for each of the sixteen metals. For a rigorous analysis of this issue, see Chen (2012). If we consider the reciprocal case of regressing volumes on prices, the estimated slope coefficient, $\hat{\lambda}$ say, would be different to the inverse of $\hat{\beta}$ from equation (5.10) or $\hat{\beta}'$ from equation (5.12), but the two regressions would have the same R^2 values, and the slopes would satisfy $\hat{\lambda} \times \hat{\beta} = R^2$. Thus the better the fit, the closer one slope would approximate the inverse of the other. See Berndt (1976) for details on these issues.

Appendix 5A

5A.1 The data

Figure 5A.1 plots the price and volume data for each of the sixteen metals. To facilitate comparisons across metals, the same scale is used for all price and volume log changes. These plots reveal several features. First, for a given metal, the volume tends to increase more steadily than the price. In other words, prices are usually more volatile than volumes, as mentioned in the text. Second, there is a tendency for prices to be more volatile in the second half of the period, a pattern previously identified by Chen (2010). Third, towards the end of the period (2010), the prices of most metals were at or near their peak. Finally, in the last several years, there were large spikes in sulphur prices.

Figure 5A.2 shows histograms of the price and volume changes for the individual metals, whereas Figure 5A.3 contains corresponding histograms for the two indexes.

5A.2 Matrix comparisons

Suppose that we have n numbers ranked in descending order, $y_1, ..., y_n$. This appendix, which is based on Clements and Izan (2012), considers a matrix approach that systematically compares each of these n numbers with all others. Let us compare one value with another in terms of the difference $y_i - y_j$. We can express all pairwise differences in the form of an $n \times n$ matrix:

$$\mathbf{X} = \mathbf{y}\boldsymbol{\iota}' - \boldsymbol{\iota}\mathbf{y}' \qquad (5A.1)$$

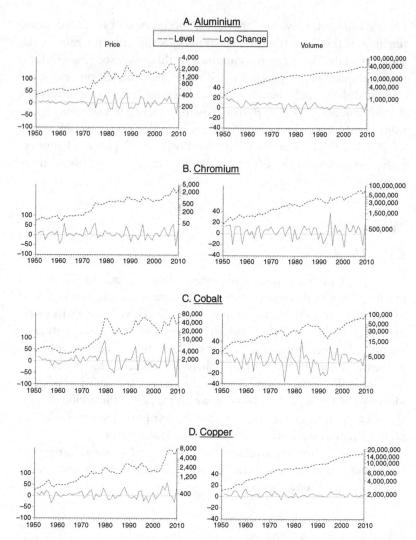

Figure 5A.1 Metal prices and volumes, 1950–2010.
Notes:
1. Prices are nominal in terms of $/tonne, and volumes refer to world production in tonnes.
2. Right-hand axis (log scale) refers to levels; left-hand axis refers to annual log changes × 100.
3. To facilitate presentation, observations with annual logarithmic changes (×100) in price and volume lying outside the ranges [−100, 100] and [−40, 40], respectively, are omitted.

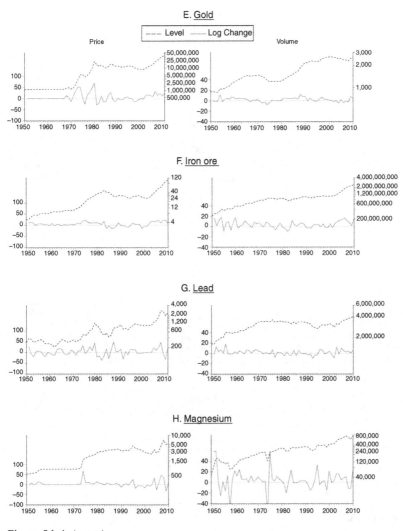

Figure 5A.1 (cont.)

where $\mathbf{y} = [y_1, \ldots, y_n]'$ and $\iota = [1, \ldots, 1]'$ is a vector of n unit elements. Equation (5A.1) defines a comparison matrix.

Consider the ith row of $\mathbf{X}$, $[x_{i1}, \ldots, x_{in}]$. One way in which the information contained in this row can be summarised in terms of one number, call it x_i, is by the value that minimises the sum of squared deviations, $\sum_{j=1}^{n} (x_{ij} - x_i)^2$. This leads to x_i being the mean of the

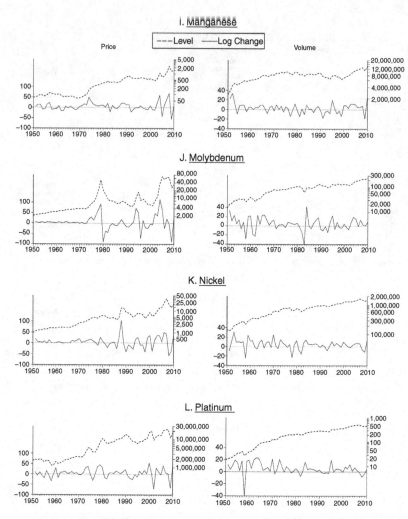

Figure 5A.1 (cont.)

row, which we denote by $\bar{x}_i = (1/n) \sum_{j=1}^{n} x_{ij}$ or $\bar{\mathbf{x}} = (1/n)\mathbf{X}\boldsymbol{\iota}$ for the corresponding vector of n row means. The vector $\bar{\mathbf{x}}$ is a desirable centre-of-gravity measure of the $\mathbf{X}$ matrix in a least-squares sense. Denoting the mean of $y_1, \ldots, y_n$ by

$$\bar{y} = \frac{1}{n} \sum_{j=1}^{n} y_j = \frac{1}{n}\boldsymbol{\iota}'\mathbf{y}$$

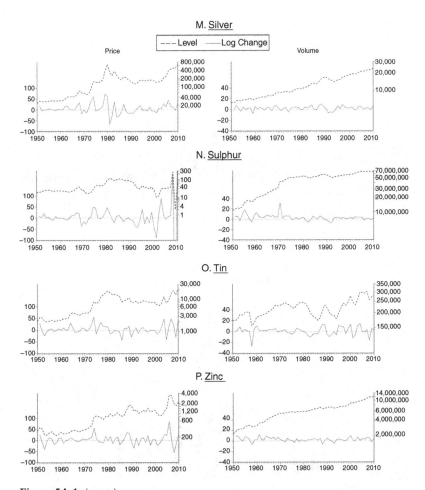

Figure 5A.1 (cont.)

it then follows from definition (5A.1) that the row averages of **X** take the form

$$\bar{\mathbf{x}} = \frac{1}{n}\mathbf{X}\iota = \frac{1}{n}\left(\mathbf{y}\iota' - \iota\mathbf{y}'\right)\iota = \mathbf{y} - \bar{y}\iota \qquad (5A.2)$$

which shows that the averages of the rows of **X** are just the deviations of each element of **y** from the overall mean. Equation (5A.2) can be expressed more compactly as

$$\bar{\mathbf{x}} = \mathbf{M}\mathbf{y}, \qquad \text{with } \mathbf{M} = \mathbf{I} - \frac{1}{n}\iota\iota' \qquad (5A.3)$$

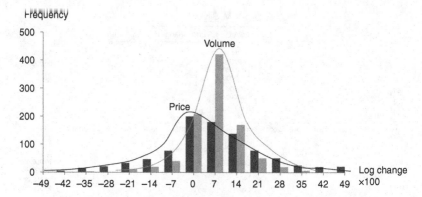

Figure 5A.2 Histogram of logarithmic changes in prices and volumes for sixteen metals, 1950–2010.

Notes: To facilitate presentation, observations with annual logarithmic changes (×100) lying outside the range [−49, 49] are omitted. As a result, forty-eight price and five volume observations are excluded.

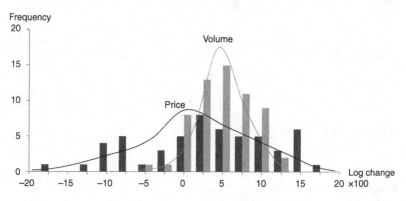

Figure 5A.3 Histogram of logarithmic changes in price and volume indexes, 1950–2010.

Notes: To facilitate presentation, observations with annual logarithmic changes (×100) lying outside the range [−20, 20] are omitted. As a result, six observations are excluded for the price index.

where $\mathbf{M}$ is a symmetric idempotent matrix $\left(\mathbf{M}^2 = \mathbf{M}\right)$ of order $n \times n$ that satisfies $\mathbf{M}\iota = 0$. As $\mathbf{M}$ is symmetric, $\iota'\mathbf{M} = 0'$, which implies that $\iota'\bar{\mathbf{x}} = \iota'\mathbf{M}y = 0$. Thus the sum over all deviations from the mean is zero.

The variance of the elements of **y** is one measure of dispersion:

$$\sigma^2 = \frac{1}{n}\sum_{i=1}^{n}(y_i - \bar{y})^2 = \frac{1}{n}(\mathbf{y} - \bar{y}\iota)'(\mathbf{y} - \bar{y}\iota) = \frac{1}{n}\bar{\mathbf{x}}'\bar{\mathbf{x}} = \frac{1}{n}\sum_{i=1}^{n}\bar{\mathbf{x}}_i^2 \quad (5A.4)$$

where the third step follows from equation (5A.2). Accordingly, the variance of $y_1, \ldots, y_n$ is the average of the sum of the squared row averages of the comparison matrix **X**. Note also that equations (5A.3) and (5A.4) imply that the variance can also be expressed as $\sigma^2 = (1/n)\mathbf{y}'\mathbf{M}'\mathbf{M}\mathbf{y}$, or, since **M** is idempotent,

$$\sigma^2 = \frac{1}{n}\mathbf{y}'\mathbf{M}\mathbf{y} \quad (5A.5)$$

Next, consider the dispersion of the elements of the ith row of **X** about their centre of gravity, as well as their comovement with the elements of some other row. The following variance and covariance provide convenient ways to measure these concepts:

$$\sigma_{ii} = \frac{1}{n}\sum_{j=1}^{n}(x_{ij} - \bar{x}_i)^2, \qquad \sigma_{ik} = \frac{1}{n}\sum_{j=1}^{n}(x_{ij} - \bar{x}_i)(x_{kj} - \bar{x}_k)$$

This σ_{ii} is the variance of the ith row of the **X** matrix, whereas σ_{ik} is the covariance between rows i and k. The matrix $\mathbf{X} - \bar{\mathbf{x}}\iota'$ is **X** expressed as a deviation from the mean vector $\bar{\mathbf{x}}$. The covariance matrix $(1/n)(\mathbf{X} - \bar{\mathbf{x}}\iota')(\mathbf{X} - \bar{\mathbf{x}}\iota')'$ contains on the diagonal the n row variances $\sigma_{11}, \ldots, \sigma_{nn}$ and the cross-row covariances σ_{ik} as the off-diagonal elements. In view of equations (5A.3) and (5A.5), as well as the idempotence of **M**, the covariance matrix takes the form

$$\frac{1}{n}\left(\mathbf{X} - \bar{\mathbf{x}}\iota'\right)\left(\mathbf{X} - \bar{\mathbf{x}}\iota'\right)' = \sigma^2\iota\iota' \quad \text{or} \quad \sigma_{ii} = \sigma_{ik} = \sigma^2, \quad i, k = 1, \ldots, n$$

In words, each row of **X** has a common variance σ^2, and each of the distinct $\frac{1}{2}[n(n-1)]$ covariances also takes this value. The corresponding correlation matrix is $\iota\iota'$, so each correlation is unity.

Definition (5A.1) implies that the mean of the n^2 elements of **X** is zero: $1/n \cdot \sum_{i=1}^{n}\sum_{j=1}^{n}x_{ij} = 1/n \cdot (\iota'\mathbf{X}\iota) = 1/n \cdot (\iota'\mathbf{y}\iota'\iota - \iota'\iota\mathbf{y}'\iota) = 0$. Thus the average sum of squares of these elements is their variance, and it can be shown that this takes the form $(1/n^2)\sum_{i=1}^{n}\sum_{j=1}^{n}x_{ij}^2 = 2\sigma^2$. The multiple 2 here derives from the structure of **X**, which involves all the bivariate comparisons (y_i, y_j), $i, j = 1, \ldots, n$. This means that

y_i is compared with y_j, and reciprocally, y_j is compared with y_i, so the whole matrix contains $x_{ij} = y_i - y_j$ and $x_{ji} = y_j - y_i = -x_{ij}$ for i, $j = 1, ..., n$. Thus, when we square the elements of $\mathbf{X}$, the minus signs disappear, and in essence, each distinct pair (i, j) is included twice in the average sum of squares $(1/n^2) \sum_{i=1}^{n} \sum_{j=1}^{n} x_{ij}^2$.

For some additional results on smoothness, see Clements and Izan (2012).

References

Balk, B. M. (1978). 'Inflation and its Variability: Some Comments and the Dutch Case'. *Economics Letters* 1: 357–60.

Berndt, E. R. (1976). 'Reconciling Alternative Estimates of the Elasticity of Substitution'. *Review of Economic Studies* 58: 50–68.

Chen, M.-H. (2010). 'Understanding World Metals Prices – Returns, Volatility and Diversification'. *Resources Policy* 35: 127–40.

    (2012). 'The Economics of World Metals Markets'. PhD thesis, The University of Western Australia.

Clements, K. W., and H. Y. Izan (2012). 'The Pay Parity Matrix: A Tool for Analysing the Structure of Pay'. *Applied Economics* 44: 4515–25.

Clements, K. W., and P. Nguyen (1981). 'Inflation and Relative Prices: A System-Wide Approach'. *Economics Letters* 7: 131–7.

Foster, E. (1978). 'The Variability of Inflation'. *Review of Economics and Statistics* 60: 346–50.

Glejser, H. (1965). 'Inflation, Productivity and Relative Prices: A Statistical Study'. *Review of Economics and Statistics* 47: 76–80.

Greene, W. H. (2008). Econometric Analysis, 6th edn. Upper Saddle River, NJ: Pearson Education.

Nutting, J. (1977). 'Metals as Materials'. *Metals and Materials*, July–August: 30–4.

Parks, R. W. (1978). 'Inflation and Relative Price Variability'. *Journal of Political Economy* 86: 79–95.

Theil, H. (1967). Economics and Information Theory. Amsterdam: North-Holland and Rand McNally.

Vining, D. R., Jr., and T. C. Eltwertowski (1976). 'The Relationship Between Relative Prices and the General Price Level'. *American Economic Review* 66: 699–708.

PART III

International patterns of incomes, prices and consumption

6 | Disparities in incomes and prices internationally

KENNETH W. CLEMENTS, GRACE GAO AND
THOMAS SIMPSON

6.1 Introduction

This chapter investigates how and why economies differ. This is, of course, a large, multidimensional issue because economies differ with respect to incomes, factor endowments, overall scale, institutions and policy, as well as noneconomic attributes such as geography, climate and, possibly, the historical and cultural context. Many of these factors are linked in one way or another, but they need to be compressed to keep things manageable. We focus on differences across countries in incomes and the structure of relative prices and their interactions. While it is an exaggeration to describe incomes and prices as 'sufficient statistics' for the economy, they do summarise much information in a compact, convenient and economically relevant way.

Perhaps the most famous approach to understanding cross-country differences in incomes and prices is the Balassa (1964)–Samuelson (1964) productivity-bias model. Here relative to poor countries, high-income countries are taken to be more productive in all commodities but relatively more so in the tradeables sector and less so in non-tradeables. The reason for the asymmetry is that tradeables (such as agricultural goods and minerals) are supposed to be more amenable to productivity improvement than nontradeables (services such as education and medical care). The higher marginal productivity of labour in the traded-goods sector means that higher wages are paid there, and if labour is sufficiently mobile across sectors, wages are higher in the nontraded sector also. The higher costs in nontradeables are passed on in terms of higher prices, whereas traded-goods prices are fixed at world values. The result is that tradeables are relatively cheaper in rich countries or nontradeables are more expensive. For more recent discussions of systematic patterns in prices across countries, see Bhagwati (1984), Bergin et al. (2006), Hsieh and Klenow (2007), Simonovska (2010) and Summers and Heston (1991).

In addition to the productivity-bias hypothesis, there are two other streams of literature on the structure of relative prices internationally. First, Theil (1967, chap. 5) uses Divisia-type concepts to measure how prices and quantities differ across six European countries and regions. This involves comparison of the price of commodity i in country a with that in b, p_{ia}/p_{ib}, which leads to a bilateral index of the price level in a relative to b. For this purpose, Theil uses the weighted geometric mean, the logarithm of which is $\Sigma_{i=1}^{n} w_{i,ab} \log(p_{ia}/p_{ib})$, where n is the number of commodities and $w_{i,ab}$ is the weight that reflects the relative importance of commodity i in the two countries. Also considered is the analogous bilateral variance, which measures the dispersion of the individual prices around the average. If prices in one country are proportional to those in another, the variance is zero, and the structure of relative prices is the same in the two countries. For further developments along these lines, see Theil (1996, chap. 5).

The second stream of this literature is due to Kravis et al. (1982, pp. 104–9), who group countries on the basis of several criteria, one of which is the similarity of the structure of prices. They introduce a 'bilateral similarity index', defined as the weighted correlation coefficient between prices in two countries. Another similarity measure the authors use is the 'Paasche–Laspeyres spread', defined as the ratio of the Paasche to the Laspeyres price index (Kravis et al., 1982, pp. 105, 109–10). It can be shown that this spread increases with the variance of relative prices and so is related to the correlation coefficient. Diewert (2009) presents an axiomatic approach to similarity indexes of prices across countries; see also Cuthbert (2009) and Sergeev (2009).[1]

This chapter advances both the theory and measurement of cross-country differences in incomes and prices. In Section 6.2 we first measure the dispersion of prices within a country by the cross-commodity weighted variance and then show in Section 6.3 how this concept is linked to the law of one price. Section 6.4 applies this dispersion measure to data from the International Comparison Program (2008) for more than 130 countries, which leads to the 'world' price distribution. An attractive feature of our approach is that the variance of the world distribution is simply the average of that in each country, with the between-country effect vanishing. Next, in Section 6.5,

---

[1] For a recent study of patterns of relative prices across countries that emphasises the traded- versus nontraded-goods distinction, see Thomas et al. (2011).

we propose a simple pricing model that shows that under not unreasonable conditions, the relative prices of luxuries (necessities) increase (decrease) with income growth. We identify a systematic difference in pricing behaviour for rich and poor countries. This model provides a link between price dispersion and income that leads to several interesting concepts, including the minimum-variance (MV) value of income and dispersion-equivalent income, the additional income that compensates for higher dispersion in the poor countries; these issues are explored in Sections 6.6 and 6.7. Section 6.8 analyses the welfare economics of price dispersion, and Section 6.9 contains concluding comments.

6.2 The distribution of prices

This section introduces measures that summarise the distribution of prices in the form of its centre of gravity and dispersion.

For good $i(i = 1, ..., n)$ in country c $(c = 1, ..., C)$, let p_{ic}, q_{ic} and $w_{ic} = p_{ic}q_{ic}/M_c$ be the price, quantity consumed and budget share, respectively, where $M_c = \sum_{i=1}^{n} p_{ic}q_{ic}$ is total expenditure. Consider the probability distribution of the prices of the n commodities in country c, $p_{ic}, ..., p_{nc}$. A simple way of summarising this distribution is to use the first two moments. It is appropriate to use a weighting scheme that recognises that some goods are more important than others in terms of spending. We use the weighted geometric mean, with the budget shares as weights to represent the relative importance of each good. The logarithm of this mean is

$$\log P_c = \sum_{i=1}^{n} w_{ic} \log p_{ic} \tag{6.1}$$

As $\log P_c$ weights prices in proportion to expenditure, it is a cost-of-living index. This index has an attractively simple sampling interpretation (Theil, 1967, pp. 136–7). For convenience, we write $\log p_{ic}$ as x_{ic} and consider a discrete random variable X_c that can take the n possible values $x_{1c}, ..., x_{nc}$. Regarding the probabilities attached to these n realisations, suppose that the names of goods are drawn at random from this distribution such that each dollar of spending has an equal chance of being selected. This means that the probability of drawing x_{ic} is its budget share w_{ic}. Accordingly, the expected value of the random variable X_c is $E(X_c) = \sum_{i=1}^{n} w_{ic} x_{ic}$, which coincides with index (6.1). Thus the index $\log P_c$ can be interpreted as the expected value of the (logarithmic) price, so it is an appealing way of summarising the cost of the budget.

The preceding index is a weighted first-order moment of the cross-commodity distribution of prices. The corresponding second-order moment is

$$\Pi_c = \sum_{i=1}^{n} w_{ic} (\log p_{ic} - \log P_c)^2 \tag{6.2}$$

which, for country c, is a measure of the dispersion of the distribution of prices. If each of the n prices coincides with the mean, then $\Pi_c = 0$.

6.3 Prices at home and abroad

This section considers aspects of the way in which prices are measured and their implications. We start with price comparisons within a country and then turn to bilateral relationships.

Expensive and cheap goods

In what sense is it possible to identify goods that are expensive and those which are cheap? As the price p_{ic} is measured in terms of domestic-currency units of country c per unit of good i, the use of this price in cross-country comparisons is unsatisfactory. The relative price $\log p_{ic} - \log P_c$ is a pure number, independent of currency units, but not independent of the unit of measurement of good i. To see this, consider, for example, the case of $i = $ food, and suppose that we initially measure its volume (q_i^{old}) in terms of kilograms per year. This means that the corresponding price (p_i^{old}) is in terms of local dollars per kilogram to satisfy the accounting identity $p_i^{\text{old}} \times q_i^{\text{old}} = X$, where X is given food expenditure (dollars per year). If we now switch to grams, then as $1,000 \text{ g} = 1 \text{ kg}$, $p_i^{\text{new}} = p_i^{\text{old}}/1,000$ and $q_i^{\text{new}} = q_i^{\text{old}} \times 1,000$, which satisfy $p_i^{\text{new}} \times q_i^{\text{new}} = X$. Furthermore, the index of prices under the new measurement regime satisfies $\log P^{\text{new}} = \log P^{\text{old}} - w_i \log(1,000)$, so the difference between the corresponding relative prices is

$$(\log p_i^{\text{new}} - \log P^{\text{new}}) - (\log p_i^{\text{old}} - \log P^{\text{old}})$$

$$= -(1 - w_i) \log(1,000)$$

for $0 < w_i < 1$; this difference is nonzero, which establishes a lack of invariance of relative prices to choice of the unit of measurement for the quantities.

This problem can be resolved by fixing on the quantity units. One approach would be to measure the quantity consumed of good i as its value in US dollars so that the corresponding price is the domestic-currency cost of \$1 worth of the good. In fact, as the currency unit is not present in the relative price $\log p_i - \log P$, this does not depend on the US dollar as the base, so we could equally well use the euro for this purpose. Subsequently, we use International Comparison Program (2008) data, where consumption of each of the n goods is expressed in terms of US dollars. An implication of measuring quantities in terms of US dollars is that the n prices $(p_{1c}, ..., p_{nc})$ are directly comparable across commodities. That is, as p_{ic} is the domestic-currency price of \$1 worth of good i, if $p_{ic} > p_{jc}$, then good i is more expensive than good j in country c. For comparison of prices in different countries, currency units have to be removed, and we can use the relative price $\log p_{ic} - \log P_c$. Good i is then relatively more expensive in country c than in country d when $\log p_{ic} - \log P_c > \log p_{id} - \log P_d$.

The law of one price

In the context of prices in different countries, it is relevant to mention the law of one price (LOP). Here arbitrage equalises prices across countries when prices are expressed in terms of a common currency.[2] To examine the implications of the LOP, let S_c be the market exchange rate for c, defined as the domestic-currency cost of \$1, so an increase in S_c represents a depreciation of the currency of c, and let p_i^* be the cost of good i in the United States in US dollars (the 'world price').[3]

---

[2] The literature on the LOP and its close cousin, purchasing power parity, is large and growing. For modern surveys, see Froot and Rogoff (1995), Lan and Ong (2003), MacDonald (2007), Rogoff (1996), Sarno and Taylor (2002), Taylor and Taylor (2004) and Taylor (2006).

[3] This discussion is simplified in the interest of clarity. In fact, the International Comparison Program (2008) evaluates consumption at 'international prices', which are cross-country averages, expressed in terms of US dollars. Thus, strictly speaking, p_i^* is not the price in the United States but the international price measured in US dollars. This simplification does not affect the logic of the argument, however.

If k_{ic} is the 'spread' between the domestic and world prices of good i that measures all factors that account for deviations from the LOP (e.g., trade barriers, pricing to market, nontraded goods, etc.), then we have $p_{ic} = k_{ic} \times S_c \times p_i^*$, with $k_{ic} = 1$ representing no deviations. When quantities are measured in terms of US dollars and prices are the cost of \$1 worth, the price of each good in the United States is unity, so $p_{ic} = k_{ic} \times S_c$ or

$$\log p_{ic} = \log k_{ic} + \log S_c \qquad (6.3)$$

Multiplying both sides of this equation by w_{ic} and then summing over $i = 1, ..., n$ yields

$$\log P_c = \log K_c + \log S_c \qquad (6.4)$$

where $\log K_c = \sum_{i=1}^{n} w_{ic} \log k_{ic} = \sum_{i=1}^{n} w_{ic} \log(p_{ic}/S_c)$ is the average spread. The term $\log K_c$ can be interpreted as the degree to which the currency is mispriced: When $\log K_c > 0$, domestic prices are too high in relation to world prices, and the market exchange rate overvalues the currency by $100 \times (K_c - 1)$ per cent, whereas it is undervalued if $\log K_c < 0$. A sufficient condition for no currency mispricing is when each of the n prices is equalised ($\log k_{ic} = 0, i = 1, ..., n$), which could be termed the 'strong form' of the LOP. The complete, or absolute, equalisation of the n prices is clearly a very stringent condition that is most unlikely to be satisfied in practice.

Subtracting both sides of equation (6.4) from equation (6.3) yields

$$\log p_{ic} - \log P_c = \log k_{ic} - \log K_c \qquad (6.5)$$

This states that the logarithmic relative price of i is the deviation of its spread from the average. The 'weak version' of the LOP states that domestic prices are proportional to world prices, so $\log k_{ic} = \log K_c$ and, from equation (6.5), $\log p_{ic} - \log P_c = 0, i = 1, ..., n$. In this case, the price variance $\Pi_c = 0$. More generally, the (weighted) variance of departures from the LOP is

$$\sum_{i=1}^{n} w_{ic}(\log k_{ic} - \log K_c)^2 = \sum_{i=1}^{n} w_{ic}[\log(p_{ic}/S_c) - (\log P_c/S_c)]^2 = \Pi_c$$

where Π_c is the variance of relative prices (6.2). It is therefore evident that a measure of departure from the LOP in its weak form is the degree of dispersion of relative prices. Moreover, as the price variance involves relative prices, for which currency units play no role, the variance is comparable across countries.

6.4 Incomes and prices in 132 countries

We use data on the prices and per-capita consumption of twelve commodities in 132 countries from the International Comparison Program (2008). Tables 6.1 and 6.2 list the countries and commodities.[4] Countries are listed in terms of decreasing real income per capita, defined as the total real volume of per-capita consumption measured in US dollars, scaled such that United States = 100. There is great variation in income, which ranges from 100 in the United States, the richest country, to 0.4 in the Democratic Republic of Congo, the poorest. Table 6.1 also contains the standard deviations of the prices $\sqrt{\Pi_c}$. There is a broad tendency for the standard deviation to be higher in low-income countries; from the last two entries of the last column of the table, the standard deviation of prices is approximately twice as high for the poor group of countries as for the rich (61 versus 30 per cent), but other than that, there is no clear pattern, most likely because noise in the price data is necessarily attenuated in any measure of dispersion.

In addition to the dispersion of n prices within a country, it is of interest to consider the dispersion across C countries:

$$\Pi = \frac{1}{C}\sum_{c=1}^{C}\sum_{i=1}^{n} w_{ic}\left[\log p_{ic} - \log P_c - \frac{1}{C}\sum_{c=1}^{C}\sum_{i=1}^{n} w_{ic}(\log p_{ic} - \log P_c)\right]^2 \quad (6.6)$$

Here commodities are weighted by their budget shares to reflect their relative importance, whereas countries are unweighted to reflect the idea that we have C independent readings on the structure of prices. This world variance Π can be decomposed into within- and between-country components:

---

[4] For details of the data, see Appendix 6A.1.

Table 6.1 *Incomes and dispersion of prices in 132 countries in 2005*

Country	Income per capita	SD of prices
1. United States	100.0	0.0
2. Luxembourg	92.2	16.8
3. Iceland	80.7	29.1
4. Norway	77.7	31.3
5. United Kingdom	76.9	26.7
6. Austria	76.4	24.9
7. Switzerland	74.6	18.9
8. Canada	74.4	21.8
9. Netherlands	72.4	25.1
10. Sweden	72.0	25.3
11. France	71.5	23.0
12. Australia	70.6	23.3
13. Denmark	69.8	25.2
14. Belgium	68.4	22.5
15. Germany	67.5	21.3
16. Hong Kong	66.3	38.4
17. Ireland	66.2	24.6
18. Japan	66.0	35.6
19. Taiwan	64.5	56.0
20. Cyprus	63.4	33.7
21. Finland	63.0	24.6
22. Spain	61.9	28.5
23. Italy	61.6	20.3
24. Greece	59.4	30.1
25. NZ	57.7	23.3
26. Israel	54.7	34.4
27. Malta	54.3	42.5
28. Singapore	53.6	47.8
29. Qatar	50.5	61.5
30. Slovenia	50.0	31.9
31. Portugal	49.0	25.6
32. Brunei	48.7	55.6
33. Kuwait	47.0	35.8
34. Czech Rep	46.3	45.5
35. Hungary	42.6	48.1
36. Bahrain	41.6	45.6

Table 6.1 (*cont.*)

Country	Income per capita	SD of prices
37. Korea	40.4	41.7
38. Estonia	39.4	47.2
39. Slovakia	38.8	49.5
40. Lithuania	38.3	54.2
41. Poland	36.7	48.8
42. Croatia	36.1	50.0
43. Macao	36.1	44.4
44. Latvia	33.4	54.9
45. Lebanon	32.0	56.0
46. Mexico	28.7	35.3
47. Belarus	27.3	73.1
48. Kazakhstan	26.5	72.9
49. Mauritius	26.3	55.3
50. Russia	26.3	63.1
51. Bulgaria	26.1	62.8
52. Iran	25.2	69.1
53. Romania	24.4	53.5
54. Oman	24.2	37.7
55. Argentina	24.0	42.9
56. Serbia	23.7	58.3
57. Saudi Arabia	23.6	36.6
58. Chile	23.3	36.0
59. Uruguay	22.1	36.3
60. Bosnia Herz.	21.9	55.9
61. Macedonia	20.5	60.6
62. Ukraine	19.8	78.8
63. South Africa	19.3	41.7
64. Malaysia	19.3	51.6
65. Turkey	18.9	51.3
66. Montenegro	18.7	55.8
67. Brazil	18.7	39.8
68. Venezuela	17.1	46.9
69. Thailand	16.1	60.4
70. Albania	14.6	58.5
71. Colombia	14.5	48.4
72. Ecuador	13.7	43.0

Table 6.1 (*cont.*)

Country	Income per capita	SD of prices
73. Jordan	13.7	52.4
74. Tunisia	13.7	49.9
75. Peru	13.6	40.0
76. Egypt	13.5	66.3
77. Moldova	13.0	83.6
78. Maldives	12.9	101.4
79. Gabon	12.7	78.4
80. Fiji	12.6	57.6
81. Georgia	12.1	94.2
82. Botswana	11.9	62.7
83. Namibia	10.9	54.8
84. Swaziland	10.8	65.4
85. Syria	10.5	57.8
86. Bolivia	10.2	63.6
87. Equat. Guinea	10.1	71.9
88. Paraguay	9.9	50.4
89. Cape Verde	8.8	47.6
90. Bhutan	8.0	66.3
91. Kyrgyz	8.0	88.3
92. Sri Lanka	7.9	55.8
93. Iraq	7.8	64.6
94. Mongolia	7.7	81.9
95. Philippines	7.5	55.9
96. Indonesia	7.4	50.9
97. Pakistan	7.3	68.1
98. Morocco	7.2	42.8
99. Lesotho	7.1	76.8
100. China	7.0	66.6
101. Vietnam	6.8	91.3
102. India	5.5	70.8
103. Cambodia	5.3	79.8
104. Yemen	5.2	57.7
105. Sudan	4.5	46.2
106. Lao	4.4	82.1
107. Djibouti	4.4	70.0

Table 6.1 (*cont.*)

Country	Income per capita	SD of prices
108. Kenya	4.3	69.4
109. Sao Tome	4.3	62.6
110. Congo, R.	4.1	81.9
111. Cameroon	4.0	52.8
112. Nigeria	4.0	76.1
113. Senegal	3.9	57.7
114. Chad	3.5	75.3
115. Nepal	3.4	64.7
116. Bangladesh	3.3	54.8
117. Benin	3.3	66.3
118. Ghana	3.3	77.6
119. Cote d'Ivoire	3.1	53.4
120. S. Leone	3.1	89.5
121. M'gascar	3.0	80.2
122. Togo	2.7	68.0
123. Burkina Faso	2.5	60.7
124. Guinea	2.4	80.5
125. Mali	2.3	62.4
126. Angola	2.3	64.9
127. Rwanda	2.1	62.1
128. C. Africa	1.9	63.2
129. M'bique	1.7	61.6
130. Niger	1.3	58.5
131. G–Bissau	1.2	61.3
132. Congo, D. R.	0.4	61.3
Mean–All	27.4	52.9
–Rich	67.9	30.3
–Poor	15.5	60.7

Notes:

1. Standard deviations (SDs) are to be divided by 100.
2. 'Poor' countries are those numbered 29 and 32 to 132, excluding 34, 37 and 39, whereas the remainder are 'rich'.
3. Poor countries coincide with 'Emerging and Developing Economies' of the IMF 2010 World Economic Outlook; see www.imf.org/external/pubs/ft/weo/2010/01/weodata/groups.htm#oem.

Table 6.2 *Relative prices and incomes in 132 countries in 2005* $[w_{ic}\log(p_{ic}/P_c) = \alpha_i + \gamma_i D_c + \beta_i \log(Q_c/\overline{Q}) + \varepsilon_{ic}]$

Commodity	Intercept α_i (×100)	Poor-country Dummy γ_i (×100)	Income β_i (×100)	Income elasticity β_i/w_i	R^2	SEE (×100)
Food	9.71 (0.99)	0.22 (1.21)	−5.31 (0.44)	−0.19	0.68	4.34
Alcoholic beverages	0.08 (0.21)	−0.11 (0.26)	0.11 (0.10)	0.03	0.03	0.94
Clothing	−0.55 (0.44)	2.71 (0.54)	0.88 (0.20)	0.17	0.18	1.93
Housing	−5.34 (1.40)	2.38 (1.71)	2.70 (0.62)	0.18	0.15	6.15
Furnishings	−0.09 (0.26)	0.91 (0.32)	0.49 (0.12)	0.10	0.12	1.15
Health	−4.53 (0.67)	−2.41 (0.82)	−0.24 (0.30)	−0.03	0.08	2.94
Transport	3.84 (0.63)	0.12 (0.77)	0.19 (0.28)	0.02	0.00	2.76
Communication	−0.14 (0.24)	0.84 (0.29)	−0.03 (0.11)	−0.01	0.12	1.05
Recreation	0.39 (0.17)	0.50 (0.20)	0.17 (0.07)	0.03	0.05	0.74
Education	−4.39 (0.87)	−5.23 (1.06)	0.28 (0.39)	0.03	0.30	3.83
Restaurants	1.48 (0.27)	0.09 (0.32)	0.47 (0.12)	0.11	0.17	1.17
Miscellaneous	−0.47 (0.21)	−0.02 (0.26)	0.29 (0.09)	0.04	0.13	0.93

Notes:
1. Standard errors in parentheses.
2. Regressions exclude the United States, the base country.
3. Elasticities in the third-last column are evaluated at means.

$$\underbrace{\Pi}$$

Total variance =

$$
= \frac{1}{C} \sum_{c=1}^{C} \sum_{i=1}^{n} w_{ic} \left[\underbrace{\log p_{ic} - \log P_c}_{\substack{\text{Relative price of good } i \\ \text{in country } c}} - \underbrace{\Sigma_{i=1}^{n} w_{ic}(\log p_{ic} - \log P_c)}_{\text{Mean for country } c} \right]^2
$$

Variance for country c

Mean variance over countries; 'within' component

$$
+ \frac{1}{C} \Sigma_{c=1}^{C} \left[\underbrace{\Sigma_{i=1}^{n} w_{ic}(\log p_{ic} - \log P_c)}_{\textit{Mean} \text{ for country } c} - \underbrace{1/C \cdot \Sigma_{c=1}^{C} \Sigma_{i=1}^{n} w_{ic}(\log p_{ic} - \log P_c)}_{\textit{Mean} \text{ over all countries}} \right]^2
$$

+ Variance across countries; 'between' component

As $\sum_{i=1}^{n} w_{ic}(\log p_{ic} - \log P_c) = 0$, the between-country variance vanishes, and the following simple result emerges on application of equation (6.2):

$$
\Pi = \frac{1}{C} \cdot \sum_{c=1}^{C} \Pi_c \tag{6.7}
$$

Thus the world variance is just the average of that in the C countries, which is a convenient result. Figure 6.1 presents histograms of relative prices of the $n = 12$ goods for the two groups of countries. Consistent with the preceding approach, prices are weighted by budget shares. It is evident that prices are clearly less disperse in the rich countries.[5]

Next, we investigate informally the dependence of prices on income. Let $\log(Q_c/\bar{Q})$ be income in country c relative to the geometric mean income for all countries. Figure 6.2 plots each relative price $\log(p_{ic}/P_c)$

[5] Note that the standard deviations of the histograms, corresponding to $\sqrt{\Pi}$, with ? defined by equation (6.6), are close to the mean SDs given at the bottom of Table 6.1 but not identical. Identical results are obtained if we first square the SD for each country in Table 6.1, average and then take the square root. That is to say, the results satisfy equation (6.7).

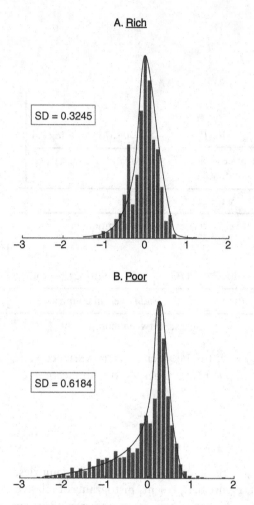

A. <u>Rich</u>

SD = 0.3245

B. <u>Poor</u>

SD = 0.6184

Figure 6.1 Relative prices in rich and poor countries.

against relative income for the 132 countries. As discussed earlier, p_{ic} is the price of \$1 worth of good i in country c, whereas P_c is the weighted geometric mean; accordingly, if $p_{ic}/P_c > 1$, then i is relatively expensive in c, and $\log(p_{ic}/P_c) > 0$. The term 'relatively more expensive' in this context means that \$1 worth of i costs more than the average over all goods. It should be noted that as $\sum_{i=1}^{12} w_{ic} \log(p_{ic}/P_c) = 0$, some of the logarithmic relative prices must be positive and others negative, averaging out to zero. Panel 1 of Figure 6.2 indicates that food prices

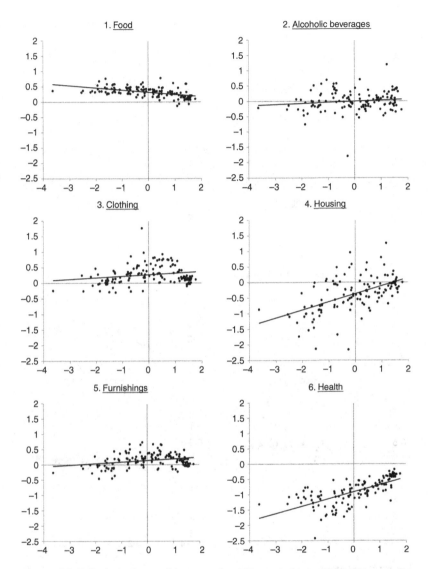

Figure 6.2 Relative prices and incomes for 132 countries in 2005. *Notes:* 1. In panel i ($i = 1, \ldots, 12$), the ith relative price, $(\log p_{ic} - \log P_c) \times 100$, is plotted against relative income per capita, $\log(Q_c / \bar{Q}) \times 100, c = 1, \ldots, 132$, where $\bar{Q}$ is geometric mean income. The solid line is the LS regression line. 2. As it is an outlier, country number 114, Chad, is excluded from the 'Education' plot but is included in the regression line. 3. The United States, the base country, is excluded from all scatter plots.

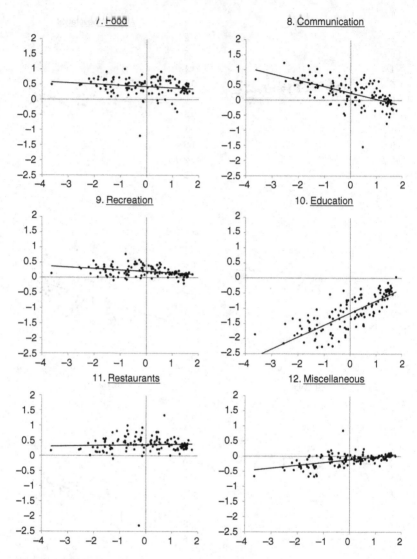

Figure 6.2 (*cont.*)

exhibit three patterns. First, as most of the points lie above the zero horizontal line, food is relatively expensive in the majority of countries. The other panels of the figure show that housing, health and education tend to be cheap, whereas clothing, transport and restaurants are expensive. Second, food prices tend to become cheaper as income increases, as indicated by the negative slope of the regression line in the panel. Third, in a number of instances there is clear visual evidence of the dependence of prices on income, a topic that is explored further in the next section.

6.5 A simple model of relative prices

Suppose that the quantity of good i supplied (q_i^s) is a log-linear function of its relative price (p_i/P), whereas its consumption depends on the relative price and real income (Q):

$$\log q_i^s = \phi_i^s + \eta_i^s (\log p_i - \log P),$$

$$\log q_i^d = \phi_i^d + \eta_i^d (\log p_i - \log P) + \theta_i \log Q$$

where $\phi_i^s (\phi_i^d)$ is the intercept of the supply (demand) function, $\eta_i^s > 0 (\eta_i^d < 0)$ is the price elasticity of supply (demand) and θ_i is the income elasticity. Market clearing implies that

$$\log p_i - \log P = \alpha_i' + \beta_i' \log Q \qquad (6.8)$$

where $\alpha_i' = (\phi_i^d - \phi_i^s)/\Delta_i$, with $\Delta_i = \eta_i^s - \eta_i^d > 0$ the excess supply elasticity, and $\beta_i' = \theta_i/\Delta_i$. This reduced form is not a completely satisfactory formulation for the following reason: If good i is normal, then the income elasticity θ_i and the reduced-form income coefficient β_i' are both positive. If each of the n goods is normal, which is entirely possible, then equation (6.8) states that the impact of income growth is to increase all relative prices, which is logically impossible; as a budget-share-weighted average of relative prices is zero, some would have to increase and others decrease.

To rectify this problem, we proceed in two steps. First, we multiply both sides of equation (6.8) by the budget share of good i and sum both sides over $i = 1, ..., n$. As $\sum_{i=1}^{n} w_i(\log p_i - \log P) = 0$, we have $A + B \log Q = 0$, where $A = \sum_{i=1}^{n} w_i \alpha_i'$ and $B = \sum_{i=1}^{n} w_i \beta_i'$ are weighted averages of the coefficients of equation (6.8). Second, we subtract $A + B \log Q$ from both sides of equation (6.8) and then multiply both sides by w_i to give

$$w_i(\log p_i - \log P) = \alpha_i + \beta_i \log Q \qquad (6.9)$$

where $\alpha_i = w_i(\alpha_i' - A)$ and $\beta_i = w_i(\beta_i' - B)$ are weighted deviations from weighted means that satisfy $\sum_{i=1}^{n} \alpha_i = \sum_{i=1}^{n} \beta_i = 0$. According to model

(6.9), growth in income leads an increase in the relative price of good i if its $\beta_i > 0$. As $w_i > 0$, this occurs when its $\beta_i' = \theta_i/(\eta_i^s - \eta_i^d)$ is greater than the average, B. Accordingly, income growth increases the relative price of i when the ratio of its income elasticity to the excess supply elasticity is greater than average and vice versa. On dividing both sides of equation (6.9) by w_i, it is evident that β_i/w_i is the income elasticity of the relative price of good i and that a budget-share-weighted average of these elasticities, $\sum_{i=1}^{n} w_i(\beta_i/w_i)$, is zero, as required.

To analyse further the working of model (6.9), suppose that the excess supply elasticity is the same for each commodity: $\eta_i^s - \eta_i^d = \Delta_i = \Delta > 0$. The income coefficient in equation (6.9) then takes the form

$$\beta_i = \frac{1}{\Delta} w_i \left(\theta_i - \sum_{j=1}^{n} w_j \theta_j \right) = \frac{1}{\Delta} w_i (\theta_i - 1) \tag{6.10}$$

where the second step follows from the requirement that a budget-share-weighted average of the income elasticities is unity. As $1/\Delta$ and w_i are both positive, equation (6.10) reveals that the sign of β_i is positive for goods that are luxuries ($\theta_i > 1$) and negative for necessities ($\theta_i < 1$). Thus, under the stated conditions, income growth increases the relative prices of luxuries and decreases those of necessities, which is perfectly reasonable.

The variance of the income elasticities of the relative prices is $\sum_{i=1}^{n} w_i(\beta_i/w_i)^2 = \sum_{i=1}^{n} \beta_i^2/w_i$, which is a cross-commodity weighted variance and is exactly analogous to the price variance (6.2). From definition (6.10), this variance takes the form

$$\sum_{i=1}^{n} \frac{\beta_i^2}{w_i} = \frac{1}{\Delta^2} \sum_{i=1}^{n} w_i (\theta_i - 1)^2 \tag{6.11}$$

As a budget-share-weighted mean of the income elasticities is unity, their weighted variance is $\sum_{i=1}^{n} w_i(\theta_i - 1)^2$. This is the third cross-commodity variance that we have encountered. Equation (6.11) shows that the variance of the income elasticities of prices β_i/w_i is proportional to the variance of the income elasticities of demand θ_i with proportionality factor $1/\Delta^2$. A greater diversity of goods implies greater dispersion of income elasticities and, from equation (6.11), greater variability of the price elasticities. For example, when all goods are the same, the income elasticities are all unity, and there is no dispersion among the price elasticities (each $\beta_i = 0$, so relative prices are independent of income).

We apply model (6.9) to the twelve commodities and 132 countries discussed in the preceding section. To do this, we make three adjustments. First, to allow for excluded factors, we add a zero-mean disturbance term for good i and country c, ε_{ic}, with $E(\varepsilon_{ic})^2 = \sigma_i^2$. Second, we recognise that there may be systematic differences in pricing patterns in rich and poor countries. For example, rich economies may have access to more advanced technologies and thus lower costs of production. This implies a greater intercept for the supply function ϕ_i^s for such countries, which has a consequential impact on the intercept α_i in model (6.9). To allow for this possibility, we specify that this intercept takes different values for the rich and poor groups of countries. Third, for convenience, we measure income as a deviation from the geometric mean $\bar{Q}$, as in the preceding section. Thus we estimate a system of twelve equations, the ith member of which is

$$w_{ic}\log(p_{ic}/P_c) = \alpha_i + \gamma_i D_c + \beta_i \log(Q_c/\bar{Q}) + \varepsilon_{ic}, \quad c = 1,\ldots,132 \quad (6.12)$$

where $D_c = 1$ if c refers to a poor economy and zero otherwise.

The least-squares estimates of equation (6.12) for $i = 1, \ldots, 12$ are given in Table 6.2. These estimates (denoted by a circumflex) satisfy the aggregation constraints $\sum_{i=1}^{12}\hat{\alpha}_i = \sum_{i=1}^{12}\hat{\beta}_i = \sum_{i=1}^{12}\hat{\gamma}_i = 0$. It is evident that five of the twelve coefficients of the poor-country dummy are significant, especially those for clothing and education; these coefficients indicate that clothing is more expensive and education is cheaper in these countries when incomes are held constant. The income coefficient for food is negative and highly significant, so food becomes cheaper as affluence increases. As food is a necessity, the negative sign of this coefficient agrees with the discussion following equation (6.10). The third-last column of the table shows that the income elasticity of the price of food is –0.19, so a doubling of income leads to an approximately 20 per cent decrease in prices. The largest income elasticity is 0.18 for housing prices (clothing is a close second).

Table 6.3 explores relation (6.10) by presenting the income elasticities of demand implied by the estimates of β_i from Table 6.2. To

Table 6.3 *Income elasticities of prices and demand*

Commodity	Income elasticity of price β_i/w_i	Income elasticity of demand			
		Value of excess supply elasticity Δ			Directly estimated
		1	2	3	
(1)	(2)	(3)	(4)	(5)	(6)
Food	−0.19	0.81	0.62	0.43	0.66
Alcohol	0.03	1.00	0.06	1.09	0.93
Clothing	0.17	0.17	1.34	1.51	0.96
Housing	0.18	1.18	1.36	1.54	1.04
Furnishings	0.10	1.10	1.20	1.30	1.07
Health	−0.03	0.97	0.94	0.91	1.16
Transport	0.02	1.02	1.04	1.06	1.18
Communication	−0.01	0.99	0.98	0.97	1.22
Recreation	0.03	1.03	1.06	1.09	1.36
Education	0.03	1.03	1.06	1.09	0.99
Restaurants	0.11	1.11	1.22	1.33	1.28
Miscellaneous	0.04	1.04	1.08	1.12	1.30

Sources: Column 2 is from Table 6.2; column 6 is derived from Clements and Chen (2012).

do this, the excess supply elasticity Δ is required, and in columns 3 through 5 we use three 'central' values 1, 2 and 3. The implied elasticities can then be compared to directly estimated ones (derived from Clements and Chen [2012] with the same data), which are given in column 6. Although the agreement is not exact, the implied elasticities of column 4, corresponding to $\Delta = 2$, seem to be closest, especially for the important case of food: For this good, the implied income elasticity is 0.62, which is close to the estimated value of 0.66. The excess supply elasticity of $\Delta = 2$ is consistent with supply and demand elasticities of 1 and −1, respectively. As these computations are based on the simplifying assumption that the excess supply elasticities are the same for all goods, the results should not be taken to be hard and fast. Nonetheless, the broad agreement between the implied and estimated elasticities can be interpreted as providing some reassurance that pricing model (6.12) makes economic sense.

6.6 Price dispersion and income

The parameter β_i in model (6.12) represents the sensitivity of the relative price of good i to changes in income. This dependence of prices means that income has a systematic impact on price dispersion. Use of the pricing equations to analyse dispersion has the effect of eliminating much of the noise in the variance of prices and gives rises to several interesting concepts, including the value of income that leads to a MV, as well as variance-equivalent incomes. This and the next section address these issues.

Dispersion quadratic in income

We divide both sides of equation (6.12) by w_{ic} and then substitute the expression for the relative price of good i, $\log p_{ic} - \log P_c$, into the definition of the variance [equation (6.2)]. Taking the expectation and writing $y_c = E(\Pi_c)$ and $x_c = \log(Q_c/\bar{Q})$, we obtain an expression for the dispersion of relative prices that is quadratic in income:

$$y_c = \lambda_0 + \lambda_1 x_c + \lambda_2 x_c^2, \quad \text{with } \lambda_0 = \sum_{i=1}^{12} \frac{\tilde{\alpha}_i^2 + \sigma_i^2}{w_{ic}},$$

$$\lambda_1 = \sum_{i=1}^{12} \frac{2\tilde{\alpha}_i \beta_i}{w_{ic}} \quad \text{and} \quad \lambda_2 = \sum_{i=1}^{12} \frac{\beta_i^2}{w_{ic}} \tag{6.13}$$

where $\tilde{\alpha}_i = \alpha_i + \gamma_i D_c$ is the intercept of pricing equation (6.12) for good i in country c, and $\sigma_i^2 = E(\varepsilon_{ic})^2$ is the variance of the disturbance term of that equation. To implement equation (6.13), we use the estimates of Table 6.2 and the shares of countries that are representative of the poor and rich groups. Table 6.4 and Figure 6.3 present the results, which are discussed in detail below.

Meanland and MV income

As income is measured relative to the mean, the intercept in equation (6.13), λ_0, represents the variance of prices corresponding to mean income. This is dispersion in 'Meanland', the hypothetical country at the centre of the world with mean income. As $dy/dx = \lambda_1 + 2\lambda_2 x_c$ and $\lambda_2 > 0$, $x^* = -\lambda_1/2\lambda_2$ is the variance-minimising value of income. In terms of the basic parameters of equation (6.12), this MV income takes

Table 6.4 *Implied price dispersion and income* ($y_c = \lambda_0 + \lambda_1 x_c + \lambda_2 x_c^2$).

Country group (1)	Order of quadratic coefficients			Minimum variance		Country nearest MV income		
	Second λ_2 (2)	First λ_1 (3)	Zero λ_0 (4)	Income $x^* = -\lambda_1/2\lambda_2$ (5)	Variance y_{x^*} (6)	Country (7)	Income (8)	Variance (9)
Poor	2.47	−6.55	33.36	132.71	29.01	24. Greece	133.19	9.08
	(0.43)	(2.60)	(1.24)	(54.23)	(1.68)			
Rich	3.38	−11.23	26.41	166.28	17.07	3. Iceland	163.85	8.44
	(0.49)	(1.85)	(2.36)	(14.70)	(0.98)			
Difference	−0.91	4.68	6.95	−33.57	11.94			
	(0.16)	(0.98)	(2.13)	(14.25)	(1.41)			

Notes:
1. Asymptotic standard errors in parentheses.
2. 'Country nearest minimum variance' is restricted to those of the corresponding category (rich/poor).
3. Budget shares for Chile and France are used to represent the rich and poor-country groups, respectively. These are listed in column 2 of Table 6.5.
4. All entries are to be divided by 100.

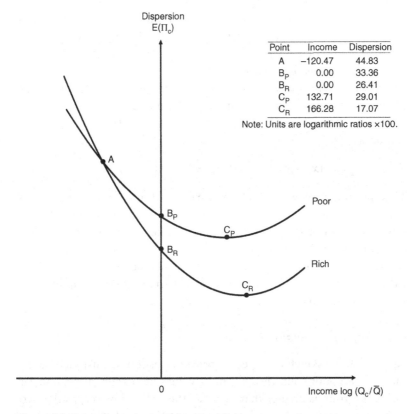

Note: Units are logarithmic ratios ×100.

Point	Income	Dispersion
A	−120.47	44.83
B_P	0.00	33.36
B_R	0.00	26.41
C_P	132.71	29.01
C_R	166.28	17.07

Figure 6.3 Price dispersion and income (1).

the form

$$\log \frac{Q^*}{\bar{Q}} = -\sum_{i=1}^{12} \kappa_i \frac{\tilde{\alpha}_i}{\beta_i}, \quad \text{with } \kappa_i = \frac{\beta_i^2/w_{ic}}{\sum_{i=1}^{12} \beta_i^2/w_{ic}} > 0, \quad \sum_{i=1}^{12} \kappa_i = 1 \quad (6.14)$$

Thus MV income is a weighted average of ratios of the inter-cept to the slope in equation (6.12), with the signs changed, $-\tilde{\alpha}_1/\beta_1, \ldots, -\tilde{\alpha}_{12}/\beta_{12}$. The weight for good i in equation (6.14), κ_i, is proportional to $\beta_i^2/w_{ic} = w_{ic}(\beta_i/w_{ic})^2$, which is the square of the income elasticity of the relative price of i weighted by its share w_{ic}. In view of the discussion preceding result (6.11), κ_i is proportional to the contribution of the good in question to the variance of the income elasticities of the relative prices. From equation (6.11), κ_i is also proportional to the contribution of good i to the variance of the income elasticities of demand under the condition that the excess supply elasticity is the same for each good.

Another interesting way to express the quadratic (6.13) is in terms of the deviation of income from its MV value. It follows from $x^* = -\lambda_1/2\lambda_2$ that $\lambda_2(x - x^*)^2 = \lambda_2 x^2 + \lambda_1 x + \lambda_1^2/4\lambda_2$, so equation (6.13) can be written as

$$y_c = \lambda_0' + \lambda_2(x_c - x^*)^2, \quad \text{with } \lambda_0' = \lambda_0 - \lambda_1^2/4\lambda_2$$

This shows that when $x_c = x^*$, the variance of prices is minimised and takes the value $\lambda_0 - \lambda_1^2/4\lambda_2$. As $\lambda_2 > 0$, the variance is higher for all other values of income and increases with the square of the deviation of income from MV income. In view of the logarithmic formulation, this deviation is the difference between the income of country c and the MV value, $\log(Q_c/Q^*)$. The excess of the variance over its minimum is $y_c - \lambda_0'$; the income elasticity of this excess is 2.

A picture of dispersion

Figure 6.3 is a sketch of expected price dispersion against income for the rich and poor countries. For most values of income, dispersion for the poor group is greater than that for the rich. However, as the two curves are not parallel, they intersect at point A, and for incomes below this critical value, dispersion for the rich countries exceeds that for the poor. Relative income at this point is

$$\frac{-(\lambda_1^P - \lambda_1^R) \pm \sqrt{(\lambda_1^P - \lambda_1^R)^2 - 4(\lambda_2^P - \lambda_2^R)(\lambda_0^P - \lambda_0^R)}}{2(\lambda_2^P - \lambda_2^R)} \tag{6.15}$$

where λ_i^g is the quadratic coefficient of order i in equation (6.13) for country group g ($g = R$ for rich, P for poor). In the figure, we use the positive root in equation (6.15) because this is closest to mean income.

The point of intersection of the curve with the vertical axis is dispersion in Meanland. This is B_P for the poor and B_R for the rich countries, with $B_P > B_R$, which again reflects that, on average, dispersion is greater in poorer countries. The MV points are C_P and C_R, which show that for rich compared with poor countries, (1) this variance is lower and (2) the corresponding income is higher (C_R lies to the right of C_P).

In terms of the quadratic coefficients, the points of intersection with the vertical axis are $B_P = \lambda_0^P$ and $B_R = \lambda_0^R$, so these coefficients determine the overall 'height' of each curve. The sensitivity of dispersion to variations in income is given by the slope of the quadratic. This slope is expressed in terms of the change in variance for a 1 per cent increase in income; the income elasticity of the variance (the slope divided by the variance) is proportional to this slope. For country group g ($g = R$, P), the slope is $\lambda_1^g + 2\lambda_2^g \log(Q^c/\bar{Q})$. Thus, for income less than MV in the poor countries (given by point C_P in the figure), the difference in slope between the two groups, $(\lambda_1^R - \lambda_1^P) + 2(\lambda_2^R - \lambda_2^P) \log(Q^c/\bar{Q})$, is always negative. This establishes that in this range, a proportionate increase in income decreases dispersion by more in the rich than in the poor countries.

Finally, the change in income sensitivity of dispersion is $2\lambda_2$, which is a measure of the curvature of the quadratic. It follows from equations (6.10), (6.11) and (6.13) that the ratio of this coefficient for the rich to that for the poor countries is the ratio of the variances of the income elasticities of demand:

$$\frac{\lambda_2^R}{\lambda_2^P} = \frac{d(\text{income sensitivity of dispersion in rich})}{d(\text{income sensitivity of dispersion in poor})}$$

$$= \frac{\text{variance of income elasticities in rich}}{\text{variance of income elasticities in poor}} \qquad (6.16)$$

This result holds under the condition that the excess supply elasticities are the same. From column 2 of Table 6.4, the estimate of λ_2^R is almost 40 per cent greater than that for the poor group, which implies that there is substantially more diversity among the income elasticities of demand for the rich compared with the poor countries. By identifying the differences in goods in the basket by the dispersion of the income elasticities of demand, result (6.16) agrees with the idea that for the rich countries consumption patterns are more diversified and relatively less intensive for food in particular (Engel's law).

More on meanland and MV income

The estimates of the zero-order coefficient in the quadratic (6.13), λ_0, contained in column 4 of Table 6.4, are 0.33 and 0.26 for the poor and rich countries, respectively. Thus dispersion at mean income is $\sqrt{0.33} = 0.57$ and $\sqrt{0.26} = 0.51$, or approximately 57 and 51 per cent for the poor and rich groups, respectively. The last two entries in this column of the table establish that these values are significantly different.

Column 5 of Table 6.4 reveals that in the poor (rich) countries, variance is a minimum when income is approximately 132 (166) per cent above the mean. The last two entries in this column show that the difference between these two income values is significant. From column 6, the MV is 29 (17) per cent for the poor (rich) group, and again, this difference is significant. The next several columns indicate that Greece has income closest to the MV for the poor group, whereas Iceland has income closest to the MV for the rich group.

Equation (6.14) defines MV income as a weighted average of ratios of the intercept to slope coefficients (with the signs changed) in pricing model (6.12). This income can thus be decomposed commodity-wise, as in Table 6.5. This shows that for both groups of countries, food and housing are the dominant contributors to MV income.[6]

6.7 Dispersion-equivalent income

As price dispersion depends on income, it is natural to ask, What change in income has the effect of equalising dispersion? We call this

---

[6] It should be noted that we explored two extensions to check the results. First, some of the relative prices for Lebanon, Iran and Georgia seem to be outlying observations. As a robustness check, we recalculated the results in Table 6.4 with the data for these three countries omitted; this had only a very marginal impact on the results. Second, in Table 6.2, poor countries are distinguished from rich countries by an intercept dummy. This treatment was reexamined graphically by plotting each relative price against income and then fitting separate regression lines for the rich and poor groups of countries. For most commodities, the scatter plots show something approximating an intercept shift. Clothing and furnishings are exceptions to this general rule, but as these goods each account for approximately 5 per cent of the budget for an average country, they are unlikely to substantially affect the overall results, which are weighted by budget shares. However, when pricing model (6.12) was estimated separately for the two groups of countries and the quadratic (6.13) was reevaluated, the results changed. There may be a case to keep the two groups separate, but owing to the relatively small sample size for the rich group, it is not possible to be hard and fast on this issue. For details, see Appendix 6A.1.

Table 6.5 *Commodity decomposition of minimum-variance income*

Commodity	Budget share $\bar{w}_i$ (×100)	Weight in equation (6.14) $\kappa_i = \dfrac{\beta_i^2/w_i}{\sum_{i=1}^{12}\beta_i^2/w_i}$ (×100)	Ratio of intercept to slope $-\dfrac{\bar{\alpha}_i}{\beta_i}$	Contribution to MV income $-\kappa_i \cdot \dfrac{\bar{\alpha}_i}{\beta_i}$ (×100)
(1)	(2)	(3)	(4)	(5)
		A. Poor		
Food	16.22	70.44 (12.13)	1.87 (0.21)	131.73 (21.03)
Alcohol	2.65	0.19 (0.32)	0.27 (1.28)	0.05 (0.19)
Clothing	7.09	4.43 (1.95)	-2.45 (0.49)	-10.86 (3.22)
Housing	15.37	19.22 (6.38)	1.10 (0.43)	21.07 (4.86)
Furnishings	7.32	1.33 (0.65)	-1.67 (0.37)	-2.22 (0.81)
Health	10.57	0.22 (0.54)	-28.92 (34.81)	-6.39 (7.93)
Transport	13.59	0.11 (0.31)	-20.84 (30.06)	-2.24 (3.39)
Communication	2.91	0.01 (0.08)	23.33 (99.84)	0.29 (1.22)
Recreation	4.03	0.29 (0.26)	-5.24 (2.18)	-1.52 (0.79)
Education	9.00	0.35 (0.97)	34.36 (48.64)	12.13 (16.67)
Restaurants	2.98	3.00 (1.55)	-3.34 (0.77)	-10.03 (3.28)
Miscellaneous	8.26	0.41 (0.27)	1.69 (0.76)	0.70 (0.24)
Total	100.00	100.00		132.71 (54.23)
		B. Rich		
Food	10.58	78.93 (5.77)	1.83 (0.15)	144.33 (14.88)
Alcohol	2.37	0.15 (0.27)	-0.73 (2.32)	-0.11 (0.25)
Clothing	3.71	6.18 (2.74)	0.63 (0.42)	3.86 (3.65)
Housing	19.72	10.95 (4.64)	1.98 (0.42)	21.65 (8.99)
Furnishings	4.58	1.55 (0.75)	0.18 (0.51)	0.29 (0.87)
Health	12.04	0.14 (0.35)	-18.88 (24.92)	-2.67 (3.05)
Transport	11.35	0.09 (0.27)	-20.21 (31.92)	-1.90 (2.63)
Communication	2.15	0.01 (0.07)	-4.67 (25.43)	-0.06 (0.20)
Recreation	8.83	0.10 (0.09)	-2.29 (1.81)	-0.22 (0.10)
Education	7.11	0.33 (0.91)	15.68 (20.10)	5.12 (7.83)
Restaurants	4.77	1.37 (0.72)	-3.15 (1.23)	-4.32 (1.05)
Miscellaneous	12.80	0.19 (0.13)	1.62 (0.56)	0.32 (0.22)
Total	100.00	100.00		166.28 (14.70)

Note: Asymptotic standard errors in parentheses.

change 'dispersion-equivalent income' (DEI). This section investigates the nature of DEI and applies the idea to the two groups of countries.

As discussed earlier, dispersion in the poor countries is mostly higher than in rich countries, and usually, dispersion decreases as income increases. These two characteristics are satisfied in the shaded region of Figure 6.4. The left-hand boundary of the region is defined by the intersection of the two curves, where income is x_1; for incomes below this value, dispersion of the rich group exceeds that of the poor group. The right-hand boundary of the region corresponds to the minimum point for the poor group, associated with income x_2; when income exceeds x_2, the rich group continues to decrease (which is satisfactory), but that for the poor group increases (not satisfactory). Within the shaded

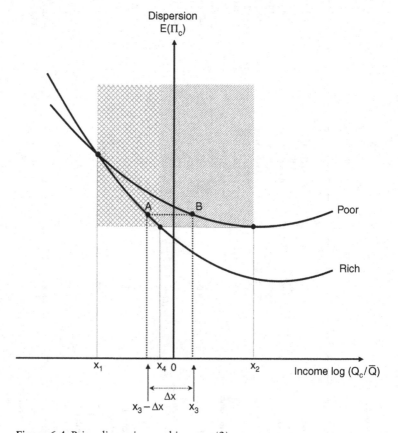

Figure 6.4 Price dispersion and income (2).

region, we can ask by how much the income of the rich group needs to be decreased to eliminate the difference in dispersion. Consider, for example, the case in which income for each group is x_3. Here dispersion in the two groups is equalised when the income of the rich group is decreased by $\Delta x > 0$ to $x_3 - \Delta x$. This Δx is DEI corresponding to x_3.

In the preceding, we commenced with the poor group and then determined the income adjustment required to increase the dispersion for the rich group to equal that for the poor group; in this sense, the latter is the base group. We could just as well reverse things and start with the rich group. Thus, when the income of the rich group is $x_3 - \Delta x$, by how much does the income of the poor group need to be increased? The answer is by the same Δx, which establishes that the analysis is symmetric with respect to the base group. However, there is an additional consideration when we start with the rich group: A positive DEI exists only within the smaller, cross-hatched subregion of Figure 6.4, where income falls in the range $x_1 \leq x \leq x_4$. The new boundary value x_4 is income when dispersion for the rich group equals the minimum value for the poor group. For income exceeding x_4, no addition to the income of the poor group will equalise dispersion. To summarise, it is legitimate to use either the rich or the poor as the base group for analysis of DEI, but given the way the two curves are drawn in Figure 6.4, the feasible income range is smaller when the rich group is used for this purpose.

It is clear from Figure 6.4 that the nonlinearities mean that DEI varies with income; as shown below, DEI is quadratic in income. This is further illustrated by Figure 6.5, which plots DEI against income.[7] The curve to the right, which refers to the case in which the base is the poor group, is derived from the left curve (base = rich) by adding the DEI for the rich group, the height of the curve, to income for the rich group to obtain the income of the poor group. For example, when the income of the rich group is $x_3 - \Delta x$, DEI $= \Delta x$. As point A on the curve for the rich group lies above the 45-degree line, $\Delta x > |x_3 - \Delta x|$. The associated point on the curve for the poor group is B, where DEI is the same Δx as before, whereas income is the previous value, $x_3 - \Delta x$, plus DEI, Δx, or x_3. Figure 6.5 reveals three patterns for DEI. First, DEI increases with

---

[7] For clarity, this figure is not drawn on the same scale as Figure 6.4.

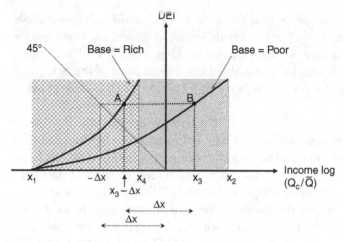

Figure 6.5 DEI and income.

income, which reflects the increasing difference in dispersion for the rich and poor countries. Second, in the range $x_1 \leq x \leq x_4$, the DEI curve for the rich group lies everywhere above that for the poor group. This means that when the income of the poor group is increased to equalise dispersion, DEI is greater than when the income of the rich group is reduced. Finally, for a given income within the range $x_1 \leq x \leq x_4$, the marginal DEI, $d(\text{DEI})/dx$, for the rich group exceeds that for the poor group.

To formulate DEI algebraically, we apply equation (6.13) to the rich and poor groups of countries explicitly by defining the quadratic coefficients as λ_k^g, for $k = 0, 1, 2$ (for the order) and $g = R, P$ (for the rich and poor). Thus we now have

$$y_c = \lambda_0^R + \lambda_1^R x_c + \lambda_2^R x_c^2, \quad \text{with } \lambda_0^R = \sum_{i=1}^{12} \frac{\alpha_i^2 + \sigma_i^2}{w_{ic}},$$

$$\lambda_1^R = \sum_{i=1}^{12} \frac{2\alpha_i \beta_i}{w_{ic}} \quad \text{and} \quad \lambda_2^R = \sum_{i=1}^{12} \frac{\beta_i^2}{w_{ic}},$$

if $c \in \text{Rich}$,

$$y_c = \lambda_0^P + \lambda_1^P x_c + \lambda_2^P x_c^2, \quad \text{with } \lambda_0^P = \sum_{i=1}^{12} \frac{\tilde{\alpha}_i^2 + \sigma_i^2}{w_{ic}},$$

$$\lambda_1^P = \sum_{i=1}^{12} \frac{2\tilde{\alpha}_i\beta_i}{w_{ic}} \quad \text{and} \quad \lambda_2^P = \sum_{i=1}^{12} \frac{\beta_i^2}{w_{ic}},$$

if $c \in$ Poor

These equations for the two groups differ for two reasons. First, the zero-order coefficients contain the respective intercepts of equation (6.12), $\tilde{\alpha}_i = \alpha_i + \gamma_i$ for the poor group and α_i for the rich group. Second, the budget shares in the coefficients are different across countries.

We write the variance for country c belonging to group g as a function of income as $y_c = f_g(x_c)$. Then DEI, Δx, solves $f_R(x_c) = f_P(x_c + \Delta x)$. If we use the preceding, this becomes

$$\lambda_0^R + \lambda_1^R x_c + \lambda_2^R x_c^2 = \lambda_0^P + \lambda_1^P(x_c + \Delta x) + \lambda_2^P(x_c + \Delta x)^2$$

or $\phi_0 + \phi_1 \Delta x + \phi_2(\Delta x)^2 = 0$

with $\phi_0 = \lambda_0^P - \lambda_0^R + (\lambda_1^P - \lambda_1^R)x_c + (\lambda_2^P - \lambda_2^R)x_c^2, \phi_1 = \lambda_1^P + 2\lambda_2^P x_c$ and $\phi_2 = \lambda_2^P$. The roots of this equation are

$$\Delta x = \frac{-\phi_1 \pm \sqrt{\phi_1^2 - 4\phi_2\phi_0}}{2\phi_2}$$

We evaluate this equation with the quadratic coefficients of Table 6.4 and use the smaller root. When the rich group is used as the basis for comparison, the admissible income range is $-1.11 \le x \le -0.26$, which is equivalent to income for the poor group falling within the range 33 to 77 per cent of the mean. Table 6.6 gives values of DEI, and it is evident that it is sensitive to income: DEI is 3 per cent of income when income in the poor group is 33 per cent of the mean, whereas DEI is 61 per cent when income increases to 56 per cent of the mean.

6.8 The cost of dispersion

Consider two countries with the same income, and suppose that because of flawed institutions and/or policies, price dispersion is higher in one than in the other. This will distort economic decisions and impose a welfare cost on the high-dispersion economy. In this section

Table 6.6 *Dispersion-equivalent income: illustrative calculations*

Income (relative to mean)		Dispersion-equivalent income (additional income relative to the base income of the poor)	
Logarithmic (×100) (1)	Percentage (2)	Logarithmic (×100) (3)	Percentage (4)
−111	33	3	3
−76	47	28	33
−57	56	47	61
−26	77	113	208

we analyse the welfare implications of higher dispersion in the poor group of countries. This analysis takes place under several simplified conditions: The excess dispersion is taken to be distortionary, and the implications are confined to consumption in the context of a simple demand structure. For these reasons, the results that follow should be viewed as illustrations of the issues involved rather than precise quantification.

Suppose that distortions change the vector of n prices by $\Delta\mathbf{p}$, which leads to changes in consumption of $\mathbf{S}\Delta\mathbf{p}$, where $\mathbf{S}$ is the substitution matrix. The associated welfare cost can be expressed as $W = -\frac{1}{2}\Delta\mathbf{p}'\mathbf{S}\Delta\mathbf{p}$ (Harberger, 1964). It can be shown that the welfare cost as a fraction of income M is

$$\frac{W}{M} = -\frac{\kappa}{2}\Pi \tag{6.17}$$

where $\kappa < 0$ is the negative of the elasticity of substitution, and Π is price dispersion (6.2).[8] In words, the welfare cost is proportional to the price variance, where the proportionality factor is half the elasticity of substitution. The cost of the higher dispersion in the poor compared with the rich countries is then $\Delta(W/M) = -(\kappa/2)\Delta\Pi$, where $\Delta\Pi > 0$ is the increase in dispersion.

---

[8] For the derivation of result (6.17), based on Selvanathan's (1985) model, see Appendix 6A.2.

In view of the broad nature of the commodity groups, there is not likely to be much substitutability between them, so a low value of the elasticity of substitution would be appropriate. Thus, if this elasticity is 0.5, then the welfare cost is a quarter of the increase in the variance. One way to measure $\Delta \Pi$ is by the increase in the variance at mean income, which from the last entry in column 4 of Table 6.4 is 6.95 ($\times 100^{-1}$). Thus the welfare cost for the poor countries, expressed as a proportion of their income, is $6.95/4 \approx 2$ percentage points higher than that for the rich countries. Although apparently quite modest, for some countries this figure could be close to the economic growth for one year. As the cost repeats itself each year, the implication is that in some cases elimination of the underlying distortions could lead to a nontrivial acceleration of growth. However, as our estimate of the cost depends on the demand structure used, the value of the elasticity of substitution, and exactly how the increase in dispersion is measured, it should be clear that it provides only a back-of-the-envelope indication of the order of magnitude involved.

6.9 Concluding comments

This chapter has dealt with the theory and measurement of differences in income and prices across countries. Using data for more than 130 countries published by the International Comparison Program (2008), we found that the distribution of prices within poor countries was substantially more disperse than that in the rich group. As the prices of some commodities are strongly related to income, we developed a simple analytical model to understand this phenomenon. This model provides a novel link between prices and the income sensitivity of consumption patterns. This approach implies that price dispersion is quadratic in income and gives rise to several interesting concepts, including the value of income that minimises dispersion, as well as dispersion-equivalent income (DEI). Finally, we carried out some illustrative calculations regarding the welfare cost of dispersion. In summary, this framework facilitates an understanding of price dispersion and its determinants and provides some useful new concepts.

Rather than reiterating the findings in detail, we conclude with some broader issues raised by the analysis. If higher dispersion entails a welfare cost, we could ask, What is the source of the distortion? If it were the result of bad policy (e.g., taxes, import tariffs, misaligned exchange rate, etc.) or mispricing of factor inputs (i.e., underpriced natural resources, labour costs that are too high because of unions, etc.), then a genuine distortion exists that imposes avoidable damage on the economy, as measured by the welfare cost. However, if the distribution of prices is more disperse because of natural factors such as climate, geography or factor endowments, then there is no distortion. The associated cost is not a welfare cost as is usually understood but a cost that simply has to be lived with.

What if the higher dispersion results from poor infrastructure such as low-quality ports, roads and telecommunications? Here the higher costs could result in higher prices at home for imported commodities and lower prices of goods that are exported, thus increasing overall dispersion. Without further information, it is not clear if this is a distortion that carries a welfare cost; for example, the infrastructure of a country may be inferior by international standards, but it may still be appropriate if there is a limited pool of investable funds. Another difficulty occurs when the lack of access to modern technology causes the cost of certain goods to be higher than would otherwise be the case while that of others is lower. The interpretation of the higher price dispersion is unclear here also. A final broader issue relates to how the economy responds to shocks of all kinds. When the economy is better able to adjust to shocks, supply and demand schedules are more price-elastic, and relative prices are more stable. Accordingly, for a given disturbance, such as an oil-price shock, price dispersion will be lower because of the greater flexibility of the economy, other things remaining unchanged.

Appendix 6A

6A.1 The data and further results

Data

The data used are budget shares, relative prices and real income per capita. Tables 6A.1 and 6A.2 contain the budget and shares prices, whereas Table 6.1 contains income. These data come from the World Bank's International Comparison Program (2008).

Table 6A.1 *Budget shares in 132 countries in 2005* (×100)

	Country	Food	Alcoholic beverages	Clothing	Housing	Furnishing	Health	Transport	Communication	Recreation	Education	Restaurant	Miscellaneous
1.	United States	6.24	1.96	4.19	16.01	4.40	18.26	10.62	1.55	8.61	8.50	5.64	14.02
2.	Luxembourg	6.88	7.66	2.81	15.50	5.38	10.63	13.67	0.97	7.60	9.97	5.38	13.54
3.	Iceland	8.94	3.04	3.45	15.40	4.94	12.65	13.51	1.91	10.95	9.76	5.93	9.51
4.	Norway	9.73	3.10	4.07	14.94	4.47	13.48	10.71	2.37	10.95	7.72	4.17	14.29
5.	UK	7.13	2.96	4.64	15.50	4.60	10.02	11.92	1.77	10.83	5.99	9.38	15.25
6.	Austria	8.74	2.39	5.22	16.69	6.06	9.85	10.75	2.16	10.25	7.81	9.77	10.32
7.	Switzerland	9.27	3.05	3.52	20.48	3.94	13.26	6.94	2.37	8.50	7.91	7.01	13.74
8.	Canada	7.69	3.18	3.77	19.21	5.01	11.78	11.56	1.90	9.11	7.91	5.69	13.20
9.	Netherlands	8.19	2.19	4.01	17.64	4.83	10.67	8.90	3.49	8.83	7.46	3.93	19.87
10.	Sweden	8.27	2.43	3.65	19.21	3.57	11.74	9.15	2.20	9.69	10.20	3.53	16.36
11.	France	10.58	2.37	3.71	19.72	4.58	12.04	11.35	2.15	8.83	7.11	4.77	12.80
12.	Australia	8.55	3.53	3.22	18.32	5.62	11.83	10.15	2.44	10.21	9.40	6.77	9.97
13.	Denmark	8.08	2.79	3.50	19.33	4.20	11.02	9.96	1.55	9.23	9.10	3.62	17.63
14.	Belgium	10.29	2.75	4.16	17.73	4.26	13.01	11.36	1.74	7.85	8.95	3.98	13.92
15.	Germany	9.14	2.88	4.30	19.77	5.63	12.65	11.24	2.25	8.29	5.84	4.38	13.63
16.	Hong Kong	8.90	0.72	9.87	17.79	5.06	8.50	6.35	2.95	11.47	7.60	9.19	11.60
17.	Ireland	4.60	4.08	4.07	16.60	5.40	10.11	9.77	2.71	6.85	10.11	12.30	13.41
18.	Japan	12.26	2.51	2.81	20.43	4.73	11.50	8.98	2.69	7.77	6.15	6.47	13.70
19.	Taiwan	14.82	2.22	3.63	15.12	5.67	8.37	10.14	3.17	8.31	10.82	7.60	10.12
20.	Cyprus	13.71	5.42	5.57	12.83	4.91	5.99	12.74	1.76	7.74	7.29	11.09	10.95

Table 6A.1 (*cont.*)

Country	Food	Alcoholic beverages	Clothing	Housing	Furnishing	Health	Transport	Communication	Recreation	Education	Restaurant	Miscellaneous
21. Finland	9.31	3.76	3.61	18.87	4.08	11.71	9.62	2.11	9.81	8.06	4.87	14.18
22. Spain	11.77	2.42	4.67	13.71	4.45	10.43	9.88	2.20	8.67	6.48	15.60	9.72
23. Italy	12.31	2.19	6.60	17.09	6.35	11.83	11.08	2.32	6.29	6.50	8.14	9.32
24. Greece	13.84	4.24	9.27	14.18	5.70	8.30	7.85	2.20	5.66	5.90	17.00	5.86
25. New Zealand	11.47	4.13	3.69	18.17	5.36	10.09	11.38	2.40	11.53	7.31	6.25	8.22
26. Israel	12.88	2.04	2.79	19.34	5.74	9.70	9.60	3.16	7.80	11.77	4.07	11.10
27. Malta	13.91	2.62	5.21	9.35	7.56	7.89	11.85	4.02	9.78	6.74	11.30	9.76
28. Singapore	8.22	2.29	3.54	14.18	5.99	8.44	16.58	2.35	12.20	7.99	7.53	10.70
29. Qatar	13.63	0.25	6.16	17.19	6.44	8.82	15.31	4.62	3.27	17.98	1.55	4.77
30. Slovenia	11.93	4.09	4.72	15.59	4.91	10.81	12.97	2.90	9.01	8.42	5.36	9.29
31. Portugal	13.15	2.94	5.97	11.45	5.58	12.19	11.60	2.41	7.30	8.55	8.57	10.29
32. Brunei	18.36	0.53	4.41	12.13	4.38	5.29	15.10	5.48	7.67	15.95	5.08	5.64
33. Kuwait	14.77	0.20	8.07	18.37	13.40	5.60	12.33	2.55	4.09	12.80	2.38	5.43
34. Czech Rep.	13.09	6.45	3.95	18.08	4.26	10.57	9.37	2.82	10.61	7.48	5.33	7.98
35. Hungary	13.32	6.59	2.85	14.68	5.28	10.81	12.55	3.59	7.89	7.73	3.96	10.75
36. Bahrain	18.96	0.52	6.83	18.19	9.33	11.11	9.97	2.25	3.38	11.59	2.19	5.69
37. Korea	13.66	2.13	3.74	15.12	3.59	8.28	9.66	4.90	6.66	10.54	6.69	15.03
38. Estonia	15.36	6.81	6.12	16.10	4.67	7.61	10.65	2.57	8.78	7.39	5.79	8.16
39. Slovakia	15.66	4.48	3.67	22.30	4.67	9.17	7.50	3.12	8.61	5.79	5.82	9.23
40. Lithuania	22.92	5.70	7.05	12.16	4.84	9.06	12.86	2.27	6.38	6.92	2.68	7.17

292

41.	Poland	17.81	5.60	4.03	20.19	3.82	8.68	7.42	2.85	7.06	7.94	2.42	12.17
42.	Croatia	19.28	3.87	4.62	14.75	7.41	9.39	9.06	2.89	7.70	6.89	7.50	6.63
43.	Macao	13.25	0.89	4.91	13.93	2.22	8.10	8.71	5.63	15.33	8.35	12.26	6.42
44.	Latvia	19.22	6.09	6.11	18.22	3.15	7.66	9.72	3.62	8.32	8.19	4.69	5.00
45.	Lebanon	27.77	2.07	6.01	10.02	6.27	8.01	7.23	1.36	2.92	17.15	5.17	6.03
46.	Mexico	21.98	2.34	2.57	15.40	6.84	7.03	15.90	1.79	3.00	8.80	6.45	7.89
47.	Belarus	34.67	4.59	5.86	11.39	3.35	9.06	6.26	3.62	4.33	10.36	2.08	4.42
48.	Kazakhstan	18.61	2.90	8.76	25.72	2.78	9.64	8.44	2.03	4.79	9.22	2.73	4.37
49.	Mauritius	23.44	6.75	4.73	19.90	6.27	5.21	10.91	2.47	5.26	7.72	2.79	4.56
50.	Russia	25.53	6.13	9.36	9.64	4.05	7.74	10.92	4.27	6.26	5.67	2.83	7.61
51.	Bulgaria	19.51	3.29	2.87	18.10	3.54	7.82	16.07	5.46	5.22	5.75	8.00	4.37
52.	Iran	23.39	0.67	6.24	24.52	5.58	8.42	9.24	2.45	3.59	7.64	1.55	6.70
53.	Romania	24.95	4.37	3.08	19.78	4.29	8.21	14.78	1.76	4.35	6.02	4.40	4.00
54.	Oman	22.11	0.49	6.32	17.26	5.11	5.39	12.20	3.82	2.18	11.70	2.26	11.17
55.	Argentina	22.49	3.64	4.27	14.38	4.86	10.68	9.14	3.68	6.42	6.00	6.98	7.46
56.	Serbia	25.64	4.62	3.84	21.49	4.47	8.18	8.27	3.35	4.48	5.34	2.37	7.95
57.	Saudi Arabia	18.46	0.36	6.38	14.78	8.75	9.03	9.70	2.33	3.48	19.12	3.97	3.63
58.	Chile	16.22	2.65	7.09	15.37	7.32	10.57	13.59	2.91	4.03	9.00	2.98	8.26
59.	Uruguay	19.02	3.54	4.86	19.52	6.05	11.39	11.70	3.04	4.44	5.51	4.45	6.48
60.	Bosnia	28.51	5.68	5.17	13.32	6.44	8.34	7.65	2.45	4.18	5.27	6.56	6.42

Table 6A.1 (cont.)

Country	Food	Alcoholic beverages	Clothing	Housing	Furnishing	Health	Transport	Communication	Recreation	Education	Restaurant	Miscellaneous
61. Macedonia	30.91	3.09	5.50	17.88	3.86	6.79	8.96	6.55	2.31	5.54	3.39	5.21
62. Ukraine	32.05	5.08	4.32	8.84	3.25	8.69	10.90	3.69	5.30	9.56	2.70	5.62
63. South Africa	17.61	5.03	5.02	11.17	6.67	10.88	15.09	2.09	4.06	10.16	2.28	9.95
64. Malaysia	17.28	1.48	2.21	17.46	4.66	4.85	12.67	5.23	4.13	9.02	7.62	13.40
65. Turkey	23.06	3.84	5.75	24.02	6.28	3.80	11.68	4.00	2.36	5.80	4.06	5.34
66. Montenegro	32.15	3.62	5.15	23.02	3.62	7.06	6.58	4.32	2.76	4.53	1.25	5.95
67. Brazil	15.50	2.25	4.10	16.27	5.67	12.00	11.87	4.03	4.32	8.39	3.68	11.90
68. Venezuela	26.07	2.92	3.98	11.07	5.18	8.83	9.08	4.61	4.17	10.44	8.15	5.49
69. Thailand	15.87	4.41	6.96	7.17	6.06	8.32	14.59	1.32	5.91	8.92	14.86	5.62
70. Albania	24.63	4.78	4.51	19.13	5.43	5.59	11.82	4.01	5.50	3.41	5.35	5.83
71. Colombia	24.32	3.98	4.40	14.17	5.19	10.66	10.74	2.81	3.52	8.53	5.79	5.87
72. Ecuador	25.92	2.08	6.23	11.43	6.83	7.08	14.13	4.47	6.01	8.89	2.97	3.97
73. Jordan	28.87	3.06	5.40	17.10	3.95	7.73	8.93	3.66	1.69	11.67	2.85	5.10
74. Tunisia	24.78	3.60	8.62	12.96	7.17	5.94	9.00	0.96	2.34	6.06	12.77	5.80
75. Peru	29.24	1.91	5.96	8.50	5.15	7.03	8.39	2.47	4.62	9.64	8.01	9.08
76. Egypt	41.65	2.74	7.71	12.88	3.63	4.89	3.96	2.61	2.53	7.51	3.09	6.80
77. Moldova	24.20	7.76	4.49	15.33	6.98	4.87	9.92	4.65	6.19	7.58	1.65	6.38
78. Maldives	22.95	2.02	3.54	29.70	3.49	9.44	3.41	3.12	3.52	14.04	1.10	3.68
79. Gabon	36.34	2.01	5.21	14.75	3.12	6.71	6.37	4.07	2.54	10.74	2.88	5.26
80. Fiji	26.25	2.97	2.35	25.80	9.49	5.51	7.61	0.39	4.96	7.36	2.84	4.49

81.	Georgia	36.70	0.90	8.54	4.16	3.79	7.63	2.48	1.88	6.01	23.43	0.45	4.03
82.	Botswana	21.94	8.81	6.18	9.04	7.40	6.49	13.02	2.92	2.42	16.57	0.19	5.03
83.	Namibia	25.96	2.65	5.14	12.15	5.08	8.41	9.67	0.71	2.67	14.32	4.29	8.95
84.	Swaziland	41.90	0.88	6.17	13.56	7.08	7.30	6.85	1.32	3.24	8.27	0.64	2.78
85.	Syria	41.72	0.26	8.69	23.91	3.17	8.15	3.29	0.31	1.36	6.80	1.83	0.50
86.	Bolivia	27.75	1.54	3.08	12.07	5.31	7.56	17.89	2.16	1.36	11.18	7.38	2.72
87.	Eq. Guinea	39.49	2.37	5.39	14.28	3.96	7.40	8.35	3.91	1.64	3.91	3.56	5.73
88.	Paraguay	32.30	2.50	7.88	11.68	5.17	5.24	11.37	2.41	6.19	5.41	4.19	5.67
89.	Cape Verde	28.84	1.69	3.39	26.96	4.87	3.52	6.11	3.00	3.06	11.73	2.75	4.08
90.	Bhutan	34.53	2.60	6.40	16.59	5.57	12.95	1.90	0.40	3.39	5.97	0.07	9.63
91.	Kyrgyzstan	40.82	8.32	7.92	7.04	3.00	4.19	9.16	2.65	2.43	5.98	2.71	5.78
92.	Sri Lanka	36.42	4.08	9.17	7.52	6.26	3.36	16.76	0.96	3.72	2.92	1.69	7.15
93.	Iraq	32.12	0.79	5.20	15.73	7.66	15.19	9.25	1.16	1.00	9.17	0.72	2.01
94.	Mongolia	35.88	2.30	10.81	16.80	3.65	5.26	6.31	1.88	3.28	10.41	0.55	2.87
95.	Philippines	43.90	1.96	2.16	13.94	1.86	3.41	5.49	3.98	1.09	9.05	3.14	10.02
96.	Indonesia	41.60	1.87	3.55	20.20	2.64	3.02	6.52	1.83	1.72	5.56	6.17	5.33
97.	Pakistan	48.77	0.93	7.49	13.67	2.40	7.24	5.18	1.94	2.69	4.53	0.69	4.47
98.	Morocco	31.09	2.85	5.03	13.00	4.29	5.36	8.83	5.06	3.17	10.44	5.69	5.20
99.	Lesotho	35.48	3.51	12.55	7.35	6.57	7.28	5.75	1.79	1.60	13.31	0.20	4.63
100.	China	24.12	2.05	6.30	14.66	3.92	6.21	4.03	4.17	4.65	9.79	5.23	14.86

Table 6A.1 (*cont.*)

Country	Food	Alcoholic beverages	Clothing	Housing	Furnishing	Health	Transport	Communication	Recreation	Education	Restaurant	Miscellaneous
101. Vietnam	31.34	2.28	3.54	15.15	4.81	8.13	9.58	0.86	4.80	9.22	6.74	3.54
102. India	33.69	2.13	5.21	12.13	2.76	7.32	15.32	1.52	1.91	5.71	1.86	10.44
103. Cambodia	47.20	3.78	1.82	12.55	1.77	7.64	7.22	0.25	2.42	6.00	4.76	4.59
104. Yemen	41.06	2.03	8.73	16.49	4.04	3.78	5.16	0.68	1.26	6.43	2.42	7.92
105. Sudan	55.60	1.50	4.69	14.30	5.82	2.02	8.17	0.10	2.95	1.68	0.10	3.06
106. Laos	47.35	5.57	1.75	12.37	2.86	3.09	10.54	0.44	2.97	6.84	2.97	3.25
107. Djibouti	33.64	12.98	2.51	16.32	6.94	4.25	7.91	0.45	0.35	7.91	4.04	2.69
108. Kenya	33.27	3.11	2.96	7.35	4.48	7.73	11.67	2.77	5.86	11.80	4.53	4.47
109. Sao Tome	53.71	4.44	3.86	9.00	3.32	5.40	9.63	1.25	1.44	4.69	1.25	2.00
110. Congo, Rep.	37.52	3.87	2.45	13.03	3.38	5.95	7.90	4.91	2.12	8.09	7.72	3.06
111. Cameroon	43.37	2.53	9.97	8.79	10.43	2.34	7.04	1.28	1.62	4.12	6.13	2.37
112. Nigeria	56.67	1.02	5.85	11.35	7.03	3.04	4.71	0.33	1.31	4.30	0.71	3.69
113. Senegal	48.93	3.05	5.24	9.96	6.20	5.24	3.89	5.39	2.29	5.12	0.97	3.72
114. Chad	55.05	1.49	1.62	2.31	7.16	1.37	19.42	0.85	4.71	1.81	0.52	3.69
115. Nepal	48.72	3.24	6.20	13.84	2.30	8.81	3.94	0.30	1.02	4.56	2.40	4.69
116. Bangladesh	49.92	2.37	5.78	17.37	3.67	3.65	4.09	0.47	0.77	5.65	2.23	4.04
117. Benin	43.59	2.39	9.19	10.34	3.16	2.91	7.34	1.74	2.17	4.57	7.89	4.72
118. Ghana	49.15	2.12	9.14	6.64	6.44	5.70	5.89	0.30	2.97	8.14	0.03	3.47
119. Cote d'Ivoire	43.28	3.21	3.54	9.71	8.42	4.22	11.14	2.93	3.53	3.99	1.46	4.58
120. Sierra Leone	42.42	2.79	7.22	6.58	2.56	14.35	2.68	2.56	3.12	9.87	1.11	4.75

121. Madagascar	57.03	3.08	4.06	14.21	4.60	4.41	3.13	0.45	0.70	5.87	1.32	1.14
122. Togo	48.59	4.19	5.22	6.56	2.70	3.77	16.02	2.04	1.95	3.94	2.32	2.70
123. Burkina Faso	41.98	9.19	3.28	9.35	8.51	2.86	7.81	1.09	1.82	4.42	5.64	4.06
124. Guinea	44.04	2.01	6.86	7.49	5.55	12.08	7.84	0.23	1.16	6.73	2.02	3.98
125. Mali	46.70	1.64	4.81	11.18	6.38	4.41	9.91	0.89	3.07	6.19	1.83	3.00
126. Angola	40.70	4.41	4.92	8.89	5.67	5.60	5.13	0.82	2.12	5.51	2.99	13.24
127. Rwanda	42.65	13.18	3.41	14.18	5.09	3.46	5.12	0.55	1.20	6.79	1.71	2.67
128. CAR	56.84	8.98	7.74	5.01	5.09	1.73	3.55	0.85	1.75	3.43	1.91	3.13
129. Mozambique	60.09	3.23	5.90	6.85	2.67	4.73	4.03	0.16	2.13	7.52	0.45	2.26
130. Niger	46.41	2.28	7.12	8.47	4.79	4.59	7.95	0.78	5.23	3.48	5.15	3.75
131. Guinea–Biss.	52.27	1.72	8.33	13.54	7.26	2.74	6.50	0.53	3.91	2.25	0.48	0.45
132. Congo, D.R.	62.22	2.02	5.00	11.95	2.80	3.99	3.41	0.82	0.91	2.99	1.39	2.50
Mean: All	27.57	3.34	5.27	14.67	5.11	7.70	9.40	2.42	4.94	7.99	4.46	7.13
Rich	10.53	3.22	4.42	16.86	5.03	10.58	10.57	2.48	8.98	8.08	7.23	12.02
Poor	33.08	3.38	5.55	13.97	5.14	6.77	9.02	2.40	3.63	7.96	3.56	5.54

Note: Means exclude the United States.

Table 6A.2 Relative prices in 132 countries in 2005

Country	Food	Alcoholic beverages	Clothing	Housing	Furnishing	Health	Transport	Communication	Recreation	Education	Restaurant	Miscellaneous
1. United States	0.00	0.00	0.00	0.00	0.00	0.00	0.00	0.00	0.00	0.00	0.00	0.00
2. Luxembourg	9.61	-28.28	11.01	-0.37	1.23	-32.30	20.54	-34.09	10.48	3.29	19.45	-0.20
3. Iceland	19.83	30.93	21.76	-14.45	3.12	-34.24	26.65	-31.14	16.49	-53.79	51.10	3.63
4. Norway	20.15	42.92	14.99	-33.22	-4.78	-34.36	51.29	-28.87	12.30	-43.80	39.28	10.46
5. UK	6.58	39.28	1.12	-22.86	1.95	-43.13	42.56	-26.94	2.60	-31.70	34.09	-0.56
6. Austria	13.31	-14.57	9.93	-19.53	2.37	-40.48	44.08	-10.54	8.22	-32.70	25.53	4.61
7. Switzerland	15.73	-35.15	-3.20	14.00	-6.05	-31.54	20.77	-11.70	1.31	-25.58	22.06	3.51
8. Canada	19.86	39.84	20.59	-20.01	17.87	-17.71	23.23	-0.27	3.77	-40.05	32.11	-1.66
9. Netherlands	-7.15	-5.83	8.18	7.64	-1.14	-42.95	53.09	-7.08	7.51	-40.72	29.93	1.99
10. Sweden	12.35	9.37	14.05	-9.69	8.19	-32.76	46.06	-44.23	14.50	-38.34	37.93	9.66
11. France	7.03	1.37	-2.99	0.99	6.67	-38.49	33.52	-0.27	10.25	-45.27	35.88	2.12
12. Australia	15.50	35.77	0.13	-6.32	18.79	-27.98	26.42	16.70	9.25	-50.20	22.86	-0.45
13. Denmark	10.07	-15.66	-1.20	-3.01	-4.72	-31.84	50.18	-55.12	8.02	-38.44	40.87	6.17
14. Belgium	11.40	-10.74	14.83	0.86	6.19	-35.54	36.01	1.89	6.83	-36.87	32.76	0.35
15. Germany	8.06	-9.98	10.52	-2.30	-1.27	-43.50	37.33	-2.74	11.08	-15.27	20.96	0.33
16. Hong Kong	31.95	46.24	-4.63	35.11	17.29	-78.15	38.37	6.55	-19.90	-67.54	33.83	-13.10
17. Ireland	8.46	35.16	-10.15	0.10	-4.18	-37.02	29.01	-11.19	0.85	-42.77	33.68	0.99
18. Japan	58.71	-31.19	23.24	-3.34	23.25	-71.57	20.26	-4.16	-8.75	-37.39	29.87	0.62
19. Taiwan	58.81	16.25	10.28	24.07	47.36	-121.10	37.99	-17.67	-6.80	-93.78	27.27	-2.83
20. Cyprus	16.92	7.34	17.95	-45.05	8.56	-40.93	39.66	-77.02	9.72	-55.25	39.52	-6.49

21.	Finland	8.50	9.79	13.28	-3.42	-0.58	-34.55	40.97	-45.26	10.88	-45.04	35.66	6.50
22.	Spain	5.22	-29.14	13.47	-5.17	14.08	-50.65	37.06	3.98	11.66	-56.31	29.57	-9.30
23.	Italy	15.69	-6.65	8.39	-14.53	6.38	-24.36	30.61	-8.32	7.88	-39.59	25.37	-6.08
24.	Greece	14.08	-9.78	20.76	-21.19	11.13	-53.57	26.43	13.69	10.61	-71.24	30.40	-9.94
25.	New Zealand	20.06	29.63	15.82	-3.79	16.95	-40.79	23.25	3.25	7.06	-51.67	5.89	-4.18
26.	Israel	18.24	11.53	13.06	-12.21	13.65	-39.22	59.04	-13.28	21.53	-60.79	56.22	3.37
27.	Malta	14.87	22.15	40.48	-68.56	33.14	-68.23	55.81	17.25	11.10	-71.26	18.85	-12.23
28.	Singapore	29.16	118.74	18.70	20.88	26.26	-86.86	41.34	-36.86	-13.37	-96.11	23.69	-13.56
29.	Qatar	-6.37	-40.37	6.30	125.73	-23.08	-68.78	-40.99	10.87	1.12	-38.15	41.56	-31.96
30.	Slovenia	21.92	-10.89	41.50	-26.85	15.29	-46.89	45.30	-8.61	18.59	-48.24	18.43	1.62
31.	Portugal	7.50	-12.26	14.89	-24.90	8.43	-40.68	46.93	11.13	13.72	-25.89	17.53	-1.77
32.	Brunei	45.77	30.48	35.42	22.28	32.98	-89.11	14.98	30.75	19.55	-109.13	45.91	1.25
33.	Kuwait	-13.30	-47.53	34.68	56.18	-15.73	-57.43	-30.09	9.08	18.66	-32.72	60.76	-5.13
34.	Czech Rep.	27.76	13.38	70.97	-33.87	40.76	-67.14	67.11	61.92	10.50	-76.54	20.80	-4.35
35.	Hungary	26.40	8.37	57.20	-45.05	22.79	-61.72	74.90	39.72	16.02	-84.69	35.40	-5.20
36.	Bahrain	3.66	-26.34	2.17	80.20	-14.81	-54.44	-14.91	16.54	9.85	-60.41	55.77	-22.78
37.	Korea	60.99	3.57	31.97	-4.92	-5.75	-83.25	29.25	-34.73	12.42	-53.77	46.45	-7.66
38.	Estonia	26.69	0.41	60.21	-20.90	22.77	-71.77	54.43	26.69	11.36	-115.59	34.13	-11.90
39.	Slovakia	33.04	10.71	58.75	-34.72	39.64	-68.86	76.74	65.35	16.58	-111.05	31.37	-2.39
40.	Lithuania	23.23	3.97	72.89	-50.84	27.34	-72.57	62.44	11.29	9.99	-123.66	37.39	-8.68

Table 6A.2 (*cont.*)

Country	Food	Alcoholic beverages	Clothing	Housing	Furnishing	Health	Transport	Communication	Recreation	Education	Restaurant	Miscellaneous
41. Poland	26.22	10.38	80.68	−35.36	33.76	−72.27	75.96	55.06	26.26	−87.86	51.94	2.33
42. Croatia	31.70	17.25	53.33	−63.09	27.17	−64.05	61.77	8.87	16.71	−91.36	49.43	−7.41
43. Macao	34.48	2.64	4.69	13.46	33.81	−95.73	28.97	17.11	0.19	−93.47	40.06	−4.85
44. Latvia	30.58	−4.95	74.67	−32.44	29.12	−77.31	61.72	63.64	12.94	−120.40	43.64	−15.70
45. Lebanon	21.55	4.71	76.02	−3.35	23.77	−74.61	−0.40	54.49	31.56	−83.76	132.57	0.84
46. Mexico	12.59	−18.70	12.06	19.37	2.30	−41.47	23.34	44.14	15.06	−98.04	25.03	−10.17
47. Belarus	46.63	17.01	77.73	−91.74	64.06	−89.69	91.14	−34.79	43.10	−127.97	40.01	23.66
48. Kazakhstan	45.31	−10.70	93.06	−15.73	65.55	−105.94	62.76	83.54	33.87	−157.52	53.89	13.39
49. Mauritius	36.51	35.79	17.76	−47.18	5.38	−87.55	73.79	−18.21	48.26	−117.45	21.27	2.90
50. Russia	26.40	−16.50	74.63	−83.55	42.21	−100.06	50.92	39.12	17.59	−152.36	44.00	5.83
51. Bulgaria	33.24	0.03	55.32	−48.61	33.73	−92.66	68.78	74.60	13.84	−156.76	7.01	−14.25
52. Iran	77.39	−4.41	22.95	−7.86	46.10	−142.18	17.41	−154.81	30.25	−99.66	77.47	−9.75
53. Romania	34.73	−2.63	52.05	−28.95	17.82	−97.40	61.19	42.34	4.00	−122.10	20.42	−17.32
54. Oman	5.51	−16.64	1.91	62.82	−12.88	−61.60	−12.31	25.88	4.85	−53.51	56.45	−24.45
55. Argentina	25.05	−33.01	30.44	−25.73	30.72	−81.41	35.63	−24.52	42.10	−64.50	61.92	−4.58
56. Serbia	47.39	−12.99	75.97	−45.94	54.37	−84.39	80.76	−39.72	15.86	−118.46	50.53	−13.36
57. Saudi Arabia	16.20	−26.31	1.30	39.02	−15.96	−65.68	−3.07	68.18	41.41	−35.44	77.58	−12.50
58. Chile	20.94	−26.51	31.73	−27.35	30.85	−58.42	40.56	41.81	15.80	−54.57	35.45	−4.03
59. Uruguay	15.48	−19.61	29.44	−6.91	18.58	−69.91	46.71	−1.28	23.51	−68.12	45.77	−3.69
60. Bosnia	34.95	−13.48	72.87	−71.83	22.76	−69.14	74.28	−3.44	12.27	−126.05	37.33	−15.85

61.	Macedonia	34.10	−19.66	57.59	−67.25	38.34	−101.49	75.71	52.19	28.57	−120.37	30.05	−16.82
62.	Ukraine	39.00	−2.19	82.46	−117.16	66.48	−88.19	75.08	57.93	34.89	−159.99	66.07	22.33
63.	South Africa	25.78	6.57	26.25	−39.10	32.00	−55.33	44.80	33.18	28.29	−76.71	50.71	0.94
64.	Malaysia	33.87	70.30	12.67	21.98	18.55	−111.41	19.85	10.68	−3.52	−129.10	39.67	−5.77
65.	Turkey	30.98	20.50	30.75	−55.43	9.29	−54.89	74.00	37.83	15.34	−109.71	41.55	−13.58
66.	Montenegro	40.27	−26.85	80.99	−35.16	33.02	−98.26	72.04	−15.09	16.07	−132.97	47.22	−23.93
67.	Brazil	16.33	−53.92	44.63	3.39	25.10	−69.91	55.74	9.55	36.89	−62.88	14.73	−5.01
68.	Venezuela	41.00	−44.31	62.35	−54.43	38.00	−69.86	19.00	−4.73	39.39	−70.03	35.53	−7.02
69.	Thailand	40.14	42.43	22.63	−40.32	36.92	−111.67	39.49	25.78	15.46	−134.97	33.23	3.66
70.	Albania	34.23	−6.44	57.97	−38.39	25.82	−141.58	59.36	41.88	8.65	−168.21	26.32	−29.61
71.	Colombia	42.17	−9.12	38.31	−44.36	20.57	−80.63	54.57	12.68	39.67	−73.10	10.52	4.25
72.	Ecuador	28.05	−19.21	27.50	−18.48	8.44	−102.25	26.80	4.61	42.12	−78.93	35.81	−9.48
73.	Jordan	19.87	−4.44	5.33	57.98	14.07	−90.38	−7.72	−1.22	21.64	−99.89	91.97	0.57
74.	Tunisia	30.73	19.21	70.80	−70.47	−8.61	−82.57	51.88	13.12	46.33	−86.99	−1.09	−3.84
75.	Peru	30.90	−1.97	17.36	−49.58	19.76	−69.24	28.27	13.76	24.18	−73.44	34.74	−16.54
76.	Egypt	40.52	30.45	21.53	−25.98	−0.98	−148.38	−5.06	80.25	31.82	−167.08	75.21	−17.63
77.	Moldova	48.88	−16.72	97.92	−89.53	72.62	−108.60	81.26	50.15	31.37	−195.15	59.09	7.68
78.	Maldives	37.85	4.69	17.86	95.92	19.95	−147.47	53.57	−12.73	5.92	−188.82	52.18	−10.07
79.	Gabon	63.32	−14.51	40.47	−52.31	27.31	−105.92	49.01	70.21	51.86	−163.29	48.01	−38.03
80.	Fiji	14.08	12.00	−25.43	47.23	−0.36	−133.77	29.28	−49.89	−2.21	−143.47	51.25	−23.53

Table 6A.2 (cont.)

	Country	Food	Alcoholic beverages	Clothing	Housing	Furnishing	Health	Transport	Communication	Recreation	Education	Restaurant	Miscellaneous
81.	Georgia	40.60	-179.62	176.39	-216.17	64.62	-155.82	-120.73	-44.07	22.30	-41.66	-230.98	84.03
82.	Botswana	57.49	8.76	30.23	-57.82	40.14	-50.80	55.89	25.58	57.92	-110.75	52.69	-17.50
83.	Namibia	47.57	-19.23	31.39	-23.95	8.89	-84.95	46.79	50.62	45.06	-89.11	77.17	-5.35
84.	Swaziland	36.83	17.36	56.14	-22.70	12.67	-172.73	46.03	54.73	45.64	-107.77	36.01	-33.59
85.	Syria	23.36	-2.46	29.31	24.42	9.93	-113.94	18.80	28.75	1.78	-160.02	62.58	-29.38
86.	Bolivia	41.83	11.04	57.19	-40.75	26.07	-95.81	39.06	38.25	52.28	-134.31	46.69	10.35
87.	Eq. Guinea	48.69	-52.32	53.22	-64.23	6.42	-128.00	37.54	81.54	43.87	-209.60	20.27	-35.60
88.	Paraguay	15.23	-22.33	48.34	-66.36	17.25	-88.40	54.76	-16.21	44.47	-122.28	35.66	-2.35
89.	Cape Verde	33.17	-0.37	46.12	1.09	21.77	-107.06	32.44	20.43	33.02	-103.46	40.50	-31.47
90.	Bhutan	48.02	34.42	33.22	-9.27	49.75	-127.62	70.22	47.23	36.67	-134.14	70.47	9.13
91.	Kyrgyzstan	40.11	-3.58	86.33	-168.06	66.42	-151.98	54.43	56.91	17.92	-225.39	34.79	-18.97
92.	Sri Lanka	26.31	57.26	-26.79	-78.80	15.12	-161.05	36.66	16.79	6.80	-189.32	37.30	-10.28
93.	Iraq	46.94	34.22	24.26	47.88	-10.82	-107.95	14.28	63.33	54.69	-110.47	98.75	-5.11
94.	Mongolia	42.40	25.09	31.45	19.06	38.56	-167.21	52.58	25.57	26.11	-198.46	82.05	19.05
95.	Philippines	33.74	-39.36	15.83	-6.26	7.25	-96.79	36.58	36.69	11.07	-152.44	25.14	-9.33
96.	Indonesia	27.48	41.65	-13.59	-6.41	1.42	-90.96	31.11	44.94	-7.26	-181.74	13.71	-22.39
97.	Pakistan	45.27	37.98	8.93	-56.09	19.28	-142.78	48.29	-12.52	8.09	-185.51	62.12	-1.34
98.	Morocco	27.12	55.93	29.97	-73.58	-19.19	-53.78	37.21	30.61	18.85	-53.74	42.54	-9.69
99.	Lesotho	56.36	10.06	35.61	-80.09	20.32	-138.77	66.62	91.52	77.48	-128.76	48.30	3.64
100.	China	42.89	47.00	64.69	-6.57	38.26	-165.74	50.90	-13.55	-3.57	-126.01	63.48	13.93

101.	Vietnam	47.12	23.18	27.36	3.03	44.14	−154.84	100.10	21.55	13.62	−219.69	44.85	15.05
102.	India	28.73	68.71	5.27	−25.18	36.01	−166.55	71.64	9.63	14.95	−169.83	52.94	1.35
103.	Cambodia	39.88	−0.36	18.12	9.62	13.88	−170.50	47.34	49.81	1.00	−226.94	47.71	4.85
104.	Yemen	30.41	−33.13	3.01	3.00	17.72	−140.07	11.72	81.10	33.18	−173.81	80.60	−4.27
105.	Sudan	31.91	56.11	−29.87	−70.94	−36.69	−103.30	20.61	44.70	−10.09	−133.05	−10.66	−65.60
106.	Laos	40.70	23.31	13.87	−74.06	18.79	−183.46	72.65	45.24	1.72	−228.98	40.01	1.53
107.	Djibouti	57.77	−35.81	31.34	−57.39	43.68	−91.08	65.40	41.14	23.65	−154.29	75.67	−61.46
108.	Kenya	46.18	18.71	1.76	−96.87	−10.52	−115.84	70.80	102.60	51.98	−103.84	3.42	−33.65
109.	Sao Tome.	35.41	−13.02	35.32	−90.18	−11.99	−115.41	29.32	49.81	33.74	−183.00	23.03	−34.97
110.	Congo, Rep.	56.89	0.37	39.33	−76.07	3.20	−106.57	57.74	81.30	42.27	−202.18	25.08	−39.36
111.	Cameroon	31.10	−14.82	12.47	−88.34	−11.16	−107.80	25.69	79.72	37.53	−167.93	23.18	−35.41
112.	Nigeria	55.14	−17.05	−15.06	−108.26	−45.55	−135.69	9.02	42.48	7.44	−206.72	20.78	−67.71
113.	Senegal	43.38	−19.92	4.97	−88.35	−19.19	−106.70	40.46	8.39	9.48	−131.87	32.25	−29.54
114.	Chad	27.12	−17.06	−28.78	−213.14	−12.97	−242.25	20.95	55.35	1.08	−416.35	8.33	−57.77
115.	Nepal	27.64	51.18	8.42	−1.02	19.41	−152.23	90.28	26.00	5.84	−167.72	55.31	1.92
116.	Bangladesh	25.33	−12.38	13.77	−13.65	6.45	−140.85	65.23	14.42	16.73	−172.63	49.46	−2.00
117.	Benin	43.71	−12.46	2.09	−118.58	−10.62	−128.03	33.11	92.40	20.16	−165.54	28.10	−37.29
118.	Ghana	58.24	−1.45	−3.21	−145.26	−9.38	−126.82	42.31	53.43	25.23	−145.80	44.52	−67.78
119.	Cote d'Ivoire	32.18	−16.69	−4.11	−99.04	−19.84	−90.92	45.15	66.36	34.51	−122.78	10.65	−34.23
120.	Sierra Leone	75.89	0.40	8.27	−126.84	12.98	−118.22	66.40	113.15	41.62	−140.87	54.78	−10.63

Table 6A.2 (cont.)

Country	Food	Alcoholic beverages	Clothing	Housing	Furnishing	Health	Transport	Communication	Recreation	Education	Restaurant	Miscellaneous
121. Madagascar	46.98	35.68	1.32	-75.45	-3.14	-103.93	63.30	44.41	26.86	-251.04	14.42	-28.20
122. Togo	34.51	-40.75	8.46	-153.34	-20.15	-77.10	34.72	81.12	14.30	-213.22	11.09	-50.15
123. Burkina Faso	34.28	-4.81	-25.47	-100.23	-1.98	-113.77	73.46	81.55	32.74	-167.39	26.17	-40.00
124. Guinea	67.36	-75.05	-1.82	-100.74	-46.15	-77.45	64.86	58.36	1.14	-188.05	11.03	-34.33
125. Mali	41.95	-45.95	-3.83	-79.18	-7.32	-108.53	43.23	60.31	29.95	-158.17	12.71	-24.40
126. Angola	53.81	-30.09	27.74	-109.76	-1.02	-87.95	44.69	57.30	41.54	-138.28	47.78	-35.12
127. Rwanda	31.69	4.63	46.51	-34.58	26.97	-126.89	68.02	72.18	54.74	-182.90	26.80	-13.80
128. CAR	35.80	-26.59	-7.86	-173.75	-28.14	-110.17	56.28	49.02	11.64	-189.50	0.59	-45.98
129. Mozambique	31.58	6.15	20.22	-128.90	-0.82	-99.59	67.09	71.94	33.59	-133.37	39.69	-21.99
130. Niger	36.77	-14.28	-25.65	-109.86	-12.33	-108.34	49.17	62.30	28.90	-151.68	20.92	-46.66
131. Guinea-Biss.	30.64	-27.05	24.54	-102.19	-2.83	-130.62	46.86	122.50	32.60	-216.19	18.79	-37.05
132. Congo, D.R.	36.46	-21.36	-24.58	-86.92	-26.34	-131.51	49.21	68.73	12.77	-186.20	16.18	-66.76
Mean: All	31.31	-0.22	26.65	-36.76	13.64	-90.87	42.20	23.82	19.74	-115.13	36.14	-11.43
Rich	19.19	9.50	16.20	-10.33	11.25	-48.14	39.28	-9.64	7.40	-49.80	30.29	-1.28
Poor	35.55	-3.36	30.30	-45.68	14.56	-105.60	43.57	34.87	23.92	-137.41	38.39	-14.83

Notes:
1. The elements in this table are the logarithmic relative price of good i in country c, $(\log p_i^c - \log p^c) \times 100$.
2. Means exclude the United States.

Possible outliers

The International Comparison Program price data contain some outliers for Lebanon (country number 45), Iran (52) and Georgia (81).
Lebanon has a high relative price for restaurants, whereas this price is
low in Georgia; these two observations stand out in panel 11 of Figure
6.2. In addition, in Georgia, prices are low for alcoholic beverages,
housing and transport and high for clothing, furnishings and miscella-
neous. Finally, in Iran, prices seem to be (marginally) high for food and
substantially low for communication. In view of the sample size, these
outliers are unlikely to have any material impact on the results. Nevertheless, as a robustness check, we redo the results in Table 6.4 with
the data for these three countries omitted. It is evident from panel *B* of
Table 6A.3 that this has only a very marginal impact on the results.

More on rich versus poor

In Table 6.2, poor countries were distinguished from rich countries
by means of a shift in the intercept for each commodity, whereas the
slope was taken to be the same. We examine this treatment in Figure
6A.1, which extends Figure 6.2 by allowing both the slope and intercept to vary across country groups. For most commodities, the scatter
plot shows something approximating an intercept shift. There are some
exceptions to this general rule: For clothing and furnishings, the slopes
of the regression lines differ for the two country groups. Although they
do not change sign, the slopes for health, communication and education also seem to differ across country groups. Clothing and furnishing,
the two commodities that seem to depart most from the common slope
assumption, each account for slightly more than 5 per cent of the budget for an average country. As they are only modest-sized components
of the overall budget, even these cases may not substantially affect the
results.

Next, we redo the results of Table 6.2 by allowing both the intercepts
and slopes to vary, which amounts to estimating separate equations for
the rich and poor countries. Panel *A* of Table 6A.4 reproduces the previous results when the two country groups are combined. It is evident
from panel *B* of the table that the intercepts for the poor countries
generally approximate the sum of the intercept and the poor-country
dummy shown in panel *A*, as expected. Similarly, the slopes are not

Table 6A.3 *Implied price dispersion and income with and without outliers* ($y_c = \lambda_0 + \lambda_1 x_c + \lambda_2 x_c^2$)

Country group	Order of quadratic coefficients			Minimum variance	
	Second	First	Zero	Income	Variance
	λ_2	λ_1	λ_0	$E(\Pi_c)$	y_{x^*}
(1)	(2)	(3)	(4)	(5)	(6)
	A. No countries omitted				
Poor	2.47	−6.55	33.36	132.71	29.01
	(0.43)	(2.60)	(1.24)	(54.23)	(1.68)
Rich	3.38	−11.23	26.41	166.28	17.07
	(0.49)	(1.85)	(2.36)	(14.70)	(0.98)
Difference	−0.91	4.68	6.95	−33.57	11.94
	(0.16)	(0.98)	(2.13)	(14.25)	(1.41)
	B. Three countries omitted				
Poor	2.53	−6.75	32.49	133.47	27.99
	(0.43)	(2.76)	(1.27)	(51.27)	(1.74)
Rich	3.47	−11.63	26.25	167.44	16.51
	(0.50)	(1.88)	(2.37)	(14.31)	(0.96)
Difference	−0.95	4.89	6.25	−33.96	11.48
	(0.16)	(1.02)	(2.03)	(15.61)	(1.42)

Notes:
1. Asymptotic standard errors in parentheses.
2. All entries are to be divided by 100.
3. Panel A is from Table 6.4.
4. Georgia, Lebanon and Iran are omitted in panel B.

substantially different between panels A and B, with all signs being the same. Panel C of the table gives the results for the rich countries, and there are some differences here. Table 6A.5 reveals that there are significant differences in slope between the two groups for clothing, furnishings, health and education, and a joint test of the hypothesis that the twelve slopes are pairwise equal is rejected. However, the differences are not too large for the important commodity, food.

We return to Table 6A.4 to consider further the differences between the poor and rich country groups. It follows from equation (6.10) that the income elasticity of the relative price of good i is

$$\frac{\beta_i}{w_i} = \frac{1}{\Delta}(\theta_i - 1)$$

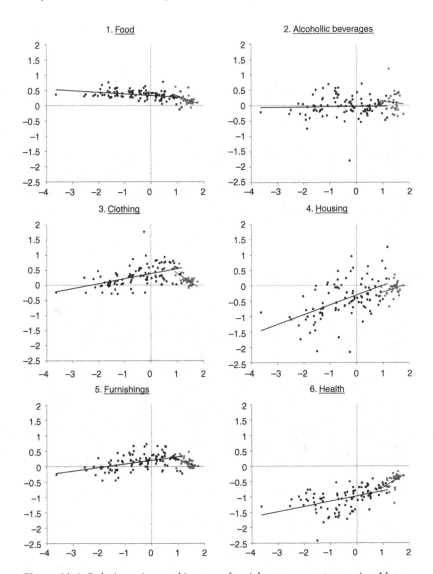

Figure 6A.1 Relative prices and incomes for rich versus poor countries. *Notes:*
1. In panel i ($i = 1, ..., 12$), the ith relative price, $(\log p_i^c - \log P^c) \times 100$, is
plotted against relative per-capita income, $\log(Q^c/\bar{Q}) \times 100, c = 1, ..., 132$,
where $\bar{Q}$ is the geometric mean income. The black solid line is the LS regression
line for poor countries, whereas the grey line is for rich countries. 2. As it is
an outlier, country number 114, Chad, is excluded from the 'Education' plot
but is included in the regression line. 3. The United States, the base country, is
excluded from all scatter plots.

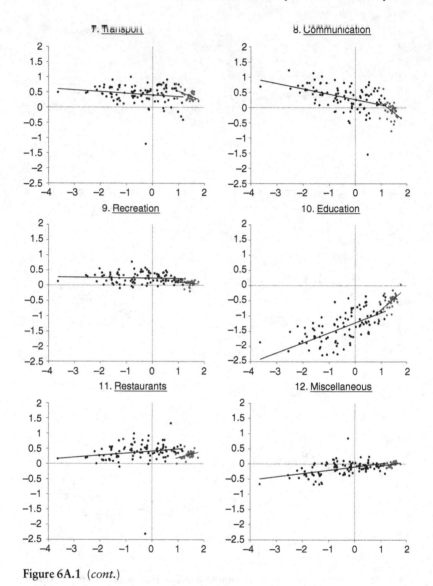

Figure 6A.1 (*cont.*)

where $\Delta > 0$ is the excess supply elasticity (for simplicity, this is taken to be the same for all goods), and θ_i is the conventional income elasticity of demand. This shows that β_i/w_i is proportional to the difference between θ_i and the weighted mean over all goods of these elasticities, *viz.*, unity. Accordingly, for necessities ($\theta_i < 1$), the price elasticity β_i/w_i

is negative. From panel *B* of Table 6A.4, the income elasticity of the relative price of food in the poor countries is estimated to be −0.16, whereas it is −0.53 in the rich countries (panel *C*). Food is a necessity in both groups, as expected, but it is more of a necessity or less of a luxury for the rich. It can be readily appreciated that this is reasonable by considering the implausibility of the alternative, whereby food is more of a luxury as income increases. The qualification to the discussion is that the estimated income coefficient for food for the rich countries has a relatively high standard error (more than three times greater than that for the poor countries). This issue is further addressed in the next paragraph. Another pattern in the results is that in eleven of twelve cases, the income coefficients for the rich countries are greater in absolute value than those for the poor countries. This is reflected in the greater dispersion of the income elasticities β_i/w_i for the rich group, which implies greater dispersion of the income elasticities of demand. As discussed in Section 6.6, this agrees with the idea that relative to the poor countries, the consumption basket of the rich countries is more diversified and less specialised in food in particular.

As stated earlier, the results for the poor countries (panel *B* of Table 6A.4) are quite similar to those for all countries combined (panel *A*), but the rich countries (panel *C*) differ substantially from all countries. One reason for this asymmetry is that ninety-nine countries belong to the poor group, whereas the rich group comprises only thirty-two countries, so the weight for the poor group in the 'world' is approximately three times that for the rich group. As the world is a weighted average of the two groups, the results in panel *A* are skewed towards the poor. This is also the reason why the standard errors of the estimated coefficients for the rich are all substantially greater than those for the poor. Thus, while a case could be made that the two groups should be kept separate, the problem is that the relatively small sample size for the rich leads to imprecise estimates for this group. In short, there is a tradeoff between more detailed modelling of individual responses and the precision of estimates.

Panel *A* of Table 6A.6 gives the implied quadratic coefficients when all countries are combined; this is reproduced from Table 6.4. Again, the quadratic coefficients for the poor group (panel *B*) are not substantially different from those for the combined case (panel *A*). For the rich group, the coefficients change, but not their sign. The zero-order coefficient λ_0 for the rich group is now larger than that for the

Table 6A.4 *Relative prices and incomes for rich and poor countries separately in 2005* $[w_{ci}\log(p_{ci}/P_c) = \alpha_i + \gamma_i D_c + \beta_i\log(Q_c/\bar{Q}) + \varepsilon_{ci}, \; w_{ci}\log(p_{ci}/P_c) = \alpha_i + \beta_i\log(Q_c/\bar{Q}) + \varepsilon_{ci}]$

Commodity	Intercept α_i (×100)		Poor-country dummy γ_i (×100)		Income β_i (×100)		Income elasticity β_i/w_i	R^2	SEE (×100)
A. All countries (C = 131)									
Food	9.71	(0.99)	0.22	(1.21)	−5.31	(0.44)	−0.19	0.68	4.34
Alcoholic beverages	0.08	(0.21)	−0.11	(0.26)	0.11	(0.10)	0.03	0.03	0.94
Clothing	−0.55	(0.44)	2.71	(0.54)	0.88	(0.20)	0.17	0.18	1.93
Housing	−5.34	(1.40)	2.38	(1.71)	2.70	(0.62)	0.18	0.15	6.15
Furnishings	−0.09	(0.26)	0.91	(0.32)	0.49	(0.12)	0.10	0.12	1.15
Health	−4.53	(0.67)	−2.41	(0.82)	−0.24	(0.30)	−0.03	0.08	2.94
Transport	3.84	(0.63)	0.12	(0.77)	0.19	(0.28)	0.02	0.00	2.76
Communication	−0.14	(0.24)	0.84	(0.29)	−0.03	(0.11)	−0.01	0.12	1.05
Recreation	0.39	(0.17)	0.50	(0.20)	0.17	(0.07)	0.03	0.05	0.74
Education	−4.39	(0.87)	−5.23	(1.06)	0.28	(0.39)	0.03	0.30	3.83
Restaurants	1.48	(0.27)	0.09	(0.32)	0.47	(0.12)	0.11	0.17	1.17
Miscellaneous	−0.47	(0.21)	−0.02	(0.26)	0.29	(0.09)	0.04	0.13	0.93
B. Poor countries (C = 99)									
Food	9.93	(0.54)			−5.31	(0.50)	−0.16	0.54	4.87
Alcoholic beverages	−0.02	(0.11)			0.12	(0.10)	0.04	0.02	0.95
Clothing	2.17	(0.24)			0.92	(0.22)	0.17	0.15	2.16
Housing	−2.97	(0.76)			2.67	(0.70)	0.19	0.13	6.87
Furnishings	0.84	(0.14)			0.52	(0.13)	0.10	0.15	1.24
Health	−6.96	(0.36)			−0.29	(0.33)	−0.04	0.01	3.23
Transport	3.99	(0.34)			0.23	(0.31)	0.03	0.01	3.06
Communication	0.71	(0.13)			−0.01	(0.12)	0.00	0.00	1.13
Recreation	0.89	(0.08)			0.17	(0.07)	0.05	0.06	0.68
Education	−9.65	(0.47)			0.22	(0.43)	0.03	0.00	4.25
Restaurants	1.58	(0.13)			0.48	(0.12)	0.13	0.14	1.17
Miscellaneous	−0.51	(0.11)			0.28	(0.10)	0.05	0.07	0.98
C. Rich countries (C = 32)									
Food	10.12	(2.52)			−5.60	(1.77)	−0.53	0.25	1.94
Alcoholic beverages	1.40	(1.20)			−0.82	(0.84)	−0.25	0.03	0.92
Clothing	4.27	(0.76)			−2.54	(0.54)	−0.57	0.43	0.59
Housing	−8.55	(3.82)			4.98	(2.69)	0.30	0.10	2.94
Furnishings	3.05	(0.91)			−1.74	(0.64)	−0.34	0.20	0.70
Health	−9.95	(2.06)			3.60	(1.45)	0.34	0.17	1.59
Transport	8.07	(1.77)			−2.80	(1.25)	−0.27	0.14	1.37
Communication	1.61	(0.93)			−1.27	(0.65)	−0.51	0.11	0.71
Recreation	1.27	(1.16)			−0.46	(0.82)	−0.05	0.01	0.89
Education	−11.17	(2.33)			5.09	(1.64)	0.63	0.24	1.79
Restaurants	2.34	(1.52)			−0.14	(1.07)	−0.02	0.00	1.17
Miscellaneous	−2.46	(0.88)			1.70	(0.62)	0.14	0.20	0.68

Notes:
1. Standard errors in parentheses.
2. All regressions exclude United States, the base country.
3. Elasticities in the third-last column are evaluated at means.
4. Panel A reproduces Table 6.2.

Table 6A.5 *Wald tests of equality of coefficients across country groups*

Commodity	Intercept	Slope
A. Individual commodities		
Food	0.01 (0.94)	0.03 (0.87)
Alcoholic beverages	1.39 (0.24)	1.25 (0.26)
Clothing	6.88 (0.01)	35.75 (0.00)
Housing	2.05 (0.15)	0.69 (0.41)
Furnishings	5.76 (0.02)	11.89 (0.00)
Health	2.05 (0.03)	6.89 (0.01)
Transport	5.12 (0.02)	5.56 (0.02)
Communication	0.93 (0.34)	3.61 (0.01)
Recreation	0.11 (0.74)	0.60 (0.44)
Education	0.41 (0.52)	8.27 (0.00)
Restaurants	0.25 (0.62)	0.33 (0.56)
Miscellaneous	4.85 (0.03)	5.17 (0.02)
B. All commodities		
	29.77 (0.00)	80.05 (0.00)

Note: The test statistics in panel *A* (*B*) follow a χ^2 distribution with one (twelve) degrees of freedom. *p*-values are in parentheses.

poor group, whereas the relative sizes of λ_1 and λ_2 for the two groups remain unchanged. Figure 6A.2 shows the corresponding plots, and it is evident that when the two groups are separated, the curve for the rich has substantially more curvature and there are now two intersection points within the relevant range. While the curve for the rich seems to change appreciably when the two groups are separated, it needs to be kept in mind that there is now substantially more sampling variability underlying that curve due to the smaller number of observations, as discussed earlier.

A weighted scatter

Figure 6A.3 repeats the scatter plots of Figure 6.2, but with each relative price weighted by its budget share to reflect its relative importance. These scatter plots, which correspond to the regressions of Table 6.2, are not appreciably different from their unweighted counterparts.

Table 6A.6 *Implied price dispersion and income for rich and poor countries separately* $(y_c = \lambda_0 + \lambda_1 x_c + \lambda_2 x_c^2)$

Country group	Order of quadratic coefficients			Minimum variance		Intersection	
	Second λ_2	First λ_1	Zero λ_0	Income $E(\Pi_c)$	Variance y_x	Income	Variance
(1)	(2)	(3)	(4)	(5)	(6)	(7)	(8)
A. All countries combined							
Poor	2.47	−6.55	33.36	132.71	29.01	−120.47	44.83
	(0.43)	(2.60)	(1.24)	(54.23)	(1.68)		
Rich	3.38	−11.23	26.41	166.28	17.07	(45.68)	(3.10)
	(0.49)	(1.85)	(2.36)	(14.70)	(0.98)		
Difference	−0.91	4.68	6.95	−33.57	11.94		
	(0.16)	(0.98)	(2.13)	(14.25)	(1.41)		
B. Rich and poor countries separately							
Poor	2.48	−6.26	16.38	126.54	12.41	128.98	12.41
	(0.49)	(3.17)	(0.64)	(65.25)	(0.71)		
Rich	13.32	−52.91	58.50	198.62	5.96	(47.12)	(0.62)
	(3.75)	(12.80)	(10.79)	(10.31)	(0.90)		
Difference	−10.84	46.64	−42.12	−72.08	6.45		
	(3.52)	(11.98)	(10.57)	(25.74)	(0.47)		

Notes:
1. Asymptotic standard errors in parentheses.
2. All entries are to be divided by 100.
3. Panel *A* reproduces Table 6.4 and intersection values from Figure 6.3.

6A.2 The welfare cost of price dispersion

This appendix derives the expression for the welfare cost [equation (6.17)] that is implied by Selvanathan's (1985) model. To place the model in context, we start with general differential demand equations.

Demand equations

Let $p_i q_i$ be the price and quantity consumed of good i ($i = 1, \ldots, n$) so that $M = \Sigma_{i=1}^n p_i q_i$ is total expenditure ('income' for short), and $w_i = p_i q_i / M$ is the budget share of i. A Marshallian demand equation for good i is $q_i = q_i(M, p_1, \ldots, p_n)$, which can be written in differential form as $dq_i = (\partial q_i / \partial M) dM + \sum_{j=1}^n (\partial q_i / \partial p_j) dp_j$. Defining s_{ij} as the compensated price slope of the demand equation, and using the Slutsky

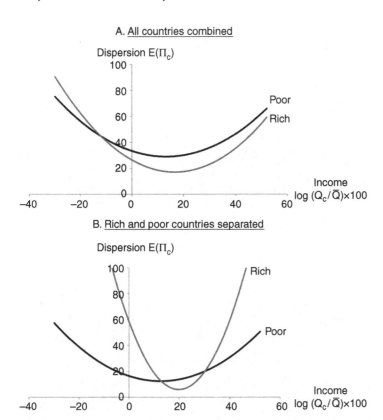

Figure 6A.2 Two versions of the dispersion and income relation.
Note: Panel A is Figure 6.3 on a different scale.

decomposition $\partial q_i/\partial p_j = s_{ij} - q_j(\partial q_i/\partial M)$, we have

$$dq_i = \frac{\partial q_i}{\partial M}(dM - \sum_j q_j dp_j) + \sum_{j=1}^n s_{ij} dp_j$$

Multiplying both sides of this equation by p_i/M and using the identity $dx/x = d(\log x)$, we obtain

$$w_i d(\log q_i) = \theta_i d(\log Q) + \sum_{j=1}^n \pi_{ij} d(\log p_j)$$

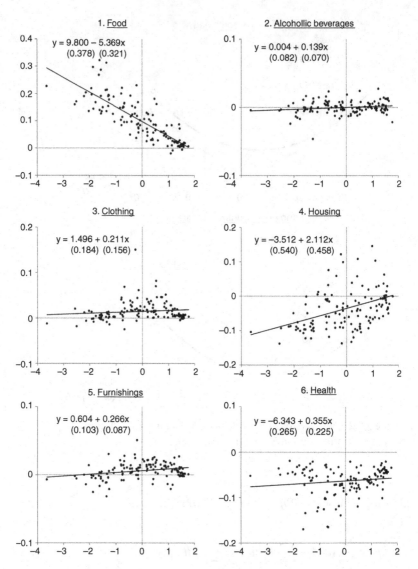

Figure 6A.3 Weighted relative prices and incomes in 132 countries in 2005.
Notes: 1. In panel i ($i = 1, ..., 12$), the ith relative price, weighted by the corresponding budget share, $w_i(\log p_i^c - \log P) \times 100$, is plotted against relative income per capita, $\log(Q^c/\bar{Q}) \times 100, c = 1, ..., 132$, where $\bar{Q}$ is geometric mean income. The solid line is the LS regression line. 2. The United States, the base country, is excluded from all scatter plots. 3. All estimates and standard errors are to be divided by 100.

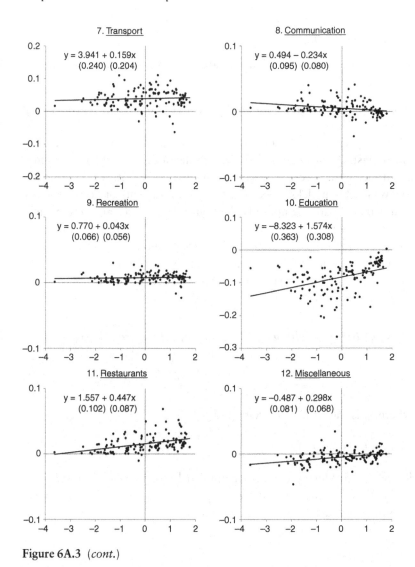

Figure 6A.3 (*cont.*)

where $\theta_i = \partial(p_i q_i)/\partial M$ is the ith marginal share, $d(\log Q) = d(\log M) - d(\log P)$ is the change in real income, with $d(\log P) = \sum_{j=1}^{n} w_j d(\log p_j)$ the Divisia price index, and $\pi_{ij} = (p_i p_j / M) s_{ij}$ is the (i, j)th Slutsky coefficient. In this formulation, the income effects of price changes transform money income into real income.

Selvanathan's model

The ith equation of the infinitesimal-change version of Selvanathan's (1985) model is

$$w_i\left[d(\log q_i) - d(\log Q)\right] = \beta_i d(\log Q) + \kappa w_i\left[d(\log p_i) - d(\log P)\right] \quad (6A.1)$$

where $\beta_i = \theta_i - w_i$ is an income coefficient, and $\kappa < 0$ is the negative of the elasticity of substitution. The whole model comprises n demand equations of the preceding form, and an attractive feature is its simplicity: While the model satisfies the usual requirements of homogeneity, symmetry and adding up, only the own-relative price appears in each equation. Moreover, the model is linear in the parameters, and as it contains only n free parameters, it is parsimonious.

The substitution term in model (6A.1) is expressed in terms of relative prices. This can also be formulated in absolute prices by writing the substitution term as

$$\kappa w_i\left[d(\log p_i) - d(\log P)\right] = \kappa w_i\left[d(\log p_i) - \sum_{j=1}^{n} w_j d(\log p_j)\right]$$

$$= \kappa w_i \sum_{j=1}^{n}\left[\delta_{ij} - w_j\right]d(\log p_j) = \sum_{j=1}^{n} \pi_{ij} d(\log p_j)$$

where δ_{ij} is the Kronecker delta and

$$\pi_{ij} = \kappa w_i(\delta_{ij} - w_j) \quad (6A.2)$$

is the (i, j)th Slutsky coefficient implied by this model. For $i, j = 1, \ldots, n$, these coefficients satisfy $\Sigma_{j=1}^{n}\pi_{ij} = 0$ (homogeneity), $\pi_{ij} = \pi_{ji}$ (symmetry) and $\Sigma_{i=1}^{n}\pi_{ij} = 0$ (adding up).

The welfare cost

If, on account of some distortion, the n prices change by $dp_1, \ldots, dp_n$, then the Harberger (1964) measure of the welfare cost is $W = -(1/2)\sum_{i=1}^{n}\sum_{j=1}^{n}(dp_i)s_{ij}(dp_j)$. Using $\pi_{ij} = (p_i p_j/M)s_{ij}$, we can express this equivalently as

$$\frac{W}{M} = -\frac{1}{2}\sum_{i=1}^{n}\sum_{j=1}^{n}d(\log p_i)\pi_{ij}d(\log p_j) \quad (6A.3)$$

This states that the welfare cost (measured as a fraction of income) is proportional to a quadratic form of the n price log changes, with proportionality factor $-1/2$. The matrix in this quadratic form is the $n \times n$ Slutsky matrix $[\pi_{ij}]$. As this matrix is negative semidefinite with rank $n - 1$ (it is singular because of homogeneity), the welfare cost is nonnegative; it is zero when all prices change proportionately.

When the Slutsky coefficients take the form of equation (6A.2), the cost (6A.3) becomes

$$\frac{W}{M} = -\frac{\kappa}{2} \sum_{i=1}^{n} \sum_{j=1}^{n} d(\log p_i) w_i (\delta_{ij} - w_j) d(\log p_j)$$

$$= -\frac{\kappa}{2} \sum_{i=1}^{n} w_i d(\log p_i) [d(\log p_i) - d(\log P)]$$

The term on the far right can be written as

$$-\frac{\kappa}{2} \left\{ \sum_{i=1}^{n} w_i [d(\log p_i) - d(\log P)]^2 \right.$$

$$\left. + \sum_{i=1}^{n} w_i d(\log P) [d(\log p_i) - d(\log P)] \right\}$$

As $\sum_i w_i d(\log P) [d(\log p_i) - d(\log P)] = 0$, we have

$$\frac{W}{M} = -\frac{\kappa}{2} \sum_{i=1}^{n} w_i \left[d(\log p_i) - d(\log P) \right]^2 = -\frac{\kappa}{2} \Pi \qquad (6A.4)$$

where Π is the variance of prices. This verifies equation (6.17).

An alternative approach

Another way of establishing result (6A.4) is as follows: The Slutsky matrix implied by the Selvanathan model is $\kappa \mathbf{W}(\mathbf{I} - \iota'\mathbf{W})$, where $\mathbf{W}$ is an $n \times n$ diagonal matrix with the budget shares on the main diagonal, $\mathbf{I}$ is an identity matrix, and ι is a vector of unit elements. Let $\mathbf{p} = [d(\log p_i)]$ be a vector of the n price log changes so that

$\mathbf{p'Wp} = \sum_{i=1}^{n} w_i [d(\log p_i)]^2$ and $\mathbf{p'W}u'\mathbf{Wp} = [d(\log P)]^2$. Then

$$\frac{W}{M} = -\frac{\kappa}{2}\mathbf{p'W}(I - u'W)\mathbf{p} = -\frac{\kappa}{2}\left\{\sum_{i=1}^{n} w_i[d(\log p_i)]^2 - [d(\log P)]^2\right\}$$

which equals $-(\kappa/2)\Pi$.

References

Balassa, B. (1964). 'The Purchasing Power Parity Doctrine: A Reappraisal'. *Journal of Political Economy* 72: 584–96.

Bergin, P. R., R. Glick and A. M. Taylor (2006). 'Productivity, Tradability and the Long-Run Price Puzzle'. *Journal of Monetary Economics* 53: 2041–66.

Bhagwati, J. N. (1984). 'Why Are Services Cheaper in the Poor Countries?' *Economic Journal* 94: 279–86.

Clements, K. W., and D. Chen (2012). 'Affluence and Food: A Simple Way to Infer Incomes'. Chapter 7 of this volume.

Cuthbert, J. (2009). 'Implicit Data Structures and Properties of Selected Additive Indices'. In D. S. P. Rao (ed), *Purchasing Power Parities of Currencies: Recent Advances in Methods and Approaches*. Cheltenham, UK: Edward Elgar. Pp. 160–80.

Diewert, W. E. (2009). 'Similarity Indexes and Criteria for Spatial Linking'. In D. S. P. Rao (ed), *Purchasing Power Parities of Currencies: Recent Advances in Methods and Approaches*. Cheltenham, UK: Edward Elgar. Pp. 183–216.

Froot, K. A., and K. Rogoff (1995). 'Perspectives on PPP and Long-Run Real Exchange Rates'. In G. Grossman and K. Rogoff (eds), *Handbook of International Economics*, Vol. 3. Amsterdam: North-Holland. Pp. 1647–88.

Harberger, A. C. (1964). 'Taxation, Resource Allocation, and Welfare'. In National Bureau of Economic Research and the Brookings Institution, *The Role of Direct and Indirect Taxes in the Federal Reserve System*. Princeton University Press. Pp. 25–75.

Hsieh, C.-T., and P. J. Klenow (2007). 'Relative Prices and Relative Prosperity'. *American Economic Review* 97: 562–85.

International Comparison Program (2008). 'Global Purchasing Power Parities and Real Expenditures'. Available at www.worldbank.org.

Kravis, I. B., A. Heston and R. Summers (1982). *World Product and Income: International Comparisons of Real Gross Product*. Baltimore: Johns Hopkins University Press for the World Bank.

Lan, Y., and L. L. Ong (2003). 'The Growing Evidence on Purchasing Power Parity'. In L. L. Ong (ed), *The Big Mac Index: Applications of Purchasing Power Parity*. Basingstoke, UK: Palgrave Macmillan. Pp. 29–50.

MacDonald, R. (2007). *Exchange Rate Economics: Theories and Evidence*. Milton Park, UK: Routledge.

Rogoff, K. (1996). 'The Purchasing Power Parity Puzzle'. *Journal of Economic Literature* 34: 647–68.

Samuelson, P. A. (1964). 'Theoretical Notes on Trade Problems'. *Review of Economics and Statistics* 46: 145–54.

Sarno, L., and M. P. Taylor (2002). *The Economics of Exchange Rates*. Cambridge University Press.

Selvanathan, E. A. (1985). 'An Even Simpler Differential Demand System'. *Economics Letters* 19: 343–47.

Sergeev, S. (2009). 'Aggregation Methods Based on Structural International Prices'. In D. S. P. Rao (ed), *Purchasing Power Parities of Currencies: Recent Advances in Methods and Approaches*. Cheltenham, UK: Edward Elgar. Pp. 274–97.

Simonovska, I. (2010). 'Income Differences and Prices of Tradables'. Working Paper 16233, National Bureau of Economic Research.

Summers, R., and A. Heston (1991). 'The Penn World Table (Mark 5): An Expanded Set of International Comparisons, 1950–1988'. *Quarterly Journal of Economics* 106: 327–68.

Taylor, A. M., and M. P. Taylor (2004). 'The Purchasing Power Parity Debate'. *Journal of Economic Perspectives* 18: 135–58.

Taylor, M. P. (2006). 'Real Exchange Rates and Purchasing Power Parity: Mean Reversion in Economic Thought'. *Applied Financial Economics* 16: 1–17.

Theil, H. (1967). *Economics and Information Theory*. Amsterdam: North-Holland and Rand McNally.

(1996). *Studies in Global Econometrics*. Dordrecht: Kluwer.

Thomas, C., J. Marquez, S. Fahle and J. Coonan. (2011). 'International Relative Price Levels: An Empirical Analysis'. In D. S. Prasada Rao and F. Vogel (eds), *Measuring the Size of the World Economy: A Framework, Methodology and Results from the International Comparison Program (ICP)*. Washington, DC: World Bank.

7 | Affluence and food: A simple way to infer incomes

KENNETH W. CLEMENTS AND DONGLING CHEN

7.1 Introduction

The fascination that economists have for international income differences goes back to at least 1776 and Adam Smith's *The Wealth of Nations*. The most popular approach to measuring incomes in different countries is to use the purchasing power parity (PPP)–based estimates of the International Comparison Program of the World Bank. As market exchange rates are volatile and are known to reflect the prices of nontraded goods (especially services) less than adequately, the PPP method is a substantial improvement over older approaches that make currency conversions on the basis of market exchange rates. However, the disadvantage of PPP is that numerous matched goods and services have to be priced in many countries, so it is demanding in its data requirements, and thus PPP estimates can be subject to long publication delays. This chapter investigates a short-cut method of measuring real incomes across countries.

Engel's law states that food has an income elasticity of less than unity or, equivalently, that the share of food in the consumption basket declines with income. We use Engel's law in reciprocal form by inferring income from the value of the food share. Such an approach is consistent with Engel (1857, pp. 28–9), who writes, '[T]he poorer a family, the greater the proportion of its total expenditure that must be devoted to the provision of food' and then goes on to argue that the richer a country, the smaller is the food share (Stigler, 1954). This approach has several advantages. First, as the food share is dimensionless, it can be compared across time, regions and countries without any adjustment for differing currency values. Second, the food share is objective, is not subject to great controversy and is readily available for many time periods in a large number of countries. Third, the link between the food share and income as enshrined in Engel's law is well established and is arguably the most widely accepted empirical regularity in all economics. Finally, as the approach uses just one share and two parameters to make inferences regarding incomes, it is attractive in its simplicity. We analyse jointly the determinants of all elements in the consumption basket and embed Engel's law in a systemwide demand model and thereby allow for the dependence of the food share on relative prices (in addition to income). The food share, adjusted for differing relative price structures across countries, is then used to infer income.

While the basic idea of using the food share as an inverse measure of welfare has been used by others (e.g., Orshansky, 1965, 1969; Van Praag et al., 1982; Rao, 1981), the approach of including food in a microeconomic demand model and then using the price-adjusted share as the basis for inferring income has been relatively unexplored, especially in a cross-country context. Chua (2003) made a preliminary investigation of estimating 'true income' in different countries from information on the food share but did not allow for international differences in relative prices. For related studies that deal with the consumer price index (CPI) bias and economic performance in the United States, see Costa (2001), Hamilton (2001) and Nakamura (1996).

It is also appropriate to mention two other short-cut approaches proposed in the early literature for countries (or regions) that do not have reliable information of real incomes. The first is the use of 'nonmonetary factors', such as calories consumed, infant mortality, the number of physicians, etc. Countries are ranked according to each factor, and these rankings are then averaged to yield an overall index (Bennett, 1951). The problem with this approach is that the equal weighting of indicators has no economic justification (Beckerman and Bacon, 1966). The second approach is to estimate income on the basis of easily observed physical indicators such as the consumption of steel, energy, electricity, cement, etc. (Beckerman and Bacon, 1966; Ehrlich, 1969; Janossy, 1963). The basic idea behind this approach is a type of reciprocal demand relation that excludes the usual relative price term. For countries that have all the required data, income is regressed on the consumption variable, and then the estimated relationship is extrapolated to yield income estimates for other countries.[1] Heston (1973) is critical

---

[1] Variations on this theme are provided by Duggar (1969), who uses money holdings instead of consumption variables, and Sahn and Stifel (2003), who use the stock of consumer durables.

of this approach as it tends to (1) give rise to large errors for low-income countries and countries least well-endowed with real-income information and (2) gives rise to too little dispersion of the cross-country income distribution. Conversely, results reported by Barlow (1977) are more favourable to the physical-indicator approach.[2]

As they are the basic building blocks of our approach, some discussion of the nature of the data published on food share is warranted. There are two basic sources of the food budget share for a country, the national accounts (NAS) and household sample surveys. Usually NAS are published quarterly in rich countries and annually in poor countries (for more on this, see below). Household sample surveys take place less frequently, perhaps every five years. As the two data sources have fundamentally different origins, they yield difference estimates. Ravallion (2003) compares these differences and writes, 'Survey and processing practices vary greatly, with implications for the comparability of the results over time and across countries. There is also heterogeneity in national income accounting practices; although standards are set internationally, they are implemented unevenly. NAS consumption numbers are rarely based on household consumption numbers'. Ravallion attributes the differences to the underestimation of income and expenditure in household surveys; measurement errors in the NAS relating to illegal, informal, household-based and subsistence activities; and differences in coverage and accounting practices (income in kind is an example). This leads Ravallion to conclude that '[T]here can be no presumption that the NAS is right and the surveys wrong, or vice versa, since they are not measuring the same thing, and both are prone to error'.[3]

While it is not easy to be precise about the reliability of published food budget shares, it is clear that, like all economic data, they are less than perfect. However, there are several reasons to believe their quality is 'reasonable'. First, the response rates in household surveys

[2] It is also worth mentioning that in the fields of economic history and economic development, the link between stature and real incomes and the degree to which the former can be inferred from the latter have been studied; for a survey, see Steckel (1995). More recently, Henderson et al. (2009) use satellite data on the intensity of artificial light emitted from a country to measure economic activity.

[3] For an analysis of these issues for US data, see Triplett (1997) and Slesnick (1998).

tend to be high, which, other things being equal, points to more reliable estimates. Deaton and Grosh (2000), for example, report response rates in the developing country surveys of the World Bank Living Standards Measurement Study of 'nearly always higher than 80 per cent and often closer to 100 per cent'. Second, there is some evidence that the two sources of data on food consumption are not too disparate. Deaton (1997, p. 27) writes, 'Minhas (1988) and Minhas and Kansal (1989) have compared various item totals from the Indian NSS consumption surveys with the independently obtained production-based totals of the amounts of various foods available for human consumption. While the results vary somewhat from food to food, and while it is important not to treat the production figures as necessarily correct, there is typically very close agreement between the two sets of estimates'.[4] Third, our inquiries with experts on Australian, Chinese and Indian data reveal that they place considerable confidence in the published food share data.[5]

Related to the quality of published food data is the issue of their timeliness – what is their periodicity, and how long is the publication lag? To investigate this issue, we examined the national accounts for twenty representative countries and found that (1) these accounts are usually published annually for poor countries, with an average publication lag of the order of seven months, and (2) for rich countries, the accounts are quarterly and have a publication lag of approximately three months. The International Comparison Program, currently the dominant source of PPP-based estimates of across-country incomes, produces estimates with an irregular periodicity that are subject to an average publication lag of more than five years.[6]

---

[4] As a possible qualification to this statement, Deaton and Kozel (2005) note an increasing gap between the estimate of total consumption from the NSS surveys and that from the national accounts. However, in referring to work by Kulshrestha and Kar (2005) and Sundaram and Tendulkar (2003), Deaton and Kozel (2005) also note that this gap is greater for nonfood items than for food. See also Deaton (2005).

[5] Our sources of advice are as follows: Australia, Judy Hensen and Bob McColl, Prices Branch, Australian Bureau of Statistics; China, Zhang Hongtao, Chief of Section, Research Department, Economic and Information Technology Commission, Shanghai Municipal People's Government; and India, Ranjan Ray, Department of Economics, Monash University. We thank these individuals for their advice.

[6] For details, see Appendix 7A.

7.2 Consumption, income and prices

In this section we set out the dependence of consumption on income and prices. As this material is well known, the presentation is brief. For more details, see Theil (1975/76, 1980) or Theil and Clements (1987).

Let p_i be the price of good i and let q_i be the corresponding quantity demanded. Then, if there are n goods, $M = \sum_{i=1}^{n} p_i q_i$ is total expenditure ('income' for short), and $w_i = p_i q_i / M$ is the budget share of i. The Marshallian demand equation for good i is $q_i = q_i(M, p_1, \ldots, p_n)$ or, using a circumflex to denote a proportional change (so that $\hat{x} = dx/x$),

$$\hat{q}_i = \eta_i \hat{M} + \sum_{j=1}^{n} \eta'_{ij} \hat{p}_j \tag{7.1}$$

where η_i is the income elasticity of demand for i and η'_{ij} is the (i, j)th uncompensated price elasticity. If we define the change in the cost of living index as a budget-share-weighted average of the n price changes, $\hat{P} = \sum_{j=1}^{n} w_j \hat{p}_j$, then the change in real income is the excess of the change in money income over this index, $\hat{Q} = \hat{M} - \hat{P}$, and the Slutsky demand equation takes the form

$$\hat{q}_i = \eta_i \hat{Q} + \sum_{j=1}^{n} \eta_{ij} \left(\hat{p}_j - \hat{P} \right) \tag{7.2}$$

where η_{ij} is the (i, j)th compensated price elasticity. In deriving equation (7.2) from equation (7.1), we have used (1) the Slutsky decomposition $\eta'_{ij} = \eta_{ij} - w_j \eta_i$ and (2) demand homogeneity, according to which $\sum_{j=1}^{n} \eta_{ij} = 0$.

Next, we note that $\hat{w}_i = \hat{p}_i + \hat{q}_i - \hat{M} = (\hat{p}_i - \hat{P}) + \hat{q}_i - \hat{Q}$. Combining this with equation (7.2) then yields

$$\hat{w}_i = (\eta_i - 1) \hat{Q} + \sum_{j=1}^{n} \eta_{ij} \left(\hat{p}_j - \hat{P} \right) + \left(\hat{p}_i - \hat{P} \right) \tag{7.3}$$

If the n commodities are broad aggregates, it is likely that there would only be limited substitutability among them. We thus take the utility function to be of the preference-independent form $u(q_1, \ldots, q_n) = \sum_{i=1}^{n} u_i(q_i)$, where $u_i(\bullet)$ is the subutility function for good i, so the marginal utility of i depends only on its own consumption. This form of taste implies that as an approximation, own-price elasticities are proportional to income elasticities, and cross-price elasticities are zero:

$$\eta_{ii} \approx \phi\eta_i, \quad i = 1,\ldots,n, \quad \eta_{ij} \approx 0, \quad i,j = 1,\ldots,n, i \neq j \qquad (7.4)$$

where ϕ is the reciprocal of the income elasticity of the marginal utility of income ('income flexibility' for short). Equations (7.3) and (7.4) then imply that

$$\hat{w}_i \approx (\eta_i - 1)\hat{Q} + (\phi\eta_i + 1)\left(\hat{p}_i - \hat{P}\right) \qquad (7.5)$$

which shows the dependence of the budget share on income and the relative price of the good. The two parameters in equation (7.5) are the income elasticity and the income flexibility.

7.3 Income and food

On the basis of budget shares, food is the most important single commodity in most poor countries. Thus, in what follows, we concentrate on this commodity. In this section we analyse the relationship between food consumption and income and defer a discussion of the role of the relative price of food until the next section.

We apply equation (7.5) to $i =$ food and subsequently omit the commodity subscript for simplicity. When the relative price of food is constant, this equation implies that $dw \approx \beta\hat{Q}$, with $\beta = w(\eta - 1)$. The marginal share of food is $\partial(pq)/\partial M$, which answers the question: If income increases by \$1, what fraction of this is spent on food? As $w\eta = \partial(pq)/\partial M$, it follows that the coefficient β is the excess of the marginal share over the corresponding budget share w. Using $\hat{x} = d(\log x)$, the preceding suggests that a convenient way to relate food consumption and income in countries a and b is

$$w^a - w^b = \beta \log\left(\frac{Q^a}{Q^b}\right) \qquad (7.6)$$

Table 7.1 gives real per-capita total consumption for 132 countries in 2005, which we interpret as Q, and the food budget share.[7] It is evident that on the basis of Q, the United States is the richest country

---

[7] The data are from the International Comparison Program (2008). It should be noted that the commodity 'food' in the ICP data refers to food consumed in the home only. For details of the data, see Appendix 7A.

Table 7.1 *Real incomes and food budget shares in 132 countries, 2005*

Country	Income per capita	Food share	Country	Income per capita	Food share	Country	Income per capita	Food share
1. USA	100.0	6.2	45. Lebanon	32.0	27.8	89. Cape Verde	8.8	28.8
2. Luxembourg	92.2	6.9	46. Mexico	28.7	22.0	90. Bhutan	8.0	34.5
3. Iceland	80.7	8.9	47. Belarus	27.3	34.7	91. Kyrgyz	8.0	40.8
4. Norway	77.7	9.7	48. Kazakhstan	26.5	18.6	92. Sri Lanka	7.9	36.4
5. United Kingdom	76.9	7.1	49. Mauritius	26.3	23.4	93. Iraq	7.8	32.1
6. Austria	76.4	8.7	50. Russia	26.3	25.5	94. Mongolia	7.7	35.9
7. Switzerland	74.6	9.3	51. Bulgaria	26.1	19.5	95. Philippines	7.5	43.9
8. Canada	74.4	7.7	52. Iran	25.2	23.4	96. Indonesia	7.4	41.6
9. Netherlands	72.4	8.2	53. Romania	24.4	25.0	97. Pakistan	7.3	48.8
10. Sweden	72.0	8.3	54. Oman	24.2	22.1	98. Morocco	7.2	31.1
11. France	71.5	10.6	55. Argentina	24.0	22.5	99. Lesotho	7.1	35.5
12. Australia	70.6	8.5	56. Serbia	23.7	25.6	100. China	7.0	24.1
13. Denmark	69.8	8.1	57. Saudi Arabia	23.6	18.5	101. Vietnam	6.8	31.3
14. Belgium	68.4	10.3	58. Chile	23.3	16.2	102. India	5.5	33.7
15. Germany	67.5	9.1	59. Uruguay	22.1	19.0	103. Cambodia	5.3	47.2
16. Hong Kong	66.3	8.9	60. Bosnia Herz.	21.9	28.5	104. Yemen	5.2	41.1
17. Ireland	66.2	4.6	61. Macedonia	20.5	30.9	105. Sudan	4.5	55.6

18. Japan	66.0	12.3	62. Ukraine	19.8	32.1	106. Lao	4.4	47.3
19. Taiwan	64.5	14.8	63. South Africa	19.3	17.6	107. Djibouti	4.4	33.6
20. Cyprus	63.4	13.7	64. Malaysia	19.3	17.3	108. Kenya	4.3	33.3
21. Finland	63.0	9.3	65. Turkey	18.9	23.1	109. Sao Tome	4.3	53.7
22. Spain	61.9	11.8	66. Montenegro	18.7	32.2	110. Congo, R.	4.1	37.5
23. Italy	61.6	12.3	67. Brazil	18.7	15.5	111. Cameroon	4.0	43.4
24. Greece	59.4	13.8	68. Venezuela	17.1	26.1	112. Nigeria	4.0	56.7
25. NZ	57.7	11.5	69. Thailand	16.1	15.9	113. Senegal	3.9	48.9
26. Israel	54.7	12.9	70. Albania	14.6	24.6	114. Chad	3.5	55.0
27. Malta	54.3	13.9	71. Colombia	14.5	24.3	115. Nepal	3.4	48.7
28. Singapore	53.6	8.2	72. Ecuador	13.7	25.9	116. Bangladesh	3.3	49.9
29. Qatar	50.5	13.6	73. Jordan	13.7	28.9	117. Benin	3.3	43.6
30. Slovenia	50.0	11.9	74. Tunisia	13.7	24.8	118. Ghana	3.3	49.2
31. Portugal	49.0	13.1	75. Peru	13.6	29.2	119. Cote d'Ivoire	3.1	43.3
32. Brunei	48.7	18.4	76. Egypt	13.5	41.6	120. S. Leone	3.1	42.4
33. Kuwait	47.0	14.8	77. Moldova	13.0	24.2	121. M'gascar	3.0	57.0
34. Czech Rep	46.3	13.1	78. Maldives	12.9	22.9	122. Togo	2.7	48.6

Table 7.1 (*cont.*)

Country	Income per capita	Food share	Country	Income per capita	Food share	Country	Income per capita	Food share
35. Hungary	42.6	13.3	79. Gabon	12.7	36.3	123. Burkina Faso	2.5	42.0
36. Bahrain	41.6	19.0	80. Fiji	12.6	26.3	124. Guinea	2.4	44.0
37. Korea	40.4	13.7	81. Georgia	12.1	36.7	125. Mali	2.3	46.7
38. Estonia	39.4	15.4	82. Botswana	11.9	21.9	126. Angola	2.3	40.7
39. Slovakia	38.8	15.7	83. Namibia	10.9	26.0	127. Rwanda	2.1	42.7
40. Lithuania	38.3	22.9	84. Swaziland	10.8	41.9	128. C. Africa	1.9	56.8
41. Poland	36.7	17.8	85. Syria	10.5	41.7	129. M'bique	1.7	60.1
42. Croatia	36.1	19.3	86. Bolivia	10.2	27.8	130. Niger	1.3	46.4
43. Macao	36.1	13.3	87. Equat. Guinea	10.1	39.5	131. G-Bissau	1.2	52.3
44. Latvia	33.4	19.2	88. Paraguay	9.9	32.3	132. Congo, D. R.	0.4	62.2

Notes:
1. Income is real total consumption expenditure per capita in US dollars with United States = 100.
2. Food shares are in percentage form.

and Congo is the poorest, with a ratio of $100/0.4 = 250$, whereas the food budget share ranges from 5 per cent to more than 60 per cent. The budget share of each country can be systematically compared with that of all others via the 132×132 skew-symmetric matrix $[w^a - w^b]$. To keep things manageable, the upper triangle of this matrix is given in panel A of Table 7.2 in the form of six groups of countries, with twenty-two countries in each group. Thus, for example, moving from left to right along the first row, we compare the average food budget share for the twenty-two richest countries with that for poorer groups arranged in decreasing poverty; the share for the poorest group is forty points above that for the richest, the share for the second poorest group is twenty-nine points above, etc. As the diagonal elements of this table would be all zero, these elements are suppressed. As we move further away from where the diagonal would have been in a northwesterly direction, groups differ more on the income scale, and the budget shares differ by more. For each pairwise comparison in this move, the share for the poorer group is greater than that for the richer group, which is a reflection of Engel's law.

Panel B of Table 7.2 gives the corresponding matrix comparisons of incomes, which for groups G and H we write as $\Delta \log Q^{GH} = \log(Q^G/Q^H)$. Panel C contains the ratios $\Delta w^{GH}/\Delta \log Q^{GH}$, where $\Delta w^{GH} = w^G - w^H$. These ratios can be interpreted as 'readings' of the coefficient β in equation (7.6). Figure 7.1 shows that while there are a few outliers at the country level (associated with near zeros in the denominators for countries with very similar incomes), the distribution has a reasonably well-defined median of approximately -0.11. This result is confirmed by the corresponding scatter of Figure 7.2.[8] When $\beta = -0.11$, a country that is 25 per cent richer than another has a food budget share approximately 2.5 percentage points lower. If we only used information on the food share, we could use this relationship in reciprocal form, whereby $\Delta \log Q^{ab} = (1/\beta)\Delta w^{ab}$, to make inferences regarding income differences. In Section 7.5 we extend this basic relationship to allow for the role of differences in relative prices and demonstrate the importance of allowing for the impact of this additional factor.

[8] By integration, equation (7.6) is consistent with the Working (1943)–Leser (1963) Engel curve, $w = \alpha + \beta \log Q$, where α is a constant. Figure 7.2 reveals that this model fits the ICP data reasonably well.

Table 7.2 *Matrix of food and income changes for six country groups*

| | ← Poorer | | Richer → | | |
	Group 6	Group 5	Group 4	Group 3	Group 2
		A. Changes in food budget share $\left(\Delta w^{GH} \times 100\right)$			
Group 1	−39.89	−29.31	−19.60	−14.65	−5.63
Group 2	−34.26	−23.68	−13.97	−9.02	
Group 3	−25.24	−14.66	−4.95		
Group 4	−20.28	−9.71			
Group 5	−10.58				
		B. Changes in income $\left(\Delta \log Q^{GH} \times 100\right)$			
Group 1	339.38	245.42	172.33	112.14	46.04
Group 2	293.34	199.38	126.29	66.09	
Group 3	227.25	133.29	60.20		
Group 4	167.05	73.09			
Group 5	93.96				

← Poorer→Richer

← Poorer→Richer

C. Ratios of changes in food budget share to income changes
$$\left(\Delta w^{GH} \middle/ \Delta \log Q^{GH} \times 100 \right)$$

Group 1	−11.89	−11.93	−11.20	−13.33	−13.03
	(−11.75)	(−11.94)	(−11.37)	(−13.06)	(−12.23)
Group 2	−11.86	−11.86	−10.68	−15.40	
	(−11.68)	(−11.88)	(−11.06)	(−13.64)	
Group 3	−11.44	−11.05	4.62		
	(−11.11)	(−11.00)	(−8.23)		
Group 4	−12.57	−12.01			
	(−12.14)	(−13.28)			
Group 5	−17.36				
	(−11.25)				

Richer ←

Poorer →

Notes:

1. The 132 countries are ranked by income per capita and then divided into six groups of twenty-two countries each, according to the grid lines in Table 7.1.

2. The (i, j)th element of the matrix in panel A is the change in the food budget share of country a relative to country b, where country a belongs to group G and country b belongs to group H, $G \neq H$ averaged over all countries within the respective groups. Similarly for panels B and C. The entries in brackets in panel C are the ratios of the corresponding elements of panel A to those of panel B.

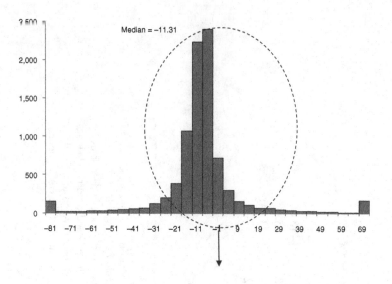

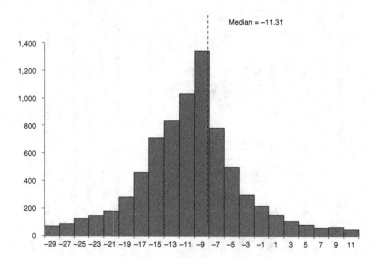

Figure 7.1 Ratio of changes in the food budget share to changes in income $(\Delta w^{ab}/\Delta \log Q^{ab} \times 100)$.

7.4 Modelling the consumption basket

As indicated by equation (7.5), the change in the budget share of good i is related to the change in income and, under the assumption of preference independence, the change in the relative price of the good. The

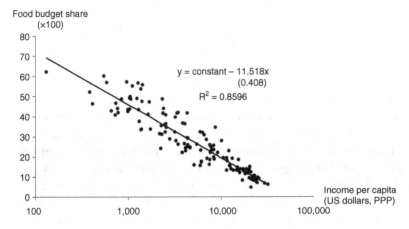

Figure 7.2 Scatter plot of food budget share against income.

parameters in this relationship are the income elasticity and the income flexibility. To efficiently estimate these parameters, we need to consider the demand for all n goods simultaneously by jointly modelling the determinants of the consumption basket. There are a number of alternative models that could be used for this purpose, including the linear expenditure system, the almost-ideal demand model, the translog, etc. We choose the Florida model (Theil et al., 1989) because it is probably the most extensively applied and assessed in a cross-country context.

In this section we reinstate the commodity subscript $i = 1, \ldots, n$ and denote countries by $c = 1, \ldots, C$. The Florida model is based on Working's (1943) model:

$$w_i^c = \alpha_i + \beta_i \log Q^c \tag{7.7}$$

where α_i and β_i are coefficients satisfying $\sum_{i=1}^n \alpha_i = 1$, $\sum_{i=1}^n \beta_i = 0$. If we denote the logarithm of real income in country c by $q^c = \log Q^c$, it can easily be shown that model (7.7) implies that the marginal share of good i takes the form $a_i + \beta_i q^{*c}$, where $q^{*c} = 1 + q^c$. The Florida model supposes that equation (7.7) holds at world prices, measured as geometric means, $\log \bar{p}_i = (1/C)\sum_{c=1}^C \log p_i^c$. Equation i of the model takes the form

$$w_i^c = \alpha_i + \beta_i q^c + (\alpha_i + \beta_i q^c)\left[\log\frac{p_i^c}{\bar{p}_i} - \sum_{j=1}^n (\alpha_j + \beta_j q^c)\log\frac{p_j^c}{\bar{p}_j}\right]$$

$$+ \phi\left(\alpha_i + \beta_i q^{*c}\right) \left[\log \frac{p_i^c}{\bar{p}_i} - \sum_{j=1}^{n}\left(\alpha_j + \beta_j q^{*c}\right) \log \frac{p_j^c}{\bar{p}_j} \right] \qquad (7.8)$$

$$+ \varepsilon_i^c$$

where ϕ is the income flexibility (as before), and ε_i^c is a zero-mean disturbance term, drawn from a multivariate normal distribution with a constant covariance matrix. The second term on the right-hand side of this equation, $\beta_i q^c$, is related to the role of real income in determining the budget share of good i, whereas the first term in square brackets is the relative price of the good compared with the world relative price. When the relative price changes, the budget share changes, even when the corresponding quantity demanded is unchanged; this 'direct' effect is measured by the term

$$\left(\alpha_i + \beta_i q^c\right) \left[\log \frac{p_i^c}{\bar{p}_i} - \sum_{j=1}^{n}\left(\alpha_j + \beta_j q^c\right) \log \frac{p_j^c}{\bar{p}_j} \right]$$

The second line of equation (7.8) is related to the substitution effect of a change in the relative price of the good; the weights used in this relative price are marginal shares $\alpha_j + \beta_j q^{*c}$, whereas in the first line of the equation they are budget shares $\alpha_j + \beta_j q^c$. The final thing to note about the Florida model is that it holds under preference independence, so it is consistent with the analysis of the preceding section.

We estimate model (7.8) using a modification of the maximum-likelihood (ML) procedure set out in Theil et al. (1989) with data from the International Comparison Program (2008) for $n = 12$ goods listed in Table 7.3 and the $C = 132$ countries listed in Table 7.1. The modification is to allow for heteroskedasticity across countries by having the disturbance covariance matrix take one value for the richest sixty-nine countries and another for the remaining sixty-three.[9] The results

---

[9] Country 69, the least affluent member of the rich group, is Thailand. As the income per capita for this country is close to the geometric mean income for all 132 countries, the two groups are interpreted as those with incomes greater than the mean and those with less. See Appendix 7A for more details on the data and the covariance matrices. If the nonfood data were of poor quality, what might the implications be for estimates of the food demand equation? Although it is not possible to provide iron-clad guarantees, some insights can be obtained as follows: The assumption of preference independence means that the cross-prices only appear in the equations in the form of the overall

Table 7.3 *The Florida model: estimates and simulation results*

$$u_i^c = \alpha_i + \beta_i q^c + (\alpha_i + \beta_i q^c)\left[\log\frac{p_i^c}{p_i} - \sum_{j=1}^{12}(\alpha_j + \beta_j q^c)\log\frac{p_j^c}{p_j}\right]$$
$$+ \phi(\alpha_i + \beta_i q^{*c})\left[\log\frac{p_i^c}{p_i} - \sum_{j=1}^{12}(\alpha_j + \beta_j q^{*c})\log\frac{p_j^c}{p_j}\right] + \varepsilon_i^c$$

	Data based				Monte Carlo simulation					
	Intercept α_i		Slope β_1		Intercept α_i			Slope β_i		
Commodity	Point estimate	ASE	Point estimate	ASE	Mean	RMSE	RMASE	Mean	RMSE	RMASE
(1)	(2)	(3)	(4)	(5)	(6)	(7)	(8)	(9)	(10)	(11)
1. Food	0.1007	0.0064	−0.0917	0.0034	0.1011	0.0064	0.0061	−0.0915	0.0036	0.0033
2. Alcohol and tobacco	0.0291	0.0028	−0.0023	0.0015	0.0291	0.0028	0.0027	−0.0023	0.0016	0.0015
3. Clothing	0.0490	0.0028	−0.0019	0.0015	0.0489	0.0028	0.0027	−0.0019	0.0015	0.0014
4. Housing	0.1590	0.0061	0.0064	0.0029	0.1588	0.0060	0.0060	0.0063	0.0028	0.0028
5. Durables	0.0590	0.0028	0.0036	0.0014	0.0589	0.0029	0.0027	0.0035	0.0014	0.0013
6. Health	0.0996	0.0033	0.0125	0.0019	0.0995	0.0033	0.0032	0.0125	0.0020	0.0018

335

Table 7.3 (*cont.*)

Commodity	Data based					Monte Carlo simulation					
	Intercept α_i		Slope β_1			Intercept α_i			Slope β_i		
	Point estimate	ASE	Point estimate	ASE		Mean	RMSE	RMASE	Mean	RMSE	RMASE
(1)	(2)	(3)	(4)	(5)		(6)	(7)	(8)	(9)	(10)	(11)
7. Transport	0.1276	0.0044	0.0171	0.0021		0.1275	0.0045	0.0042	0.0170	0.0022	0.0021
8. Communication	0.0356	0.0019	0.0056	0.0008		0.0356	0.0021	0.0019	0.0056	0.0008	0.0008
9. Recreation	0.0815	0.0035	0.0177	0.0013		0.0816	0.0038	0.0033	0.0177	0.0014	0.0013
10. Education	0.0811	0.0049	−0.0008	0.0027		0.0812	0.0050	0.0047	−0.0009	0.0028	0.0026
11. Restaurants	0.0676	0.0049	0.0126	0.0020		0.0677	0.0050	0.0047	0.0126	0.0020	0.0019
12. Other	0.1103	0.0048	0.0213	0.0021		0.1102	0.0048	0.0047	0.0214	0.0021	0.0020
Income flexibility	Point estimate = −0.6782 , ASE = 0.0243					Mean = −0.6783, RMSE = 0.0261, RMASE = 0.0219					

Notes:

1. $q^{*c} = 1 + q^c$.
2. The Monte Carlo simulation involves 1,000 trials.
3. ASE = asymptotic standard error.
4. RMSE is the root mean squared error over the 1,000 trials.
5. $\text{RMASE} = \sqrt{(1/1{,}000)\sum_{s=1}^{1,000}\left(\text{ASE}^{(s)}\right)^2}$, where $\text{ASE}^{(s)}$ is the asymptotic SE of a given parameter at trial s.

are given in columns 2 through 5 in Table 7.3. The largest estimate of β_i (in absolute value) is for food at -0.09, a value that is highly significant. That this value is approximately 20 per cent lower than the estimate of the same coefficient discussed in the preceding section indicates the importance of controlling for differences in the relative price of food across countries. As discussed in Chapter 6, food prices tend to decrease with income, so omitting the price has the effect of biasing upwards the estimate of $|\beta_i|$ for food (Gao, 2012).

To assess the quality of the estimates, we conduct a Monte Carlo experiment that involves the following steps: First, we write model (7.8) for $i = 1,\ldots,11$ as[10]

$$\mathbf{w}^c = \mathbf{f}\left(\mathbf{X}^c, \boldsymbol{\theta}\right) + \boldsymbol{\varepsilon}^c \tag{7.9}$$

where $\mathbf{w}^c$ and $\boldsymbol{\varepsilon}^c$ are vectors of budget shares and disturbances for country c, $\mathbf{X}^c$ is a matrix of the observed values of the independent variables and $\boldsymbol{\theta}$ is a vector of parameters. We simulate the budget vector for country c from equation (7.9) by (1) drawing $\boldsymbol{\varepsilon}^c$ from a normal distribution with mean vector zero and covariance matrix equal to its data-based ML estimate, (2) using the data-based estimate for $\boldsymbol{\theta}$ and (3) using the observed values of $\mathbf{X}^c$. Repeating this for each of the 132 countries leads to 132 values of the simulated vector of budget shares $\mathbf{w}^{c(s)}$, $c = 1,\ldots,132$, which are used together with the observed values of the independent variables to reestimate the model by the same ML procedure. Second, we repeat the procedure 1,000 times to

---

deflators. That is, in equation (7.8) for $i =$ food, the terms

$$\left[\log \frac{p_i^c}{\bar{p}_i} - \sum_{j=1}^{n} (\alpha_j + \beta_j q^c) \log \frac{p_j^c}{\bar{p}_j}\right] \quad \text{and} \quad \left[\log \frac{p_i^c}{\bar{p}_i} - \sum_{j=1}^{n} (\alpha_j + \beta_j q^{*c}) \log \frac{p_j^c}{\bar{p}_j}\right]$$

are two versions of the relative price of food, the nominal price deflated by indexes of the prices of all goods. The index in the first relative price is of the Divisia form, which uses budget shares as weights $(\alpha_j + \beta_j q^c)$, whereas the index in the second is a Frisch form, which uses marginal shares $(\alpha_j + \beta_j q^{*c})$ as weights. The n prices enter these indexes in a constrained manner in that they involve weighted sums, and the preceding relative prices have zero-weighted sums over commodities, where the weights are budget and marginal shares, respectively. If the nonfood prices are poorly measured, then the structured way in which they enter the food demand equation via the two relative prices and the constraints implied by this structure mean that the impact on the food estimates is likely to be relatively minor.

[10] We omit the twelfth equation because $\sum_{i=1}^{12} \varepsilon_i^c = 0$.

yield 1,000 simulated values of the vector of estimated parameters $\theta^{(s)}$, $s = 1, \ldots, 1,000$. Columns 6 through 11 in Table 7.3 summarise the results in the form of the mean, root mean square error (RMSE), and root mean asymptotic standard error (RMASE) for each parameter. It is evident that all the estimates are unbiased, whereas the asymptotic standard errors tend to understate the sampling variability of the estimates, but not by a huge amount.

7.5 Simulating income

In this section we draw inferences on cross-country incomes from the behaviour of the food budget share after controlling for the influence of the relative price. As before, we concentrate exclusively on food and drop the commodity subscript.

We return to equation (7.5) and write it as

$$\hat{Q} = \frac{\hat{w}}{\eta - 1} - \frac{(\phi\eta + 1)\left(\hat{p} - \hat{P}\right)}{\eta - 1} \tag{7.10}$$

where $\hat{Q}$ is the change in income, $\hat{w}$ is the change in the food budget share, η is the income elasticity of food, ϕ is the income flexibility and $\hat{p} - \hat{P}$ is the change in the relative price of food, and where we have ignored the approximation error. This equation states that the change in income is equal to the difference between a term involving the change in the food share and a term that adjusts for the change in the relative price of food. To apply equation (7.10) to countries a and b, we could express it as

$$\log\left(\frac{Q^a}{Q^b}\right) = \frac{\log\left(w^a/w^b\right)}{\eta^{ab} - 1}$$

$$- \frac{\left(\phi\eta^{ab} + 1\right)\left[\log\left(p^a/p^b\right) - \log\left(P^a/P^b\right)\right]}{\eta^{ab} - 1} \tag{7.11}$$

where $\eta^{ab} = (1/2)(\eta^a + \eta^b)$ is the average income elasticity of food in the two countries. To allow for uncertainty in the budget shares and the elasticities of equation (7.11), we embed it in the Monte Carlo simulation described earlier and define the base country as the geometric mean for the 132 countries, which now plays the role of country b.

Thus we can write the realization at trial s as

$$
\log\left(\frac{Q^a}{Q^*}\right)^{(s)} = \frac{\log\left(w^{a(s)}/w^*\right)}{\eta^{a*(s)} - 1}
$$
$$
- \frac{\left(\phi^{(s)}\eta^{a*(s)} + 1\right)\left[\log\left(p^a/p^*\right) - \log\left(P^a/P^*\right)\right]}{\eta^{a*(s)} - 1} \tag{7.12}
$$

where an asterisk denotes the geometric mean over the 132 countries, and $\eta^{a*(s)} = (1/2)(\eta^{a(s)} + \eta^{*(s)})$ is the average income elasticity in a and the base country in trial s.

The experiment yields 1,000 values of the right-hand side of equation (7.12) for $a = 1, \ldots, 132$ countries, which are summarised in Table 7.4. Take the case of India (country 102) as an example. According to column 2, the observed log ratio of India's income to geometric mean (over all countries) income is -1.05, so its income is $\exp(-1.05) \approx 0.35$ times the average. On the basis of the mean of the 1,000 trials of the adjusted food shares (column 3) for India, the log ratio is estimated to be -1.08, or 0.34 times the average. The situation is not quite as good for China (country 100), for which the actual and estimated log ratios are -0.80 and -0.58, respectively; these values imply that actual income is 0.45 times the average income, whereas it is estimated to be 0.56 times the average. Column 7 of Table 7.4 gives the logarithmic errors, the difference between observed and estimated income. The mean error is 3.1 per cent, and the mean absolute value is 15.8 per cent; 81 per cent of the errors fall in the range ± 30 per cent, 61 per cent in the range ± 20 per cent, and 51 per cent in the range ± 10 per cent. The predictions tend to be worse for very high-income (VHI) countries (those in the top half of the rich group), as observed in Figure 7.3, which plots actual and predicted income.[11] However, Figure 7.3 also reveals that, on average, the predictions are reasonable, as confirmed by a regression of actual on predicted ($\text{actual}_c = \kappa + \lambda \cdot \text{predicted}_c$), from which we are unable to reject the unbiassedness hypothesis $H_0: \kappa = 0, \lambda = 1$. Table 7.4 also shows that the distribution of income in the VHI countries has more skewness and

---

[11] Our approach underestimates income in the VHI countries because the Florida model tends to underpredict food shares in those countries. In subsequent research, it would be useful to explore this issue further by devising an Engel curve that is steeper in this region than that implied by the model of Working (1943).

Table 7.4 A cross-country income comparison

Country	Observed	log(Q^a/Q^*) Simulated					Components of simulated log(Q^a/Q^*)			
		Mean	SD	Skewness	Kurtosis	Error	Food share		Food relative price	
							Mean	SD	Mean	SD
(1)	(2)	(3)	(4)	(5)	(6)	(7)	(8)	(9)	(10)	(11)
1. United States	185.3	115.2	25.9	−2.33	9.58	70.1	148.0	28.6	−32.8	5.0
2. Luxembourg	177.2	127.4	22.0	−2.04	8.09	49.8	151.1	23.0	−23.7	3.5
3. Iceland	163.9	137.6	20.8	−2.14	9.65	26.2	151.1	20.5	−13.4	1.7
4. Norway	160.1	135.7	22.1	−1.69	7.04	24.4	148.9	21.7	−13.2	1.8
5. United Kingdom	159.1	122.5	21.5	−1.95	8.22	36.6	151.1	20.8	−28.6	3.9
6. Austria	158.4	127.6	22.7	−1.82	7.62	30.8	148.7	22.2	−21.1	2.9
7. Switzerland	156.0	131.6	21.1	−1.58	6.12	24.4	150.0	20.4	−18.5	2.4
8. Canada	155.8	136.0	20.9	−1.51	6.12	19.8	149.7	20.2	−13.7	1.7
9. Netherlands	153.0	108.9	23.5	−2.47	10.54	44.2	151.3	24.9	−42.4	6.1
10. Sweden	152.4	127.4	21.9	−1.77	7.24	25.1	149.7	21.1	−22.4	3.0
11. France	151.7	121.3	22.2	−1.73	7.11	30.4	149.8	21.3	−28.4	3.8
12. Australia	150.6	129.8	21.4	−1.40	5.48	20.8	148.8	20.3	−19.0	2.3
13. Denmark	149.4	124.1	21.9	−1.62	6.56	25.3	149.3	21.2	−25.1	3.3
14. Belgium	147.4	125.0	21.8	−1.36	5.02	22.4	148.7	20.5	−23.7	3.0
15. Germany	146.1	120.5	23.6	−1.69	6.95	25.6	148.1	22.6	−27.7	3.7
16. Hong Kong	144.2	139.5	26.8	−1.24	4.58	4.7	138.7	26.9	0.8	0.1

17. Ireland	144.1	120.2	23.9	−1.50	5.72	23.9	147.6	22.5	−27.5	3.5
18. Japan	143.8	156.9	29.9	−0.76	3.22	−13.0	119.5	32.9	37.3	3.6
19. Taiwan	141.5	153.0	30.6	−0.65	3.31	−11.4	115.0	33.5	37.9	3.4
20. Cyprus	139.7	120.1	27.0	−0.96	3.68	19.6	138.5	25.5	−18.4	2.0
21. Finland	139.2	119.2	24.6	−1.42	5.28	20.0	146.9	22.9	−27.7	3.4
22. Spain	137.3	113.8	25.6	−1.42	5.59	23.5	145.7	23.4	−32.0	3.9
23. Italy	136.9	123.2	25.6	−1.11	3.96	13.7	142.8	24.2	−19.6	2.2
24. Greece	133.2	117.7	26.4	−0.88	3.40	15.5	139.6	24.7	−21.9	2.4
25. NZ	130.4	122.9	27.7	−1.06	4.02	7.5	137.3	26.6	−14.5	1.5
26. Israel	125.0	119.8	26.8	−0.88	3.58	5.3	136.5	25.5	−16.8	1.9
27. Malta	124.3	108.1	31.1	−0.75	3.07	16.2	129.8	29.3	−21.7	2.3
28. Singapore	123.0	123.0	30.7	−0.70	3.16	0.0	125.9	30.5	−2.9	0.3
29. Qatar	117.0	99.1	26.6	−1.16	4.24	17.9	145.1	23.3	−46.0	5.9
30. Slovenia	116.1	113.2	31.7	−0.75	3.18	2.9	125.8	30.8	−12.6	1.2
31. Portugal	114.0	106.4	29.1	−0.96	3.78	7.6	137.0	26.7	−30.6	3.3
32. Brunei	113.4	129.7	31.9	−0.55	3.04	−16.3	109.5	33.3	20.2	1.6
33. Kuwait	109.8	91.0	27.4	−1.42	5.48	18.8	145.6	24.0	−54.6	6.7
34. Czech Rep	108.2	116.4	31.9	−0.64	3.25	−8.2	121.2	31.5	−4.8	0.4
35. Hungary	100.1	105.1	35.9	−0.73	3.58	−4.9	111.9	35.4	−6.8	0.6
36. Bahrain	97.6	96.6	31.5	−0.91	3.71	1.1	132.7	28.5	−36.1	3.8
37. Korea	94.7	118.9	37.5	−0.20	2.83	−24.2	74.6	40.3	44.3	3.3
38. Estonia	92.3	99.8	35.9	−0.47	2.95	−7.6	106.4	35.4	−6.5	0.6
39. Slovakia	90.7	103.7	35.3	−0.49	3.20	−13.0	101.2	35.5	2.5	0.2
40. Lithuania	89.3	87.9	36.8	−0.50	3.28	1.4	99.5	36.0	−11.5	0.9

Table 7.4 (*cont.*)

Country	Observed	log(Q^a/Q^*) Simulated					Components of simulated log(Q^a/Q^*)			
		Mean	SD	Skewness	Kurtosis	Error	Food share		Food relative price	
							Mean	SD	Mean	SD
(1)	(2)	(3)	(4)	(5)	(6)	(7)	(8)	(9)	(10)	(11)
41. Poland	85.0	98.8	36.0	−0.51	3.07	−13.9	106.0	35.5	−7.2	0.6
42. Croatia	83.6	89.3	38.3	−0.42	2.98	−5.8	88.8	38.3	0.6	0.0
43. Macao	83.3	93.0	38.0	−0.33	2.71	−9.7	88.4	38.3	4.6	0.4
44. Latvia	75.5	83.6	40.4	−0.29	2.85	−8.1	84.7	40.3	−1.1	0.1
45. Lebanon	71.4	86.2	37.8	−0.39	2.74	−14.8	100.1	36.8	−13.9	1.1
46. Mexico	60.4	63.7	38.4	−0.30	2.84	−3.3	90.9	36.7	−27.2	2.0
47. Belarus	55.3	71.4	40.4	−0.17	2.68	−16.1	47.7	41.7	23.8	1.6
48. Kazakhstan	52.7	78.5	38.5	−0.28	2.86	−25.8	57.0	39.7	21.5	1.5
49. Mauritius	51.8	59.3	39.9	−0.07	2.69	−7.4	51.3	40.4	8.0	0.5
50. Russia	51.7	44.6	40.7	−0.11	2.77	7.1	52.2	40.3	−7.6	0.5
51. Bulgaria	51.0	52.6	41.2	−0.10	2.72	−1.6	49.6	41.3	3.0	0.2
52. Iran	47.5	76.4	39.9	0.11	2.91	−28.8	1.0	43.1	75.4	4.6
53. Romania	44.1	52.1	42.0	−0.13	2.81	−8.0	46.8	42.3	5.3	0.4
54. Oman	43.5	50.3	40.6	−0.27	3.04	−6.9	87.9	38.2	−37.6	2.9
55. Argentina	42.7	50.7	41.2	−0.08	2.92	−8.0	60.3	40.7	−9.6	0.7
56. Serbia	41.2	58.5	42.3	−0.15	2.69	−17.3	33.1	43.7	25.4	1.7
57. Saudi Arabia	40.8	56.7	41.5	−0.13	2.64	−15.9	79.1	40.1	−22.4	1.7

58. Chile	39.8	50.9	39.1	-0.14	2.96	-11.0	66.5	38.2	-15.7	1.1
59. Uruguay	34.2	43.9	41.6	-0.21	2.71	-9.7	67.8	40.2	-23.9	1.7
60. Bosnia Herz.	33.2	38.3	42.4	-0.13	2.76	-5.1	32.6	42.7	5.8	0.4
61. Macedonia	26.9	31.0	41.5	-0.13	2.94	-4.1	26.6	41.7	4.4	0.3
62. Ukraine	23.4	28.0	43.3	-0.05	2.70	-4.7	15.6	43.9	12.4	0.8
63. South Africa	20.6	33.4	42.5	-0.04	2.73	-12.8	42.0	42.1	-8.6	0.6
64. Malaysia	20.6	32.5	42.7	-0.27	3.03	-11.9	28.5	42.9	4.1	0.3
65. Turkey	18.5	26.4	42.6	0.01	2.73	-7.9	26.9	42.6	-0.5	0.0
66. Montenegro	17.8	30.9	42.1	0.06	2.68	-13.1	16.5	42.8	14.4	0.9
67. Brazil	17.4	31.6	43.1	-0.27	2.81	-14.2	54.6	41.9	-23.0	1.5
68. Venezuela	8.7	21.7	42.9	-0.15	2.78	-13.0	5.9	43.6	15.8	0.9
69. Thailand	2.9	9.1	41.2	-0.08	3.16	-6.2	-5.4	41.8	14.5	0.9
70. Albania	-7.2	-13.9	65.8	-0.04	2.88	6.7	-18.7	66.1	4.8	0.4
71. Colombia	-7.5	10.3	66.2	-0.02	2.67	-17.8	-7.5	67.4	17.8	1.4
72. Ecuador	-13.1	-5.7	68.3	-0.14	2.95	-7.4	-0.4	67.9	-5.3	0.5
73. Jordan	-13.6	1.8	65.7	-0.19	2.83	-15.4	20.1	64.3	-18.2	1.6
74. Tunisia	-13.8	-10.4	67.7	-0.04	2.72	-3.4	-9.4	67.7	-1.0	0.1
75. Peru	-14.1	-12.1	67.3	-0.03	2.82	-2.0	-11.4	67.3	-0.7	0.1
76. Egypt	-15.0	-24.3	66.7	0.14	2.73	9.3	-39.9	67.6	15.6	1.2
77. Moldova	-18.7	-7.2	63.6	-0.08	2.85	-11.6	-36.9	65.3	29.7	2.2
78. Maldives	-19.1	-0.7	66.7	0.00	2.64	-18.4	-11.5	67.4	10.8	0.9
79. Gabon	-20.8	-1.6	63.8	-0.05	2.76	-19.2	-56.6	66.9	55.0	3.9
80. Fiji	-21.9	-28.3	72.1	0.03	2.59	6.4	-0.3	70.0	-28.0	2.5

Table 7.4 (*cont.*)

Country	$\log(Q^a/Q^*)$ Observed	Simulated					Components of simulated $\log(Q^a/Q^*)$			
							Food share		Food relative price	
	Observed	Mean	SD	Skewness	Kurtosis	Error	Mean	SD	Mean	SD
(1)	(2)	(3)	(4)	(5)	(6)	(7)	(8)	(9)	(10)	(11)
81. Georgia	−26.0	−72.8	66.1	0.20	2.83	46.9	−89.2	66.9	16.4	1.1
82. Botswana	−27.2	−2.1	66.9	0.07	2.79	−25.2	−46.6	69.8	44.6	3.4
83. Namibia	−36.7	−7.4	65.0	−0.14	2.72	−29.3	−34.9	66.6	27.4	2.0
84. Swaziland	−37.6	−28.9	64.4	0.03	2.65	−8.7	−38.2	64.9	9.3	0.7
85. Syria	−39.8	−40.5	66.7	−0.04	2.98	0.8	−27.2	65.9	−13.3	1.0
86. Bolivia	−42.6	−26.8	64.6	−0.03	2.99	−15.7	−44.7	65.6	17.9	1.3
87. Equat. Guinea	−44.1	−54.2	64.0	0.06	2.93	10.1	−84.7	65.5	30.5	2.0
88. Paraguay	−45.5	−60.4	69.6	0.02	2.80	14.9	−33.3	67.9	−27.1	2.0
89. Cape Verde	−57.4	−43.4	66.2	0.08	3.10	−14.0	−46.6	66.3	3.2	0.2
90. Bhutan	−67.1	−38.9	65.7	0.19	2.77	−28.2	−67.8	67.3	29.0	2.0
91. Kyrgyz	−67.8	−97.6	62.8	0.10	2.85	29.8	−113.4	63.6	15.8	1.0
92. Sri Lanka	−68.0	−98.1	66.0	0.08	2.97	30.1	−89.3	65.6	−8.8	0.6
93. Iraq	−69.8	−35.9	65.4	0.02	2.84	−33.9	−62.9	66.9	27.0	1.9
94. Mongolia	−71.1	−60.4	64.5	0.18	2.76	−10.7	−79.8	65.5	19.4	1.3
95. Philippines	−73.5	−69.8	65.0	0.15	2.92	−3.7	−74.1	65.2	4.2	0.3
96. Indonesia	−74.8	−79.7	65.6	0.07	2.93	4.9	−73.0	65.3	−6.7	0.4
97. Pakistan	−76.3	−79.5	63.3	0.08	2.96	3.2	−104.4	64.4	24.9	1.6
98. Morocco	−78.2	−69.7	65.9	0.17	3.15	−8.5	−62.4	65.5	−7.2	0.5

99. Lesotho	−79.0	−63.6	62.0	0.05	2.81	−15.4	−108.4	64.0	44.8	2.8
100. China	−80.1	−58.3	67.5	0.05	2.82	−21.8	−78.5	68.6	20.2	1.4
101. Vietnam	−83.5	−67.2	64.8	0.05	3.16	−16.3	−95.2	66.2	28.0	1.8
102. India	−105.1	−108.1	67.2	0.12	2.88	3.0	−103.5	67.0	−4.6	0.3
103. Cambodia	−108.3	−108.7	64.2	0.21	3.03	0.5	−124.2	64.9	15.5	1.0
104. Yemen	−111.1	−115.0	65.5	0.12	2.90	3.9	−113.4	65.4	−1.6	0.1
105. Sudan	−125.7	−140.2	66.0	0.10	2.93	14.5	−141.3	66.1	1.1	0.1
106. Lao	−126.4	−143.1	62.1	0.15	3.01	16.7	−160.4	62.8	17.3	1.0
107. Djibouti	−127.7	−110.5	62.6	0.14	3.00	−17.3	−159.3	64.4	48.8	2.9
108. Kenya	−129.1	−125.1	63.0	0.15	3.21	−4.0	−152.5	64.0	27.3	1.6
109. Sao Tome	−129.4	−146.0	61.0	0.20	2.96	16.6	−153.5	61.2	7.5	0.4
110. Congo, R.	−133.8	−126.7	61.5	0.12	2.84	−7.1	−174.3	63.3	47.6	2.8
111. Cameroon	−135.7	−159.0	64.1	0.08	3.03	23.3	−158.6	64.1	−0.4	0.0
112. Nigeria	−135.9	−158.9	59.5	0.22	3.04	23.0	−204.0	61.1	45.1	2.6
113. Senegal	−138.8	−145.8	63.6	0.27	3.15	7.0	−168.2	64.5	22.4	1.3
114. Chad	−150.0	−261.3	57.2	0.13	2.86	111.4	−253.2	56.9	−8.1	0.5
115. Nepal	−154.1	−143.8	64.9	0.05	3.21	−10.3	−137.1	64.6	−6.7	0.4
116. Bangladesh	−156.5	−164.7	62.4	0.19	2.95	8.3	−153.7	62.0	−11.0	0.6
117. Benin	−157.0	−173.7	60.4	0.10	2.92	16.8	−197.1	61.2	23.4	1.4
118. Ghana	−157.3	−162.5	56.6	0.20	3.00	5.2	−213.7	58.2	51.2	2.8
119. Cote d'Ivoire	−161.9	−173.3	64.2	0.27	3.47	11.4	−174.9	64.3	1.6	0.1
120. S. Leone	−162.0	−136.9	58.3	0.09	2.97	−25.1	−222.1	61.1	85.2	4.9

Table 7.4 (*cont.*)

Country (1)	Observed (2)	log(Q^a/Q^*) Simulated Mean (3)	SD (4)	Skewness (5)	Kurtosis (6)	Error (7)	Components of simulated log(Q^a/Q^*) Food share Mean (8)	SD (9)	Food relative price Mean (10)	SD (11)
121. M'gascar	−164.6	−172.3	58.4	0.09	2.93	7.7	−201.9	59.5	29.6	1.7
122. Togo	−176.9	−217.4	58.1	0.23	2.90	40.6	−223.5	58.3	6.1	0.3
123. Burkina Faso	−185.4	−204.6	62.1	0.08	2.68	19.2	−210.2	62.2	5.6	0.3
124. Guinea	−186.7	−174.7	56.1	0.09	3.11	−12.0	−244.4	58.0	69.7	3.8
125. Mali	−191.5	−194.5	60.1	0.02	2.99	3.0	−214.8	60.8	20.3	1.2
126. Angola	−192.7	−180.9	59.6	0.10	3.03	−11.8	−224.0	60.8	43.0	2.4
127. Rwanda	−202.4	−193.3	60.1	0.16	3.11	−9.2	−194.0	60.1	0.7	0.0
128. C. Africa	−213.4	−249.8	57.9	0.31	3.01	36.4	−258.6	58.2	8.7	0.5
129. M'bique	−220.3	−228.3	57.7	0.02	2.75	8.0	−228.8	57.8	0.5	0.0
130. Niger	−249.2	−259.4	56.1	0.00	2.70	10.1	−270.0	56.4	10.7	0.6
131. G–Bissau	−254.9	−272.0	57.4	0.16	3.30	17.1	−270.7	57.3	−1.3	0.1
132. Congo, D. R.	−363.3	−352.4	50.3	0.21	3.24	−10.9	−362.9	50.6	10.5	0.6

Notes:
1. All entries, except those in columns 5 and 6, are to be divided by 100.
2. $Q^* =$ geometric mean of Q_c; SD = standard deviation.
3. Column 7 = column 2 − column 3.

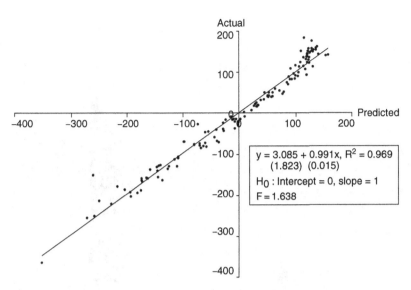

Figure 7.3 Actual and predicted income (logarithmic ratios to geometric mean ×100). *Note:* The points above the horizontal axis represent countries in the rich group (countries 1–69 in Table 7.4). The points below the horizontal represent the poor countries (countries 70–132).

kurtosis than in the other countries. Figure 7.4 provides a plot of the observed and simulated income differences for each pair of countries. The simulated 'income mountain' is more uneven than its observed counterpart, which is due in part to use of the same ranking of countries in the two panels of the figure (observed incomes). Nevertheless, the two shapes match quite well in general. As the estimated mountain for the poor countries is 'bumpy' in comparison with its rich counterpart, there is more uncertainty regarding incomes for the poor countries. This is also evident in column 4 of Table 7.4, where the average standard deviation for poor countries is approximately twice that for the rich countries. We further discuss the uncertainty of incomes in the next section.

Next, we use equation (7.12) to decompose simulated income into two components:

$$\log\left(\frac{Q^a}{Q^*}\right)^{(s)} = \text{food share}^{a(s)} + \text{relative price}^{a(s)}$$

where the components for country a in trial s are

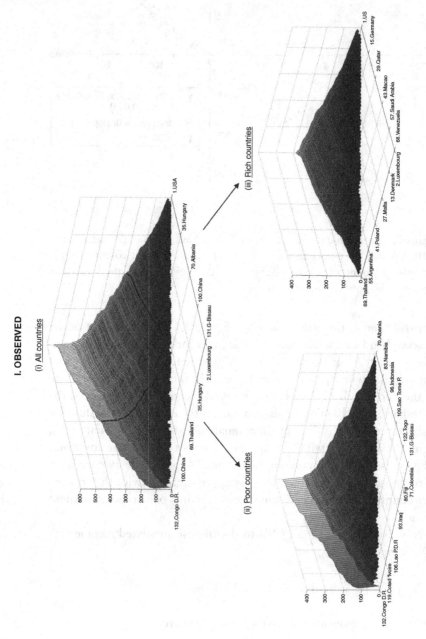

I. OBSERVED

(i) <u>All countries</u>

(ii) <u>Poor countries</u>

(iii) <u>Rich countries</u>

Figure 7.4 Further cross-country income comparisons (logarithmic ratios ×100).

II. SIMULATED

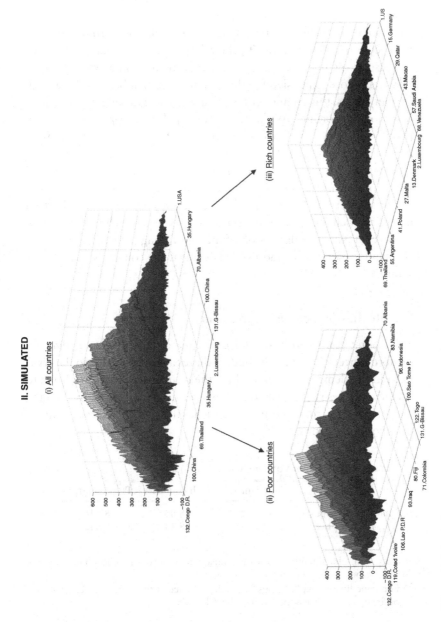

Figure 7.4 (*cont.*)

$$\text{food share}^{a(s)} = \frac{\log\left(w^{a(s)}/w^*\right)}{\eta^{a*(s)} - 1},$$

$$\text{relative price}^{a(s)} = -\frac{\left(\phi^{(s)}\eta^{a*(s)} + 1\right)\left[\log\left(p^a/p^*\right) - \log\left(P^a/P^*\right)\right]}{\eta^{a*(s)} - 1}$$

Column 10 in Table 7.4 reveals that within the rich group of countries (countries 1 through 69), the relative price component tends to increase as income decreases, which reflects that, on average, food is relatively more expensive for the less affluent members of the group. In many cases, this component is substantial, so ignoring it would lead to serious distortion. As the term $-(\phi^{(s)}\eta^{a*(s)} + 1)/(\eta^{a*(s)} - 1)$ in the preceding is most likely to be positive, the food share decreases with its price. Consequently, for countries within the top half of rich group, ignoring the cheaper food prices leads to an underestimate of the food share and an overestimate of income, at least on average. This tendency to overestimate income is weaker for counties in the bottom half of the rich group, where food is more expensive. Thus, ignoring of prices overstates the dispersion of income among the rich countries.[12] No similar pattern in food prices is evident for countries in the poor group.[13]

7.6 Stochastic income comparisons

The income comparisons provided by equation (7.12) involve two elements of uncertainty: (1) The budget shares are random due to the error term in the demand model, and (2) the estimation procedure leads to elasticity values that are also random. In this section we show how the incorporation of this randomness enriches the analysis of cross-country income comparisons.

[12] The standard deviations of log income ($\times 100$) are

	All countries	Rich countries	Poor countries
Unadjusted for prices	130.98	48.06	86.18
Adjusted for prices	118.24	38.14	83.12

There is a related tendency for the adjustment for prices to smooth out some of the sharp spikes in the income differences.

[13] For some further explorations of the dependence of the relative price of food on income, see Appendix 7A. See also Chapter 6.

We start with a summary picture for the six groups of countries, each comprising twenty-two members, as indicated by the grid lines of Table 7.1 (as before). We denote these groups by $G = 1, ..., 6$ and order them in terms of increasing average income. If S_G denotes the set of countries in group G, then in trial s the average income in this group is $\log(Q^G/Q^*)^{(s)} = (1/22) \sum_{c \in S_G} \log(Q^c/Q^*)^{(s)}$. The income of group G relative to group H is then $\log(Q^G/Q^H)^{(s)} = \log(Q^G/Q^*)^{(s)} - \log(Q^H/Q^*)^{(s)}$. Figure 7.5 shows histograms of the relative income for the $s = 1, ..., 1,000$ trials for all pairs of groups. Consider the first row, which refers to the richest group of countries. As we move from left to right along this row, we compare groups that become closer together on the income scale. Thus, as expected, the centre of gravity of the histograms moves in the direction of zero along the journey from left to right. The same pattern applies to the subsequent three rows of the figure, as well as to the columns, for the same reason. Note also that the dispersion tends to increase as we move down a diagonal from right to left as the difference in mean income increases. In addition, there is little evidence of skewness or excess kurtosis in the income distributions.[14]

Next, we descend from high-level income comparisons involving groups and consider more detail by applying the same approach to individual countries. We compare the distribution of income in richer country a with that in a poorer country b by means of the probability $P(Q^a > Q^b)$. When this probability is close to 1, there is little overlap in the income distributions of the two countries, so they are more distinct on the income scale. Figure 7.6 plots these probabilities for all pairs of countries. The one-step-removed diagonal elements of this figure refer to comparisons of adjacent countries, and the probability

---

[14] The simulations can also be used to determine the estimated probability that an ostensibly richer country group is more affluent than its poorer neighbour. For all pairs of groups, these probabilities are close to 1, which means that there is little stochastic overlap of country groups. We can also compare income distributions by testing for stochastic dominance. That is, if we denote by $F_G(Q)$ the income distribution of group G, we test $H_0 : F_G(Q)$ stochastically dominates $F_H(Q)$, $G, H = 1, ..., 6$, $G < H$. Using the Anderson (1996) test as modified by Barrett and Donald (2003), we reject the null for first-, second- and third-order stochastic dominance for all pairs of country groups at conventional significance levels. This finding is perhaps not unexpected given the lack of overlap of the distributions in Figure 7.5.

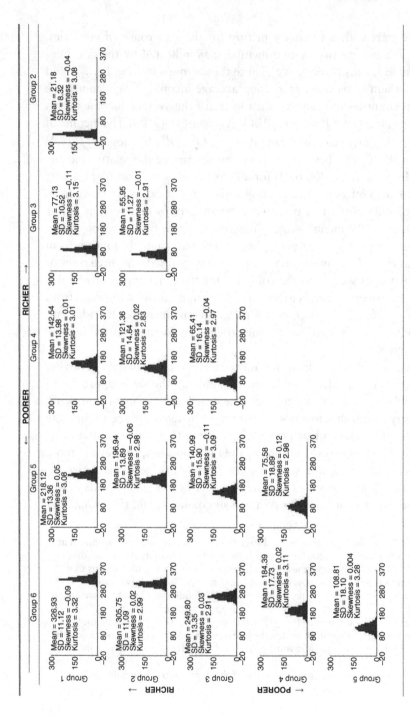

Figure 7.5 Matrix of histograms of simulated income differences for six country groups (logarithmic ratios ×100). *Note:* The 132 countries are ranked by income per capita and then divided into six groups of 22 countries each, according to the grid lines in Table 7.1.

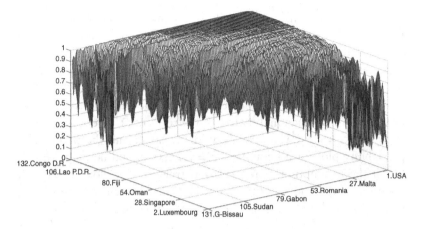

Figure 7.6 Probability of income differences.

of income differences among these pairs is of the order of 0.5. Thus, in contrast to the result for groups, this shows that these countries are not really distinct at all. In other words, as the precise ranking of individual countries is not too reliable, for income comparisons, it makes more sense to locate countries in broad groups. As countries become more distant from each other, the probability of income differences increases. In Figure 7.6, as we move away from the diagonal (which compares neighbouring countries) and travel in a northerly or easterly direction, or any linear combination thereof, we encounter pairs of countries more distant on the income scale. There is a distinct tendency for the probability surface in the figure to increase with such a move, which reflects the fact that incomes are more likely to differ the greater the distance between countries or the more 'exotic' or 'foreign' they are.[15]

It should be kept in mind that the stochastic income comparisons of this section are based on the assumption that the disturbances in demand equation (7.8) are multivariate normal. While this is a convenient assumption, it cannot be completely true because the dependent variable of equation (7.8) is a budget share, which has a [0, 1] domain. All the estimated food shares fall in the [0, 1] range, which provides some reassurance that normality is not grossly violated, however. To

---

[15] For a further analysis, see Appendix 7A.

examine this issue in more detail, we follow Theil (1975–6) and let $\tilde{r}^c$ be a vector of eleven residuals from the demand model (7.8) for $i = 1,\ldots,11$ goods (as the twelve residuals have a zero sum, we need only consider the first eleven) for country c, and let Ω be the corresponding covariance matrix. This Ω can be expressed as $C\Lambda^2 C'$, where C is an orthogonal matrix in which columns are the characteristic vectors of Ω and Λ^2 is a diagonal matrix of the roots of Ω. The standardised residuals $r^c = C\Lambda^{-1}C'\tilde{r}^c$ are then uncorrelated, and the points of a probability plot for all countries $c = 1,\ldots,C$ should lie on a straight line if the assumption of normality is true. Such a plot for the rich countries is not too far from a straight line between the probability levels 0.01 and 0.90, but for the poor countries this range is reduced to [0.05, 0.80]. Accordingly, as the assumption of normality is shakier for the poor countries, this represents a qualification of our results.[16]

7.7 Concluding comments

This chapter has reconsidered the old but fundamental problem of measuring the wealth of nations. We argued that the share of total consumption expenditure devoted to food (the food budget share) has several attractive features as an inverse measure of affluence. As it is a pure number that is independent of the price level and currency units, it is readily comparable across time and countries. In addition, fairly reliable information on the food budget share is available in most countries within a reasonable timeframe. Finally, the relation between this share and income is one of the most studied in economics and is enshrined in Engel's law. We demonstrated that once differences in food prices are allowed for, the food budget share provides a method of estimating incomes across countries that is a viable alternative to that provided by the PPP measures of the International Comparison Program of the World Bank.

---

[16] Such a finding is corroborated by the Shapiro-Wilk test. However, when this test is applied to each commodity individually, interestingly, the p-value for normality of the residuals of the food equation is 0.42 for rich and 0.026 for poor countries, so in both cases we are unable to reject the null hypothesis for this commodity at the usual significance levels. A probability plot of the residuals for food in the rich countries reveals that the points are not too far from a straight line between the probability levels 0.20 and 0.80; for the poor countries, this range is [0.08, 0.80].

Table 7.5 *Illustrative comparison of food shares and incomes, Nigeria and Indonesia.*

Ratio of food shares:	
(i) Observed, w^N/w^I	1.36
(ii) Adjusted for prices,	
$\exp\left[\log\left(\dfrac{w^N}{w^I}\right) - \Delta\log\left(\dfrac{w^N}{w^I}\right)\right]$	1.19
Income difference (logarithmic ratio):	
(iii) Estimated, unadjusted for prices,	
$\dfrac{1}{\eta^{NI}-1}\log\left(\dfrac{w^N}{w^I}\right)$	−1.20
(iv) Estimated, adjusted for prices,	
$\dfrac{1}{\eta^{NI}-1}\left[\log\left(\dfrac{w^N}{w^I}\right) - \Delta\log\left(\dfrac{w^N}{w^I}\right)\right]$	−0.69
(v) Observed	−0.61

Our rule for measuring international income differences is given by equation (7.11). This implies that the estimate of per-capita income of country *a* in terms of country *b* can be formulated as

$$\frac{1}{\eta^{ab}-1}\left[\log\left(\frac{w^a}{w^b}\right) - \Delta\log\left(\frac{w^a}{w^b}\right)\right]$$

where η^{ab} is the average food income elasticity, w^a and w^b are the food budget shares in the two countries, $\Delta\log(w^a/w^b) = (\phi\eta^{ab}+1)\left[\log(p^a/P^a) - \log(p^b/P^b)\right]$ is the change in the log ratio of the shares on account of the different relative food prices, and φ is the income flexibility (the reciprocal of income elasticity of the marginal utility of the income). Thus our measure of income differences is attractive in its simplicity because it just depends on two basic elements: (1) food budget shares and prices and (2) two parameters, the food income elasticity and the income flexibility, for which many estimates are available.

The workings of this rule can be illustrated using the case of *a* = Nigeria (denoted by *N*) and *b* = Indonesia (*I*). The observed food budget shares are $w^N = 0.567$ and $w^I = 0.416$, so their ratio is $w^N/w^I = 1.36$, as indicated by item (i) in Table 7.5. The log ratio of the relative price of food for the two countries is 0.28, so food is more than 30 per cent more expensive in Nigeria. For illustration, we use $\eta^{NI} = 0.75$, the average value of food income elasticity in poor countries, and $\varphi = -0.68$, the estimate of the income flexibility in Table 7.3. Adjusting for the higher food prices in Nigeria, the ratio of shares decreases from 1.36 to 1.19, as shown in item (ii) of Table 7.5. Taking the price differences into account, we estimate the log ratio of per-capita income in Nigeria, in terms of that in Indonesia, to be -0.69 [item (iv)], so on average Nigerians are approximately 50 per cent poorer. On a PPP basis, the observed log ratio of incomes is -0.61 [item (v)]. Although the agreement is not perfect, the discrepancy is modest and points to the practical usefulness of our short-cut approach when comprehensive data are lacking.

Appendix 7A

7A.1 Dates and data

Table 7A.1 contains information regarding the publication of national accounts data in twenty selected countries. This table reveals that, on average, there is a publication lag of the order of 80 days for quarterly estimates (which are produced mostly in rich countries) and more than 200 days for annual estimates. Table 7A.2 shows that the publication activities of the International Comparisons Program are speeding up, but the most recent estimates were still subject to a three-year publication lag.

7A.2 Data source

All data are from the International Comparison Program (2008), which refers to 146 countries. Eight of these countries are excluded because of missing data, and a further six were excluded on the basis that they represented significant outliers in a regression of the food budget share on the log of income per capita, as indicated in Figure 7A.1. This leaves $146 - 8 - 6 = 132$ countries. Table 5 of the International Comparison Program (2008) gives per-capita expenditures on twelve consumption commodities valued at US dollar prices, from which the budget shares are computed. The sum of these expenditures over the twelve commodities yields total per-capita consumption Q^c. The budget shares are listed in Table 6A.1, whereas Table 7.1 gives Q^c with the United States $= 100$. For the prices p_i^c we use the 'PPP prices' of Table 1

Table 7A.1 *National accounts data for twenty selected countries*

Country	Periodicity	Timeliness	Estimated publication lag (calendar days)	Analytical framework	Statistical agency and reference
(1)	(2)	(3)	(4)	(5)	(6)
1. United States	Quarterly	Advance estimates are released after thirty days; preliminary estimates are published after sixty days. The third release is referred to as final and is published after eighty-five days.	85	SNA 1993	Bureau of Economic Analysis (BEA) www.bea.gov/newsreleases/news_release_sort_national.htm
2. Canada	Quarterly	Released after ten weeks and revised in accordance with an established revision practice. A particular quarter's estimate can be revised in other quarters in the same year but cannot be revised in subsequent years except at the time the first quarter estimates for those years are published. These annual revisions are limited to four years, after which the estimates are considered final.	70	SNA 1993	Statistics Canada www.statcan.gc.ca/bsolc/olc–cel/olc–cel?catno=13–010–X&lang=eng www.statcan.gc.ca/bsolc/olc–cel/olc–cel?catno=13–010–X&chropg=1&lang=eng
3. Australia	Quarterly	Initial estimates are released about eight to ten weeks after and no later than three months. New information is incorporated into the accounts as soon as it is available.	63	SNA 1993	Australian Bureau of Statistics (ABS) www.abs.gov.au/AUSSTATS/abs@.nsf/mf/5206.0

357

Table 7A.1 (*cont.*)

Country (1)	Periodicity (2)	Timeliness (3)	Estimated publication lag (calendar days) (4)	Analytical framework (5)	Statistical agency and reference (6)
4. Taiwan	Quarterly	Released within seven to eight weeks. A comprehensive revision is released every five years.	53	SNA 1993	Republic of China (Taiwan) National Statistics http://win.dgbas.gov.tw/dgbas03/bs7/sdds/english/3d/na.htm
5. Singapore	Quarterly	The advance estimates are released after ten days and within eight weeks for the preliminary estimates. The data become final two years after their first release.	56	SNA 1993	Singapore Department of Statistics www.singstat.gov.sg/stats/arc.html http://unstats.un.org/unsd/EconStatKB/Attachment75.aspx
6. Estonia	Quarterly	Publishes flash estimates of GDP growth after sixty-five days and provides full data at 120 days. Improved data are incorporated as soon as they become available. The final quarterly estimates are released eighteen months after the end of the reference year.	120	SNA 1993 & ESA 95	Statistics Estonia www.stat.ee/release-calendar?id=11707&cover=2009&type=501&display=1&area=all http://dsbb.imf.org/Applications/web/sddsctycatbaselist/?strcode=EST&strcat=NAG00
7. Russia	Quarterly	The first preliminary estimates are disseminated after fifty working days; revised estimates are released after eighty working days and finalised twenty-four months after the end of the calendar year.	112	SNA 1993	Russian Federal State Statistics Service (Rosstat) www.gks.ru/bgd/free/B00_25/IssWWW.exe/Stg/dvvp/I000140R.HTM

	Country	Frequency	Description	Timeliness	Standard	Source
8.	Oman	Annually	Provisional estimates of annual data are disseminated after eight to nine months. Preliminary estimates of annual data, derived as the sum of the quarterly data, are disseminated after two to three months.	255	SNA 1993	Ministry of National Economy (MONE) www.imf.org/external/pubs/ft/scr/2005/cr05429.pdf
9.	Turkey	Quarterly	Three months after for the first and fourth quarters, seventy days after for the second and third quarters. Data are preliminary when first released, and revised data are published in the press release for the fourth quarter.	80 (on average)	ESA 95	Turkish Statistical Institute (Turkstat) http://dsbb.imf.org/Applications/web/sddsctycatbaselist/?strcode=TUR&strcat=NAG00
10.	Brazil	Quarterly	Published after seventy days.	70	SNA 1993	Instituto Brasileiro de Geografia e Estatística (IBGE) www.bcb.gov.br/sddsi/ctasnac_i.htm www.imf.org/external/np/loi/2000/bra/02/
11.	Egypt	Quarterly	Released after three months.	90	SNA 1993	Ministry of Economic Development (MOED) and the Central Agency for Public Mobilization and Statistics (CAPMAS) http://dsbb.imf.org/Applications/web/sddsctycatbaselist/?strcode=EGY&strcat=NAG00
12.	Moldova	Quarterly	Estimates are published within three months, except for the fourth quarter, for which data are disseminated within six months.	120 (on average)	SNA 1993	National Bureau of Statistics (NBS) http://dsbb.imf.org/Applications/web/sddsctycatbaselist/?strcode=MDA&strcat=NAG00

Table 7A.1 (*cont.*)

Country (1)	Periodicity (2)	Timeliness (3)	Estimated publication lag (calendar days) (4)	Analytical framework (5)	Statistical agency and reference (6)
13. Fiji	Annually	Estimates are released after six months, on the last working day in June.	180	SNA 1968	Fiji Islands Bureau of Statistics http://dsbb.imf.org/Applications/web/gdds/gddscountrycategorycfreport/?strcode=FJI&strcat=NAG00
14. Kyrgyz	Quarterly	Data are released after ninety days.	90	SNA 1993	National Statistical Committee www.stat.kg/nsdp/calendar.htm
15. Philippines	Quarterly	Estimates are released no later than two months for the first, second and third quarters and no later than one month for the fourth quarter.	60 (on average)	SNA 1968	National Statistical Coordination Board www.nscb.gov.ph/sna/schedule.asp
16. China	Annually	First estimates are published in February of the following year in *China's Statistical Communiqué* and then with more detail in May in *A Statistical Survey of China*. These are preliminary estimates. In September, first confirmed estimates are published in the *Statistical Yearbook*. The next year's issue of *A Statistical Survey of China* contains the second confirmed estimates. This concludes the cycle of regular revisions.	270	SNA 1968	National Bureau of Statistics of China (NBS) www.oecd.org/dataoecd/44/1/1850377.pdf (pg. 11) www.stats.gov.cn/english/statisticaldata/yearlydata/

#	Country	Frequency	Description		SNA	Source
17.	Kenya	Annually	Released within six to twelve months.	270	SNA 1968	Kenya National Bureau of Statistics (KNBS) http://unstats.un.org/unsd/dnss/docViewer.aspx?docID=2122
18.	Ghana	Annually	Released within three months (switching to quarterly estimates when data become available).	90	SNA 1968	Ghana Statistical Service www.imf.org/external/np/loi/2009/gha/062609.pdf
19.	Rwanda	Annually	Released within nine months.	270	SNA 1993	National Institute of Statistics of Rwanda (NISR) http://statistics.gov.rw/index.php?option=com_content&task=view&id=1428&Itemid=189
20.	Niger	Annually	Published within six months. Revisions are normally released after another eight weeks.	180	SNA 1968	Institut National de la Statistique www.imf.org/external/np/loi/2009/ner/042709.pdf
	Mean		Rich countries: Quarterly estimates	80		
			Poor countries: Quarterly estimates	86		
			Annual estimates	210		

Table 7A.1 (*cont.*)

Country	Periodicity	Timeliness	Estimated publication lag (calendar days)	Analytical framework	Statistical agency and reference
(1)	(2)	(3)	(4)	(5)	(6)
	All countries: Quarterly estimates		82		
	All countries: Annual estimates		217		

Notes:

1. SNA 1968, SNA 1993 and ESA 95 denote the United Nations System of National Accounts 1969, United Nations System of National Accounts 1993 and the European System of Accounts 1995, respectively.

2. The estimated publication lag shown in column 4 is expressed in terms of calendar days. It is assumed that 1 month = 30 days and 1 week = 7 days. Working days are converted to calendar days by multiplying by 7/5. Information shown in column 4 is, to some degree, subjective in that it generally refers to the time taken before the final estimates are released. In cases for which information on the type of release (advance, preliminary, etc.) is unavailable, the release is assumed to be the 'final' release.

3. Rich and poor countries (at the bottom of the table) refer to countries 1–9 and 10–20 of column 1, respectively.

Table 7A.2 *International Comparison Program data*

Benchmark year and phase (1)	Publication year (2)	Publication lag (years) (3)	Number of countries (4)	Statistical agency and reference (5)
1. 1967/70 Phase I	1975	5	10 (6 in 1967, 10 in 1970)	The United Nations Statistical Office, the World Bank and the University of Pennsylvania (Kravis et al. 1975) www–wds.worldbank.org/external/default/WDSContentServer/WDSP/IB/2001/01/10/000178830_98101911364270/Rendered/PDF/multi_page.pdf
2. 1970/73 Phase II	1978	5	16 (10 in 1970, 16 in 1973)	The United Nations Statistical Office, the World Bank and the University of Pennsylvania (Kravis et al., 1978)
3. 1975 Phase III	1982	7	34	The United Nations Statistical Office, the World Bank and the University of Pennsylvania (Kravis et al., 1982) http://siteresources.worldbank.org/ICPINT/Resources/worldproductandincome.pdf
4. 1980 Phase IV	1986	6	60	The United Nations, the Statistical Office of the European Communities (EUROSTAT) and the World Bank (ICP, 1986, 1987)
5. 1985 Phase V	1994	9	64	The United Nations and EUROSTAT (ICP, 1994) http://siteresources.worldbank.org/ICPINT/Resources/worldcomparisongdp1985.pdf
6. 1993 Phase VI	1996/97	3–4	117	ICP (1997a, 1997b, 1999) and Mouyelo-Katoula and Munnsad (1996)

Table 7A.2 (cont.)

Benchmark year and phase (1)	Publication year (2)	Publication lag (years) (3)	Number of countries (4)	Statistical agency and reference (5)
7. 2005 ICP	2008	3	146	International Bank for Reconstruction and Development and the World Bank (ICP, 2008) http://siteresources.worldbank.org/ICPINT/Resources/icp–final.pdf
Mean		5.5		

Note: References to works cited:

ICP (1986). *World Comparisons of Purchasing Power and Real Product for 1980*, Part One: *Summary Results for 60 Countries* New York: United Nations and Eurostat.

ICP (1987). *World Comparisons of Purchasing Power and Real Product for 1980*, Part Two: *Detailed Summary Results for 60 Countries*. New York: United Nations and Eurostat.

ICP (1994). *World Comparisons of Purchasing Power and Real Product, 1985: Phase V of the International Comparison Program* New York: United Nations.

ICP (1997a). *Purchasing Power Parities: Volume and Price Level Comparisons for the Middle East, 1993*. Amman: Economic Commission for Western Asia and the World Bank.

ICP (1997b). *International Comparison of Gross Domestic Product in Europe 1993*. New York: United Nations.

ICP (1999). *ESCAP Comparisons of Real Gross Domestic Product and Purchasing Power Parities, 1993*. Bangkok: United Nations

ICP (2008). 'Global Purchasing Power Parities and Real Expenditures'. Available at www.worldbank.org.

Kravis, I., Z. Kenessey, A. Heston and R. Summers (1975). *A System of International Comparisons of Gross Product and Purchasing Power*. Baltimore, MD: Johns Hopkins University Press.

Kravis, I., Z. Kenessey, A. Heston and R. Summers (1978). *International Comparisons of Real Product and Purchasing Power*. Baltimore, MD: Johns Hopkins University Press.

Kravis, I., Z. Kenessey, A. Heston and R. Summers (1982). *World Product and Income, International Comparisons of Real Product and Purchasing Power*. Baltimore, MD: Johns Hopkins University Press.

Mouyelo–Katoula, M., and K. Munnsad (1996). *Comparisons of Price Levels and Economic Aggregates: The Results of 22 African Countries*. Luxembourg: Eurostat.

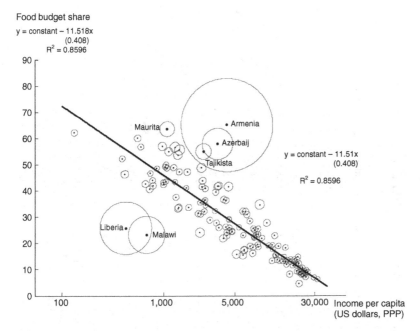

Figure 7A.1 Further scatter plot of food budget share against income for 138 countries. Notes: 1. This plot has 138 points, one for each country. Each country is represented by a point (its observed share and income) at the centre of a circle. The area of the circle is proportional to the reciprocal square root of the *p*-value for the dummy variable for this country in a regression of food share on the logarithm of income. Accordingly, the larger the area, the greater is the probability that the country is an outlier. 2. We declare a country an outlier if its *p*-value is less than 0.02. This yields six outlier countries (i.e., Armenia, Liberia, Malawi, Azerbaijan, Tajikistan and Mauritania) that are excluded from the regression.

of the International Comparison Program (2008); these are listed in Table 7A.3.

7A.3 Disturbance covariance matrix

Let $\boldsymbol{\varepsilon}^c = \left[\varepsilon_i^c\right]$ be a 12×1 vector of disturbances for country c. Countries 1 through 69 are classified as rich and countries 70 through 132 as poor, denoted by R and P, respectively. The disturbances for the rich countries have covariance matrix Σ^R, whereas that for the poor countries it is Σ^P, both of which are estimated by mean squares and

Table 7A.3 Prices of 12 commodities in 132 countries (domestic currency prices for US$1 worth of commodity)

Country	Food	Alcohol and tobacco	Clothing	Housing	Durables	Health	Transport	Communication	Recreation	Education	Restaurants	Other
(1)	(2)	(3)	(4)	(5)	(6)	(7)	(8)	(9)	(10)	(11)	(12)	(13)
1. United States	1.00	1.00	1.00	1.00	1.00	1.00	1.00	1.00	1.00	1.00	1.00	1.00
2. Luxembourg	1.04	0.71	1.05	0.94	0.96	0.68	1.16	0.67	1.05	0.98	1.15	0.94
3. Iceland	123.96	138.51	126.37	87.98	104.89	72.19	132.71	74.46	119.89	59.37	169.47	105.42
4. Norway	11.70	14.69	11.11	6.86	9.11	6.78	15.97	7.16	10.81	6.17	14.16	10.61
5. United Kingdom	0.71	0.98	0.67	0.53	0.68	0.43	1.01	0.51	0.68	0.48	0.93	0.66
6. Austria	1.00	0.76	0.97	0.72	0.90	0.59	1.37	0.79	0.95	0.63	1.13	0.92
7. Switzerland	2.08	1.25	1.72	2.05	1.68	1.30	2.19	1.58	1.80	1.38	2.22	1.84
8. Canada	1.48	1.81	1.49	1.00	1.45	1.02	1.53	1.21	1.26	0.82	1.68	1.20
9. Netherlands	0.80	0.81	0.94	0.93	0.85	0.56	1.47	0.80	0.93	0.57	1.16	0.88
10. Sweden	10.14	9.84	10.32	8.14	9.73	6.46	14.21	5.76	10.36	6.11	13.10	9.87
11. France	0.96	0.90	0.87	0.90	0.95	0.61	1.25	0.89	0.99	0.57	1.28	0.91
12. Australia	1.61	1.97	1.38	1.29	1.66	1.04	1.80	1.63	1.51	0.83	1.73	1.37
13. Denmark	9.61	7.43	8.58	8.43	8.29	6.32	14.35	5.01	9.41	5.91	13.07	9.24
14. Belgium	0.99	0.79	1.02	0.89	0.94	0.62	1.26	0.90	0.94	0.61	1.22	0.89
15. Germany	0.96	0.80	0.98	0.86	0.87	0.57	1.28	0.86	0.99	0.76	1.09	0.88
16. Hong Kong	8.82	10.17	6.12	9.10	7.62	2.93	9.40	6.84	5.25	3.26	8.99	5.62
17. Ireland	1.14	1.49	0.95	1.05	1.01	0.73	1.40	0.94	1.06	0.68	1.47	1.06
18. Japan	238.42	97.04	167.23	128.20	167.25	64.80	162.33	127.16	121.45	91.21	178.69	133.38
19. Taiwan	34.96	22.84	21.52	24.70	31.17	5.78	28.39	16.27	18.14	7.60	25.50	18.87
20. Cyprus	0.54	0.49	0.55	0.29	0.50	0.31	0.68	0.21	0.51	0.26	0.68	0.43
21. Finland	1.10	1.12	1.16	0.98	1.01	0.72	1.53	0.64	1.13	0.65	1.45	1.08
22. Spain	0.83	0.59	0.90	0.75	0.90	0.47	1.14	0.82	0.88	0.45	1.06	0.72

23. Italy	1.05	0.84	0.98	0.78	0.96	0.71	1.22	0.83	0.97	0.61	1.16	0.85
24. Greece	0.88	0.70	0.94	0.62	0.86	0.45	1.00	0.88	0.85	0.38	1.04	0.69
25. NZ	1.87	2.06	1.80	1.48	1.82	1.02	1.94	1.58	1.65	0.91	1.63	1.47
26. Israel	4.41	4.13	4.19	3.25	4.21	2.48	6.63	3.22	4.56	2.00	6.45	3.80
27. Malta	0.33	0.35	0.42	0.14	0.39	0.14	0.49	0.33	0.31	0.14	0.34	0.25
28. Singapore	1.77	4.34	1.60	1.63	1.72	0.56	2.00	0.92	1.16	0.51	1.68	1.16
29. Qatar	2.77	1.97	3.15	10.40	2.35	1.49	1.96	3.30	2.99	2.02	4.48	2.15
30. Slovenia	190.73	137.39	231.98	117.11	178.51	95.85	240.97	140.55	184.48	94.57	184.20	155.69
31. Portugal	0.80	0.66	0.86	0.58	0.81	0.49	1.19	0.83	0.85	0.57	0.89	0.73
32. Brunei	1.49	1.28	1.35	1.18	1.31	0.39	1.10	1.29	1.15	0.32	1.50	0.96
33. Kuwait	0.22	0.16	0.36	0.45	0.22	0.14	0.19	0.28	0.31	0.18	0.47	0.24
34. Czech Rep	18.03	15.61	27.77	9.73	20.53	6.98	26.72	25.37	15.17	6.35	16.82	13.08
35. Hungary	161.99	135.26	220.42	79.28	156.25	67.11	263.11	185.07	146.02	53.34	177.25	118.10
36. Bahrain	0.29	0.21	0.28	0.62	0.24	0.16	0.24	0.33	0.31	0.15	0.49	0.22
37. Korea	1515.00	853.15	1133.40	783.71	777.29	358.08	1102.96	581.71	932.11	480.86	1309.98	762.56
38. Estonia	10.42	8.01	14.57	6.47	10.02	3.89	13.75	10.42	8.94	2.51	11.22	7.08
39. Slovakia	22.67	18.13	29.31	11.51	24.21	8.18	35.09	31.31	19.23	5.37	22.29	15.91
40. Lithuania	1.94	1.60	3.18	0.92	2.02	0.74	2.87	1.72	1.70	0.45	2.23	1.41
41. Poland	2.37	2.02	4.09	1.28	2.56	0.89	3.90	3.16	2.37	0.76	3.07	1.87
42. Croatia	5.83	5.04	7.24	2.26	5.57	2.24	7.87	4.64	5.02	1.70	6.96	3.94
43. Macao	8.32	6.05	6.18	6.74	8.26	2.26	7.87	6.99	5.90	2.31	8.80	5.61
44. Latvia	0.41	0.29	0.64	0.22	0.41	0.14	0.56	0.58	0.35	0.09	0.47	0.26
45. Lebanon	1149.93	971.76	1982.64	896.54	1175.80	439.62	923.37	1598.59	1271.01	401.16	3490.05	934.83
46. Mexico	8.16	5.97	8.12	8.74	7.37	4.75	9.09	11.19	8.37	2.70	9.25	6.50
47. Belarus	1024.38	761.80	1398.15	256.78	1219.48	262.09	1598.69	453.81	988.82	178.72	958.78	814.14
48. Kazakhstan	71.24	40.69	114.84	38.69	87.22	15.70	84.82	104.41	63.54	9.37	77.62	51.77

Table 7A.3 (*cont.*)

Country (1)	Food (2)	Alcohol and tobacco (3)	Clothing (4)	Housing (5)	Durables (6)	Health (7)	Transport (8)	Communication (9)	Recreation (10)	Education (11)	Restaurants (12)	Other (13)
49. Mauritius	23.50	23.33	19.48	10.18	17.21	6.80	34.12	13.60	26.43	5.04	20.18	16.79
50. Russia	16.58	10.80	26.86	5.52	19.42	4.68	21.19	18.83	15.18	2.78	19.77	13.50
51. Bulgaria	0.96	0.69	1.20	0.42	0.97	0.27	1.37	1.45	0.79	0.14	0.74	0.60
52. Iran	5664.84	2500.05	3286.78	2415.29	4143.06	630.39	3109.57	555.59	3535.75	964.43	5669.35	2369.92
53. Romania	2.24	1.54	2.67	1.19	1.89	0.60	2.92	2.42	1.65	0.47	1.94	1.33
54. Oman	0.27	0.22	0.26	0.48	0.23	0.14	0.23	0.33	0.27	0.15	0.45	0.20
55. Argentina	1.70	0.95	1.80	1.02	1.80	0.59	1.89	1.04	2.02	0.69	2.46	1.27
56. Serbia	48.03	26.26	63.92	18.89	51.50	12.86	67.06	20.10	35.04	9.15	49.56	26.16
57. Saudi Arabia	3.02	1.97	2.60	3.79	2.19	1.33	2.49	5.08	3.89	1.80	5.58	2.27
58. Chile	453.99	282.46	505.74	280.11	501.26	205.31	552.38	559.34	431.23	213.37	524.90	553.68
59. Uruguay	16.93	11.92	19.47	13.54	17.47	7.21	23.14	14.32	18.35	7.34	22.93	13.98
60. Bosnia Herz.	1.19	0.74	1.75	0.41	1.06	0.42	1.77	0.81	0.95	0.24	1.22	0.72
61. Macedonia	31.30	18.29	39.59	11.36	32.66	8.07	47.46	37.51	29.62	6.68	30.06	18.81
62. Ukraine	2.20	1.46	3.40	0.46	2.90	0.62	3.16	2.66	2.11	0.30	2.89	1.86
63. South Africa	5.53	4.56	5.56	2.89	5.89	2.46	6.69	5.95	5.67	1.98	7.10	4.31
64. Malaysia	2.76	3.98	2.24	2.45	2.37	0.65	2.40	2.19	1.90	0.54	2.93	1.86
65. Turkey	1.29	1.17	1.29	0.55	1.04	0.55	1.99	1.39	1.11	0.32	1.44	0.83
66. Montenegro	0.66	0.34	0.99	0.31	0.61	0.17	0.91	0.38	0.52	0.12	0.71	0.35
67. Brazil	1.68	0.83	2.23	1.48	1.84	0.71	2.50	1.57	2.07	0.76	1.66	1.36
68. Venezuela	1833.68	781.31	2270.24	706.12	1779.57	605.17	1471.64	1160.72	1804.35	604.15	1736.17	1134.45
69. Thailand	25.14	25.72	21.10	11.24	24.34	5.51	24.97	21.77	19.64	4.36	23.46	17.45
70. Albania	82.09	54.66	104.09	39.71	75.47	14.15	105.54	88.62	63.56	10.84	75.85	43.35

71. Colombia	1738.52	1040.89	1672.66	731.79	1400.78	509.14	1968.01	1294.54	1695.48	548.99	1266.79	1189.83
72. Ecuador	0.66	0.41	0.66	0.41	0.54	0.18	0.65	0.52	0.76	0.23	0.71	0.45
73. Jordan	0.51	0.40	0.45	0.75	0.49	0.17	0.39	0.42	0.52	0.16	1.06	0.42
74. Tunisia	1.01	0.90	1.51	0.37	0.68	0.33	1.25	0.85	1.18	0.31	0.73	0.71
75. Peru	2.28	1.64	1.99	1.02	2.04	0.84	2.22	1.92	2.13	0.80	2.37	1.42
76. Egypt	3.00	2.71	2.48	1.54	1.98	0.45	1.90	4.46	2.75	0.38	4.24	1.68
77. Moldova	6.35	3.30	10.37	1.59	8.05	1.32	8.78	6.43	5.33	0.55	7.03	4.21
78. Maldives	11.30	8.11	9.25	20.20	9.45	1.77	13.22	6.81	8.21	1.17	13.04	7.00
79. Gabon	751.51	345.11	598.03	236.46	524.26	138.33	651.34	805.12	670.16	77.95	644.85	272.76
80. Fiji	1.78	1.74	1.20	2.48	1.54	0.41	2.07	0.94	1.51	0.37	2.58	1.22
81. Georgia	3.35	0.37	13.04	0.26	4.27	0.47	0.67	1.44	2.79	1.47	0.22	5.18
82. Botswana	5.43	3.33	4.13	1.71	4.56	1.84	5.34	3.94	5.45	1.01	5.17	2.56
83. Namibia	7.03	3.60	5.98	3.44	4.78	1.87	6.98	7.25	6.86	1.79	9.45	4.14
84. Swaziland	5.64	4.65	6.85	3.11	4.43	0.69	6.19	6.75	6.16	1.33	5.60	2.79
85. Syria	28.17	21.76	29.90	28.47	24.63	7.14	26.92	29.73	22.70	4.50	41.70	16.63
86. Bolivia	3.61	2.65	4.21	1.58	3.08	0.91	3.51	3.48	4.01	0.62	3.79	2.64
87. Equat. Guinea	736.79	268.32	770.92	238.18	482.76	125.89	659.00	1023.23	702.07	55.67	554.50	317.15
88. Paraguay	2621.77	1800.97	3650.97	1159.47	2675.51	930.20	3893.15	1914.50	3512.50	662.83	3216.28	2199.24
89. Cape Verde	97.06	69.40	110.48	70.42	86.61	23.88	96.36	85.46	96.91	24.76	104.44	50.85
90. Bhutan	25.39	22.16	21.90	14.32	25.83	4.38	31.70	25.19	22.66	4.11	31.78	17.21
91. Kyrgyz	18.69	12.07	29.67	2.33	24.31	2.74	21.56	22.11	14.97	1.31	17.72	10.35
92. Sri Lanka	59.95	81.69	35.25	20.96	53.60	9.21	66.49	54.51	49.32	6.94	66.91	41.58
93. Iraq	820.46	722.45	653.99	828.21	460.50	174.33	591.87	966.58	886.65	169.99	1377.42	487.58
94. Mongolia	697.11	586.29	624.83	551.99	670.86	85.70	771.86	589.16	592.31	62.70	1036.36	551.94
95. Philippines	33.61	16.18	28.09	22.53	25.78	9.11	34.57	34.61	26.79	5.22	30.84	21.85
96. Indonesia	5817.55	6703.02	3857.99	4145.21	4483.12	1779.72	6032.79	6927.66	4110.24	717.99	5069.14	3533.10
97. Pakistan	33.44	31.09	23.25	12.14	25.79	5.10	34.47	18.76	23.06	3.33	39.58	20.98

Table 7A.3 (cont.)

Country	Food	Alcohol and tobacco	Clothing	Housing	Durables	Health	Transport	Communication	Recreation	Education	Restaurants	Other
(1)	(2)	(3)	(4)	(5)	(6)	(7)	(8)	(9)	(10)	(11)	(12)	(13)
98. Morocco	7.82	10.43	8.04	2.86	4.92	3.48	8.65	8.09	7.20	3.48	9.12	5.41
99. Lesotho	5.66	3.56	4.60	1.45	3.95	0.80	6.28	8.05	6.99	0.89	5.22	3.34
100. China	5.52	5.75	6.86	3.36	5.27	0.68	5.98	3.14	3.47	1.02	6.78	4.13
101. Vietnam	8351.70	6573.71	6853.98	5373.74	8106.22	1108.27	14186.43	6467.28	5974.33	579.48	8163.96	6060.04
102. India	21.13	31.52	16.71	12.33	22.73	3.00	32.46	17.46	18.41	2.90	26.92	16.07
103. Cambodia	2304.24	1540.82	1853.60	1702.49	1776.67	281.10	2482.62	2544.70	1561.96	159.85	2491.73	1623.23
104. Yemen	114.72	60.77	87.22	87.21	101.05	20.85	95.16	190.44	117.94	14.88	189.49	81.10
105. Sudan	209.26	266.55	112.81	74.82	105.38	54.14	186.90	237.81	137.48	40.20	136.70	78.92
106. Lao	5999.57	5041.84	4587.66	1904.26	4819.33	637.70	8257.96	6278.17	4062.99	404.52	5958.62	4055.22
107. Djibouti	185.38	72.72	142.32	58.60	161.00	41.84	200.07	156.98	131.78	22.24	221.71	56.27
108. Kenya	54.14	41.13	34.72	12.95	30.71	10.71	69.25	95.17	57.37	12.08	35.30	24.37
109. Sao Tome	10467.07	6449.36	10458.29	2981.50	6516.16	2316.53	9849.02	12088.91	10294.54	1178.41	9248.32	5178.40
110. Congo, R.	632.74	359.54	530.85	167.41	369.89	123.41	638.12	807.72	546.69	47.43	460.36	241.67
111. Cameroon	471.31	297.78	391.20	142.76	308.86	117.51	446.50	766.45	502.63	64.41	435.45	242.37
112. Nigeria	159.01	77.25	78.81	31.03	58.10	23.59	100.27	140.11	98.70	11.59	112.77	46.55
113. Senegal	522.49	277.43	355.86	139.96	279.47	116.50	507.48	368.25	372.29	90.57	467.48	251.99
114. Chad	597.45	384.07	341.60	54.06	400.12	40.40	561.69	792.33	460.47	7.08	495.08	255.63
115. Nepal	34.09	43.14	28.13	25.60	31.40	5.64	63.79	33.54	27.41	4.83	44.96	25.36
116. Bangladesh	34.28	23.52	30.54	23.22	28.39	6.51	51.10	30.74	31.46	4.74	43.64	25.09

117. Benin	495.42	282.52	326.75	97.76	287.76	88.94	445.58	806.15	391.47	61.12	423.84	220.39
118. Ghana	8920.78	4911.35	4825.45	1165.78	4536.90	1401.83	7607.26	8502.22	6413.31	1159.52	7777.54	2530.02
119. Cote d'Ivoire	528.53	324.22	367.70	142.30	314.18	154.33	601.75	743.95	541.03	112.23	426.18	272.06
120. S. Leone	2758.53	1296.55	1402.75	363.26	1470.41	395.95	2508.55	4003.91	1958.04	315.72	2233.36	1161.20
121. M'gascar	1367.95	1221.71	866.50	402.10	828.67	302.47	1610.40	1333.14	1118.57	69.47	987.76	645.02
122. Togo	506.07	238.44	390.03	77.34	292.98	165.77	507.12	806.55	413.45	42.49	400.41	217.03
123. Burkina Faso	388.14	262.55	213.55	101.12	270.08	88.31	574.31	622.73	382.21	51.66	357.89	184.68
124. Guinea	2947.23	709.52	1475.62	548.76	947.20	692.68	2874.54	2693.64	1519.97	229.19	1677.91	1066.10
125. Mali	482.74	200.44	305.43	143.76	294.94	107.20	488.93	580.03	428.14	65.26	360.33	248.63
126. Angola	126.79	54.79	97.70	24.70	73.27	30.72	115.74	131.28	112.14	18.57	119.36	52.10
127. Rwanda	333.21	254.21	386.42	171.75	317.85	68.23	479.17	499.53	419.56	38.97	317.29	211.41
128. C. Africa	566.15	303.39	365.87	69.65	298.71	131.52	694.85	646.21	444.67	59.49	398.11	249.92
129. M'bique	18411.35	14276.50	16433.88	3699.26	13316.04	4959.22	26261.13	27563.55	18785.04	3537.72	19965.90	10774.73
130. Niger	460.81	276.58	246.84	106.35	282.01	107.97	521.66	594.81	425.91	70.00	393.25	200.07
131. G–Bissau	461.33	259.08	434.01	122.21	330.08	91.97	542.54	1155.94	470.45	39.09	409.77	234.43
132. Congo, D. R.	542.73	304.40	294.77	158.02	289.61	101.18	616.52	749.44	428.23	58.56	443.09	193.32

Table 7A.4 *Ratios of the standard deviation of residuals for poor to rich countries*

Commodity	Ratio
1. Food	1.62
2. Alcohol and tobacco	1.53
3. Clothing	1.43
4. Housing	0.91
5. Durables	1.15
6. Health	1.44
7. Transport	1.35
8. Communication	1.07
9. Recreation	0.72
10. Education	1.17
11. Restaurants	0.75
12. Other	0.86
Budget-share-weighted average	1.25

Note: Countries 1–69 (70–132) in Table 7.1 are the rich (poor) countries.

cross-products of the residuals. Table 7A.4 contains the square roots of the ratios of the corresponding diagonal elements of these matrices. Thus the standard deviation of the residuals for food are approximately 60 per cent higher in poor countries relative to the rich countries; averaging over all commodities, residuals for the poor countries are 25 per cent more variable that those for the rich countries.

7A.4 Food prices for the rich and poor countries

For good i in country c, let w_i^c be the budget share and $\log p_i^c - \sum_{j=1}^{12} w_j^c \log p_j^c$ be the relative price. Figure 7A.2 contains scatter plots of the relative price of food against income. Regardless of whether income is measured as inversely proportional to the food budget share, $\log Q^c$ or Q^c, the pattern is clear: For rich countries, the relative price of food decreases as income increases but is more or less unrelated to income for poor countries.

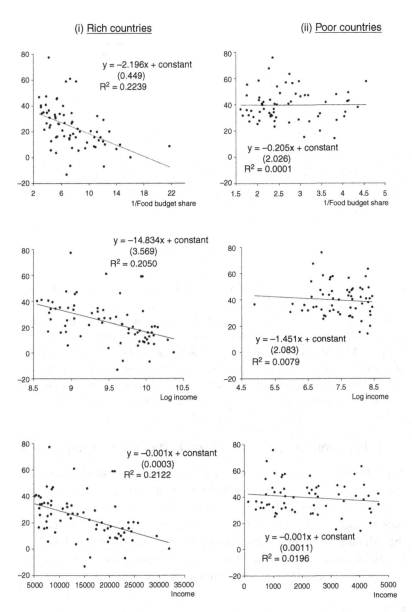

Figure 7A.2 Food prices and incomes (log relative price of food ×100 on vertical axes).

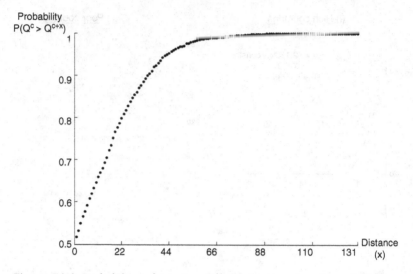

Figure 7A.3 Probability of income differences as a function of distance between countries. *Note:* Countries are indexed by $c = 1, \ldots, 132$ and ranked in terms of decreasing per-capita income. This figure shows the relative frequency for which country c is richer than country $c + x$ ($x \geq 0$, the 'bandwith') for $c = 1, \ldots, 132$. Alternatively, in the 1,000 realizations of the 132×132 matrix, $Q^{(s)} = [Q^{a(s)} - Q^{b(s)}]$, $s = 1, \ldots, 1,000$, the point corresponding to bandwidth x is the average (over trials and countries) of the relative frequencies on the subdiagonal x steps away from the main diagonal once removed.

7A.5 Economic geography and stochastic income comparisons

The idea of stochastic income comparisons is pursued further in Figure 7A.3. This gives the probability of income differences by the distance separating countries, with distance interpreted as the difference in income ranking. These multistep comparisons show that as the distance increases, so does the probability that countries have different incomes, but the rate of increase decreases and the probability converges to unity for countries sufficiently far removed.

References

Anderson, G. (1996). 'Nonparametric Tests for Stochastic Dominance'. *Econometrica* 64: 1183–93.
Barlow, R. (1977). 'A Test of Alternative Methods of Making GNP Comparisons'. *Economic Journal* 87: 450–9.

Barrett, G. F., and S. G. Donald (2003). 'Tests for Stochastic Dominance'. *Econometrica* 71: 71–104.

Beckerman, W., and R. Bacon (1966). 'International Comparisons of Income Levels: A Suggested New Measure'. *Economic Journal* 76: 519–36.

Bennett, M. K. (1951). 'International Disparities in Consumption Levels'. *American Economic Review* 41: 632–49.

Chua, G. (2003). 'Food and Cross-Country Income Comparisons'. Economics Discussion Paper 03.14, Business School, The University of Western Australia.

Costa, D. L. (2001). 'Estimating Real Income in the United States from 1888 to 1994: Correcting CPI Bias Using Engel Curves'. *Journal of Political Economy* 109: 1288–310.

Deaton, A. (1997). *The Analysis of Household Surveys*. Baltimore, MD: Johns Hopkins University Press.

Deaton, A. (2005). 'Measuring Poverty in a Growing World (Or Measuring Growth in a Poor World)'. *Review of Economics and Statistics* 87: 1–19.

Deaton, A., and M. Grosh (2000). 'Consumption'. In M. Grosh and P. Glewwe (eds), *Designing Household Survey Questionnaires for Developing Countries: Lessons from Ten Years of LSMS Experience*. Washington, DC: World Bank.

Deaton, A., and V. Kozel (2005). 'Data and Dogma: The Great Indian Poverty Debate'. *World Bank Research Observer* 20: 177–99.

Duggar, J. W. (1969). 'International Comparisons of Income Levels: An Additional Measure'. *Economic Journal* 79: 109–16.

Ehrlich, E. (1969). 'Dynamic International Comparison of National Incomes Expressed in Terms of Physical Indicators'. *Osteuropa Wirtschaft* 14, 1.

Engel, E. (1857). 'Die Productions- und Consumptionsverhaltnisse des Konigreichs Sachsen'. Reprinted in Engel (1895). *Die Lebenskosten belgischer Atbeiter-Familien*. Dresden: Heinrich.

Gao, G. (2012). 'World Food Demand'. *American Journal of Agricultural Economics* 94: 25–51.

Hamilton B. W. (2001). 'Using Engel's Law to Estimate CPI Bias'. *American Economic Review* 91: 619–30.

Henderson, V., A. Storeygard and D. N. Weil (2009). 'Measuring Economic Growth from Outer Space'. Working paper, Brown University and National Bureau of Economic Research.

Heston, A. (1973). 'A Comparison of Some Short-Cut Methods of Estimating Real Product per Capita'. *Review of Income and Wealth* 19: 79–104.

International Comparison Program (2008). 'Global Purchasing Power Parities and Real Expenditures'. Available at www.worldbank.org.

Janossy, F. (1963). *A Gazdasagi Fejlettseg Merhetosege es uj Meresi Modszere (The Measurability and a New Measuring Method of Economic Development Level)*. Budapest: Kozgazdasagi es Jogi Konyvkiado.

Kulshrestha, A. C., and A. Kar (2005). 'Consumer Expenditure from the National Accounts and National Sample Survey'. In A. Deaton and V. Kozel (eds), *The Great Indian Poverty Debate*. New Delhi: Macmillan.

Leser, C. E. V. (1963). 'Forms of Engel Functions'. *Econometrica* 31: 694–703.

Minhas, B. S. (1988). 'Validation of Large-Scale Sample Survey Data: The Case of NSS Household Consumption Expenditure'. *Sankhya Series B* 50(suppl.): 1–63.

Minhas, B. S., and S. M. Kansal (1989). 'Comparison of NSS and CSO Estimates of Private Consumption: Some Observations Based on 1983 Data'. *Journal of Income and Wealth* 11: 7–24.

Nakamura, L. (1996). 'Is US Economic Performance Really that Bad?' Working Paper No. 95, Federal Reserve Bank of Philadelphia.

Orshansky, M. (1965). 'Counting the Poor: Another Look at the Poverty Profile'. *Social Security Bulletin* 28: 3–29.

Orshansky, M. (1969). 'How Poverty is Measured'. *Monthly Labor Review* 92: 37–41.

Rao, V. V. B. (1981). 'Measurement of Deprivation and Poverty Based on the Proportion Spent on Food: An Exploratory Exercise'. *World Development* 9: 337–53.

Ravallion, M. (2003). 'Measuring Aggregate Welfare in Developing Countries: How Well Do National Accounts and Surveys Agree?' *Review of Economics and Statistics* 85: 645–52.

Sahn, D. A., and D. Stifel (2003). 'Exploring Alternative Measures of Welfare in the Absence of Expenditure Data'. *Review of Income and Wealth* 49: 463–89.

Slesnick, D. T. (1998). 'Are Our Data Relevant to the Theory? The Case of Aggregate Consumption'. *Journal of Business and Economic Statistics* 16: 52–61.

Steckel, R. H. (1995). 'Stature and the Standard of Living'. *Journal of Economic Literature* 33: 1903–40.

Stigler, G. J. (1954). 'The Early History of Empirical Studies in Consumer Behavior'. *Journal of Political Economy* 62: 95–113.

Sundaram, K., and S. Tendulkar (2003). 'NAS-NSS Estimates of Private Consumption for Poverty Estimation: A Further Comparative Examination'. *Economic and Political Weekly*, January 25: 376–84.

Theil, H. (1975/76). *Theory and Measurement of Consumer Demand*, Vols. 1 and 2. Amsterdam: North-Holland.

Theil, H. (1980). *The System-Wide Approach to Microeconomics*. The University of Chicago Press.

Theil, H., C.-F. Chung and J. L. Seale, Jr. (1989). *International Evidence on Consumption Patterns*. Greenwich, CT: JAI Press.

Theil, H., and K. W. Clements (1987). *Applied Demand Analysis: Results from System-Wide Approaches*. Cambridge, MA: Ballinger Publishing Co.

Triplett, J. (1997). 'Measuring Consumption: The Post-1973 Slowdown and the Research Issues'. *Federal Reserve Bank of St Louis Review*, May–June: 9–42.

Van Praag, B. M. S., J. S. Spit and H. Van de Stadt (1982). 'A Comparison Between the Food Ratio Poverty Line and the Leyden Poverty Line'. *Review of Economics and Statistics* 64: 691–4.

Working, H. (1943). 'Statistical Laws of Family Expenditure'. *Journal of the American Statistical Association* 38: 43–56.

Index

Printed in the United States
by Baker & Taylor Publisher Services